CONSUMER BEHAVIOR 2014

10th Edition

RKMA MARKET RESEARCH HANDBOOK SERIES

By: Richard K. Miller and Kelli Washington

Published by:

Richard K. Miller & Associates
4132 Atlanta Highway, Suite 110
Loganville, GA 30052
(888) 928-RKMA (7562)
www.rkma.com

Richard K. Miller & Associates
since 1972

CONSUMER BEHAVIOR 2014

10th Edition

RKMA MARKET RESEARCH HANDBOOK SERIES

ISBN Number: 9781577831945

Richard K. Miller & Associates
4132 Atlanta Highway, Suite 110
Loganville, GA 30052
(888) 928-RKMA (7562)
www.rkma.com

CONTENTS

PART I: THE AMERICAN CONSUMER

1

DEMOGRAPHIC OVERVIEW

1.1 Population Distribution

Census 2010 counted the U.S. population on April 1, 2010 at 308,745,538, a 9.7% increase over the count of 281,421,906 from Census 2000.

The U.S. Census Bureau (www.census.gov) estimated the U.S. population as of November 2013 at 317,143,580.

There is in the United States, on average, one birth every 8 seconds, one death every 12 seconds, one international migrant (net) every 44 seconds, and a net population gain of one person every 14 seconds.

The following is the population distribution by gender and age at year-end 2011 (most recent data available as of November 2013):

Age	Male	Female
• 0:	0.66%	0.63%
• 1:	0.65%	0.62%
• 2:	0.65%	0.62%
• 3:	0.67%	0.64%
• 4:	0.68%	0.65%
• 5:	0.67%	0.64%
• 6:	0.67%	0.64%
• 7:	0.67%	0.64%
• 8:	0.66%	0.64%
• 9:	0.66%	0.63%
• 10:	0.68%	0.65%
• 11:	0.69%	0.66%
• 12:	0.68%	0.65%
• 13:	0.68%	0.65%
• 14:	0.68%	0.65%
• 15:	0.68%	0.65%
• 16:	0.70%	0.66%
• 17:	0.71%	0.68%
• 18:	0.73%	0.68%
• 19:	0.74%	0.70%
• 20:	0.75%	0.72%
• 21:	0.75%	0.72%
• 22:	0.72%	0.69%
• 23:	0.71%	0.68%
• 24:	0.69%	0.67%
• 25:	0.70%	0.67%
• 26:	0.70%	0.68%
• 27:	0.68%	0.66%
• 28:	0.69%	0.68%
• 29:	0.69%	0.68%
• 30:	0.68%	0.68%
• 31:	0.70%	0.69%
• 32:	0.65%	0.65%
• 33:	0.64%	0.64%
• 34:	0.63%	0.63%
• 35:	0.61%	0.61%
• 36:	0.63%	0.63%
• 37:	0.61%	0.62%
• 38:	0.62%	0.63%
• 39:	0.65%	0.66%
• 40:	0.69%	0.70%
• 41:	0.70%	0.71%
• 42:	0.66%	0.67%
• 43:	0.65%	0.66%
• 44:	0.65%	0.66%
• 45:	0.66%	0.67%
• 46:	0.70%	0.72%
• 47:	0.72%	0.73%
• 48:	0.72%	0.74%

- 49: 0.71% 0.74%
- 50: 0.72% 0.75%
- 51: 0.73% 0.75%
- 52: 0.71% 0.73%
- 53: 0.70% 0.73%
- 54: 0.69% 0.73%
- 55: 0.67% 0.70%
- 56: 0.66% 0.70%
- 57: 0.63% 0.67%
- 58: 0.61% 0.65%
- 59: 0.58% 0.63%
- 60: 0.57% 0.61%
- 61: 0.55% 0.60%
- 62: 0.54% 0.58%
- 63: 0.53% 0.58%
- 64: 0.56% 0.60%
- 65: 0.41% 0.45%
- 66: 0.40% 0.45%
- 67: 0.39% 0.44%
- 68: 0.40% 0.45%
- 69: 0.35% 0.40%
- 70: 0.32% 0.37%
- 71: 0.30% 0.35%
- 72: 0.28% 0.33%
- 73: 0.27% 0.32%
- 74: 0.25% 0.30%
- 75: 0.24% 0.29%
- 76: 0.22% 0.28%
- 77: 0.20% 0.26%
- 78: 0.19% 0.25%
- 79: 0.18% 0.25%
- 80: 0.17% 0.24%
- 81: 0.17% 0.24%
- 82: 0.15% 0.22%
- 83: 0.14% 0.21%
- 84: 0.12% 0.20%
- 85: 0.11% 0.18%
- 86: 0.10% 0.17%
- 87: 0.08% 0.15%
- 88: 0.07% 0.14%
- 89: 0.06% 0.12%
- 90: 0.05% 0.10%
- 91: 0.04% 0.09%
- 92: 0.03% 0.07%
- 93: 0.02% 0.06%
- 94: 0.02% 0.04%
- 95: 0.01% 0.03%
- 96: 0.01% 0.03%
- 97: 0.01% 0.02%
- 98: 0.00% 0.01%
- 99: 0.00% 0.01%
- 100+: 0.00% 0.02%

The median age was reported by Census 2010 as follows:

- Female: 38.5
- Male: 35.8
- Both genders: 37.2

The following is the distribution by race reported by Census 2010 and change from Census 2000:

	Census 2010	Change
• White alone:	74.4%	5.7%
• Black or African American alone:	12.6%	12.3%
• Asian alone:	4.8%	43.3%
• American Indian or Alaska Native alone:	0.9%	18.4%
• Native Hawaiian or other Pacific Islander alone:	0.2%	35.4%
• Some other race alone:	6.2%	24.4%
• Two or more races:	2.9%	32.2%

As reported in Census 2010, 50.5 million people, or 16% of the total population, identify themselves as Hispanic or Latino. The Hispanic population increased from 35.3 million in 2000, when this group made up 13% of the total population. The Hispanic population increased 43.0% between Census 2000 and Census 2010, while the non-Hispanic population increased 4.9% during that period.

Ethnic demographics are further assessed in Part VI of this handbook.

Regional populations at year-end 2012 were as follows (source: Census Bureau):

	Population	Distribution
• South:	117,257,221	37.4%
• West:	73,579,431	23.4%
• Midwest:	67,316,297	21.4%
• Northeast:	55,761,091	17.8%

1.2 Households

An August 2013 report by the U.S. Census Bureau estimated there were 114.99 million households in the U.S. at year-end 2011. Distribution was as follows:

- Family households, married couple: 55.52 million
- Non-family households (a person living alone, unrelated people living together, or people in group settings): 38.91 million
- Family households, husband or wife only present: 20.56 million

Household composition has undergone significant shifts in recent decades. Distributions since 1970 have been as follows:

	1970	1980	1990	2000	2010
• Married couples with children:	40.3%	30.9%	26.3%	24.1%	20.9%
• Married couples without children:	30.3%	29.9%	29.8%	18.7%	28.8%
• Other family households:	10.6%	12.9%	14.8%	16.0%	17.4%
• Men living alone:	5.6%	8.6%	9.7%	10.7%	11.9%
• Women living alone:	11.5%	14.0%	14.9%	14.8%	14.8%
• Other non-family households:	1.7%	3.6%	4.6%	5.7%	6.2%

According to the *Current Population Survey*, by the Census Bureau, households grew an average of about 500,000 per year from 2007 through 2010. This is less than half the 1.2 million annual pace averaged 2000 through 2007, and lower than that averaged in the 1990s when Generation X matured to become heads of households.

By Metropolitan Statistical Area, households in 2010 were as follows:

- Inside principal cities of Metropolitan Statistical Areas: 39.47 million
- Outside principal cities of Metropolitan Statistical Areas: 59.79 million
- Outside Metropolitan Statistical Areas: 19.42 million

Note: Metropolitan Statistical Areas are defined in Chapter 69 of this handbook.

1.3 Generational Demographics

Marketers typically categorize consumers into five generations, as follows:

	Year of Birth	Age (in 2013)	Population
• Seniors:	1945 and prior	68 and older	36 million
• Baby Boomers:	1946-1964	49-to-67	76 million
• Generation X:	1965-1979	34-to-48	61 million
• Millennials (Gen Y):	1980-2000	13-to-33	93 million
• Generation Z:	2001-present	12 and younger	53 million

Generational assessments explore how the era in which consumers live influences their behavior. Many consumers who lived through the Great Depression of 1929, for example, remained frugal their entire lives because of the profound impact it had on them. Baby Boomers grew up without psychological scars from the Depression and generally spend more freely than their parents' generation. Subsequent generations have grown up in an age of abundance, easy credit, and a taste for luxury. Spending and lifestyles of Generation Z will likely be influenced by the Great Recession of 2008-2009.

Spending is also influenced by life cycles. Most Generation Xers are now in their peak earning and spending years. Baby Boomers, some looking toward retirement or semi-retirement, are beginning to spend less.

Generational demographics are further assessed in Part VIII of this handbook.

1.4 Urban, Suburban and Rural Populations

Metropolitan and micropolitan statistical areas, or metro and micro areas, are geographic entities defined by the U.S. Office of Management and Budget (www.omb.gov) for use by federal statistical agencies in collecting, tabulating, and publishing federal statistics. A metro area contains a core urban area population of 50,000 or more. A micro area contains a core urban area population of at least 10,000 but less than 50,000. Census 2010 reported the population distribution by core statistical area as follows:

- Metropolitan Statistical Area: 83.7%
- Micropolitan Statistical Area: 10.0%
- Outside core area: 6.3%

Geodemographics are further assessed in Part X of this handbook.

1.5 Market Resources

U.S. Population Clock, U.S. Census Bureau; provides U.S. population estimate on a daily basis. (www.census.gov/main/www/popclock.html)

2

CONSUMER SPENDING

2.1 Consumer Contribution to the GDP

According to the Bureau of Economic Analysis (www.bea.gov), real gross domestic product (GDP) – the output of goods and services produced by labor and property located in the United States – was $16.24 trillion in 2012. Consumer spending (i.e., personal consumption expenditures) was $11.15 trillion, or 68.7% of GDP.

2.2 Spending Assessment

According to the Bureau of Labor Statistics (BLS, www.bls.gov), there were 124.42 million consumer units (which are similar to households) in 2012, with an average income before taxes of $65,596, a 3.0% increase from the year prior. There were 2.5 persons per consumer unit, on average, with 1.3 income earners. Sixty-four percent (64%) were homeowners.

Average spending per consumer unit was $51,442 in 2012, a 3.5% increase from the previous year. Spending was distributed as follows (change from previous year in parenthesis):

- Housing: $16,887 (0.5%)
- Transportation: $ 8,998 (8.5%)
- Food: $ 6,599 (2.2%)
  - At home: $ 3,921 (2.2%)
  - Away from home: $ 2,678 (2.2%)
- Personal insurance and pensions: $ 5,591 (3.1%)
- Healthcare: $ 3,556 (7.3%)
- Entertainment: $ 2,605 (1.3%)
- Cash contributions: $ 1,913 (11.2%)
- Apparel and services: $ 1,736 (-0.2%)
- All other expenditures: $ 3,557 (5.2%)

The BLS provides regional consumer spending surveys for the following metropolitan areas: Atlanta, Baltimore, Boston, Chicago, Cleveland, Dallas-Fort Worth, Detroit, Houston, Los Angeles, Miami, Minneapolis, New York, Phoenix, Philadelphia, San Diego, San Francisco, Seattle, and Washington, D.C., available online at www.bls.gov/cex/csxregreleases.htm.

2.3 Consumer Price Index

The Consumer Price Index (CPI) is a measure of the average change in prices over time of goods and services purchased by households. The CPI assessment was initiated by the Census Bureau in 1977 with the CPI set at 100.0 as a point of reference. The CPI throughout the past decade has been as follows:

- 2001: 260.0
- 2002: 264.2
- 2003: 270.1
- 2004: 277.4
- 2005: 286.7
- 2006: 296.1
- 2007: 304.5
- 2008: 316.2
- 2009: 315.0
- 2010: 320.2
- 2011: 329.8
- 2012: 335.4

The CPI rose 1.7% in 2012 after a 3.0% increase in 2011. This was the third smallest December-December increase of the past ten years and compares to a 2.4% average annual increase over the span.

The BLS reports changes in the CPI on a monthly basis (www.bls.gov/cpi). The overall CPI increased 1.0% for the 12-month period ending October 2013. Changes for select items were as follows:

- Apparel: -0.2%
- Energy: -4.8%
  - Gasoline (all types): -10.1%
  - Fuel oil: -4.6%
  - Electricity: 3.0%
  - Utility (piped) gas service: 4.4%
- Food: 1.3%
  - Food at home: 0.8%
  - Food away from home: 1.9%
- Medical care services: 2.9%
- Medical care commodities: 0.5%
- Shelter: 2.3%
- Transportation services: 2.5%
- Vehicles, new: 1.0%
- Vehicles, used: 1.4%

2.4 Daily Spending

The Gallup Organization (www.gallup.com) surveys consumers bi-monthly about their daily spending (excluding housing and vehicle purchases). Self-reported daily spending has been as follows:

- October 2008: $91
- October 2009: $66
- October 2010: $83
- October 2011: $70
- October 2012: $72
- October 2013: $88

Average daily spending among upper-income Americans – those earning $90,000 or more annually – was $156 in October 2013. Daily spending among those with lower incomes was $76.

By demographic, average daily spending in October 2013 was as follows:

Gender

- Female: $ 73
- Male: $103

Age

- 18-to-29: $ 75
- 30-to-49: $103
- 50-to-64: $ 90
- 65 and older: $ 74

Region

- East: $ 82
- Midwest: $ 84
- South: $ 89
- West: $ 94

2.5 Market Resources

Consumer Expenditures 2012, Bureau of Labor Statistics, September 2013. (www.bls.gov/news.release/cesan.nr0.htm)

Consumer Price Index Summary, Bureau of Labor Statistics (www.bls.gov/cpi)

3

RETAIL SPENDING

3.1 The U.S. Retail Sector

The U.S. retail industry encompasses more than 1.6 million retail establishments and employs more than 24 million people (about 1 in 5 American workers), according to the National Retail Federation (NRF, www.nrf.com).

3.2 GAFO Spending

According to the Census Bureau (www.census.gov) of the U.S. Department of Commerce, total U.S. retail sales were $4.89 trillion in 2012, a 1.05% gain over 2011.

Sales at GAFO (general merchandise, apparel, furnishings, and other) stores were $1.19 trillion in 2012, a 1.02% gain from 2011. GAFO sales were distributed by month in 2012 as follows (change from 2011 in parenthesis):

- January: $ 84.9 billion (4.6%)
- February: $ 91.5 billion (8.3%)
- March: $ 99.2 billion (6.4%)
- April: $ 92.3 billion (-0.2%)
- May: $ 98.0 billion (3.9%)
- June: $ 95.6 billion (2.6%)
- July: $ 93.6 billion (0.4%)
- August: $101.7 billion (5.5%)
- September: $ 91.8 billion (0.2%)
- October: $ 93.8 billion (0.4%)
- November: $108.9 billion (1.6%)
- December: $142.4 billion (-0.9%)

Retail sales in 2012 for stores in the GAFO categories were as follows (change from previous year in parenthesis):

- General merchandise stores, including leased departments (NAICS 452): $631.8 billion (0.4%)
  - Superstores and warehouse clubs (NAICS 45291): $389.5 billion (-0.3%)
  - Discount department stores, including leased departments (NAICS 452112): $119.9 billion (-1.4%)
  - Conventional and national chain department stores, including leased departments (NAICS 452111): $ 64.4 billion (-2.9%)
  - Variety stores and miscellaneous (NAICS 45299): $ 59.5 billion (11.3%)

- Apparel and accessories stores (NAICS 448): $239.2 billion (5.5%)
  - Family clothing (NAICS 44814): $ 93.2 billion (5.1%)
  - Women's ready-to-wear (NAICS 44812): $ 41.6 billion (7.8%)
  - Jewelry stores (NAICS 44831): $ 30.8 billion (5.8%)
  - Shoe stores (NAICS 4482): $ 28.7 billion (4.7%)
  - Men's and boy's clothing (NAICS 44811): $ 8.7 billion (2.3%)

- Sporting goods, hobby, book, and music stores (NAICS 451): $ 90.1 billion (6.4%)
  - Sporting goods stores (NAICS 45111): $ 42.6 billion (6.8%)
  - Book stores (NAICS 451211): $ 15.2 billion (-0.6%)
  - Hobby, toy, and game stores (NAICS 45112): $ 19.5 billion (10.8%)

- Furniture and home furnishings (NAICS 442): $ 95.6 billion (7.7%)

- Electronics and appliance stores (NAICS 443): $ 99.2 billion (-0.8%)

- Office supplies and stationary stores (NAICS 45321): $ 19.1 billion (-4.0%)

- Gift, novelty, and souvenir stores (NAICS 45322): $ 19.0 billion (13.8%)

Retail sales in non-GAFO retail categories in 2012 were as follows:

- Motor vehicles and parts stores (NAICS 441): $891.2 billion (7.9%)

- Food and beverage stores, not including restaurants (NAICS 445): $634.3 billion (3.3%)

- Restaurants and drinking places (NAICS 722): $529.6 billion (7.3%)

- Building materials, home improvement and gardening equipment, and supplies dealers (NAICS 444): $294.2 billion (5.5%)

- Gasoline stations (NAICS 447): $546.9 billion (10.8%)

- Health and personal care stores, including pharmacies and drug stores (NAICS 446): $274.9 billion (1.0%)

- Non-store retailers (NAICS 454): $439.7 billion (11.7%)

3.3 E-Commerce

Sixty-percent (60%) of U.S. adults shop online at lease once every three months, according to Forrester Research (www.forrester.com).

Those ages 45-to-54 are the biggest spenders online, spending an average $647 online every three months.

According to the U.S. Department of Commerce, e-commerce sales in the U.S. have been as follows:

	E-commerce Sales	Percent of Total Retail Sales	Growth
• 2005:	$ 86.3 billion	2.3%	25%
• 2006:	$114.6 billion	2.8%	33%
• 2007:	$132.8 billion	3.2%	16%
• 2008:	$132.3 billion	3.3%	no change
• 2009:	$134.9 billion	3.7%	2%
• 2010:	$167.7 billion	4.3%	24%
• 2011:	$194.7 billion	4.7%	16%
• 2012:	$225.5 billion	5.0%	16%

"Despite all this growth, online purchases remain a very small portion of retail sales. Over 90% of all United States retail commerce still takes place in physical stores."

Bill Martin, Founder
ShopperTrak
The New York Times, 11/30/13

E-commerce sales by quarter in 2012 were as follows (change from previous year in parenthesis):

- First quarter: $50.3 billion (-18.6%)
- Second quarter: $51.2 billion (1.8%)
- Third quarter: $52.5 billion (2.5%)
- Fourth quarter: $71.6 billion (36.3%)

eMarketer (www.emarketer.com) provides the following projections for e-commerce sales in the U.S.:

	E-commerce Sales	Growth
• 2013:	$256.0 billion	14.2%
• 2014:	$289.8 billion	13.2%
• 2015:	$325.2 billion	12.2%
• 2016:	$361.9 billion	11.3%

According to eMarketer, the number of U.S. consumers shopping online has been and is projected as follows:

	Number	Sales Per Digital Buyer
• 2011:	143.4 million	$2,104
• 2012:	149.8 million	$2,293
• 2013:	156.1 million	$2,466
• 2014:	162.6 million	$2,626
• 2015:	168.7 million	$2,785
• 2016:	175.0 million	$2,937

Forrester Research estimates that online auctions generate about $60 billion in sales annually.

3.4 Back-to-School

The back-to-school season typically is the second-biggest consumer spending event for retailers – behind the winter holidays – and can account for up to 15% of retailers' annual sales. It is sometimes used to gauge the health of the upcoming holiday shopping season.

Back-to-school (K-12) spending and back-to-college spending each dropped in 2013 from 2012, which was a record year. Total spending in 2013 was $72.5 billion, distributed as follows (change from previous year in parenthesis):

- Back-to-school: $26.7 billion (-11%)
- Back-to-college: $45.8 billion (-14%)

The National Retail Federation estimated 2013 back-to-school spending (excluding college) at $26.7 billion, a drop from $30.3 billion in 2012. According to NRF's *2013 Consumer Intentions and Actions Survey*, conducted by Prosper Business Development (www.goprosper.com), students and parents reported average spending of $635 on back-to-school merchandise.

Back-to-school spending was distributed by category as follows:

	Avg. Per Student	Total Spending
• Apparel:	$231	$9.7 billion
• Electronics/computers:	$199	$8.4 billion
• Shoes:	$114	$4.8 billion
• School supplies:	$ 90	$3.8 billion

The National Retail Federation estimated 2013 back-to-college spending (excluding textbooks) at $45.8 billion, a decline from $53.8 billion the previous year. According to NRF's *2013 Consumer Intentions and Actions Survey*, students and parents reported average spending of $837 on back-to-college merchandise, a drop from $907 in 2012.

Back-to-college spending was distributed by category as follows:

	Avg. Per Student	Total Spending
• Electronics/computers:	$203	$11.1 billion
• Apparel:	$123	$ 6.7 billion
• Dorm/apartment furnishings:	$105	$ 5.7 billion
• Food, snacks and beverages:	$104	$ 5.7 billion
• Shoes:	$ 66	$ 3.6 billion
• Gift cards/pre-paid cards:	$ 65	$ 3.6 billion
• Personal care items:	$ 65	$ 3.6 billion
• School supplies:	$ 63	$ 3.4 billion
• Collegiate branded gear:	$ 43	$ 2.3 billion

3.5 Christmas Season Holiday Spending

According to the U.S. Census Bureau, year-over-year growth of December retail sales has been as follows:

	Total Retail*	GAFO**
• 2006:	3.0%	3.7%
• 2007:	3.1%	-0.3%
• 2008:	-6.8%	-6.0%
• 2009:	5.6%	1.4%
• 2010:	6.4%	3.2%
• 2011:	5.6%	4.0%
• 2012:	1.6%	0.6%

* excluding motor vehicle and parts dealers
** GAFO: (general merchandise, apparel, furnishings, and other)

"The holiday season generally accounts for 20% to 40% of a retailer's annual sales, according to the National Retail Federation, and Thanksgiving weekend alone typically represents about 10% to 15% of those holiday sales."

The New York Times, 11/30/13

According to the National Retail Federation, total holiday retail sales increased 3.0% to $579.8 billion in 2012. Holiday sales by category were as follows:

- Clothing and clothing accessories stores' sales increased 2.5%.
- Electronics and appliance stores' sales decreased 0.4%.
- Furniture and home furnishing stores' sales increased 3.0%.
- General merchandise stores' sales decreased 3.4%.
- Health and personal care stores' sales decreased 0.7%.
- Non-store retailers' sales increased 9.6%.
- Sporting goods, hobby, book, and music stores' sales increased 4.7%.

According to ShopperTrak (www.shoppertrak.com), retails sales for Black Friday, the Friday following Thanksgiving and typically the busiest shopping day of the year, topped $11.4 billion during the 2012 holiday season. The following were the top shopping days ranked by sales and foot traffic:

Rank by Sales

1. Friday, November 23 (Black Friday)
2. Saturday, December 22 (Super Saturday)
3. Sunday, December 23
4. Friday, December 21
5. Saturday, December 15

Rank by Foot Traffic

1. Friday, November 23 (Black Friday)
2. Saturday, December 22 (Super Saturday)
3. Saturday, December 15
4. Sunday, December 23
5. Thursday, November 24 (Thanksgiving weekend)

The Christmas/Hanukkah/Kwanzaa online shopping season is generally designated as the period from November 1 through December 31. According to comScore (www.comscore.com), online sales (excluding travel, auctions, and large corporate purchases) for this period have been as follows (change from previous year in parenthesis):

- 2003: $13.1 billion (24%)
- 2004: $16.2 billion (24%)
- 2005: $19.9 billion (23%)
- 2006: $24.6 billion (25%)
- 2007: $26.3 billion (7%)
- 2008: $25.5 billion (-3%)
- 2009: $29.1 billion (4%)
- 2010: $32.6 billion (12%)
- 2011: $37.2 billion (15%)
- 2012: $42.3 billion (14%)

Online sales for the major seasonal shopping days in 2012 were as follows (change from previous year in parenthesis):

- November 26 (Cyber Monday): $1.47 billion (17%)
- December 4 (Tuesday): $1.36 billion (22%)
- December 10 (Green Monday): $1.28 billion (13%)
- November 27 (Tuesday): $1.26 billion (13%)
- December 11 (Tuesday): $1.22 billion (15%)
- December 14 (Friday): $1.22 billion (n/a)
- November 24, 25 (Thanksgiving weekend): $1.19 billion (15%)
- December 13 (Thursday): $1.14 billion (12%)
- December 3 (Monday): $1.12 billion (-5%)
- November 28 (Wednesday): $1.11 billion (8%)
- December 5 (Wednesday): $1.11 billion (n/a)
- November 23 (Black Friday): $1.04 billion (28%)
- December 17 (Free Shipping Day): $1.01 billion (76%)
- December 25 (Christmas Day): $ 288 million (36%)

3.6 State-by-State Retail Spending

According to the National Retail Federation, retail sales are distributed by state as follows (2011 sales, most recent data available):

- Alabama: $ 36.49 billion
- Alaska: $ 6.32 billion
- Arizona: $ 54.49 billion
- Arkansas: $ 22.13 billion
- California: $289.49 billion
- Colorado: $ 41.35 billion
- Connecticut: $ 30.40 billion
- District of Columbia: $ 3.64 billion
- Delaware: $ 9.00 billion
- Florida: $177.59 billion
- Georgia: $ 73.22 billion
- Hawaii: $ 12.16 billion
- Idaho: $ 12.40 billion
- Illinois: $ 98.52 billion
- Indiana: $ 48.41 billion
- Iowa: $ 22.38 billion
- Kansas: $ 19.21 billion
- Kentucky: $ 30.65 billion
- Louisiana: $ 32.35 billion
- Maine: $ 12.40 billion
- Maryland: $ 48.41 billion
- Massachusetts: $ 56.92 billion

- Michigan: $ 75.41 billion
- Minnesota: $ 43.78 billion
- Mississippi: $ 21.65 billion
- Missouri: $ 47.92 billion
- Montana: $ 8.75 billion
- Nebraska: $ 15.08 billion
- Nevada: $ 27.73 billion
- New Hampshire: $ 16.29 billion
- New Jersey: $ 75.90 billion
- New Mexico: $ 15.08 billion
- New York: $144.26 billion
- North Carolina: $ 70.30 billion
- North Dakota: $ 6.08 billion
- Ohio: $ 82.47 billion
- Oklahoma: $ 24.32 billion
- Oregon: $ 30.89 billion
- Pennsylvania: $ 99.01 billion
- Rhode Island: $ 8.27 billion
- South Carolina: $ 33.08 billion
- South Dakota: $ 7.78 billion
- Tennessee: $ 51.08 billion
- Texas: $182.21 billion
- Utah: $ 20.43 billion
- Vermont: $ 6.08 billion
- Virginia: $ 63.98 billion
- Washington: $ 54.98 billion
- West Virginia: $ 13.13 billion
- Wisconsin: $ 43.78 billion
- Wyoming: $ 5.10 billion

3.7 Market Resources

comScore, 11950 Democracy Drive, Suite 600, Reston, VA 20190. (703) 438-2000. (www.comscore.com)

Estimates Of Monthly Retail and Food Services Sales By Kind Of Business, U.S. Department of Commerce, 2013. (www.census.gov/retail/marts/www/marts_current.pdf)

Forrester Research, Harvard Square, P.O. Box 1091, Cambridge, MA 02238. (617) 497-7090. (www.forrester.com)

International Council of Shopping Centers, 1221 Avenue of the Americas, 41st Floor, New York, NY 10020. (646) 728-3800. (www.icsc.org)

Internet Retailer, 125 South Wacker Drive, Suite 2900, Chicago, IL 60606. (312) 362-9527. (www.internetretailer.com)

National Retail Federation, 325 7th Street NW, Washington, DC 20004. (202) 783-7971. (www.nrf.com)

Retail Business Market Research Handbook 2013, 15th Edition, Richard K. Miller & Associates, June 2013. (www.rkma.com)

ShopperTrak, 200 West Monroe Street, Chicago, IL 60606. (312) 529-5300. (www.shoppertrak.com)

The State Of Retailing Online 2013: Marketing, Social, and Mobile, Shop.org, May 2013.

4

USE OF TIME

4.1 Americans' Use of Time

The *American Time Use Survey* (*ATUS*, www.bls.gov/tus/), first published in 2005 by the Bureau of Labor Statistics (BLS) of the U.S. Department of Labor and updated annually, is the most recognized source for data on use of time.

Use-of-time data is skewed because most people do not participate in all types of activities. *ATUS* accounts for this by quantifying for each type of activity the average amount of time spent both by all consumers and by only those who participate in an activity.

According to the 2012 *ATUS*, published by the BLS in June 2013, American adults' average 24-hour day, the percentage participating in various activities, and the average time spent among participants are distributed as follows:

	All Consumers	Pct.	Active Participants
• Sleeping and personal care:	9.49 hours	100%	9.49 hours
• Leisure and sports:	5.37 hours	96%	5.58 hours
• Working and work-related activities:	3.53 hours	44%	8.05 hours
• Household activities:	1.74 hours	74%	2.36 hours
• Eating and drinking:	1.25 hours	96%	1.30 hours
• Purchasing goods and services:	0.72 hours	41%	1.72 hours
• Caring for/helping household members:	0.51 hours	24%	2.09 hours
• Educational activities:	0.50 hours	8%	5.87 hours
• Organizational, civic, religious:	0.32 hours	14%	2.33 hours
• Caring for/helping non-household members:	0.18 hours	11%	1.62 hours
• Telephone calls, mail, email:	0.16 hours	20%	0.78 hours
• Other activities:	0.24 hours	14%	1.69 hours

By gender, adults' 24-hour day is distributed as follows:

	Men	Women
• Sleeping and personal care:	9.22 hours	9.74 hours
• Leisure and sports:	5.79 hours	4.97 hours
• Working and work-related activities:	4.17 hours	2.94 hours
• Household activities:	1.29 hours	2.17 hours
• Eating and drinking:	1.30 hours	1.20 hours
• Purchasing goods and services:	0.60 hours	0.84 hours
• Caring for/helping household members:	0.35 hours	0.66 hours

• Educational activities:	0.53 hours	0.47 hours
• Organizational, civic, religious:	0.26 hours	0.38 hours
• Caring for/helping non-household members:	0.16 hours	0.20 hours
• Telephone calls, mail, email:	0.11 hours	0.20 hours
• Other activities:	0.23 hours	0.25 hours

4.2 Daily Activities

The following is a summary of the *American Time Use Survey* reporting on activities in 2012:

Leisure Activities

- On an average day, nearly everyone age 15 and over (96%) engaged in some sort of leisure activity, such as watching TV, socializing, or exercising. Of those who engaged in leisure activities, men spent more time in these activities (6.0 hours) than did women (5.2 hours).
- Watching TV was the leisure activity that occupied the most time (2.8 hours per day), accounting for about half of leisure time, on average, for those age 15 and over. Socializing, such as visiting with friends or attending or hosting social events, was the next most common leisure activity, accounting for nearly three-quarters of an hour per day.
- Men were more likely than women to participate in sports, exercise, or recreation on any given day – 22% compared with 17%. On the days that they participated, men also spent more time in these activities than did women – 1.9 hours compared with 1.4 hours.
- On an average day, adults age 75 and over spent 7.7 hours engaged in leisure activities – more than any other age group; 25-to-34 year-olds spent 4.4 hours and 35-to-44-year-olds spent 4.3 hours engaged in leisure and sports activities – less than other age groups.
- Time spent reading for personal interest and playing games or using a computer for leisure varied greatly by age. Individuals age 75 and over averaged 1.0 hour of reading per weekend day and 20 minutes playing games or using a computer for leisure. Conversely, individuals ages 15-to-19 read for an average of 7 minutes per weekend day while spending 1.0 hour playing games or using a computer for leisure.
- Employed adults living in households with no children under age 18 engaged in leisure activities for 4.7 hours per day, about an hour more than employed adults living with a child under age 6.

Household Activities

- On an average day, 82% of women and 65% of men spent some time doing household activities such as housework, cooking, lawn care, or financial and other household management.
- On the days they did household activities, women spent an average of 2.6 hours on such activities, while men spent 2.0 hours.

- On an average day, 20% of men did housework – such as cleaning or doing laundry – compared with 48% of women. Thirty-nine percent (39%) of men did food preparation or cleanup, compared with 65% of women.

Care of Household Children (by adults in households with children)

- Adults living in households with children under age 6 spent an average of 2.0 hours per day providing primary childcare to household children. Adults living in households where the youngest child was between the ages of 6 and 17 spent less than half as much time providing primary childcare to household children – 47 minutes per day. Primary childcare is childcare that is done as a main activity, such as physical care of children and reading to or talking with children.
- On an average day, among adults living in households with children under age 6, women spent 1.1 hours providing physical care (such as bathing or feeding a child) to household children; by contrast, men spent 26 minutes providing physical care.
- Adults living in households with at least one child under age 6 spent an average of 5.4 hours per day providing secondary childcare – that is, they had at least one child in their care while doing activities other than primary childcare. Secondary childcare provided by adults living in households with children under age 6 was most commonly provided while doing leisure activities (2.1 hours) or household activities (1.3 hours).
- Adults living in households with children under age 6 spent more time providing primary childcare on an average weekday (2.1 hours) than on an average weekend day (1.7 hours). However, they spent less time providing secondary childcare on weekdays than on weekend days – 4.5 hours compared with 7.6 hours.

4.3 Older Americans

Among those ages 55 and older, time spent daily doing select activities was as follows:

	Ages 55-64	Ages 65-74	75 and Older
• Leisure and sports:	5.3 hours	6.7 hours	7.6 hours
• Working and related activities:	3.4 hours	1.0 hours	0.3 hours
• Household activities:	2.2 hours	2.4 hours	2.3 hours

By employment status, those ages 55 or older spent leisure time as follows:

	Not Employed	Employed
• Watching TV:	4.4 hours	2.8 hours
• Reading:	1.0 hours	0.7 hours
• Socializing and communicating:	0.7 hours	0.6 hours
• Relaxing and thinking:	0.7 hours	0.3 hours
• Other leisure:	1.1 hours	0.7 hours

4.4 Students

High school students spent the average weekday engaged in various activities as follows:

	Not Employed	Employed
• Sleeping:	8.8 hours	8.4 hours
• Education:	6.3 hours	5.6 hours
• Socializing, relaxing and leisure:	3.7 hours	3.0 hours
• Sports, exercise and recreation:	0.9 hours	0.6 hours
• Spiritual and volunteering:	0.2 hours	0.4 hours
• Working:	0.0 hours	1.6 hours

Full-time college and university students spent the average weekday engaged in various activities as follows:

- Sleeping: 8.3 hours
- Leisure and sports: 3.7 hours
- Educational activities: 3.3 hours
- Working and related activities: 3.1 hours
- Travel: 1.5 hours
- Eating and drinking: 1.0 hours
- Grooming: 0.8 hours
- Other: 2.3 hours

4.5 Market Resources

American Time Use Survey - 2012 Results, Bureau of Labor Statistics, June 2013. (www.bls.gov/news.release/atus.nr0.htm)

5

USE OF MEDIA & THE INTERNET

5.1 State Of The Media

Published annually by Deloitte (www.deloitte.com), *State of the Media Democracy* assesses media consumption preferences among U.S. adults. The following are findings of the 7th edition, published in January 2013:

- Ninety-three percent (93%) of Americans place Internet access as the most valued household subscription.
- More than half of all consumers are willing to pay a premium for faster Internet connection, with tablet and smartphone owners more inclined to do so.
- Twenty-six percent (26%) of consumers are digital omnivores (own a laptop, smartphone, and tablet).
- Tablet ownership increased 177% in 2012, with almost a third of tablet owners viewing it as one of their top three most preferred consumer electronic devices.
- Tablet owners stream movies 70% more often than non-tablet owners.
- More than 80% of consumers multi-task while watching TV.

5.2 Use Of Media

Use of media among U.S. adults has shifted toward digital platforms over the past four years. Digital media usage surpassed time spent watching TV in 2013.

According to eMarketer (www.emarketer.com), time spent by adults using media has been as follows:

- 2010: 10.77 hours
- 2011: 11.30 hours
- 2012: 11.82 hours
- 2013: 12.08 hours

The increase is attributed, in part, to multitasking.

The share of time per day spend by adults with major media has been as follows (source: eMarketer):

	2010	2011	2012	2013
• Digital:	29.6%	33.8%	38.5%	43.6%
- Mobile (non-voice):	3.6%	7.1%	13.4%	19.4%
- Online:	22.0%	22.6%	20.7%	19.2%
- Other:	3.9%	4.1%	4.4%	5.0%
• TV:	40.9%	40.4%	39.2%	37.4%
• Radio:	14.9%	13.9%	13.0%	11.9%

- Print: 7.7% 6.5% 5.4% 4.5%
- Other: 7.0% 5.5% 4.1% 2.8%

Media Use Benchmark 2013, by Temkin Group (www.temkingroup.com), reported daily media consumption as follows:

- Television: 3.9 hours
- Internet via PC, not for work: 3.8 hours
- Radio: 2.1 hours
- Internet via PC, for work: 2.0 hours
- Read a book, not online: 1.4 hours
- Read news online: 1.4 hours
- Internet or app via mobile phone: 1.4 hours
- Read newspaper, not online: 1.1 hours
- Read a book online or via tablet: 0.9 hour

5.3 Internet Use

According to the Pew Internet & American Life Project (www.pewinternet.org), adult use of the Internet is as follows:

- 18-to-29: 97%
- 30-to-49: 91%
- 50-to-64: 77%
- 65 and older: 53%

Among all adults, broadband access at home is as follows:

- 18-to-29: 75%
- 30-to-49: 77%
- 50-to-64: 82%
- 65 and older: 39%

Among adult Internet users, those going online in a typical day are as follows:

- 18-to-29: 87%
- 30-to-49: 86%
- 50-to-64: 76%
- 65 and older: 70%

Among adult Internet users, those that use social networking sites and those that do so in a typical day are as follows:

	Total	Typical Day
• 18-to-29:	86%	70%
• 30-to-49:	72%	52%
• 50-to-64:	50%	31%
• 65 and older:	34%	18%

Among adult Internet users, those that use email and those that do so in a typical day are as follows:

	Total	Typical Day
• 18-to-29:	91%	59%
• 30-to-49:	93%	61%
• 50-to-64:	90%	60%
• 65 and older:	86%	48%

5.4 Cross-Platform Consumer Behavior

According to a survey for Google (www.google.com) by Ipsos (www.ipsos.com), more than one-half of all media interactions involve multitasking, or the simultaneous use of one or more types media. Simultaneous use of media among those who use various media technologies is as follows:

TV With Another Device:	77%
• With a smartphone:	49%
• With a PC/laptop:	34%
Tablet With Another Device:	75%
• With a TV:	44%
• With a smartphone:	35%
PC With Another Device:	67%
• With a smartphone:	45%
• With a TV:	32%
Smartphone With Another Device:	57%
• With a TV:	29%
• With a PC/laptop:	28%

5.5 Online Activities

Since 2000, the Center for the Digital Future (www.digitalcenter.org) at the University of Southern California, Annenberg School for Communication and Journalism has conducted the Digital Future Project. The annual report is the longest continuing study of its kind and provides insight into the evolution of Internet use in the U.S.

The following is a summary of historical data presented in the 2013 edition:

	2000	2005	2010	2012
• Americans using the Internet:	67%	79%	82%	86%
• Time online per week:	9.4 hrs	13.3 hrs	18.3 hrs	20.4 hrs
• Time online at home:	3.3 hrs	7.8 hrs	12.3 hrs	14.1 hrs
• Time online at work:	4.6 hrs	5.6 hrs	9.2 hrs	9.2 hrs
• Households with broadband:	10%	48%	84%	83%
• Pct. Internet users who buy online:	45%	46%	68%	78%

Those who shop online have made the following types of online purchases:

- Clothes: 66%
- Travel: 66%
- Books: 63%
- Gifts: 60%
- Electronics: 51%
- Videos/DVDs: 42%
- Computers/peripherals: 40%
- Software/games: 37%
- CDs: 35%
- Products for hobbies: 34%

Fifty-six percent (56%) of users reported that they went online with a handheld device in 2013; in 2012 that figure was 33%.

People spend roughly as much time watching television as they do online. When asked about the distribution of their screen time, participants in the Digital Future Project responded as follows:

- TV: 48%
- Desktop PC or laptop: 33%
- Mobile phone: 15%
- Tablet: 4%

America At The Digital Turning Point, a 2012 report by the Annenberg School for Communication and Journalism, identified ten key findings and observations related to current use and the future of online activities, as follows:

- Americans view the Internet as an important information source, yet many Internet users do not trust much of the information they find online.
- Personal privacy is lost.
- The Internet's influence on political power is still a major question.
- The Internet will create even greater shifts in buying habits, particularly at the expense of traditional bricks-and-mortar retail.
- Most printed daily newspapers will be gone in about five years.
- As social networking continues to grow, family and friends are being linked more closely than ever. But social networking and other Internet use is affecting personal time spent with family and friends.
- Many Internet users are frustrated with the vast amount of email received and, increasingly, the encroachment on their lives.
- Over the next three years, the tablet will become the primary tool for personal computing needs. Use of a desktop PC may dwindle to only 4% to 6% of computer users and laptop use will probably decline as well.
- Because of online technology, work is increasingly a 24/7 experience.

5.6 Smartphones and Tablets

eMarketer assessed 2012 smartphone users and forecasts 2015 users as follows (total number of smartphone users, percentage of total population, and percentage among mobile phone users):

	No. Users	Pct. of Population	Pct. of Mobile Users
• 2012:	115.8 million	36.6%	47.7%
• 2015:	176.3 million	54.2%	68.8%

Time spent with mobile phones and tablets, excluding voice calls, nearly tripled between 2011 and 2013, according to eMarketer, with time spent via mobile access surpassing computer access in 2013.

According to the Pew Internet & American Life Project, as of September 2013, 56% of U.S. adults owned a smartphone; 93% of these smartphone owners use their device to go online.

The number of Americans ages 16 and older who own tablet computers increased to 35% as of September 2013; the share who have e-reading devices (e.g., Kindles and Nooks) is 24%. Overall, the number of people who have a tablet or an e-book reader among those 16 and older is 43%.

The percentage of smartphone users who go online using their phones has been as follows (source: Pew Internet & American Life Project):

	Email	Internet	Total
• 2009:	25%	25%	32%
• 2010:	34%	38%	43%
• 2011:	38%	44%	47%
• 2012:	44%	53%	55%
• 2013:	52%	60%	63%

In 2013, 34% of cell Internet users said they mostly go online using their mobile phone. That means that 21% of all adult cell owners now do most of their online browsing using their mobile phone rather than a desktop or laptop computer.

5.7 Social Networking

According to an August 2013 report by the Pew Internet & American Life Project, the percentage of U.S. adult Internet users who use social networking sites has been as follows:

- 2005: 8%
- 2006: 15%
- 2007: 23%
- 2008: 28%
- 2009: 47%
- 2010: 61%
- 2011: 64%
- 2012: 68%
- 2013: 72%

Demographics of adults who used social networking sites in 2013 are as follows (source: Pew Internet & American Life Project):

Gender

• Female:	74%
• Male:	70%

Age

• 18-to-29:	89%
• 30-to-49:	78%
• 50-to-64:	60%
• 65 and older:	43%

Race/Ethnicity

• Hispanic:	80%
• Black, non-Hispanic:	75%
• White, non-Hispanic:	70%

Education

• No high school diploma:	67%
• High school graduate:	72%
• Some college:	73%
• College degree:	72%

Household Income

• Less than $30,000:	75%
• $30,000 to $49,999:	72%
• $50,000 to $74,999:	74%
• $75,000 and higher:	71%

Community

• Urban:	74%
• Suburban:	71%
• Rural:	69%

Among adults who use social networks, preferred platforms are as follows (multiple responses allowed):

• Facebook:	67%
• LinkedIn:	20%
• Twitter:	16%
• Pinterest:	15%
• Instagram:	13%
• Tumblr:	6%

"Checking Facebook has become almost as embedded in the lives of Americans as getting a cup of coffee. On any given day, more than 40% of Americans – 128 million people – visit Facebook. Of those daily visitors, about 79%, or 101 million, use a mobile device like a smartphone or tablet to access the service."

The New York Times, 8/5/13

5.8 Online and Mobile Video

eMarketer assessed 2012 online and mobile video viewing and forecasts 2015 viewing as follows (total number of viewers, percentage of total population, and percentage among online/mobile users):

2012

	No. Viewers	Pct. of Population	Pct. of Online/Mobile
• Online:	169.3 million	53.5%	70.8%
• Mobile:	54.6 million	17.3%	22.5%

2015

	No. Viewers	Pct. of Population	Pct. of Online/Mobile
• Online:	195.5 million	60.1%	76.0%
• Mobile:	78.1 million	24.0%	30.5%

5.9 Market Resources

Digital Future Project, Center for the Digital Future at the University of Southern California, Annenberg School for Communication and Journalism, 11444 West Olympic Boulevard, Suite 120, Los Angeles, CA 90064. (www.digitalcenter.org)

eMarketer, 75 Broad Street, 32nd Floor, New York, NY 10004. (212) 763-6010. (www.emarketer.com)

Entertainment, Media & Advertising Market Research Handbook 2013-2014, Richard K. Miller & Associates, November 2012. (www.rkma.com)

Pew Internet & American Life Project, 1615 L Street NW, Suite 700, Washington, DC 20036. (202) 419-4500. (www.pewinternet.org)

State of the Media, The Nielsen Company, March 2012. (www.nielsen.com/us/en/insights/reports-downloads/2012/us-digital-consumer-report.html)

State of the Media Democracy Survey, 7th Edition, Deloitte, January 2013. (www.deloitte.com/us/mediademocracy)

The Nielsen Company, 770 Broadway, New York, NY 10003. (646) 654-5000. (www.nielsen.com)

6

CONSUMER INCOME & WEALTH

6.1 Household Income

According to the U.S. Census Bureau (www.census.gov), real median household income in the United States in 2012 was $51,017, not statistically different in real terms from the 2011 median of $51,100. This followed two consecutive annual declines. In 2012, real median household income was 8.3% lower than in 2007, the year before the Great Recession.

6.2 Income Distribution

In 2012, median household income was as follows (source: U.S. Census Bureau):

- Married-couple family households: $64,053
- Non-family households: $30,880

By region, median household income in 2012 was as follows:

- West: $55,157
- Northeast: $54,627
- Midwest: $50,479
- South: $48,033

By householder age, median household income in 2012 was as follows:

- Under 24: $30,604
- 25-to-34: $51,381
- 35-to-44: $63,629
- 45-to-54: $66,411
- 55-to-64: $58,626
- 65 and older: $33,848

By community, median household income in 2012 was as follows:

- Inside metropolitan areas: $52,988
- Outside metropolitan areas: $41,198

In 2012, the real median earnings of men and women who worked full time were $49,398 and $37,791, respectively. The 2012 female-to-male earnings ratio was 0.77, a figure that has not experienced a significant annual change since 2007.

6.3 Income by State

Median income by state in 2011 (most recent data available as of November 2013) was as follows (source: Census Bureau):

- Alabama: $41,415
- Alaska: $67,825
- Arizona: $46,709
- Arkansas: $38,758
- California: $57,287
- Colorado: $55,387
- Connecticut: $65,753
- Delaware: $58,814
- District of Columbia: $63,124
- Florida: $44,299
- Georgia: $46,007
- Hawaii: $61,821
- Idaho: $43,341
- Illinois: $53,234
- Indiana: $46,438
- Iowa: $49,427
- Kansas: $48,964
- Kentucky: $41,141
- Louisiana: $41,734
- Maine: $46,033
- Maryland: $70,004
- Massachusetts: $62,859
- Michigan: $45,981
- Minnesota: $56,954
- Mississippi: $36,919
- Missouri: $45,247
- Montana: $44,222
- Nebraska: $50,296
- Nevada: $48,927
- New Hampshire: $62,647
- New Jersey: $67,458
- New Mexico: $41,963
- New York: $55,246
- North Carolina: $43,916
- North Dakota: $51,704
- Ohio: $45,749
- Oklahoma: $43,225
- Oregon: $46,816
- Pennsylvania: $50,228
- Rhode Island: $53,636
- South Carolina: $42,367
- South Dakota: $48,321
- Tennessee: $41,693
- Texas: $49,392
- Utah: $55,869
- Vermont: $52,776
- Virginia: $61,882
- Washington: $56,835
- West Virginia: $38,482
- Wisconsin: $50,395
- Wyoming: $56,322

6.4 Household Wealth

More than two-thirds of Americans saw their net worth decline during the recession. According to the *Survey of Consumer Finances*, published every three years and most recently in 2012 by the Federal Reserve (www.federalreserve.gov), from 2007 to 2010, median inflation-adjusted net worth (e.g., wealth) fell 38.8% to $77,300, the same level as in 2001. Median net worth dropped 14.8% to $489,800, a level not seen since 1992.

Overall, net household wealth, which mostly consists of home equity, stock portfolios, and other savings, was $62.7 trillion in 2012, according to the Federal Reserve. Household wealth peaked before the recession at $67.4 trillion and reached a low of $51.2 trillion in early 2009, in the depths of the recession.

The distribution of wealth in the United States is as follows:

- The top 20% of Americans hold 84% of U.S. wealth
- The second 20% hold 11%
- The third 20% hold 4%
- The fourth 20% hold 0.2%
- The bottom 20% hold 0.1%

Twenty-five percent (25%) of American households have zero or negative net worth; 37% have a net worth of less than $12,000.

6.5 Income and Wealth Inequality

According to Robert Reich, Ph.D., an economics professor at University of California, Berkeley and author of *Inequality For All* (2013, 72 Productions), the average male U.S. worker in 1978 earned $48,000, adjusted for inflation, while the average member of the Upper One Percent earned $390,000, or eight times as much. By 2010, the middle-class male's wages had declined to $33,000, while the One Percenter was making $1.1 million, or 33 times more. Prof. Reich says that the wealthiest 400 people in the U.S. today have more money than the bottom 150 million Americans combined.

The White House's Council of Economic Advisers says that since 1970, the percentage of people designated as middle class has fallen from 50% to 42%. And a 2012 report by the Congressional Research Service says that the wealthiest 10% of households went from controlling 67% of the country's wealth in 1989 to almost 75% in 2010.

The Great Recession widened the gap between the wealthy and the rest of the U.S. population.

An ongoing assessment of income distribution at the University of California, Berkeley found that the richest 1% in America took 19% of national income in 2012, their biggest share since 1928. The top 10% of earners held a record 48.2%. During the recovery between 2009 and 2012 real family incomes rose by an average of 4.6%, though this was skewed by a 31.4% increase for the top 1%. For the other 99% incomes rose by just 0.4%.

According to an April 2013 assessment by The Pew Research Center (www.pewresearch.org), during the first two years of the economic recovery, the mean net worth of households in the upper 7% of the wealth distribution rose by an estimated 28%, while the mean net worth of households in the lower 93% dropped by 4%. From 2009 to 2011, the mean wealth of the 8 million households in the more affluent group rose to an estimated $3,173,895 from an estimated $2,476,244, while the mean wealth of the 111 million households in the less affluent group fell to an estimated $133,817 from an estimated $139,896.

"While 91% of the total household wealth lost during the crisis has been recovered, according to the St. Louis Federal Reserve, that recovery has been uneven: the richest households, more heavily invested in stocks, lost the most and regained the most. Adjusting for inflation and population growth, the average household has recovered only about 45% of its wealth."

Time, 8/19/13

Median annual household income in February 2013 was $51,404. According to Sentier Research (www.sentier.com), this is 5.6% lower than it was in June 2009, the month the recovery technically began; 7.3% lower than in December 2007, when the most recent recession officially started; and 8.4% lower than in January 2000.

6.6 Poverty and Economic Insecurity

The U.S. poverty rate in 2012 was 15.0%, with 46.5 million people classified as living in poverty, according to the Census Bureau. This was not statistically different from the two prior years.

While Census Bureau figures provide an official measure of poverty, they are only a temporary snapshot and do not capture the makeup of those who cycle in and out of poverty at different points in their lives. That snapshot shows that 12.6% of adults in their prime working-age years of 25-to-60 live in poverty. But measured in terms of a person's lifetime risk, a much higher number – four in ten adults – fall into poverty for at least a year of their lives.

According to a July 2013 assessment by the Associated Press (AP), the risks of falling into poverty have been increasing in recent decades, particularly among people ages 35-to-55, and coinciding with widening income inequality. For instance, people ages 35-to-45 had a 17% risk of encountering poverty during the 1969-1989 time period; that risk increased to 23% during the 1989-2009 period. For those ages 45-55, the risk of poverty jumped from 12% to 18%.

The AP study defines 'economic insecurity' as a year or more of periodic joblessness, reliance on government aid such as food stamps, or income below 150% of the poverty line. According to its assessment, higher recent rates of unemployment mean the lifetime risk of experiencing economic insecurity is 79%.

Poverty and economic insecurity cut across all ethnic and racial demographics. More than 19 million whites fall below the poverty line of $23,021 for a family of four, accounting for more than 41% of the nation's destitute, nearly double the number of poor blacks. Seventy-six percent (76%) of whites will experience economic insecurity by the time they turn 60.

> **"Hardship is particularly growing among whites, based on several measures. Pessimism among that racial group about their families' economic futures has climbed to the highest point since at least 1987. In the most recent AP-GfK poll, 63% of whites called the economy poor. While poverty rates for blacks and Hispanics are nearly three times higher, by absolute numbers the predominant face of the poor is white."**
>
> *Associated Press*, 7/28/13

6.7 Market Resources

Household Income Trends, Sentier Research, 2013. (www.sentier.com)

Income, U.S. Census Bureau. (U.S. Census Bureau website for income statistics) (www.census.gov/hhes/www/income/income.html)

Institute for Research On Poverty, University of Wisconsin-Madison, 1180 Observatory Drive, Madison, WI 53706. (608) 262-6358. (www.irp.wisc.edu)

Survey of Consumer Finances, a triennial survey of U.S. families by the Federal Reserve. (www.federalreserve.gov/econresdata/scf/scfindex.htm)

7

CONSUMER DEBT

7.1 Household Debt

According to the Federal Reserve (www.federalreserve.gov), total U.S. household debt at the end of the third quarter 2013 was $11.28 trillion, distributed as follows:

- Mortgages: $7.90 trillion
- Student loans: $1.21 trillion
- Motor vehicle loans: $ 862 billion
- Credit cards/ revolving credit: $ 815 billion
- Other: $ 491 billion

The third quarter 2013 showed the first substantial increase in outstanding balances since 2008, when Americans began reducing their debt, with a 1.1% increase from the prior quarter. Still, this was 11% below the peak of $12.67 trillion in the third quarter of 2008.

The percentage of 90+ day delinquent balances for all household debt declined to 5.3% during third quarter 2013, the lowest rate since Q3 2008. Debt delinquency rates were as follows:

- Auto loans: 3.4%
- Home equity lines of credit: 3.5%
- Mortgages: 4.3%
- Credit card debt: 9.4%
- Student loans: 11.8%

According to a March 2013 report by the Census Bureau (www.census.gov), 69% of U.S. households carried some type of debt at year-end 2011, a drop from 74% in 2000. Median household debt was $70,000 in 2011, an increase from $51,000 in 2000. In 2011, median household debt by age of head of household was as follows:

- Under 35: $ 45,300
- 35-to-44: $108,000
- 45-to-54: $ 86,500
- 55-to-64: $ 70,000
- 65 and older: $ 26,000

A February 2013 report by the Pew Research Center (www.pewresearch.org), reported that median total household debt declined 29% between 2007 and 2010 among households headed by young adults (younger than age 35), from $21,912 to $15,473. Among older households, debt dropped from $32,543 to $30,070, an 8% decline.

"After running up record debt-to-income ratios during the bubble economy of the 2000s, young adults shed substantially more debt than older adults did during the Great Recession and its immediate aftermath. Debt reduction among young adults during bad economic times has been driven mainly by the shrinking share who own homes and cars, but it also reflects a significant decline in the share who are carrying credit card debt."

Pew Research Center, 2/21/13

Debt rates accumulated the most among lower income households during the recession. According to The Urban Institute (www.urban.org), the average debt for households earning $20,000 a year or less more than doubled to $26,000 between 2001 and 2010. The averages for households in slightly higher brackets grew by 50% to 90% in the same period.

"Millions of Americans have been keeping the lights on through hard times with borrowed money, running a kind of shell game to keep bill collectors away."

The New York Times, 1/14/13

7.2 Mortgage Debt

Mortgage debt accounts for 70% of total consumer debt. Sixty-six percent (66%) of adults have mortgages on their homes, according to Harris Interactive (www.harrisinteractive.com).

Balances on home equity lines of credit (HELOC) were $535 billion at the end of third quarter 2013, a 0.9% drop from the prior quarter. Approximately 26% of refinancings are now 'cash in' deals, where borrowers increase their equity; less than a quarter are 'cash out.' For comparison, in 2008, 67% of borrowers who refinanced took cash out.

According to The Federal Home Loan Mortgage Corporation (FHLMC), known as Freddie Mac (www.freddiemac.com), homeowners are shortening the terms of their mortgages. Since 2011, over one-third of refinancers paid off a 30-year loan and switched to a 20- or 15-year loan.

Foreclosures have been on a declining trend since the second quarter of 2009. There were 168,000 foreclosures in the third quarter 2013, the lowest level since 2005.

7.3 Credit Card Debt

According to the Federal Reserve, approximately 47% of households had credit card debt at year-end 2012. Among those with credit card debt, the average was $15,587 per household. Many consumers have given up using credit cards entirely. According to the Federal Reserve, 32% of families had no credit cards in 2012, an increase from 27% in 2007.

Credit card debt at the end of third quarter 2013 was $814.7 billion, an increase from $813.0 a year prior.

Credit card balances typically peak in December following the holiday shopping season. Year-end revolving credit balances have been as follows (source: Federal Reserve):

- 2008: $1.005 trillion
- 2009: $ 917 billion
- 2010: $ 841 billion
- 2011: $ 842 billion
- 2012: $ 846 billion

7.4 Student Loans

About two-thirds of bachelor's degree recipients borrow money to attend college, either from the government or private lenders, according to the U.S. Department of Education.

Outstanding educational debt has been as follows (source: Federal Reserve):

- 2008: $ 731 billion
- 2009: $ 832 billion
- 2010: $ 912 billion

- 2011: $1.012 trillion
- 2012: $1.131 trillion
- 3Q 2013: $1.214 trillion

Since the peak in household debt in 2008, student loan debt has increased by $483 billion, while other forms of debt have dropped a combined $1.6 trillion.

During third quarter 2013, 11.8% of student loan balances were 90 or more days delinquent.

According to the Pew Research Center, 19% of U.S. households owe student debt, more than double the share two decades earlier and a rise from the 15% that owed such debt in 2007, just prior to the onset of the Great Recession. Forty percent (40%) of households headed by someone younger than age 35 owe such debt. Among households owing student debt, the average outstanding student loan balance is $26,682; 10% of student debtor households owe more than $61,894.

"With more than $1 trillion in student loans outstanding in this country, crippling debt is no longer confined to dropouts from for-profit colleges or graduate students who owe on many years of education, some of the over-extended debtors in years past. As prices soar, a college degree statistically remains a good lifetime investment, but it often comes with an unprecedented financial burden."

The New York Times, 5/12/12

7.5 Market Resources

The Federal Reserve Bank Of New York reports on household credit, including mortgages, at www.newyorkfed.org/regional/householdcredit.html.

Monthly short- and intermediate-term consumer credit data, excluding loans secured by real estate, is available from the Federal Reserve Bank at www.federalreserve.gov/releases/g19/current/default.htm.

Survey of Consumer Finances, a triennial survey of U.S. families by the Federal Reserve, is available at www.federalreserve.gov/econresdata/scf/scfindex.htm.

PART II: SHOPPING BEHAVIORS

8

COMPETITION BETWEEN SHOPPING CHANNELS

8.1 Overview

Today's shopping has been likened to warfare between consumers and retailers.

Consumers shop armed with tablet computers and smartphones, checking product reviews and making price comparisons. They do not hesitate to switch product brands or retailers for the slightest cost savings. A survey by GroupM Next (www.groupmnext.com) found 45% of customers shopping in-store at bricks-and-mortar locations will walk out and complete their purchase online for a discount as low as 2.5%; 60% will do so for a 5% savings.

Retailers are responding to consumers' use of technology with their own arsenal, tracking consumers online and while they are in their stores, using customer profiles to tailor offers, showing different price categories to various customers, and more.

8.2 Showrooming

"Showrooming" is the practice where customers go to a bricks-and-mortar retail location, make a decision on what item to buy, and instead of heading to the check-out aisle, use a mobile device to find a better price online where they ultimately make their purchase.

An April 2013 Harris Poll (www.harrisinteractive.com) found that 40% of U.S. adults have visited a bricks-and-mortar store to examine a product before purchasing it elsewhere online. Poll participants said the mean spending on their last such showrooming experience was $178.

> **"Despite bricks-and-mortar retailers' best efforts to keep consumers buying in-store, forty percent of Americans have showroomed."**
>
> Harris Poll, 6/4/13

The Harris Poll asked consumers about the best way retailers could get them to make their purchases in stores. Fifty-seven percent (57%) said they are more likely to make purchases in bricks-and-mortar stores that have implemented permanent price matching policies in order to compete with online retailers.

A survey by Retrevo (www.retrevo.com) found that 66% of all shoppers and 78% of smartphone owners have checked out products in a store, used their device for price comparisons or research, then bought in another store or online. By product category, those that have done so are as follows:

	All Shoppers	Smartphone Owners
• Consumer electronics:	48%	58%
• Shoes:	32%	41%
• Apparel:	31%	39%
• Appliances:	19%	23%
• Sporting goods:	16%	22%
• Home & garden:	15%	18%

"Shoppers armed with smartphones have become a major challenge for some bricks-and-mortar retailers. The showrooming phenomenon exposes two potential vulnerabilities for bricks-and-mortar retailers. First, bricks-and-mortar retailers likely have higher fixed costs than their web-only rivals, making it hard to compete on price. Second, they are dealing with consumers who are better informed, more demanding, and more aware of alternative sources of goods and services."

eMarketer

Online retailers encourage showrooming. Amazon.com, for instance, offers a 5% discount to users who try its Price Check mobile app, which allows in-store shoppers to scan product barcodes to check Amazon's prices online. Other apps such as BarCode Reader and RedLaser also let smartphone users scan a product's bar code to compare prices online or in nearby stores.

For retailers with a strong online presence, showrooming can be useful. A survey by Vibes (www.vibes.com) found that 29% of showroom shoppers later purchased a product from the website of the store they had visited; 25% bought the item from a competitor's website.

Many consumers that check prices while in a store using their mobile device typically buy a product in the same store. Vibes found that among those who did so, 48% said that scanning for product information made them feel better about their purchase.

A 2012 study by Deloitte (www.deloitte.com) found that smartphone shoppers were 14% more likely than non-smartphone shoppers to convert in-store, even when those smartphone shoppers used a mobile app or site not belonging to the retailer. Seventy-two percent (72%) of shoppers who used their smartphone on their most recent in-store trip made a purchase while there, compared with 63% of shoppers who did not use a smartphone to assist in making a purchase during their last in-store trip.

Among all retail sectors, consumer electronics (CE) has been the most impacted by showrooming. While the overall CE sector is projected to experience a -0.9% CAGR through 2016, online CE sales will increase from $48.6 billion in 2012 to $80.2 billion in 2016. CE sales accounted for 21.7% of all e-commerce revenue (excluding travel and event tickets) in 2012, a figure which is projected to grow to 22.2% by 2016.

Even for customers who make in-store CE purchases, digital channels still play a key role. The Interactive Advertising Bureau (www.iab.net) found that 91% of Internet users had researched electronics products online before making a purchase in-store.

8.3 Cross-Channel Shopping

Showrooming is only one of the cross-channel strategies used by today's consumers. Among those who said they had searched using one channel and made a purchase through another channel, a 2012 survey by Cisco Internet Business Solutions Group (www.cisco.com/web/about/ac79/) found these consumers had engaged in the following cross-channel shopping activities (percentage of respondents):

- PC-to-store: 57%
- Store-to-online: 38%
- Mobile-to-PC: 26%
- Kiosk-to-store (immediate in-store sale): 24%
- Mobile-to-store: 24%
- Kiosk-to-store (delivery to location of choice): 15%

In the *Multichannel Consumer Survey* by PricewaterhouseCoopers (PwC, www.pwc.com), 56% of U.S. adults said they are likely to spend more with multichannel retailers than with either online-only retailers or stores with only bricks-and-mortar locations.

"Our research shows that when consumers use multiple channels, they spend more. That flies in the face of conventional wisdom that launching an online store steals sales from physical stores."

Lisa Feigen Dugel, Director
PwC Retail and Consumer Advisory Practice
Marketing Daily, 5/13/13

In an October 2013 survey by VISA, 83% of adults said they would choose a retailer based on how easy it is to transact across online, in-store, and mobile.

"People expect their experiences to be seamless across devices and channels."

Kevin Burke, CMO
VISA
Advertising Age, 10/21/13

8.4 Marketshare Shifts

Competition between shopping channels is shifting the retail marketplace. Additionally, traditional mass merchants and supermarkets have yielded share to value channels (club, dollar, and supercenter) and drug stores.

The Nielsen Company (www.nielsen.com) projects the following retail sectors to have the highest compound annual growth rate (CAGR) and to gain marketshare through 2016:

- E-commerce: 8.5%
- Warehouse clubs: 4.9%
- Dollar stores: 4.8%
- Supercenters: 4.6%
- Pet stores: 4.1%
- Drug stores: 2.7%

The following sectors are projected to have a positive CAGR through 2016 but will grow slower than the overall U.S. economy, thus losing marketshare:

- Convenience/gas: 2.1%
- Supermarkets: 1.5%
- Liquor stores: 1.2%
- Discount department stores: 0.4%
- Sporting goods: 0.3%

The following sectors are projected to lose marketshare with a negative CAGR:

- Home improvement: -0.1%
- Department stores: -0.4%
- Auto stores: -0.5%
- Home, bed, bath: -0.5%
- Office supply stores: -0.5%
- Apparel: -0.8%
- Electronics: -0.9%
- Book stores: -1.1%
- Toy stores: -1.7%
- Mass merchants: -3.0%

"Retailers will be challenged as never before in the next five years to differentiate from an ever-expanding competitive set that brings novel ideas and fresh perspective to the marketplace. It should come as no surprise that e-commerce tops the list of growth channels."

Todd Hale, Senior Vice President
Consumer & Shopper Insights
The Nielsen Company, 3/21/12

9

IN-STORE SHOPPING

9.1 Preference For In-Store

The *2013 Harris Poll Equi-Trend Study*, published in June 2013 by Harris Interactive (www.harrisinteractive.com), found that consumers generally report higher satisfaction with bricks-and-mortar stores than with online shopping.

"There are many reasons why a consumer would choose to visit a location-based retailer over its online counterpart, including convenience, selection, and immediate needs. Most of all, shoppers tend to want to interact with physical merchandise before purchasing it. Trend data shows that while consumers are increasingly shopping online, their brand experience when doing so tends to score lower than their in-store experience."

Lisa Mulyk, Vice President
Harris Interactive, 6/10/13

In a May 2013 survey by Synqera (www.synqera.com), 67% of adults said they prefer to shop in traditional, bricks-and-mortar stores than online commerce sites. The survey found that 80% of shoppers are more likely to shop in a store that provides an overall customized shopping experience, and 66% are more likely to shop in a store where they receive personal suggestions while shopping.

9.2 Lifestyle Centers

According to *The State of the Shopping Center*, a May 2013 report by The Nielsen Company (www.nielsen.com), traditional shopping centers have morphed into lifestyle centers which blend traditional retail with upscale leisure options that offer shoppers a place to gather and socialize as well as to shop. The lines between shopping, entertainment, and community are increasingly becoming blurred.

> **"Despite the boom in e-commerce, U.S. consumers do most of their shopping at physical stores. In order to attract and captivate consumers, shopping centers have become much more than just places to buy things – they're social centers, places for entertainment, and employment hubs. This blending of experiences has created an opportunity for retailers to strengthen social ties within communities looking for communal experiences."**
>
> Nielsen, 5/23/13

9.3 How America Shops

Since 2004, WSL Strategic Retail (www.wslretail.com) has annually surveyed U.S. consumers about their shopping behaviors. The most recent assessment, *How America Shops*, provides insight into the behavior of today's retail shopper. The following are key findings from the study:

- Seventy-five percent (75%) of consumers say it is important to get the lowest price on everything they buy, up 12 percentage points from 2008 and an increase of 22 percentage points from 2004.
- Sixty-eight percent (68%) of shoppers say they regularly use coupons to reduce costs, an increase of seven percentage points from one year prior.
- Sixty-six percent (66%) of shoppers say they take a pause before buying to ask, "Is this a smart use of my money?" Among those with a household income of $150,000 or more, 47% do so.

- Fifty-eight percent (58%) of consumers say they manage their aspirations by sticking to brands and stores they can afford. Among those with a household income of $150,000 or more, 36% do so.
- Forty-eight percent (48%) of consumers say they are staying out of stores where they might be tempted to overspend. Among those with a household income of $150,000 or more, 28% do so.
- Forty-five percent (45%) of shoppers claim they only buy items that are on sale, an increase of seven percentage points from one year prior.
- Forty-three percent (43%) of consumers make a point to search online for store discounts before they shop, up 10 percentage points from one year prior.
- Twenty-six percent (26%) of shoppers admit that while they used to buy brand names they could not afford, they are no longer giving in to this indulgence.
- Fourteen percent (14%) of consumers say they use their mobile phones while in a store to see if they can find a lower price, before they buy.
- It takes a significantly higher income to feel financially secure in this economy, with nearly 30% of Americans in the $100,000 to $150,000 income bracket claiming they can only afford the basics. Once considered affluent, six-figure income shoppers are increasingly identifying themselves as middle-income.

9.4 Self-Service

In the May 2013 survey by Synqera, 73% of shoppers say they find waiting in the checkout line their least favorite aspect of in-store shopping.

A survey by Buzzback Market Research (www.buzzback.com) found that 66% of shoppers feel that self-service technology creates a more positive perception of the deployer's brand.

According to IHL Group (www.ihlservices.com), consumers made $255 billion in purchases through self-checkout lanes in 2012; transactions at self-service kiosks of all types were $1 trillion.

A survey by Leo J. Shapiro & Associates (www.ljs.com) found consumers divided on the benefits of self checkout. Only 43% said it shortens checkout time, while 38% feel it lengthens checkout. Still, given a choice, 39% say they prefer self-checkout over a cashier.

9.5 The In-Store Experience

According to *The Future of Retail*, by PwC (www.pwc.com), omnichannel shopping – or shopping across multiple channels such as in-store, online, on TV, on a tablet, potentially at the same time – will lead to stores being physically altered in the near future. Conventional bricks-and-mortar stores could be replaced by retail destinations that have limited merchandise, stocking only a few samples for customers who still want to touch and feel products. Stores could operate primarily using screen images and scanners to show, swipe, and sell.

"Anyone who has recently shopped or browsed on a tablet or smartphone knows that the retail experience is changing. And it's changing for both the consumer and the retailer. Within a few years, the entire shopping experience is likely to be all about the consumer, from start to finish. Buying and returning merchandise will be different – more consumer-focused, more technology-enabled, and just plain easier."

Lisa Feigen Dugel, Director
PwC Retail and Consumer Advisory Practice
Marketing Daily, 5/13/13

In a 2012 survey by Motorola Solutions (www.motorolasolutions.com), 74% of retail executives said they believe that developing a more engaging in-store experience will be critical to their business over the next five years. Survey participants foresee the following technological developments occurring in the retail marketplace by 2016:

- All transactions will be completed via mobile POS, self checkout at terminal, or on shopper's mobile device: 56%
- Sales will come from online, mobile, and commercial sites: 42%
- Will send coupons based on customer location in the store: 42%
- Will provide personalized product details to shopper's smartphone based on previous behavior: 41%
- Will recognize customer in store with geofencing or presence technology: 35%

Consumers' cross-channel shopping behaviors will change retailers' marketing strategies. *Retail USA: What's In Store for 2016*, a 2012 study from Nielsen, forecasts the retail marketplace will change in the following ways:

- Store footprints either will get supersized for one-stop-shop convenience or downsized into smaller stores for quick grab-and-go trips.
- For people who view shopping as entertainment that engages all the senses, lifestyle outlets will blur the line of demarcation between traditional formats, merging restaurants with food markets, serving up food and wine tastings, providing live music and movies, and creating places for friends and co-workers to gather and socialize.

- Technology will bring consumers into the shopping experience via options such as touchscreen ordering, QR code advertising, mobile coupons, and shopping lists.
- Store brands will mushroom to include super premium offerings joined by an increasing number of restaurant and celebrity-chef brands, while a few consumer packaged goods brands transition onto restaurant menus.
- The Big Four technology companies (i.e., Amazon, Apple, Facebook, and Google) will establish beachheads outside the tech world, challenging conventional players to re-think their business models and forge new alliances or chance seeing themselves become less relevant.
- Deep discounters will continue to keep the cap on operating costs in order to maintain their price edge, but low prices alone have not been enough to guarantee sales success.
- Retailers will expand designated stores-within-a store spaces, pulling together related items that fulfill a consumer need into a discrete space such as a cosmetics department complete with expert consultants, occasion-based home meal solution centers, or dedicated pet care areas.
- Mobile and online technologies will enable one-to-one marketing, customized shopping lists, menu plans, coupons, and other content to reflect user interests and consumption patterns.
- In-store shelf talkers will take on a new, interactive dimension with QR codes that connect directly to robust websites offering discounts and cross merchandising suggestions such as wine pairings.
- Online avatars and in-store service agents will assist consumers with meal management, entertainment, health and wellness monitoring, and fashion selections.
- The chasm between income and wealth strata will enable retailers at both the high and low ends of the price spectrum to prosper by merchandising to niche audiences.

10

ONLINE SHOPPING

10.1 Overview

According to eMarketer (www.emarketer.com), the number of U.S. consumers shopping online has been, and is projected, as follows:

	Number	Pct. of Internet Users
• 2009:	163.1 million	85.0%
• 2010:	172.3 million	87.1%
• 2011:	178.5 million	87.5%
• 2012:	184.3 million	88.1%
• 2013:	189.6 million	88.7%
• 2014:	195.4 million	89.4%
• 2015:	201.1 million	90.1%

Sixty-percent (60%) of U.S. adults shop online at lease once every three months, according to Forrester Research (www.forrester.com). The percentages by age are as follows:

- 18-to-30: 54%
- 31-to-44: 68%
- 45-to-54: 64%
- 55-to-65: 60%
- 66 and older: 48%

According to A.T. Kearney (www.atkearney.com), among those who shopped online in 2012, purchases were made online for the following product categories (percentage of respondents):

- Books: 81%
- Apparel: 74%
- Music/video/movies: 65%
- Beauty and personal care: 59%
- Footwear: 54%
- Consumer electronics: 52%
- Services (e.g., spas, salons): 34%
- Jewelry: 24%
- Furniture: 18%
- Household products: 16%
- Other: 18%

10.2 Why People Shop Online

A recent poll of Internet users by The Nielsen Company (www.nielsen.com) asking primary reasons for shopping online found the following:

- Able to shop 24 hours a day: 81%
- Saves time: 76%
- Able to comparison shop: 61%
- Easy to find what I am looking for: 56%
- Selection of items: 49%
- Can search by brands I like: 46%
- Available product information: 46%
- Low prices: 45%
- Items are in stock: 35%
- Low shipping costs: 24%
- Recommendations for items: 15%
- Customer service and communication: 12%
- Easy to return purchases: 11%
- Gift services such as cards, wrapping, or birthday/holiday reminders: 10%

A survey by Impulse Research (www.impulseresearch.com) found the primary reasons that Millennial adults, ages 18-to-34, shop online are as follows:

- Better prices: 37%
- Avoid shopping hassles and crowds: 29%
- Convenience: 18%
- Better selection: 13%
- Direct shipping to home: 3%

A survey by Accenture (www.accenture.com) found parents with children in school liked to shop online for the following reasons (percentage of respondents):

- Save money/find discounts: 70%
- To research products and prices: 63%
- Avoid going to many stores: 40%
- Avoid boring trips for kids: 28%
- Avoid kid pressure to buy items: 17%
- School works with e-retailers to ensure supplies are in stock: 7%

"Price and convenience lead many parents to shop online for back-to-school items. Web shoppers like not having to schlep from store to store, dragging kids with them."

Accenture, 7/12

10.3 Characteristics Of Online Shopping

When asked how they typically find what they're shopping for online, responses were as follows (source: Nielsen; multiple responses allowed):

- Know the site by name: 69%
- Search engines: 62%
- Comparison shopping tools: 23%
- Subscribe to an e-newsletter from retailers: 15%
- Blogs/chat rooms/consumer reviews: 5%

In its May 2013 Monthly E-Commerce Research Initiative, Shopzilla (www.shopzilla.com) asked U.S. adults how they first saw the product they most recently purchased online. Responses were as follows:

- While surfing online: 29%
- Looking for something specific: 24%
- In email from store: 11%
- While "out and about": 8%
- In friend's house: 8%
- In a magazine: 7%
- In an ad: 6%
- On blog or other website content: 4%
- On Facebook: 2%
- On Pinterest: <1%
- On Twitter: <1%

10.4 Expectations Online

According to a survey by OneUpWeb (www.oneupweb.com), Internet users expect the following from e-commerce sites (percentage of respondents):

- Pricing/shipping information clearly stated: 96%
- Site looks credible and trustworthy: 76%
- Product displayed on homepage: 71%
- Visually appealing: 67%
- Total cost calculator: 59%
- Search function: 48%
- Privacy statement: 46%
- Onsite customer reviews: 41%
- Online customer service (live chat): 32%
- Links to social networks (Facebook, Twitter): 23%

According to a survey by A.T. Kearney, the following attributes are important to consumers when shopping online (percentage of respondents):

- Finding specific products: 96%
- Free shipping: 93%
- Finding favorite brands: 92%
- Best price: 90%
- Ease of navigation: 88%
- Site security: 87%
- Special promotions: 78%
- Free samples: 67%
- Peer reviews: 59%
- New products: 55%

A June 2013 survey by comScore (www.comscore.com) asked online shoppers the factors driving them to shop with an online retailer. Responses were as follows (two responses per survey participant):

- The ability to buy online and then make returns at the store: 62%
- The push of a coupon/promotion to my smartphone: 47%
- The ability to buy online and pick up in store: 44%
- The availability of an application designed specifically for a tablet: 41%
- The option to conduct one-click check-out online: 40%
- The ability to complete a purchase in store using mobile device: 37%
- The availability of a mobile application for a smartphone: 36%
- The availability of an in-store kiosk to browse products: 25%
- The ability to start a purchase online and then complete the purchase in store: 23%
- The ability to make an appointment for an in-store consult after researching online: 18%

When asked what factors have led them to recommend an online retailer to others, responses were as follows (multiple responses allowed):

- Free shipping: 68%
- Receiving my product when expected: 47%
- Free returns: 34%
- Easy returns and exchanges: 34%
- Tracking services: 29%
- Fast credits/refunds if I return products: 25%

When asked what factors have led them to make negative recommendations about an online retailer, responses were as follows (multiple responses allowed):

- Shipping costs too high based on product price: 59%
- Shipping costs were too high based on expected delivery date: 45%
- Products arrived damaged due to shipping/packaging: 43%
- The delivery took longer than I was told: 40%
- I could not get a refund, only credits: 37%
- Bombarded with e-mail offers I didn't want: 35%
- Getting a refund/credit took too long: 34%
- Unreliable shipping made it hard to anticipate delivery dates: 31%
- Could not find a phone number to contact customer service: 31%
- Dealing with the retailer on returns was too cumbersome: 29%
- Difficulty getting package because I am not home to sign for it: 27%
- Check-out process was way too long: 24%

11

MOBILE SHOPPING

11.1 Overview

The use of a smartphone or mobile device to assist in shopping, or even to make a purchase, is becoming increasingly popular. Over half of mobile phone users now own a smartphone (see 5.6); about one-third of smartphone users have used their device in some type of shopping activity.

Product research, price comparisons, and mobile coupon redemption are the most common shopping-related uses of mobile devices by consumers. Emerging mobile shopping activities include using mobile devices to make purchases and the use of a smartphone as a mobile wallet to make payments.

11.2 In-Store Smartphone Use

A September 2013 study by shop.org, the online arm of the National Retail Federation (www.nrf.com), reported shopping-related use of smartphones as follows (percentage of survey respondents participating in each use):

• Visit same company's site or app while in store:	57%
• Visit different company's site while in store:	43%
• Search for coupons and deals:	35%
• Find a store:	24%
• Take photos of products:	23%
• Check product availability:	19%
• Send an image to family or friends:	17%
• Text or call family or friends about a product while in store:	17%

Among those who visited a company's site or app while in a store, 59% did so to see if there was an online discount. Among those who visited a different store's site, 92% did so to find a better deal.

A survey by uSamp (www.usamp.com) found the following mobile shopping activities by gender (percentage of mobile device users):

	Female	Male
• Scanned a barcode:	85%	91%
• Used mobile for payment:	32%	46%
• Made a mobile purchase:	34%	45%
• Used a mobile coupon:	44%	44%
• Commented on a purchase:	28%	35%
• Wrote review of purchase:	15%	26%

A survey by the Nielsen Company (www.nielsen.com) assessed three types of in-store smartphone uses: read reviews, scan barcodes/QR codes for product information, and request/use coupons. By store type, smartphone owners used their device as follows (percentage of respondents):

	Reviews	Scan Codes	Coupons
• Electronics store:	73%	57%	41%
• Department store:	43%	36%	41%
• Mass merchandiser:	34%	31%	39%
• Office superstore:	22%	26%	29%
• Apparel shop:	21%	20%	26%
• Furniture store:	19%	16%	17%
• Grocery/supermarket:	14%	6%	9%
• Convenience store:	7%	5%	5%
• Dollar store:	3%	2%	2%

In a survey by Deloitte (www.deloitte.com) parents reported using smartphones to assist with back-to-school shopping as follows (percentage of respondents):

• Get price information:	62%
• Get discounts or coupons:	45%
• View a retailer's ad:	44%
• Get a store location:	38%
• Obtain product information:	35%
• Locate a store carrying a particular product:	33%
• Access a retailer's website:	29%
• Shop online:	25%
• Receive a text message from a retailer:	18%
• Read product/retailer reviews:	18%
• Make a purchase:	14%

Deloitte also asked consumers about their in-store smartphone use in various types of retail stores, the frequency of use, and the influence on purchases. Responses were as follows:

	Used to Shop	Frequency of Use	Mobile Influence
• Electronics/appliances:	49%	60.9%	8.3%
• Department/warehouse:	46%	52.5%	6.7%
• Clothing/footwear:	38%	56.2%	5.9%
• Food/beverage:	35%	58.2%	5.7%
• Books & music:	33%	57.1%	5.2%
• Home improvement/garden:	31%	53.5%	4.6%
• Sporting/toys/hobby:	30%	56.7%	4.7%
• Health/personal care/drug:	27%	58.4%	4.4%
• Furniture/home furnishing:	24%	58.7%	3.9%

11.3 M-Commerce Purchases

According to a May 2013 survey by AYTM Market Research (www.aytm.com), smartphone users use their mobile device to purchase products online as follows:

- Often: 9%
- Sometimes: 27%
- Rarely: 19%
- Never: 45%

An October 2013 survey by Harris Interactive (www.harrisinteractive.com) found that 63% of smartphone users in major metropolitan areas have shopped on their device. By city, the percentages who have done so are as follows:

- San Francisco, CA: 75%
- Washington, DC: 68%
- New York, NY: 67%
- Los Angeles, CA: 66%
- Atlanta, GA: 65%
- Dallas-Ft. Worth, TX: 65%
- Houston, TX: 58%
- Boston, MA: 55%
- Chicago, IL: 50%
- Philadelphia, PA: 49%

eMarketer (www.emarketer.com) estimates that 63% of U.S. tablet users will make a purchase on the device in 2013; 78% of tablet users will do so by 2017.

11.4 M-Commerce Spending

According to comScore (www.comscore.com), m-commerce spending has been as follows:

- Second quarter 2010: $0.6 billion
- Third quarter 2010: $0.8 billion
- Fourth quarter 2010: $1.6 billion
- First quarter 2011: $2.4 billion
- Second quarter 2011: $2.6 billion
- Third quarter 2011: $3.5 billion
- Fourth quarter 2011: $4.9 billion
- First quarter 2012: $4.5 billion
- Second quarter 2012: $3.8 billion
- Third quarter 2012: $4.6 billion
- Fourth quarter 2012: $7.2 billion
- First quarter 2013: $5.9 billion
- Second quarter 2013: $4.7 billion

M-commerce spending during the first half of 2013 represented 9.5% of total U.S. e-commerce spending. By product category and platform, m-commerce spending as a percentage of total e-commerce was as follows (source: comScore):

	Smartphone	Tablet
• Total e-commerce:	6.0%	3.5%
• Apparel and accessories:	6.2%	3.5%
• Computer hardware:	3.3%	2.1%
• Consumer packaged goods:	3.0%	1.3%
• Consumer electronics:	2.6%	2.9%
• Event tickets:	10.9%	4.5%

11.5 Mobile Shopping Apps

The May 2013 survey by AYTM Market Research found that smartphone users have downloaded shopping apps to their mobile devices as follows (percentage of respondents):

- Shopping apps for particular stores: 34%
- Local store/shopping locator: 26%
- General coupon apps: 25%
- Daily deal apps: 22%
- Other shopping apps: 10%

12

PEER-TO-PEER SHOPPING

12.1 Overview

The peer-to-peer marketplace – which goes by a host of monikers such as collaborative consumption, communal consumption, asset-light lifestyle, the peer economy, and the sharing economy – lets individuals rent unused assets or services to other individuals. The economic downturn was the impetus for growth of the concept. Today there are numerous Internet-based services available to aggregate supply and demand. *Time* calls the sharing economy one of the ten most important ideas that is changing the world.

> **"Why pay through the nose for something when you can rent it more cheaply from a stranger online? That is the principle behind a range of online services that enable people to share cars, accommodations, bicycles, household appliances, and other items, connecting owners of underused assets with others willing to pay to use them. Dozens of firms such as Airbnb, which lets people rent out their spare rooms, or RelayRides, which allows other people to rent your car, act as matchmakers, allocating resources where they are needed and taking a small cut in return."**
>
> *The Economist*, 3/9/13

According to *Forbes* (February 2013), over 100 companies provide platforms that offer individuals an income stream from renting or selling physical assets or services. The 2013 peer-to-peer marketplace is estimated at $3.5 billion and growing at an annual rate of over 25%.

"Just as YouTube did with TV and the blogosphere did to mainstream media, the sharing economy blows up the industrial model of companies owning and people consuming, and allows everyone to be both consumer and producer, along with the potential for cash that the latter provides."

Forbes, 2/11/13

12.2 The Sharing Economy

The following are popular types of peer-to-peer rentals and services:

Accommodations

- Individuals offer accommodations ranging from furnished houses to spare bedrooms to couches for travelers. The largest such sites, HomeAway and VRBO, have over 500,000 listings worldwide and reported 153 million visits in 2012. Airbnb, another large such service, has been used by more than 4 million people since it launched in 2008. Other services include 9flats, Bed and Fed, Couchsurfing, One Fine Stay, and Roomorama.

Car Sharing Services

- *Forbes* (February 2013) estimates that roughly 50,000 of the tens of millions of cars idling in America's driveways are available through car-sharing services. Among providers serving this market are DriveMyCar Rentals, Getaround, RelayRides, Tamyca, and WhipCar. Exchanges like Lyft and SideCar let people monitize their road trips by carrying fee-paying passengers.

Crowdfunding

- Crowdfunding is the collective effort of individuals who network and pool their money to support businesses, organizations, and individuals. Funded projects can include startup companies, disaster relief, support of artists by fans, political campaigns, software and product development, and research projects. Massolution (www.massolution.com) estimates that $2.7 billion was raised through crowdfunding in 2012, a figure that will increase to $5 billion in 2013. Crowdfunding services include Catarse, Crowdcube, Indiegogo, Kickstarter, Pozible, and StartSomethingGood.

> **"Proponents of crowdfunding believe it has the potential to upend traditional financing models, such as loans and venture capital, and unleash a tidal wave of capital for entrepreneurs and creative types."**
>
> *Fortune*, 5/20/13

Fashion

- Several companies rent special-occasion and designer apparel online. With over three million members, 35,000 dresses, and 7,000 accessories by 170 designers, Rent the Runway is the largest in the sector. Other services include Bag Borrow or Steal, Dress Vault, and Fashion Hire.

> **"Rent the Runway has certainly redefined the fashion business, bringing high-end fashion wear to Everywoman. It is also upending storefronts big and small – why buy a dress when you can borrow at a sweet price?"**
>
> *Forbes*, 4/15/13

Lending

- Peer-to-peer lending, or social lending, brings together individual borrowers and lenders via online platforms. The two biggest lending platforms are Lending Club and Prosper, both founded in 2006 and based in San Francisco. The bulk of lending is for debt consolidation by credit-card borrowers. With little overhead, rates of 14% are attractive for individual lenders and well below standard charges of 18% for borrowers. Lending Club made possible about $150 million in loans monthly in 2013.

As the sharing economy grows, so, too, do the types of items and services being offered. No item is too small to spawn a peer-to-peer market and the list seems limitless.

"A few dozen square feet in a driveway can now produce income via Parking Panda. A pooch-friendly room in your house is suddenly a pet penthouse via DogVacay. On Rentoid, an outdoorsy type with a newborn who suddenly notices her camping tent never gets used can rent it out at $10 a day to a city slicker who'd otherwise have to buy one. On SnapGoods, a drill lying fallow in a garage can become a $10-a-day income source from a homeowner who just needs to put up some quick drywall. On Liquid, an unused bicycle becomes a way for a traveler to cheaply get around while visiting town for $20 a day."

Forbes, 2/11/13

Services

- The peer-to-peer marketplace offers an opportunity for individuals with marketable skills and talents to provide their services on a freelance basis. Sites like elance.com, guru.com, fiverr.com, TaskRabbit, Exec, and Amazon's Mechanical Turk provide a marketplace for consumers looking for technology services, creative services, or business services. Everything from web developing to bookkeeping to legal services to writing to illustrating can be provided through such sites.

"The 'gig economy,' the plethora of microjobs fueled by online marketplaces offering and filling an array of paid errands and office chores."

Forbes, 2/11/13

12.3 Economic Impact

According to Arun Sundararajan, Ph.D., a professor at the Stern School of Business at New York University, the largest question for academics is whether the sharing economy simply replaces existing businesses or creates new value. People have purchased residential properties and automobiles solely to rent them out, for example, indicating the concept has an extended impact.

While the sharing economy clearly poses a competitive threat to traditional businesses, it also has a positive economic impact on cities. A study commissioned by Airbnb found that because peer-to-peer rentals tend to be cheaper than a hotel, people often stay longer and spend 31% more than those who stay in a comparable hotel. Among those who rented an Airbnb property in San Francisco, for example, 14% said they would not have visited the city at all without Airbnb.

> **"Of course established travel companies won't go out of business as a result of this sharing revolution, but the way we travel will almost certainly become more efficient. Put differently, your next 'hotel' may be someone's spare bedroom, your next ride to the airport might be in another person's car, and you might rent a stranger's vehicle when you arrive."**
>
> *USA Today*, 9/30/13

Renting out underused assets can be profitable. Airbnb reports that hosts in San Francisco who rent out their homes do so for an average of 58 nights a year, earning a median $9,300. Car owners who rent their vehicles to others using RelayRides make an average of $250 a month; some make more than $1,000 monthly.

12.4 Outlook

The sharing economy is becoming more mainstream as it grows. Consider eBay, which started out as a peer-to-peer marketplace but is now dominated by professional 'power sellers' (many of whom started out as ordinary eBay users). The same may happen in other sharing economy segments.

Corporations are entering the sharing marketplace through acquisitions or by providing venture capital. Google, for example, has a stake in Lending Club, Relay

Rides, and Sidecar. Avis, Daimler, and General Motors, among others, have also entered the peer-to-peer marketplace.

"In the future, companies may develop hybrid models, listing excess capacity (whether vehicles, equipment or office space) on peer-to-peer rental sites. In the past, new ways of doing things online have not displaced the old ways entirely. But they have often changed them. Just as Internet shopping forced Walmart and Tesco to adapt, so online sharing will shake up transport, tourism, equipment-hire, and more."

The Economist, 3/9/13

As the sharing economy expands, it is experiencing various growing pains.

"As they become more numerous and more popular, sharing services have started to run up against snags. There are questions around insurance and legal liability. Some services are falling foul of industry-specific regulations. Landlords are clamping down on tenants who sub-let their properties in violation of the terms of their leases. Tax collectors are asking whether all the income from sharing schemes is being declared. Meanwhile, the big boys are moving in, as large companies that face disruption from sharing schemes start to embrace the model themselves."

The Economist, 3/9/13

PART III: BEHAVIORAL ANALYSES

13

AT HOME

13.1 At-Home Entertainment

With near-universal broadband connections and digital content of all types, including over 400 cable channels alone, consumers can be endlessly entertained right in their own living rooms. Michael J. Wolf, partner for the global entertainment division of McKinsey & Co. (www.mckinsey.com), calls it "cocooning in the digital age."

"Times have changed. It used to be you'd have dinner at home and go out for entertainment. Now you do entertainment at home and go out for dinner."

Fortune, 2/25/13

The expanded access of entertainment options at home has led to a significant shift in consumer behavior, impacting traditional leisure sectors. As Americans stay home more, attendance and participation figures have been flat, at best, for the majority of entertainment and sports activities. According to Parks Associates (www.parksassociates.com), 42% of Internet users are less likely to go to the movies than they were five years ago. An additional 46% are less likely to go to a concert. Likewise, participation is down in almost every recreational sport, from golf and tennis to bowling and snow skiing, according to data from the Sports & Fitness Industry Association (www.sfia.com). Americans are also increasingly less likely to go out for cultural activities. *Survey of Public Participation in the Arts* found that the share of adults who report viewing performing arts or listening to music at home remains higher than live attendance, and the gap between the two has widened over the past decade.

The shift has been a boon for the consumer electronics sector. According to the Consumer Electronics Association (CEA, www.ce.org), the average U.S. household spent $1,312 on consumer electronic (CE) devices in 2012, a 36% increase over 2011. Among adults ages 25-to-34, CE spending increased 62%.

Televisions are the most universally owned CE device. According to the *15th Annual Household CE Ownership and Market Potential Study*, published in April 2013 by the CEA, 98% of U.S. households own at least one TV; the average U.S. household owns 2.9 televisions. Seventy-four percent (74%) of U.S. households own at least one high-definition television (HDTV), 61% own at least one LCD TV. Internet-enabled TVs were found in 15% of U.S. households at year-end 2012, a six percentage point increase from twelve months prior.

According to a 2012 report by The Nielsen Company (www.nielsen.com), by age, people spend time watching TV in their home as follows:

	Living/Family Room	Bedroom	Other
• 12-to-17:	48%	47%	5%
• 18-to-34:	57%	37%	7%
• 35-to-64:	62%	31%	7%
• 65 and older:	69%	20%	10%

Among all types of CE products, mobile devices are the most rapidly growing. Household penetration of consumer electronic devices at year-end 2012 and the percentage-point increase from one year prior are as follows:

	Pct. of Households	Increase
• Tablet computer:	39%	17%
• Smartphones:	58%	12%
• E-readers:	29%	10%
• Wireless mobile hotspot:	21%	10%

13.2 Working At Home

According to a recent study published in the *American Sociological Review*, nearly half of American workers bring work home with them regularly.

The U.S. Bureau of Labor Statistics (www.bls.gov) estimates that 4.2 million adults are home-workers; about 65% of these people work full-time at home. Fifty-eight percent (58%) of stay-at-home-workers run their own business and 35% telecommute, working for private companies or nonprofits located elsewhere.

"As communication and information technologies advance, we are seeing that workers are increasingly able to perform work at home."

Peter J. Mateyka, Survey Statistician
U.S. Census Bureau

People who work exclusively from home have a median household income of $74,000, compared with $65,600 for on-site workers. Those who work both on-site and from home earn an average of $96,300.

Metropolitan areas in the southeast, southwest, and west have the largest share of home-workers, according to the Census Bureau. The following are the metropolitan areas with the highest share of people who work from home:

- Boulder, CO: 10.9%
- Medford, OR: 8.4%
- Santa Fe, NM: 8.3%
- Kingston, NY: 8.1%
- Santa Rosa, CA: 7.9%
- Mankato, MN: 7.7%
- Prescott, AZ: 7.6%
- St. Cloud, MN: 7.6%
- Athens, GA: 7.5%
- Austin, TX: 7.3%

A March 2013 Harris Poll by Harris Interactive (www.harrisinteractive.com) surveyed employed adults about working at home. Thirty-four percent (34%) said they worked at home at least part of the time. The extent of working at home was as follows:

- Work at home: 34%
  - Work primarily or exclusively from home: 9%
  - Spend about half of working time at home: 8%
  - Less than half my time working from home: 17%
- Do not currently work from home at all: 66%

Participants in the Harris Poll had the following opinions about working at home (multiple responses allowed):

- Working from home provides flexibility: 90%
- Working from home enables employees to balance work and family needs: 85%
- Working together in an office setting adds to team camaraderie: 84%
- Some of the best ideas and/or decisions can result from impromptu, in-person meetings and discussions: 83%
- The option of working from home is a significant job perk: 83%
- Working in an office setting improves communication/collaboration: 81%
- Working from home increases productivity and work output: 64%
- The option to telecommute has/would have an impact on my decision to take or stay at a job: 61%
- Working from home hurts speed and work quality: 35%

14

AWAY FROM HOME

14.1 Overview

According to Arbitron (www.arbitron.com), the following are percentages of the U.S. population (age 12 and older) that visit various venues each month:

	Pct.	Number
• Airports:	21%	54 million
• Bars:	29%	65 million
• Coffeehouses or sandwich shops:	50%	130 million
• Convenience stores:	72%	187 million
• Drug stores:	69%	179 million
• Fast food or casual dining restaurants:	79%	204 million
• Gas stations:	88%	227 million
• Grocery stores:	90%	232 million
• Health clubs:	22%	86 million
• Large retail or department stores:	72%	186 million
• Movie theaters:	41%	107 million
• Public transportation (bus, taxicab, train):	27%	69 million
• Shopping malls:	65%	169 million
• Stadiums or arenas:	20%	51 million

The following sections provide a demographic profile of visitors to each of these outlets. (note: Education and Household Composition categories are based on adults ages 18 and older; other categories are based on ages 12 and older.)

14.2 Airports

Gender

- Female: 45%
- Male: 55%

Age

- 12-to-17: 11%
- 18-to-24: 9%
- 25-to-34: 22%
- 35-to-44: 17%
- 45-to-54: 20%

- 55-to-64: 14%
- 65 and older: 8%

Race/Ethnicity
- African-American: 14%
- Asian-American/other: 10%
- Caucasian: 59%
- Hispanic: 17%

Annual Household Income
- Under $25,000: 11%
- $25,000 to $49,999: 16%
- $50,000 to $99,999: 46%
- $100,000 and above: 27%

Education
- Four-year college degree or higher: 63%

Household Composition
- Have children under age 18 living at home: 34%

14.3 Bars

Gender
- Female: 33%
- Male: 67%

Age
- 12-to-20: n/a
- 21-to-24: 21%
- 25-to-34: 26%
- 35-to-44: 26%
- 45-to-54: 13%
- 55-to-64: 9%
- 65 and older: 5%

Race/Ethnicity
- African-American: 11%
- Asian-American/other: 8%
- Caucasian: 62%
- Hispanic: 19%

Annual Household Income

- Under $25,000: 23%
- $25,000 to $49,999: 28%
- $50,000 to $99,999: 37%
- $100,000 and above: 14%

Education

- Four-year college degree or higher: 51%

Household Composition

- Have children under age 18 living at home: 39%

14.4 Coffeehouses and Sandwich Shops

Gender

- Female: 47%
- Male: 53%

Age

- 12-to-17: 14%
- 18-to-24: 16%
- 25-to-34: 20%
- 35-to-44: 19%
- 45-to-54: 13%
- 55-to-64: 12%
- 65 and older: 6%

Race/Ethnicity

- African-American: 19%
- Asian-American/other: 9%
- Caucasian: 55%
- Hispanic: 17%

Annual Household Income

- Under $25,000: 24%
- $25,000 to $49,999: 21%
- $50,000 to $99,999: 33%
- $100,000 and above: 22%

Education

- Four-year college degree or higher: 46%

Household Composition
- Have children under age 18 living at home: 44%

14.5 Convenience Stores

Gender
- Female: 43%
- Male: 57%

Age
- 12-to-17: 17%
- 18-to-24: 14%
- 25-to-34: 18%
- 35-to-44: 22%
- 45-to-54: 14%
- 55-to-64: 10%
- 65 and older: 6%

Race/Ethnicity
- African-American: 16%
- Asian-American/other: 6%
- Caucasian: 59%
- Hispanic: 17%

Annual Household Income
- Under $25,000: 29%
- $25,000 to $49,999: 26%
- $50,000 to $99,999: 33%
- $100,000 and above: 13%

Education
- Four-year college degree or higher: 41%

Household Composition
- Have children under age 18 living at home: 51%

14.6 Drug Stores

Gender
- Female: 54%
- Male: 46%

Age
- 12-to-17: 10%
- 18-to-24: 16%
- 25-to-34: 19%
- 35-to-44: 15%
- 45-to-54: 18%
- 55-to-64: 11%
- 65 and older: 11%

Race/Ethnicity
- African-American: 19%
- Asian-American/other: 4%
- Caucasian: 59%
- Hispanic: 18%

Annual Household Income
- Under $25,000: 29%
- $25,000 to $49,999: 28%
- $50,000 to $99,999: 30%
- $100,000 and above: 13%

Education
- Four-year college degree or higher: 43%

Household Composition
- Have children under age 18 living at home: 43%

14.7 Fast Food and Casual Dining Restaurants

Gender
- Female: 44%
- Male: 56%

Age
- 12-to-17: 13%
- 18-to-24: 15%
- 25-to-34: 17%
- 35-to-44: 19%
- 45-to-54: 16%
- 55-to-64: 11%
- 65 and older: 10%

Race/Ethnicity

- African-American: 19%
- Asian-American/other: 7%
- Caucasian: 60%
- Hispanic: 15%

Annual Household Income

- Under $25,000: 27%
- $25,000 to $49,999: 26%
- $50,000 to $99,999: 29%
- $100,000 and above: 17%

Education

- Four-year college degree or higher: 40%

Household Composition

- Have children under age 18 living at home: 42%

14.8 Gas Stations

Gender

- Female: 46%
- Male: 54%

Age

- 12-to-17: 13%
- 18-to-24: 13%
- 25-to-34: 18%
- 35-to-44: 21%
- 45-to-54: 19%
- 55-to-64: 10%
- 65 and older: 6%

Race/Ethnicity

- African-American: 18%
- Asian-American/other: 7%
- Caucasian: 59%
- Hispanic: 17%

Annual Household Income

- Under $25,000: 19%
- $25,000 to $49,999: 26%

- $50,000 to $99,999: 33%
- $100,000 and above: 22%

Education
- Four-year college degree or higher: 46%

Household Composition
- Have children under age 18 living at home: 50%

14.9 Grocery Stores

Gender
- Female: 49%
- Male: 51%

Age
- 12-to-17: 12%
- 18-to-24: 14%
- 25-to-34: 17%
- 35-to-44: 19%
- 45-to-54: 17%
- 55-to-64: 10%
- 65 and older: 11%

Race/Ethnicity
- African-American: 14%
- Asian-American/other: 8%
- Caucasian: 64%
- Hispanic: 14%

Annual Household Income
- Under $25,000: 26%
- $25,000 to $49,999: 29%
- $50,000 to $99,999: 30%
- $100,000 and above: 15%

Education
- Four-year college degree or higher: 40%

Household Composition
- Have children under age 18 living at home: 44%

14.10 Health Clubs

Gender
- Female: 51%
- Male: 49%

Age
- 12-to-17: 13%
- 18-to-24: 21%
- 25-to-34: 17%
- 35-to-44: 19%
- 45-to-54: 15%
- 55-to-64: 10%
- 65 and older: 7%

Race/Ethnicity
- African-American: 12%
- Asian-American/other: 10%
- Caucasian: 63%
- Hispanic: 15%

Annual Household Income
- Under $25,000: 9%
- $25,000 to $49,999: 16%
- $50,000 to $99,999: 47%
- $100,000 and above: 28%

Education
- Four-year college degree or higher: 67%

Household Composition
- Have children under age 18 living at home: 36%

14.11 Large Retail Or Department Stores

Gender
- Female: 46%
- Male: 54%

Age
- 12-to-17: 11%
- 18-to-24: 16%
- 25-to-34: 16%

- 35-to-44: 22%
- 45-to-54: 16%
- 55-to-64: 9%
- 65 and older: 10%

Race/Ethnicity
- African-American: 15%
- Asian-American/other: 6%
- Caucasian: 65%
- Hispanic: 14%

Annual Household Income
- Under $25,000: 21%
- $25,000 to $49,999: 30%
- $50,000 to $99,999: 33%
- $100,000 and above: 17%

Education
- Four-year college degree or higher: 41%

Household Composition
- Have children under age 18 living at home: 42%

14.12 Movie Theaters

Gender
- Female: 46%
- Male: 54%

Age
- 12-to-17: 21%
- 18-to-24: 18%
- 25-to-34: 21%
- 35-to-44: 16%
- 45-to-54: 12%
- 55-to-64: 9%
- 65 and older: 4%

Race/Ethnicity
- African-American: 15%
- Asian-American/other: 8%
- Caucasian: 62%
- Hispanic: 15%

Annual Household Income
- Under $25,000: 19%
- $25,000 to $49,999: 27%
- $50,000 to $99,999: 39%
- $100,000 and above: 15%

Education
- Four-year college degree or higher: 50%

Household Composition
- Have children under age 18 living at home: 42%

14.13 Public Transportation (bus, taxicab, train)

Gender
- Female: 48%
- Male: 52%

Age
- 12-to-17: 4%
- 18-to-24: 20%
- 25-to-34: 23%
- 35-to-44: 17%
- 45-to-54: 17%
- 55-to-64: 11%
- 65 and older: 8%

Race/Ethnicity
- African-American: 20%
- Asian-American/other: 12%
- Caucasian: 50%
- Hispanic: 18%

Annual Household Income
- Under $25,000: 23%
- $25,000 to $49,999: 26%
- $50,000 to $99,999: 30%
- $100,000 and above: 21%

Education
- Four-year college degree or higher: 43%

Household Composition

- Have children under age 18 living at home: 43%

14.14 Shopping Malls

Gender

- Female: 47%
- Male: 53%

Age

- 12-to-17: 16%
- 18-to-24: 18%
- 25-to-34: 15%
- 35-to-44: 20%
- 45-to-54: 14%
- 55-to-64: 8%
- 65 and older: 9%

Race/Ethnicity

- African-American: 20%
- Asian-American/other: 7%
- Caucasian: 56%
- Hispanic: 17%

Annual Household Income

- Under $25,000: 23%
- $25,000 to $49,999: 25%
- $50,000 to $99,999: 33%
- $100,000 and above: 19%

Education

- Four-year college degree or higher: 43%

Household Composition

- Have children under age 18 living at home: 44%

14.15 Stadiums and Arenas

Gender

- Female: 41%
- Male: 59%

Age
- 12-to-17: 16%
- 18-to-24: 18%
- 25-to-34: 20%
- 35-to-44: 20%
- 45-to-54: 15%
- 55-to-64: 7%
- 65 and older: 5%

Race/Ethnicity
- African-American: 11%
- Asian-American/other: 10%
- Caucasian: 71%
- Hispanic: 8%

Annual Household Income
- Under $25,000: 14%
- $25,000 to $49,999: 26%
- $50,000 to $99,999: 35%
- $100,000 and above: 25%

Education
- Four-year college degree or higher: 56%

Household Composition
- Have children under age 18 living at home: 33%

15

BRAND LOYALTY

15.1 Brand Preferences

Consumer brand preferences vary by product category. A survey by The NPD Group (www.npd.com) found brand names are relevant in some retail categories but of minimal importance in others. By category, shoppers look for a specific brand as follows:

	Always	Never
• Housewares/textiles:	4%	40%
• Furniture:	6%	44%
• Apparel:	14%	25%
• Food (grocery):	21%	12%
• Footwear:	23%	23%
• Cosmetics:	31%	22%
• Electronics:	31%	16%

The following are percentages of consumers willing to pay a lot more for premium brands:

- Electronics: 11%
- Footwear: 9%
- Cosmetics: 8%
- Furniture: 8%
- Food (grocery): 6%
- Housewares/textiles: 4%

Retailing Today, in conjunction with Leo J. Shapiro & Associates (www.ljs.com), surveyed consumers on their brand preferences. The following is a ranking of retail product categories for which consumers are most brand sensitive, based on the percentage of consumers with a brand preference:

- Beverages: 90%
- Snacks: 88%
- Health and beauty aids: 87%
- Cosmetics: 81%
- Cameras/film: 79%
- Candy: 78%
- Groceries and canned foods: 72%
- Consumer electronics: 65%

- Men's apparel: 64%
- Intimate apparel: 63%
- Toys: 58%
- Computer/entertainment software: 56%
- Greeting cards: 54%
- Women's apparel: 52%
- Children's apparel: 51%
- Domestics: 37%

In a survey by comScore (www.comscore.com), the following percentages of consumers said they buy their preferred brand of these select consumer packaged goods regardless of cost:

- Toothpaste: 57%
- Canned soup: 52%
- Shampoo: 52%
- Laundry detergent: 47%
- Pasta sauce: 45%
- Mouth rinse: 44%
- OTC medications: 43%
- Fruit juice: 40%
- Facial tissue: 39%
- Jeans: 39%
- Paper towels: 35%
- Small appliances: 34%

15.2 Store Brands

The influence of cost on brand loyalty increases as consumers are impacted by economic conditions. In a survey by Accenture (www.accenture.com), 39% of consumers said they increased their purchase of store brands or private label brands in recent years because of the economy. The study reported the following attitudes toward private label products (percentage of respondents):

- Buy because they are cheaper: 66%
- Quality is just a good: 50%
- Better variety: 48%
- Trust: 42%
- Just another brand: 36%
- Prefer store brands: 28%
- Buying private label for many years: 28%
- Don't buy/not as good: 9%
- Embarrassed to buy: 4%

In 2012, store brands garnered 19.1% of consumer spending for CPGs and a 23.1% unit share in supermarkets, according to The Nielsen Company (www.nielsen.com). In drug stores, these figures were 15.9% and 16.6%, respectively.

For several years department stores have been creating stronger private labels while also eliminating underperforming or over-distributed supplier brands to increase their consumer appeal and reduce pervasive sameness. In 2007, the percentage of sales at Macy's in exclusive or limited distribution brands, including its private label lines, was 35%. By 2012, store brands increased to 43% of sales. The percentage is even higher at Kohl's and JCPenney, where private label brands represent 48% and 50% of sales, respectively.

Consumer preference for store brands appears to be growing. According to Nielsen, store brand sales grew 3.8% during the first three quarters of 2013 while sales of national brands was flat. For comparison, sales of store brand increased 2.9% in 2012 while national brand sales grew 2.2%.

15.3 Brand Loyalty In Travel

A 2013 survey by Deloitte (www.deloitte.com) found that only 14% of travelers say they are loyal to a particular airline; just 8% say they are loyal to the same hotel brand.

Price, comfort and service are driving decisions more than loyalty programs. When picking airlines, most travelers say they look first at safety, value, and whether flights are on time. When choosing hotels, they look at price, whether there is free parking, comfort, and location. Loyalty programs rank near the bottom of influencing factors.

> **"The findings don't bode well for hotels and airlines, which invest millions to attract and reward travelers with their frequent-flier and frequent-guest programs in an effort to attract return customers. The current environment for building loyalty really isn't creating long-term sustainable loyalty. There's been a real erosion in loyalty."**
>
> Adam Weissenberg, Vice Chairman
> Travel, Hospitality and Leisure
> Deloitte, 1/19/13

15.4 Increasing Brand Loyalty

Various studies point to convenience, customer service, loyalty programs, price, and social network connections as influences on customer loyalty.

Convenience

- According to Brand Keys (www.brandkeys.com), convenience increases product and service consideration, adoption, and loyalty by 19%.

Customer Service

- Few things can affect customer loyalty like customer service. According to a survey by Accenture, in assessing loyalty related to retailers of technology products, over 80% of customers who rated their service below average said they would buy from a different company next time. Merely average service dropped customer purchasing loyalty from 51% to 27%.

Customer Surveys

- Many customers feel more loyal to a brand if it takes the time to find out their opinion. In a 2012 survey by Cint (www.cint.com), 62% of customers said they were more likely to purchase a brand's product if their opinion has been sought by the brand.

Price

- A survey by Acxiom (www.acxiom.com) found that 53% of adults would change to a new auto insurance carrier to save $300 annually.

Social Network Connections

- Studies have shown a company's social followers are more likely to buy the brand's products. In a survey by Chadwick Martin Bailey (www.cmbinfo.com), more than half of Facebook users said they are likely to purchase at least a few brands they are social friends and followers of; 67% of Twitter followers indicated the same. Also, 60% of respondents claimed their Facebook fandom increased the chance that they would recommend a brand to a friend; among Twitter followers, that percentage rose to almost 80%.

In the *2012 Brand Loyalty Survey* by ClickFox (www.clickfox.com), survey respondents identified the following as the best ways companies can build brand loyalty (percentage of respondents):

- Providing exceptional customer service: 34%
- Rewarding purchases, feedback, and referrals: 20%
- Sending exclusive and/or relevant offers and specials: 13%
- Providing personalized products or services: 12%
- Knowing the customer when they visit or call: 10%

15.5 Influence of Social Network Connections

Chadwick Martin Bailey explored why social media users become brand fans. The top reason to 'friend' a brand on Facebook is to receive discounts, followed by simply being a customer of the company and having a desire to show others one's support for the brand. Chadwick Martin Bailey found that for Facebook users, the desire to receive discounts and special offers was the top reason for liking a brand, cited by 41% of respondents. On Twitter, discounts, up-to-the-minute information, and exclusive content were the main draws; only 2% of respondents followed brands on Twitter to show their support.

A study by Syncapse (www.syncapse.com) and Hotspex (www.hotspex.com) compared average annual spending for Facebook fans and non-fans for various products as follows:

	Fans	Non-Fans
• McDonald's:	$310	$150
• Starbucks:	$235	$111
• Coca-Cola:	$190	$121
• Pringles:	$133	$ 61
• Skittles:	$129	$ 53
• Red Bull:	$114	$ 50
• Nutella:	$102	$ 53
• Oreo:	$ 84	$ 56

Syncapse and Hotspex found that the average annual value to brands for a Facebook fan is $136.38.

16

BUYING AMERICAN-MADE

16.1 Preference For U.S.-Made Products

In a poll by Harris Interactive (www.harrisinteractive.com), 61% of adults said they are more likely to purchase something when an ad touts it is 'Made in America,' and 3% said they are less likely to buy it; 35% said they are neither more nor less likely to purchase a product when an ad emphasizes it is Made in America.

Those who are more likely to purchase a product that is Made in America, by age and region, are as follows:

Age	Much More Likely	Somewhat More	Neither	Less Likely
• 18-to-34:	15%	29%	52%	4%
• 35-to-44:	20%	42%	37%	1%
• 45-to-54:	29%	37%	30%	4%
• 55 and older:	39%	37%	22%	3%
Region				
• East:	22%	38%	36%	3%
• Midwest:	32%	35%	31%	2%
• South:	25%	35%	36%	4%
• West:	26%	32%	38%	5%
Overall	26%	35%	35%	3%

Other surveys have found preference to be even higher. In a September 2012 survey by Boston Consulting Group (BGC, www.bcg.com), 80% of adults said they preferred U.S.-made goods and that they are willing to pay more for them.

When asked about factors influencing their decision to buy American-made products in a December 2012 Harris Poll, survey participants said the following were important (percentage of respondents):

- Keeping jobs in America: 90%
- Supporting American companies: 87%
- Safety concerns with products produced outside the U.S.: 82%
- Quality concerns with products produced outside the U.S.: 83%
- Patriotism: 76%
- Human rights issues with products produced outside the U.S.: 76%
- Decreasing environmental impact since products don't need to be shipped as far: 71%

Interestingly, BCG also found that many consumers in other countries also prefer U.S.-made goods. When the same question was asked of Chinese consumers, 47% said they preferred Made in America.

A 2013 poll by *The New York Times* had findings consistent with the Harris Poll.

> **"Two-thirds of Americans say they check labels when shopping to see if they are buying American goods, according to a *New York Times* poll taken early this year. Given the example of a $50 garment made overseas, almost half of respondents – 46% – said they would be willing to pay from $5 to $20 more for a similar garment made in the United States."**
>
> *The New York Times*, 11/30/13

16.2 Buying American By Product Type

When asked about various categories of products in a December 2012 Harris Poll, the following percentages of adults said it is important to buy American-made products:

- Major appliances: 75%
- Furniture: 74%
- Clothing: 72%
- Small appliances: 71%
- Automobiles: 70%
- Sports/exercise equipment: 66%
- Home electronics/TVs: 66%
- Smartphones/tablets: 66%
- Jewelry: 63%
- Motorcycles: 59%
- Novelty/gift items: 59%

By gender, responses were as follows:

	Female	Male
• Major appliances:	79%	71%
• Furniture:	78%	71%
• Clothing:	77%	67%

• Small appliances:	76%	66%
• Automobiles:	74%	65%
• Sports/exercise equipment:	69%	64%
• Home electronics/TVs:	72%	60%
• Smartphones/tablets:	71%	61%
• Jewelry:	67%	58%
• Motorcycles:	61%	58%
• Novelty/gift items:	66%	51%

By generation, responses were as follows:

	Millennials	Gen Xers	Baby Boomers	Seniors
• Major appliances:	57%	74%	86%	85%
• Furniture:	54%	76%	86%	84%
• Clothing:	56%	76%	80%	80%
• Small appliances:	53%	72%	81%	81%
• Automobiles:	58%	72%	76%	75%
• Sports/exercise equipment:	50%	70%	76%	71%
• Home electronics/TVs:	49%	69%	74%	76%
• Smartphones/tablets:	46%	69%	76%	76%
• Jewelry:	47%	67%	69%	70%
• Motorcycles:	46%	62%	67%	61%
• Novelty/gift items:	45%	64%	66%	61%

By demographic region, responses were as follows:

	Urban	Suburban	Rural
• Major appliances:	72%	74%	81%
• Furniture:	71%	73%	79%
• Clothing:	70%	72%	73%
• Small appliances:	72%	68%	76%
• Automobiles:	71%	67%	75%
• Sports/exercise equipment:	64%	65%	73%
• Home electronics/TVs:	69%	63%	71%
• Smartphones/tablets:	66%	64%	71%
• Jewelry:	62%	60%	68%
• Motorcycles:	55%	58%	63%
• Novelty/gift items:	57%	56%	61%

16.3 Buy American Initiatives

Some brands have long produced their products in the United States. Others have made recent initiatives to bring manufacturing back to the U.S. Apple, for example, announced in 2013 that it would manufacture some of its Mac product line domestically. Apparel retailer Club Monaco has launched lines and products marketed specifically as Made in America.

In early 2013, Walmart announced plans to spend an additional $50 billion on U.S.-made goods over the next decade.

"Not since the 1970s has 'Made in America' been such a hot way to market your product."

Advertising Age, 2/18/13

17

BUYING LOCAL

17.1 Buying Local

According to the Institute for Local Self-Reliance (www.ilsr.org), for every $100 spent at a locally owned store, $45 remains in the local economy, compared with about $13 per $100 spent at a national chain retailer.

> **"Locally owned businesses create more jobs locally and, in some sectors, provide better wages and benefits than chains do. Compared to chain stores, locally owned businesses recycle a much larger share of their revenue back into the local economy, enriching the whole community."**
>
> Stacy Mitchell, Senior Researcher
> Institute for Local Self-Reliance, 11/13

Civic Economics (www.civiceconomics.com) estimated that if San Francisco Bay Area consumers shifted 10% of their spending from national chains to local businesses, the impact would be $192 million in increased economic activity for the region and almost 1,300 new jobs.

According to *Time*, 82% of consumers actively support local or neighborhood businesses.

17.2 Locally Sourced Food Products

There has been a trend of increased demand for locally sourced foods at restaurants, farmers' markets, and groceries among patrons. While locally grown foods are not necessarily healthier, consumers are comforted by knowing the source of their food items. As concerns about food safety rise, the number of locavores – those who eat locally produced foods when available – is also increasing.

In a 2012 survey by the National Restaurant Association (www.restaurant.org), 64% of adults said locally sourced menu items are important when choosing a full-service restaurant (FSR). For comparison, 43% said organic or environmentally friendly food was important. In choosing a quick-service restaurant (QSR), locally sourced and organic menu items were cited as an important consideration by 63% and 45% of adults, respectfully. By gender and age, those placing a priority on locally sourced and, for comparison, organic menu items are as follows:

	Locally Sourced		Organic/Environmentally Friendly	
	FSR	**QSR**	**FSR**	**QSR**
Gender				
• Men:	59%	60%	38%	40%
• Women:	69%	65%	47%	50%
Age				
• 18-to-34:	58%	58%	46%	48%
• 35-to-44:	68%	67%	37%	40%
• 45-to-54:	63%	63%	44%	46%
• 55-to-64:	67%	64%	44%	45%
• 65 and older:	68%	65%	41%	43%

Opinions vary as to what constitutes 'local' food products. In a survey by The Hartman Group (www.hartman-group.com), consumers defined 'local product' as follows:

- Within 100 miles: 50%
- Within my state: 37%
- Within a region: 4%
- In the United States: 4%

At Whole Foods, which is recognized for its selection of locally sourced food products, each region has its own guidelines for using the term 'local' in its stores. In the northeast, for example, products are local if they are made either in-state or in a contiguous state. According to Errol Schweizer, Whole Foods' senior global grocery coordinator, 15% to 30% of the food items in a store are local.

In a 2013 survey by A.T. Kearney (www.atkearney.com), the following percentages of adults said they are willing to pay more for local foods:

- Single urban households: 95%
- Young couples w/o kids: 78%
- Affluent families: 71%
- Senior citizens: 68%
- Middle income families: 67%
- Low income families: 57%

A.T. Kearney found that grocery shoppers largely embrace local food options because they believe it helps local economies (66%), delivers a broader and better assortment of products (60%), and provides healthier alternatives (45%). Some shoppers say they buy local food to improve the carbon footprint (19%) and to help increase natural or organic production (19%).

When asked about the availability of local food at their preferred supermarket, 65% say their supermarket offers at least some kind of locally sourced food. Almost 30% of grocery shoppers say they consider purchasing food elsewhere if their preferred store does not carry local foods. Only 5% indicate they shop for local foods at big-box retailers, 15% at national supermarkets. Overwhelmingly, respondents say their main source for local food is the local farmers market and farm stores.

17.3 Buy Local Initiatives

Most states have programs that encourage residents to buy local. The following is a selection of programs:

- Alabama: www.fma.alabama.gov/buy_fresh.htm
- Alaska: www.buyalaska.com
- Arizona: http://localfirstaz.com
- Colorado: www.coloradolocalfirst.com
- Hawaii: http://hdoa.hawaii.gov/add/md/buy-local-it-matters/
- Indiana: http://mylocalindiana.com
- Montana: www.buylocalmontana.org
- New Jersey: http://njbuylocal.com/
- Utah: www.localfirst.org
- Virginia: www.buylocalvirginia.org
- Wisconsin: http://datcp.wi.gov/Business/Buy_Local_Buy_Wisconsin/

Similarly, some cities have launched initiatives to encourage residents to shop at locally owned businesses. The following are some example programs:

- Biddeford, ME: http://biddefordsacobuylocal.org
- Fayette County, PA: https://buylocalfayette.org
- Grand Junction, CO: www.gjchamber.org/bluebandwagon.asp
- Orlando, FL: www.buylocalorlando.com
- Pasadena, CA: http://cityofpasadena.net/Pasadena_First/
- Philadelphia, PA: www.sbnphiladelphia.org/initiatives/
- Portland, ME: www.portlandbuylocal.org
- Santa Monica, CA: www.buylocalsantamonica.com
- Scarborough, ME: www.buylocalscarborough.org
- Steamboat Springs, CO: www.steamboat-chamber.com/info/buy.local.asp

Buy-local advocates have gone viral with a social-network-based activity called cash mob. The purpose is to support local business by using Facebook, Twitter, and other social media to gather shoppers at the same independent business on the same designated day.

"The cash mob is gathering steam across the nation as a bona fide social phenomenon. Since a systems engineer organized the first cash mob in Buffalo last year, they've gone viral. Hundreds of cash mobs have sprung up across the U.S. – in all 50 states – as well as in large European cities such as London and Milan. Mobbers may be asked to spend $10 or $20, to show up at one time or throughout the day, but the basics are always the same: local business, cash, en masse."

Time, 11/5/12

18

CONSUMER CONFIDENCE

18.1 Overview

In general, the more confident people feel about the economy and their job and income, the less likely they are to avoid making purchases. When confidence is trending down, consumers are likely to slow their spending, thus the rate of economic growth slows. Conversely, when consumer confidence is trending up, the economy typically grows with increases in consumer spending.

There are several recognized measurements of consumer confidence. This chapter provides a review of various assessments.

18.2 Consumer Comfort Index

The Consumer Comfort Index, which began in 1985, is announced weekly by Bloomberg (www.bloomberg.com/consumer-comfort-index/).

The following three questions are used to calculate the index:

- Would you describe the state of the nation's economy these days as excellent, good, not so good, or poor?
- Would you describe the state of your own personal finances these days as excellent, good, not so good, or poor?
- Considering the cost of things today and your own personal finances, would you say now is an excellent time, a good time, a not so good time, or a poor time to buy the things you want and need?

The index is derived from telephone interviews conducted by Langer Research Associates (www.langerresearch.com). The margin of error is ±3 percentage points.

18.3 Consumer Confidence Index

The Consumer Confidence Index is calculated each month by The Conference Board (www.conference-board.org) based on a survey of consumers' opinions on present conditions and future expectations of the economy. The Consumer Confidence Index was started in 1967 and is benchmarked at a reference of 100 for 1985, a year chosen because it was neither a peak nor a trough. Opinions on current conditions make up 40% of the index, with expectations of future conditions comprising the remaining 60%.

Each month The Conference Board surveys 5,000 U.S. households. The survey consists of five questions that ask the respondents' opinions about the following:

- Current business conditions
- Business conditions for the next six months
- Current employment conditions
- Employment conditions for the next six months
- Total family income for the next six months

Survey participants are asked to answer each question as "positive," "negative," or "neutral." The "relative value" is calculated for each question separately and compared against each relative value from 1985. This comparison of the relative values results in an index value for each question. The index values for all five questions are then averaged together to form the Consumer Confidence Index. The data is calculated for the United States as a whole and for each of the country's nine census regions.

The preliminary results from the Consumer Confidence Survey are released on the last Tuesday of each month at 10:00 a.m. EST.

18.4 Consumer Sentiment Index

The Consumer Sentiment Index is one of the most recognized among several consumer confidence measures. It was devised in the late 1940s by Prof. George Katona at the University of Michigan. The index is calculated monthly based on 500 telephone household interviews conducted by the University of Michigan's Institute for Social Research (www.sca.isr.umich.edu/). Thomson Reuters published the Consumer Sentiment Index.

The University of Michigan releases three related figures each month: the Index of Consumer Sentiment (ICS, or MCSI), the Index of Current Economic Conditions (ICC), and the Index of Consumer Expectations (ICE). The ICE is an official component of the U.S. Index of Leading Economic Indicators.

18.5 Current Economic Conditions

Commonly known as the Beige Book, the *Current Economic Conditions* report is published by the Federal Reserve Board eight times per year. Each Federal Reserve Bank gathers anecdotal information on current economic conditions in its district through reports from bank and branch directors and interviews with key business contacts, economists, market experts, and other sources. The Beige Book summarizes this information by district and sector.

The *Current Economic Conditions* reports are available online at www.federalreserve.gov/monetarypolicy/beigebook/default.htm.

18.6 Economic Confidence Index

The Gallup Organization (www.gallup.com) continuously monitors consumer confidence with a two-question survey. The percentage of Americans classifying economic conditions as positive, negative, and mixed is reported daily based on a three-day rolling average of surveys of approximately 1,500 adults.

The poll, which guides the determination of Gallup's Economic Confidence Index, consists of the following questions:

- How would you rate economic conditions in this country today: as excellent, good, only fair, or poor?
- Right now, do you think that economic conditions in the country as a whole are getting better or getting worse?

Gallup reports on its website the Economic Confidence Index on a daily, weekly, monthly, and quarterly basis.

18.7 Other Measures Of Consumer Confidence

Developed by Leo J. Shapiro & Associates (LJS, www.ljs.com), the LJS National Poll has been tracking consumer trends and attitudes since 1971. Each quarterly poll provides a snapshot of American behavior and attitudes. The polls track consumer spending, purchase intent for a variety of goods and services, household income, financial outlook, job security, and attitudes toward inflation. Each month's poll is conducted by telephone with a nationally projectable sample of 450 U.S. households.

The RBC CASH (Consumer Attitudes and Spending by Household) Index is a monthly national survey of consumer attitudes on the current and future state of local economies, personal financial situations, savings, and confidence to make large investments. The survey, which has been in existence since 2002, is conducted for RBC Financial Services (www.rbc.com) by Ipsos Public Affairs (www.ipsos-pa.com). Survey results are released at the end of the first full week of each month.

Three TIPP (TechnoMetrica Institute of Policy and Politics) indices are published monthly based on a survey of 1,000 adults by TechnoMetrica Market Intelligence (www.technometrica.com) for *Investor's Business Daily*. The indices are as follows:

- Economic Optimism Index
- Presidential Leadership Index
- National Outlook Index

19

CUSTOMER SATISFACTION

19.1 Overview

Surveys by Service Management Group (SMG, www.smg.com) assess various aspects of customer satisfaction at retail stores. The surveys query customers based on their most recent retail visit and compare various factors that relate to customer satisfaction.

19.2 Factors Contributing To High Customer Satisfaction

The following are findings from recent SMG surveys:

Corporate Headquarters Markets

SMG research found chain retail stores don't have an advantage with locations in the same city as corporate headquarters. Customers rated their satisfaction at chain locations as follows:

	Overall Satisfaction	Likely To Return
• Corporate headquarters market:	71%	74%
• All other markets:	72%	75%

"Customers visiting retail stores in the same city as the brand's corporate headquarters are actually slightly less satisfied than customers visiting locations in other cities. Customers may have slightly higher expectations of brands that are headquartered close to their home."

Service Management Group

First-Time vs. Returning Customers

SMG found that first-time customers are generally more difficult to satisfy than returning customers. Survey results are as follows:

	Highly Satisfied	Highly Likely to Return	Highly Likely to Recommend
Returning customers:	70%	67%	72%
First-time customer:	67%	59%	57%

"Across retail segments, first-time customers are generally less satisfied overall than returning customers. Loyalty to a brand is generally built up over time – one experience is often not enough to create a loyal customer."

Service Management Group

Large vs. Small Stores

Based on the size of the store, customers rated their satisfaction with retail locations as follows:

	Overall Satisfaction	Likely To Return
• Smallest footprint:	64%	65%
• Smaller footprint:	63%	64%
• Larger footprint:	63%	64%
• Largest footprint:	62%	63%

"Customers in the smallest footprint stores are slightly more satisfied. As stores increase in size, customers are somewhat less satisfied and less likely to recommend the store to their friends and family. These findings support the recent move by retailers to create smaller footprint locations in order to deliver better experiences. Most typically, customer issues in larger stores center on locating products and finding assistance."

Service Management Group

Mall vs. Freestanding Locations

Based on store location, the following percentages of customers said they likely would return to or recommend a retail location:

	Likely To Return	Recommend
• Freestanding:	75%	73%
• Mall:	75%	71%

"Customers visiting a mall location of a retailer are less likely to return and recommend than customers visiting other store formats. Freestanding locations don't share brand equity or customer experience with mall properties or adjoining retailers."

Service Management Group

Newer vs. Older Locations

Based on the age of the store, the following percentages of customers said they likely would return to or recommend a retail location:

	Likely To Return	Recommend
• Store under two years old:	78%	74%
• Store 2-to-5 years old:	75%	68%
• Store 5-to-10 years old:	74%	66%
• Store more than 10 years old:	73%	65%

"Customers visiting stores more than two years old report lower scores on loyalty metrics. Infusing capital into stores is a solid investment toward improving the customer experience. By doing so, operators can showcase the latest in store design and product enhancements."

Service Management Group

Returning Merchandise

Comparing customers with returns with those not returning merchandise, those highly satisfied with their most recent shopping experience are as follows:

	Overall Satisfaction	Friendliness	Speed
• No return:	57%	56%	47%
• Return:	57%	56%	44%

> **"Customers with returns are equally satisfied with their visit when compared with those who did not return an item. Returns are an unglamourous part of the retail world and stores seem to be doing a nice job handling returns."**
>
> Service Management Group

Rural vs. Urban Locations

Based on market population, the following percentages of customers said they likely would recommend a retail location based on their most recent shopping experience:

- Population more than 50,000: 63%
- Population 10,000-to-50,000: 66%
- Population less than 10,000: 67%

> **"Rural customers are slightly more satisfied overall with their retail concepts. Rural shoppers may have a smaller number of options to shop and, as a result, a smaller frame of reference when comparing experiences."**
>
> Service Management Group

19.3 Market Resources

Service Management Group, 1737 McGee Street, Kansas City, MO 64108. (800) 764-0439. (www.smg.com)

20

ENVIRONMENTALLY CONSCIOUS CONSUMERISM

20.1 Concerns About The Environment

Since 2008, Cone Communications (www.conecomm.com) has conducted the *Green Gap Trend Tracker* survey. The 2013 survey found that 71% of American consumers routinely or sometimes consider the environment when making a purchasing decision. This is an increase from 69% and 66%, respectively, who did so a year prior and in 2008.

Since 2009, Harris Interactive (www.harrisinteractive.com) has conducted annual surveys that track adults' attitudes toward the environment as well as their engagement in various environmentally friendly activities. In the 2012 poll, and, for comparison in the 2009 poll, consumers expressed the following views:

	2009	2012
• Concerned about the planet we are leaving behind for future generations:	43%	34%
• Personally care a great deal about the current state and future of the environment:	36%	31%
• Describe themselves as environmentally conscious:	30%	27%
• Describe themselves as a conservationist:	17%	20%
• Describe themselves as "green:"	13%	17%
• Describe themselves as an environmentalist:	13%	16%

In an April 2013 survey by The Nielsen Company (www.nielsen.com), 60% of adults said they are "strongly concerned" about the environment.

20.2 Use Of Products With An Environmental Benefit

The following are findings of Cone Communications' 2013 *Green Gap Trend Tracker* survey related to the use of products with an environmental benefit:

- Ninety percent (90%) of adults say they believe it's their responsibility to properly use and dispose of products with an environmental benefit, but their actions do not aligning with intent. Only 30% say they often use products in a way that achieves the intended environmental benefit; 42% say they dispose of products in a way that fulfills the intended environmental benefit.
- Eighty-five percent (85%) of adults say they want companies to educate them on how to properly use and dispose of products.
- Seventy-eight percent (78%) say they will boycott a product if they discover an

environmental claim to be misleading.

- Seventy-one percent (71%) of consumers say they wish companies would do a better job helping them understand environmental terms.
- Seventy-one percent (71%) of adults say they regularly read and follow instructions on how to properly use a product, 66% read proper-disposal instructions, and 41% said they perform additional research to determine how best to utilize and discard a product for maximum benefit.
- Although more than 60% of respondents say they understand the environmental terms companies use in their advertising, the majority continue to erroneously believe common expressions such as "green" or "environmentally friendly" mean a product has a positive (40%) or neutral (22%) impact on the environment. Fewer were able to correctly identify these terms as meaning the product has a lighter impact than other similar products (22%) or less than it used to (2%). Despite the attention given to product development and environmental marketing, consumer misunderstanding of "green" claims has remained flat at around 60% since 2008.

Nielsen's April 2013 survey reported that 34% of adults said that within the past 30 days they had purchased a product because they perceived it as environmentally responsible.

"Any way you cut it, green is big business. Sales of environmentally friendly products in the U.S. exceeded $40 billion last year. This includes $29.2 billion for organic food, more than $10 billion for hybrid, electric and clean-diesel vehicles, more than $2 billion on energy-efficient light bulbs and $640 million on green cleaning products."

Advertising Age, 9/24/13

20.3 Paying A Premium For Green Products

While consumers are increasingly purchasing products with an environmental benefit, they are more reluctant to pay a premium for these items than they were a few years ago.

The Harris Poll found consumers' willingness to pay more for green products in 2009 and 2012 as follows:

	2009	2012
• Seek out green products as long as cost is the same:	29%	30%
• Seek out green products even if I have to pay a little extra:	26%	24%
• Seek out green products even if I have to pay a lot extra:	2%	2%

In its *Green Gauge* survey, GfK (www.gfk.com) found consumers' willingness to pay more for green products as follows:

	2008	2012
• Energy-efficient light bulbs:	70%	60%
• Food/dairy with no hormones/antibiotics:	57%	51%
• Autos that pollute less:	62%	49%
• Biodegradable plastic packaging:	58%	49%
• Electricity from renewable sources:	56%	48%
• Paper products made from recycled materials:	53%	47%
• Packaging using less plastic:	52%	47%
• Apparel made from organic/recycled content:	45%	40%

The shift is, in part, because consumers have come to expect environmental compatibility in the products they purchase; a few years ago such products were more of a novelty.

The consumer pushback is also a reaction to marketers that over-hype green products and make overly aggressive claims. Diane Crispell, Consulting Director at GfK, sees a bifurcation of the market, with the most committed and educated 'Green Indeed' consumers still being willing and able to spend more on products, while those in the mainstream grow more skeptical.

20.4 Environmentally Focused Activities

In the Harris Poll consumers said that they engage in the following environmentally focused activities in their daily lives (percentage of respondents):

• Keep unneeded lights off or turn lights off when leaving a room:	81%
• Recycle:	68%
• Reuse things that I have instead of throwing them away or buying new items:	61%
• Make an effort to use less water:	57%
• Unplug electrical appliances when I am not using them:	43%
• Purchase locally grown produce:	36%
• Buy food in bulk:	30%
• Purchase locally manufactured products:	24%
• Purchase used items rather than new:	23%
• Purchase all-natural products:	18%
• Purchase organic products:	17%
• Compost food and organic waste:	16%
• Carpool or take public transportation:	16%
• Walk or ride a bike instead of driving or using public transportation:	15%

In a survey by Ipsos (www.ipsos.com), 25% of respondents reported that they always proactively take steps to green their home or lifestyle, such as by recycling, driving energy efficient vehicles, weatherizing their home, or using eco-friendly products. An additional 60% say they sometimes take these actions, while just 15% say they never do.

Nielsen found in its April 2013 survey that 80% of consumers recycle paper, plastic, or other materials at home. Nearly one-half said they made changes to their residence that made it more energy efficient.

21

GIFT GIVING

21.1 Overview

The percentages of consumers giving gifts for holidays and occasions are as follows (sources: National Retail Federation [www.nrf.com] and VoiceQuilt [www.voicequilt.com]):

- Christmas: 96%
- Birthdays: 95%
- Religious holidays: 89%
- Valentine's Day: 72%
- Mother's Day: 71%
- Father's Day: 66%

21.2 Characteristics of Gift Giving

According to the *National Trends in Gift Giving Study*, conducted by VoiceQuilt, 47% of all U.S. women buy gifts for ten or more occasions throughout the year; 25% say they give gifts for 15 or more events, and 19% give gifts for 20 or more occasions over a 12-month period. The vast majority of U.S. women spend less than $50 on gifts regardless of the occasion.

Women have the following motivations behind their gift giving (source: VoiceQuilt):

- To say "I love you:" 65%
- Because they love giving gifts: 52%
- To surprise the gift receiver: 48%
- Because the occasion required a gift: 39%
- To thank someone: 35%
- Because it was the right thing to do: 27%
- To reciprocate: 10%
- To say "I'm sorry:" 4%
- Felt peer pressured: 1%
- To outdo someone else's gift: 1%

The following are the most important attributes of gifts (source: VoiceQuilt):

- Original: 78%
- Sentimental: 77%

- Make recipient feel its "just for them:" 74%
- Unique: 70%
- Heirloom: 54%
- Expensive: 19%

A December 2012 survey by Research Now (www.researchnow.com) found that people find the most challenging aspect of holiday shopping as follows (percentage of responses; two responses allowed per survey participant):
- Finding the right gift: 60%
- Staying within budget: 56%
- Long lines and traffic: 50%

People consider the following to be the most difficult to buy gifts for (source: Research Now):
- Someone who has everything: 68%
- Unclassified love interest (not an official significant other or ex): 33%
- Frenemies (a friend who is also a rival): 26%

21.3 Responsible Gift Giving

The Responsible Giving Survey, conducted by Ketchum Global Research Network (www.ketchum.com), studied the intent behind giving and examined how attitudes and culture shape gifting decisions and shopping habits. The survey found that 78% of adults give gifts during the holiday season because they want to and not out of a sense of obligation.

The following are other findings of the survey:
- Eighty-one percent (81%) of adults appreciate charitable donations given on their behalf in lieu of a gift; 74% would volunteer their time to charity as a gift if they thought others would value this type of responsible giving.
- Fifty-nine percent (59%) of adults prepare alternative gifts such as homemade gifts and donations of time or money to charities during the holiday season.
- Forty-nine percent (49%) of married men say their spouse takes full responsibility for purchasing holiday gifts; 75% of married women say they take full responsibility for purchasing holiday gifts.
- Thirty-three percent (33%) of married men say they and their spouse share the responsibility of purchasing holiday gifts, but only 20% of married women say the same.
- Forty percent (40%) say that giving a homemade gift is better than giving a store-bought gift.
- Parents are more likely than adults without children to say they will make gifts rather than purchase some gifts (40% of parents vs. 29% of non-parents).
- Fifty-seven percent (57%) of those employed gave a gift to coworkers; 42% gave their boss a gift.
- Women are more likely than men to give a holiday gift or tip to people at work.

- Older adults ages 65 and above are more likely than adults overall to give a holiday gift or tip to people whose services they employ, such as a hairstylist (59% vs. 41% overall), a gardener or housekeeper (57% vs. 41% overall), or a mail or newspaper carrier (54% vs. 40% overall).

Fifty-nine percent (59%) of adults say that they have never re-gifted, though a similar number of adults say that re-gifting is socially acceptable. Among those who say that re-gifting is not socially acceptable, 22% admit that despite that belief, they have re-gifted.

The majority of adults agree that it's important to set an agreed-upon spending limit for gifts between family members or friends. Half agree that you should consider how much someone else can afford to spend when purchasing a gift for them.

Thirty percent (30%) of adults think someone is being irresponsible if they do not send a note of thanks for a gift. Older adults ages 50 and above are more likely than younger adults ages 18-to-29 to agree that someone is being irresponsible if they do not send a note of thanks for a gift (44% of older adults vs. 20% of younger adults).

21.4 Self Gifting

According to the National Retail Federation, 57% of shoppers plan to set aside money to make purchases for themselves (i.e., self-gifting) while Christmas shopping in 2013, with $129.62 as the average amount to spend. During the prior holiday season these figures were 59% and $140.43, respectively.

"During the holidays, we traditionally think of it as a season for gift-giving. But self-indulgence is quickly becoming a new tradition. After several years of cutting back, people have grown weary of dismissing their own wants and needs."

Marshal Cohen, Chief Retail Analyst
The NPD Group

21.5 Wedding Gift Giving

In a survey by Claria Corporation (www.claria.com), 75% of respondents said they planned to attend one to three weddings during the coming 12-month period.

Thirty-four percent (34%) had or planned to purchase wedding gifts through online retail channels, with 80% planning to buy gifts from the bride and groom's registry.

Forty-eight percent (48%) of respondents indicated they would purchase a wedding gift in the coming three months. Of those, 43% planned to buy online and 83% planned to purchase a gift requested in the bride and groom's gift registry.

Sixty-five percent (65%) typically buy gifts for all couples who invite them to a wedding, 30% only purchase gifts for weddings they attend. Sixty percent (60%) of respondents reported spending $26 to $75 for a wedding gift.

Ninety-four percent (94%) of engaged couples are registered.

21.6 Graduation Gift Giving

According to the National Retail Federation, 30% of consumers purchase a graduation gift, spending collectively approximately $4 billion each year. The average consumer buying graduation gifts gives to two graduates and spends an average of $90 on gifts.

Fifty-nine percent (59%) of those who give graduation gifts give cash, a higher percentage than for any other occasion. Additionally, 32% give gift cards.

21.7 Returning Gifts

The downside to gift-giving and -receiving is gifts that are unwanted. According to a Western Union survey, 75% of Americans have pretended to like a gift they received.

The National Retail Federation estimates that 10% of holiday sales are returned. A survey by *Consumer Reports* found that about half of Americans include receipts with their gifts to help with returns and exchanges.

A survey by HomeGoods found that 54% of adults had re-gifted presents; 36% had done so on several occasions.

22

INFLUENCE OF GASOLINE PRICES

22.1 Overview

Gasoline prices tend to be cyclical, generally increasing in the late spring and summer, but the overall trend since 2009 has been a steady escalation in the price of fuel.

The price of gasoline is generally perceived as a indicator of economic conditions because it is so conspicuous.

"People may not remember too many numbers about the economy, but there are certain signposts they do pay attention to. As a shorthand way to assess how the economy is doing, everybody notices the price of gas. It can have a big symbolic impact."

Ethan Harris, Chief Economist
Bank of America Merrill Lynch

22.2 Impact On Consumer Spending

Credit Suisse (CS) estimates that each 1¢ uptick in a gallon of gas redirects $1 billion of consumer spending away from other goods over the course of a year.

The Monthly Consumer Survey by the National Retail Federation (www.nrf.com) asks consumers about the impact of gasoline prices. In the October 2013 survey, 33% of adults said that gasoline prices were affecting their spending. The impact on spending was as follows:

- Driving less: 37%
- Reduced dining out: 32%
- Decreased vacation/travel: 29%
- Spending less on clothing: 25%

- Delayed major purchases (car, TV, furniture, etc.): 20%
- Spending less on groceries: 18%
- Increased carpooling: 7%
- Other: 2%

"Most Americans drive to work or the supermarket, and few have any reasonable alternative. When other prices change, we can shift to different goods. It's really hard to adjust how much we drive. And the poorest Americans, for whom gas makes up a far larger share of the household budget, are hardest hit. Eventually people can move closer to their jobs or get a more fuel-efficient car, but that takes time."

Prof. Samara Gunter, Ph.D.
Colby College

23

PAYMENT PREFERENCES

23.1 How Americans Pay Their Bills

According to *2013 Online Banking and Bill-Payment Forecast*, published in September 2013 by Javelin Strategy & Research (www.javelinstrategy.com), Americans will make $2.1 trillion in payments for just seven common types of bills in 2013. Methods used for bill payment are as follows:

- Biller website: 37%
- Check payment by mail: 31%
- Primary financial institution's bill pay service: 25%
- Walk-in location: 22%
- Secondary financial institution's bill pay service: 10%
- Telephone: 8%
- Mobile device: 5%
- Third-party bill pay service: 4%
- Other: 2%

Thirty-nine percent (39%) of adults managed financial tasks on smartphones in 2013, compared with 22% in 2012. According to Javelin, 37 million people, or 26% of the adult population, use mobile bill-pay; 11 million, or 8%, bank online and use mobile banking but do not pay their bills through their banks. Another 55 million, or 39%, bank online and pay bills via their banks, but do not use mobile banking.

23.2 Credit and Debit Cards

According to The Nilson Report (www.nilsonreport.com), spending in the U.S. for goods and services on general purpose and private label consumer and commercial credit, debit, and prepaid cards reached $4.633 trillion in 2012; that figure is projected to reach $7.285 trillion by 2017. Credit cards accounted for 52.8% of spending in 2012 compared to 47.2% for debit cards. In 2011, these statistics were 52.6% and 47.4%, respectively. Credit card spending in 2012 was up $172 billion, an 8.4% increase from the prior year.

"The more than 20-year trend that had debit card purchase volume and purchase transactions gaining share versus credit cards ended in 2012."

The Nilson Report, 11/11/13

23.3 Proximity Mobile Payments

Proximity mobile payments are growing rapidly in popularity in the U.S. eMarketer (www.emarketer.com) estimates transactions using mobile devices increased 283% in 2012 and will rise a further 234% in 2013.

While only 37% of smartphone users had used a mobile payment system as of March 2013, 51% had done so by December 2013, according to JiWire (www.jiwire.com).

Proximity mobile payment users, transaction volume, and average spend per user have been and are projected as follows (source: *eMarketer*):

	2011	2012	2013	2014	2015
• Users:	2.7 million	7.9 million	13.3 million	21.3 million	34.0 million
• Transactions:	$166 million	$635 billion	$2.12 billion	$7.51 billion	$24.6 billion
• Avg. spend:	$61	$81	$160	$352	$725

Among those consumers who used a mobile payment system in 2012, the platform used was as follows (source: JiWire):

- PayPal: 64%
- Amazon Payments: 40%
- Google Wallet: 20%
- Isis: 2%
- Other: 10%

24

POST-RECESSION CONSUMER BEHAVIOR

24.1 A Recovery No Better Than The Recession

The most severe economic downturn in recent history, dubbed the Great Recession, officially began in December 2007 and ended in June 2009, according to the National Bureau of Economic Research (NBER, www.nber.org). Economic woes, however, did not end for many consumers in 2009. Many still continue to struggle financially and the spending behaviors of an even larger group continues to be affected by the downturn.

An assessment by the Social & Demographic Trends Group of the Pew Research Center (www.pewsocialtrends.org) observed that the median income of American households decreased by as much in the first two years after the official end of the Great Recession as it did during the recession itself. The decrease in household income from 2009 to 2011 nearly equaled the decrease in income in the two years of the recession, indicating that the recovery from the Great Recession is bypassing the nation's households. Median income continued to drop in 2012 and early 2013.

According to Sentier Research (www.sentierresearch.com), median annual household income (pretax and adjusted for both inflation and seasonal changes) in February 2013 was $51,404, 5.6% lower than it was in June 2009, the month the recovery technically began; 7.3% lower than in December 2007, when the most recent recession officially started; and 8.4% lower than in January 2000, the earliest date that this statistical series became available.

The Great Recession followed the 2001 recession, which also had a lingering loss in median household income. As of year-end 2012, 13 years had passed without the median exceeding the peak of $54,932 in 1999.

The drop in household income is symptomatic of broader struggles in the economic well-being of U.S. households. The share of families with at least one unemployed member nearly doubled during the Great Recession and remains at a high level.

24.2 Disproportionate Impact

Unskilled workers and older demographics have suffered the most during and after the Great Recession.

"Workers with less advanced skills have also suffered disproportionately. The pay gap between college graduates and everyone else is near a record. Despite the long economic slump – and the well-chronicled struggles of some college graduates – their unemployment rate is just 4.1%."

The New York Times, 3/29/13

According to Sentier Research, adults in their 50s and early 60s – those near retirement age who do not yet have access to Medicare and Social Security – have lost the most earnings power of any age group, with their household incomes 10% less than when the recovery began in 2009.

"In the current listless economy, every generation has a claim to having been most injured. But the Labor Department's latest jobs snapshot and other recent data reports present a strong case for crowning Baby Boomers as the greatest victims of the recession and its grim aftermath."

The New York Times, 2/2/13

24.3 Spending Plans

Harris Interactive (www.harrisinteractive.com) has tracked consumer spending plans since the Great Recession. When asked about their spending and savings plans for the upcoming six months in 2013 and, for comparison, during the prior five years, responses have been as follows:

	2008	2009	2010	2011	2012	2013
• Decrease spending eating out at restaurants:	65%	62%	66%	61%	59%	62%
• Reduce spending on entertainment:	64%	58%	62%	58%	55%	59%

• Save or invest more money:	49%	53%	52%	51%	50%	50%
• Take a vacation lasting longer than a week:	29%	35%	31%	29%	29%	35%
• Move more money to spend as desired:	25%	27%	28%	26%	30%	31%
• Buy a new computer:	22%	23%	21%	23%	24%	25%
• Move to a different residence:	18%	17%	17%	14%	16%	22%
• Buy/lease a new car, van, or truck:	12%	12%	12%	12%	13%	16%
• Purchase a condo or house:	10%	8%	10%	7%	8%	10%
• Start a new business:	9%	7%	10%	6%	8%	10%
• Buy a boat or recreational vehicle:	5%	4%	6%	3%	5%	7%

Surveys were conducted in November 2008, December 2009, September 2010, November 2011, November 2012, and June 2013.

24.4 Cutting Back

When asked by Harris Interactive about measures to save money they had done or considered during the prior six months, responses were as follows:

	2009	2010	2011	2012	2013
• Purchasing more generic brands:	64%	62%	61%	57%	62%
• Brown bagging lunch:	47%	45%	42%	41%	44%
• Going to stylist/barber less often:	43%	37%	37%	38%	39%
• Switching to refillable water bottles:	36%	37%	31%	33%	38%
• Cancelling magazine subscriptions:	34%	27%	25%	27%	29%
• Cancelling or cutting back on cable TV subscriptions:	21%	22%	21%	21%	24%
• Stop purchasing coffee in the morning:	20%	22%	17%	20%	22%
• Cut down on dry cleaning:	22%	21%	19%	18%	22%
• Cancelled newspaper subscription:	21%	17%	15%	16%	18%
• Cancelled landline telephone service:	12%	17%	14%	16%	20%
• Changed or cancelled cellphone service:	15%	17%	14%	14%	17%
• Begun carpooling or using mass transit:	14%	14%	13%	14%	15%

Surveys were conducted in October 2009, October 2010, December 2011, November 2012, and June 2013.

In a consumer sentiment survey by Prosper Business Development (www.goprosper.com), published by *Stores Magazine* in February 2013, 53.9% of adults reported cutting back on some spending in 2012, a drop from 76.4% who said they did so a year prior. Specific items consumers cut back on were as follows:

	2011	2012
• Casual dining:	54.5%	49.1%
• Daily cup of gourmet coffee:	40.8%	28.8%
• Luxury handbag purchases:	39.8%	24.6%

25

PRIVACY ISSUES

25.1 Overview

Consumers are increasingly reacting to the continuous invasion of privacy in their lives. They feel, rightfully, that marketers are watching virtually every aspect of their lives, even while they are in their own homes.

> **"A surveillance society is taking root. Video cameras peer constantly from lamp poles and storefronts. Smartphones relay a dizzying barrage of information about their owners to sentinel towers dotting cities and punctuating pasture-land. Meanwhile, on the information superhighway, every stop by every traveler is noted and stored by Internet service providers like Google, Verizon, and Comcast. Retailers scan, remember, and analyze each purchase by every consumer. Smart TVs know what we're watching – soon they will have eyes to watch us watching them – and smart meters know if we've turned out the lights."**
>
> *Time*, 8/12/13

General surveys indicate that consumers have concerns about their privacy, both online and offline. However, it is difficult to ascertain their concerns about specific actions by marketers because few people really understand what these activities are. And there is a general misconception that the government is protecting their privacy.

"My national phone surveys going back to 1999 show that the majority of Americans know companies follow them, but they have little understanding of data mining or targeting. They also think the government protects them more than it does regarding the misuse of their information and against price discrimination."

Prof. Joseph Turow, Ph.D., Associate Dean
Annenberg School For Communication
University of Pennsylvania
Advertising Age, 1/28/13

Consumers' concerns about privacy are also sometimes difficult to gauge because they are self-contradictory about marketer's use of their information.

"People may claim to worry about privacy issues but look at what they actually do online ... willingly surrendering personal information for a coupon or in a Facebook discussion. The disconnect between what people say and do shows that policymakers and academics misjudge the extent to which the public really cares about the use of data about them by marketers."

Mark Dolliver, Analyst
The Digital Privacy Dilemma
eMarketer, 12/12/12

25.2 Privacy Online

In a January 2013 survey by Ipsos (www.ipsos-na.com), 45% of adults say they feel they have little (33%) or no (12%) control over the personal information companies gather while they are browsing the web or using online services such as photo sharing, travel sites, or gaming. Twenty-one percent (21%) say that they have at least a significant amount of control over such personal information; 34% feel they have moderate control.

When asked their attitudes about online tracking by companies, responses were as follows:

- Only after an individual specifically gives the company permission to do so: 60%
- Should never be allowed to track individual's online activities: 28%
- Only if the individual gets something in return: 8%
- Tracking any individual online is okay: 5%

When asked if they understand how to protect their online privacy, responses were as follows:

- Totally understand: 11%
- Mostly understand: 29%
- Moderately understand: 40%
- Minimally understand: 17%
- Totally confused: 3%

Eight-five percent (85%) of adults have taken steps to protect their online privacy. Specific actions taken have been as follows:

- Deleting cookies: 65%
- Opting out of targeted advertising: 44%
- Uninstalling an app: 41%
- Request that websites don't track them: 39%
- Stopped using an online service: 21%
- Changed to a different website or online service: 20%

Thirty-two percent (32%) of survey participants said they always consider a company's privacy reputation, track record, or policies when choosing which websites to visit or online services to use. An additional 54% only sometimes do so. However, 13% never take these things into account when choosing which websites and online services to use.

25.3 Mobile Privacy

In a September 2013 survey by TRUSTe (www.truste.com), an online privacy management services provider, 60% of adults said they have privacy concerns about mobile app use. When asked what party is most responsible for protecting mobile privacy, responses were as follows:

- Individuals themselves: 76%
- Wireless service providers: 6%
- Device manufacturers: 5%
- Government through legislation: 4%
- Mobile operating system: 2%
- App stores: 2%
- App developers: 2%

> **"TRUSTe found that the vast majority of respondents believed they held the most responsibility for managing their own privacy protections."**
>
> *eMarketer*, 9/12/13

When mobile app users were asked what types of information they would share with a company, responses were as follows:

- Gender: 53%
- Age: 44%
- E-mail: 39%
- Full name: 31%
- No information at all: 25%

25.4 Whom Do Consumers Trust?

A July 2013 Harris Poll (www.harrisinteractive.com) asked adults how much trust they have in various entities handling their personally identified information (such as credit card information, contact information and so forth) in a properly confidential and secure manner. Responses were as follows:

	Trust	Don't Trust
• Health providers (e.g., doctors and hospitals):	79%	21%
• Major online retailers (e.g., Amazon, eBay):	74%	26%
• Banks and brokerage companies:	68%	32%
• Small and/or independent online retailers:	55%	45%
• State and local governments:	52%	48%
• Search and Portal sites (e.g., Google, Yahoo!):	49%	51%
• Federal government:	48%	52%
• Social networking sites (like Facebook or MySpace):	28%	72%

By age, adults trust the following entities handling their personal identification:

	18-to-34	35-to-44	45-to-54	55+
• Health providers (e.g., doctors and hospitals):	78%	78%	76%	82%
• Major online retailers (e.g., Amazon, eBay):	74%	72%	74%	76%
• Banks and brokerage companies:	70%	65%	63%	71%
• Small and/or independent online retailers:	55%	58%	58%	53%
• State and local governments:	61%	52%	49%	46%
• Search and portal sites (e.g., Google, Yahoo!):	55%	54%	50%	41%
• Federal government:	58%	51%	48%	39%
• Social networking sites (like Facebook or MySpace):	42%	34%	27%	14%

Adults said they view the following as a threat to their privacy:

- Cyber-criminals: 88%
- Social networking sites (e.g., Facebook, Google+): 70%
- People with wearable, camera-equipped devices: 63%
- The federal government: 60%
- People with camera-equipped phones: 59%
- State and local governments: 56%
- Search and portal sites (e.g., Google, Yahoo!): 53%
- Banks and brokerage companies: 43%
- Small and/or independent online retailers: 42%
- Major online retailers (e.g., Amazon, eBay): 35%
- Health providers (e.g., doctors and hospitals): 31%

26

PURCHASE DECISION MAKING

26.1 Top Influencers

In a survey conducted by Opinion Research Corp. (www.opinionresearch.com) for ARAnet (www.aranet.com), consumers said their buying decisions are influenced by the following (percentage of respondents):

- Personal advice from friends or family members: 59%
- TV news or other broadcasts: 40%
- Search engines: 39%
- Ads on TV: 36%
- Newspaper and magazine articles: 33%
- Newspaper and magazine ads: 31%
- Articles seen online: 28%
- Radio news or other broadcasts: 25%
- Direct mail: 24%
- Ads heard on the radio: 20%
- Emails from retailers or manufacturers: 20%
- Ads seen online: 19%
- Messages or posts on social media: 18%
- Billboards: 15%

According to a survey by Fleishman-Hillard (www.fleishman.com), for spending of $100 or more the following are influencers for women:

- Spouse/significant other: 53%
- Online reviews: 37%
- Friends: 30%
- Other family members: 26%
- Expert recommendations: 23%
- Salesperson: 15%

26.2 Trust in Shopping Recommendations

According to a survey by Edelman (www.edelman.com), credible sources of information about companies or products are as follows (percentage of respondents):

- An academic or expert: 70%
- Technical expert with the company: 64%
- Financial or industry expert: 53%

- CEO: 50%
- Non-government organization representative: 47%
- Governmental official: 43%
- Person like yourself: 43%
- Regular employee: 34%

In the *Global Online Consumer Survey*, by The Nielsen Company (www.nielsen.com), 90% of respondents said they trust recommendations from people they know. The following are percentages that trust various other sources:

- Consumer opinions posted online: 70%
- Brand websites: 70%
- Editorial content (e.g. newspaper): 69%
- Brand sponsorships: 64%
- TV: 62%
- Newspaper: 61%
- Magazines: 59%
- Billboards/outdoor advertising: 55%
- Radio: 55%
- Emails signed up for: 54%
- Ads before movies: 52%
- Search engine results ads: 41%
- Online video ads: 37%
- Online banner ads: 33%
- Text ads on mobile phones: 24%

According to a survey by Bridge Ratings (www.bridgeratings.com), consumers rate trusted sources of information as follows (rated on a scale of 1-to-10):

- Friends, family, and acquaintances: 8.6
- Strangers with expertise: 7.9
- Teachers: 7.3
- Religious leaders: 6.9
- Newspapers and magazines: 6.1
- Favorite radio personality: 5.5
- TV news reporters: 5.2
- Bloggers: 2.8
- Advertising: 2.2
- Telemarketers: 1.4

26.3 Shopper Decision Priorities

The *Brand Landscape Report* by The NPD Group (www.npd.com) explored the factors that go into purchase decisions made by shoppers. The assessment found that priorities vary by product category and the gender of the shopper.

For various product categories, consumers consider a product for purchase as follows:

Apparel

Female

1. Is a brand I've had success with
2. Has the features/benefits you want
3. Is your style
4. Offers real solutions for you
5. Fits well
6. Is comfortable
7. Has a lot of sales or special deals
8. Offers good value for the money
9. Is a brand friends wear
10. Is affordable

Male

1. Is a brand I've had success with
2. Is your style
3. Has the features/benefits you want
4. Offers good value for the money
5. Offers real solutions for you
6. Is comfortable
7. Is affordable
8. Has a lot of sales or special deals
9. Is a brand you can trust
10. Fits well

Athletic Footwear

Female

1. Is your style
2. Fits me
3. Offers real solutions for you
4. Offers real solutions for my activities
5. Is comfortable
6. Is fun to wear
7. Is growing in popularity
8. Is a brand you can trust
9. Has a fashionable look
10. Has a broad selection

Male

1. Is your style
2. Offers real solutions for you
3. Offers real solutions for my activities
4. Fits me
5. Is fun to wear
6. Is growing in popularity
7. Is comfortable
8. Offers good value for the money
9. Has a fashionable look
10. Has a broad selection

Consumer Electronics

Female

1. Is a brand currently owned
2. Works well with what I own already
3. Has the features & benefits I want
4. Is growing in popularity
5. Offers real solutions for you
6. Offers good value for the money
7. Has a fashionable look
8. Is socially responsible
9. Is a brand I can trust
10. Has a broad selection

Male

1. Is a brand currently owned
2. Is growing in popularity
3. Offers real solutions for you
4. Has the features & benefits I want
5. Offers product bundles or packages
6. Works well with what I already own
7. Has a lot of sales or special deals
8. Offers good value for the money
9. Has the latest trend
10. Is socially responsible

Toys

	Female		Male
1.	I/my child is a fan of the character	1.	I collect this brand
2.	Is growing in popularity	2.	I/my child is a fan of the character
3.	I collect this brand	3.	Is growing in popularity
4.	Has the features/benefits you want	4.	Is trendy or is "in" right now
5.	Is trendy or is "in" right now	5.	Has a broad selection
6.	Has a broad selection	6.	Has the features/benefits you want
7.	Has the latest trend	7.	Has the latest trend
8.	Has a lot of sales or special deals	8.	Has the latest technology
9.	Offers good value for the money	9.	Has a lot of sales or special deals
10.	A good gift idea	10.	A good gift idea

26.4 Deals and Bargains

According to *Time* (February 2013), 40% of items purchased by consumers are at some discount, an increase from 10% of sales in 1990 that were discounted.

"There's not a weekend where an average specialty retailer in the mall is not offering some kind of 30% to 40% off deal. It certainly feels like the consumer is not shopping unless there's some kind of deal attached to it. And it's very hard to pull back when the consumer gets used to buying things on sale."

Brad Tunick
Senior Specialty Retail Analyst
JPMorgan Chase
Bloomberg Businessweek, 10/3/13

In a survey of millennials (ages 18-to-34) by IRI (www.iriworldwide.com), item price ranked as the #1 influencer of brand selection, ahead of previous usage and trust of brands, shopper loyalty cards, and advertising. Eighty-seven percent (87%) of survey respondents said price was among the two top influencers.

A Harris Poll (www.harrisinteractive.com) found that consumers, by age, find the following most helpful when hunting for bargains:

	18-to-34	35-to-44	45-to-55	55 & older	Total
• Newspaper/magazine ads:	15%	16%	24%	33%	23%
• Online ads:	22%	26%	17%	12%	18%
• Direct mail/catalogs:	15%	13%	14%	10%	12%
• TV commercials:	17%	12%	8%	7%	11%
• Radio ads:	2%	3%	<1%	1%	2%
• All media viewed equally:	31%	31%	36%	36%	34%

Harris also found that consumers, by age, find the following most useful in deciding what products and services to purchase:

	18-to-34	35-to-44	45-to-55	55 & older	Total
• Television commercials:	50%	38%	35%	23%	37%
• Newspaper ads:	6%	13%	14%	31%	17%
• Internet search engine ads:	10%	15%	16%	16%	14%
• Radio ads:	3%	4%	3%	2%	3%
• Internet banner ads:	4%	1%	1%	<1%	1%
• All media viewed equally:	27%	29%	31%	27%	28%

27

RESPONSE TO ADVERTISING

27.1 Preferred Media For Ads

CrossView (www.crossview.com) found shoppers' preference for retail promotion delivery as follows:

- Email: 37%
- Mailer: 23%
- Text message: 18%
- In-store: 11%
- Social media: 9%
- Other: 3%

27.2 Positive Response To Advertising

A March 2013 survey by Truth Central, the thought leadership unit of McCann (www.mccann.com), found that 71% of consumers feel positive about the advertising sector, 67% of consumers feel positive about the advertising they see around them, 57% of consumers say advertising gives them something to talk about, and 39% of consumers say they love advertising. When asked how advertising benefits them, survey participants responded as follows:

- Helps me keep informed about the latest offers: 87%
- Helps me know what the latest trends are: 83%
- Entertains me and makes me laugh: 77%

Microsoft Advertising (www.advertising.microsoft.com) found attitudes toward advertising through the four formats as follows:

	Computer	TV	Smartphone	Gaming Console
• Fun to watch:	32%	54%	28%	30%
• Generally like the ads:	29%	46%	25%	26%
• Regularly notice ads:	54%	64%	39%	31%
• More meaningful and relevant:	35%	48%	29%	27%
• Helpful if targeted to preferences:	50%	54%	40%	33%
• Rarely notice ads:	36%	29%	43%	38%
• Very annoying:	58%	43%	62%	43%

27.3 Negative Response To Ads

In a recent Harris Poll (www.harrisinteractive.com), consumers, by age, said they have chosen not to purchase a certain brand for the following reasons:

	18-to-34	35-to-44	45-to-55	55 & older	Total
• Found the ads distasteful:	37%	34%	32%	37%	35%
• Didn't like the spokesperson:	29%	24%	27%	30%	28%
• Didn't like program or event sponsored by the brand:	26%	26%	26%	30%	27%

A separate Harris Poll found that 91% of consumers ignore at least some types of ads. The following are the types of ads that consumers, by age, tend to ignore or disregard the most:

	18-to-34	35-to-44	45-to-55	55 & older	Total
• Internet banner ads:	43%	50%	48%	45%	46%
• Internet search engine ads:	20%	14%	17%	15%	17%
• Television commercials:	7%	10%	15%	20%	13%
• Radio ads:	11%	10%	9%	7%	9%
• Newspaper ads:	7%	7%	5%	5%	6%
• None of these:	14%	9%	6%	8%	9%

27.4 Effectiveness of Celebrity Endorsements

In a recent Harris Poll, consumers, by age, said they found the following types of celebrities most persuasive when endorsing a product in an ad:

	18-to-34	35-to-44	45-to-55	55 & older	Total
• Business leaders:	28%	33%	38%	46%	46%
• Athletes:	24%	21%	20%	19%	19%
• Television or movie stars:	23%	21%	15%	15%	15%
• Singers or musicians:	13%	15%	17%	12%	12%
• Former political figures:	13%	9%	9%	8%	8%

For brands using celebrity endorsers, the possibility of a scandal poses a risk. But the actual impact of such scandals is actually less than might be expected. Harris found that 74% of consumers are not impacted when a celebrity endorser gets involved in a scandal. The following were opinions by age:

	18-to-34	35-to-44	45-to-55	55 & older	Total
• No impact on brand:	68%	77%	70%	81%	74%
• Feel worse about brand:	21%	18%	18%	19%	22%
• Feel better about brand:	11%	5%	1%	<1%	5%

27.5 Ad Awareness While Multitasking

According to a survey by Frank N. Magid Associates (www.magid.com), online consumers report using a computer 42% of the time they watch TV. Their responsiveness to ads when multitasking is as follows:

	Men		Women	
	Age 18-35	Age 35-54	Age 18-35	Age 35-54
• Pay more attention to TV ads:	28%	19%	19%	21%
• Pay more attention to online ads:	15%	8%	11%	9%
• Pay attention to both equally:	24%	25%	19%	20%
• Don't pay attention to either:	32%	48%	52%	50%

27.6 Response to Email

In a September 2013 survey by Kentico (www.kentico.com), respondents said they read emails to which they subscribe as follows:

- About 25%: 36%
- About 50%: 26%
- About 75%: 16%
- All: 10%
- None: 12%

Participants in the survey subscribe or have opted-in to the following number of emails:

- 1-to-5: 37%
- 6-to-10: 31%
- 11-to-15: 15%
- 16-to-20: 7%
- More than 20: 5%

Of those who subscribe to email lists, 57% stay on a list for a period of 1-to-3 years, 22% stay on a list for 4-to-6 years, 5% for 7-to-9 years, and 16% for ten or more years.

Seventy-seven percent (77%) of respondents say they are unlikely to welcome an unsolicited email even if it caters to their particular interests.

When asked how frequently they respond to marketing emails, such as learning more about a product or taking part in a sale, online consumers responded as follows:

- Once or twice a month: 45%
- 3-to-4 times per month: 21%
- 5-to-6 times per month: 8%
- 7 or more times per month: 6%
- Never: 18%

A review by Yesmail Interactive (www.yesmail.com) of 5 billion opt-in emails sent during second quarter 2013 found that 61% of consumers are now viewing email exclusively on a mobile device or using both mobile and desktop devices interchangeably. Forty-nine percent (49%) of all email opens happen on a mobile device. The average click-to-open rate across all consumer segments is 100% higher for desktop emails than it is for mobile.

According to SimpleRelevance (www.simplerelevance.com), most consumers have limited windows of time allocated for responding to emails. While people open email several times throughout the day, 62% only click through to a commercial website during one single hour per day. Email use behaviors vary by gender and income as follows:

- Men tend to open email an average of eight time-periods throughout the day, while women average seven.
- Men click more frequently in the early morning, 4 a.m. until 9 a.m., while women click more frequently in the afternoon to evening, 10 a.m. until 9 p.m.
- For all hours in which men and women open their email, 57% of men and 66% of women prefer one single hour per day in which they actually click through. Twenty-two percent (22%) of men and 19% of women have two one-hour time-periods per day to click through an email.
- People earning $150,000 or more are more likely to click in the early morning from 5 a.m. until 8 a.m., while people earning $75,000 or less are more active from 9 a.m. until 8 p.m.

27.7 Response to Irrelevant Ads

Almost every online consumer has received information while visiting a website that has nothing to do with their personal interests or demographics. The *2013 Online Personal Experience* study, conducted by Harris Interactive for Janrain (www.janrain.com), found that people are running out of patience with irrelevant ads.

When asked their response irrelevant online ads, responses were as follows:

- I get frustrated with websites when content, offers, ads, promotions, etc. appear that have nothing to do with my interests: 74%
- I would leave the site if asked for donations from a political party that I dislike the most: 67%
- I would leave the site if shown ads for a dating service (response from married survey participants only): 57%
- I would leave the site if shown a recommendation to purchase underwear that is for the opposite gender: 50%

"These results align with additional market research indicating that consumers have reached the tipping point when it comes to being shown content that isn't relevant to them. It's a wake up call for brands to fix this problem or risk losing customers and prospects."

Larry Drebes, CEO
Janrain, 7/31/13

28

RESPONSE TO CUSTOMER SERVICE

28.1 Loyalty

Good customer service can win customers and increase loyalty, and studies have shown that good customer service translates to increased sales.

In the *Brand Loyalty Survey* by ClickFox (www.clickfox.com), survey respondents said providing exceptional customer service is the #1 way companies can build brand loyalty. When asked in the survey to identify the top influence in building loyalty, responses were as follows (percentage of respondents):

- Providing exceptional customer service: 34%
- Rewarding purchases, feedback, and referrals: 20%
- Sending exclusive and/or relevant offers and specials: 13%
- Providing personalized products or services: 12%
- Knowing the customer when they visit or call: 10%

According to the *Customer Service Barometer* by American Express (www.amex.com), consumers are willing to spend, on average, 13% more with companies that deliver great customer service. But 93% of U.S. adults say that companies, in general, fail to meet their service expectations; 55% have walked away from an intended purchase in the past 12 months because of a poor customer service experience. Adults estimate that they tell about 15 people about good customer service experiences during the course of a year; they tell 24 people about bad customer service experiences. Those who use social networks tell an average of 53 people about negative experiences.

28.2 Comparison With Low Prices, Deals, and Convenience

While poor customer service compromises brand loyalty, consumers still patronize companies that offer low prices and convenience. In a survey by The NPD Group (www.npd.com), consumers said the following were extremely important factors in deciding where to shop (percentage of respondents):

- Price: 85%
- Sales and special deals: 75%
- Convenience of location: 60%
- Ease of shopping: 60%
- Customer service: 56%

"Price trumps sales and special deals, customer service, and convenience as a factor in deciding where to shop for the majority of U.S. consumers. Eighty-five percent of consumers say the price needs to be right before they shop."

The NPD Group

28.3 Impact By Segment

While customer service is important across all consumer sectors, the influence varies by segment. The following are some industry-specific influences:

Airlines

A 2013 assessment by *Forbes* found airline quality ratings (i.e., on-time arrivals, denied boardings, mishandled baggage, and customer complaints) do not seem to influence revenue.

"Rude flight attendants, delayed arrivals, stale meals. Frequent flyers have plenty to gripe about. But does better customer service actually sell more tickets? Apparent correlation: zero."

Forbes, 9/23/13

Drugstores and Pharmacies

The *National Pharmacy Study*, conducted by J.D. Power and Associates (www.jdpower.com), found customer service, not price, was most important among consumers with respect to store loyalty at drugstores and pharmacies.

E-Commerce

Customer service ranks low among attributes most important to online shoppers. In a survey by A.T. Kearney (www.atkearney.com), the ability to find specific products, free shipping, finding favorite brands, best prices, ease of navigation, site security, special promotions, free samples, peer reviews, and the availability of new products all ranked above customer service.

Still, many online shoppers do expect some level of customer service. In a survey by OneUpWeb (www.oneupweb.com), 32% of Internet users said they expect live chat. A survey by comScore (www.comscore.com) found 35% of online shoppers would like online retailers to improve the availability of live customer service.

Restaurants

Emphatica (www.empathica.com) found that 20% of consumers value good service over good food at fine- and casual-dining establishments. Even in fast-food restaurants, service trumps food quality.

A Gallup Poll (www.gallup.com) found that the biggest driver of engagement in a fast-food restaurant is being treated as a valued customer. Warmth of the greeting ranked second in the survey; taste of food ranked third. Gallup found that a fully engaged customer will spend $33.90 on fast food per month, 16% more than the $29.24 spent by a non-engaged consumer.

28.4 Factors Contributing To Good Customer Service

A 2013 survey by Dimensional Research (www.dimensionalresearch.com) asked consumers about recent interactions with customer service departments of mid-sized companies. Responses were as follows:

Good Customer Service

- The problem was resolved quickly: 69%
- The person who helped me was nice: 65%
- The problem was resolved in one interaction: 63%
- The outcome was what I was originally hoping for: 47%

Bad Customer Service

- I had to explain my problem to multiple people: 72%
- The person I dealt with was unpleasant: 67%
- My problem took too long to resolve: 65%
- The problem was not resolved: 51%

"Interestingly, [Dimensional Research] found that among those who said they had had a positive customer service experience, more said it was because they received a quick resolution to their problem, rather than a desirable outcome."

eMarketer, 4/23/13

29

RESPONSE TO REVIEWS

29.1 Online Consumer Reviews

Ratings sites – like ratemds.com to rate doctors, tripadvisor.com to rate hotels and destinations, and epinions.com to rate consumer products – have become recognized sources consumers rely on for reviews about products and services.

A survey by ChannelAdvisor (www.channeladvisor.com) found that 92% of Internet users read product reviews. Among these people, 89% have been influenced to make a purchase or deterred from purchasing a specific product as the result of reviews. Only 3% of those who have read reviews say their decisions have been unaffected by reviews.

Among those who use reviews, about a quarter also post their own opinions. According to eMarketer (www.emarketer.com), 34.4 million consumers, or 20% of the U.S. population, share advice online about products or services.

Consumers are increasingly accessing reviews while shopping. Compete (www.compete.com) reports that 45% of smartphone users have looked at third-party or consumer reviews of a product while in a store.

29.2 Online Research

According to Opinion Research Corp. (www.opinionresearch.com), the most researched product and service categories are as follows (percentage of consumers that have researched prior to purchase):

- Travel/recreation/leisure: 82%
- Electronic goods: 80%
- Household products/services: 66%
- Clothing: 55%
- Automotive: 55%
- Personal care: 40%
- Food: 24%

29.3 Travel Reviews

Among all product and service categories, travel reviews are the most used by consumers.

According to Forrester Research (www.forrester.com), approximately one-third of travelers who research trips via the Internet read reviews. Of those who book hotels online, a third have changed plans based on other travelers' comments.

Expedia-owned TripAdvisor (www.tripadvisor.com), the largest online travel review site, claims more than 30 million consumer reviews of hotels, attractions, and restaurants across the globe. Many hoteliers monitor TripAdvisor daily for feedback about their properties, and more than 300 hotels have posted TripAdvisor comments on their own sites through a TripAdvisor program that provides automatic feeds of the ten most recent consumer reviews. TripAdvisor has acquired such popular travel sites as Smartertravel.com, IndependentTraveler.com, CruiseCritic.com, and SeatGuru.com.

29.4 Consumer Electronics Reviews

Among all product and service categories, consumer electronics (CE) reviews are the second most used by consumers.

A 2013 survey by Weber Shandwick (www.webershandwick.com) found that consumers seek out opinions about consumer electronics products they are considering as follows:

- Search for reviews online: 74%
- Ask someone their opinion: 66%
- Read 'likes' or recommendations on a social networking site: 47%
- Watch an online video with someone's experiences: 37%
- Ask their social network friends or followers: 28%

Seventy-two percent (72%) conduct at least two of these activities.

Among those who use online reviews, 65% have been inspired enough by a favorable consumer review to buy a CE product they weren't considering, and 59% have been similarly inspired by a professional review.

Among those using consumer reviews, 95% report gaining confidence in a purchase decision; 86% have gained confidence because of professional reviews.

Comparing consumer and professional reviews, 77% of consumers say they pay more attention to professional reviews; 23% give preference to professional reviews.

Eighty percent (80%) of those who use reviews say they have had concerns about authenticity. Specific concerns are as follows (percentage of respondents):

- A positive review may be posted by the manufacturer's employee or agent, not an actual consumer: 51%
- A negative review may be posted by the manufacturer's employee or agent, not an actual consumer: 39%
- A review reads more like an advertisement than an objective assessment of the product's benefits and drawbacks: 39%
- A review appears to be entirely negative or entirely positive: 37%

Among sites that post CE product reviews, survey respondents said they completely or somewhat trust the following (percentage of respondents):

- Amazon.com: 84%
- BestBuy.com: 76%
- *Consumer Reports*: 72%
- Target.com: 66%
- eBay: 60%
- *PC Magazine*: 56%
- Overstock.com: 56%
- *PC World*: 54%
- Cnet: 50%
- TigerDirect: 42%
- Newegg: 23%

Note: Some responses are low because fewer consumers have used the sites for reviews, not because of a lack of trust in the sites.

30

SPENDING FOR GOODS VS. EXPERIENCES

30.1 A Shift From Goods To Experiences

As some consumers are beginning to realize they have all the material things they need, many are shifting their interests toward seeking new experiences. This is especially true for older consumers who have been accumulating all their lives.

> **"With the attitude of 'been there, done that' in buying more things, Boomers will turn away from a focus on consuming things, to a hunger for experiences and personal development. Service industries that satisfy the mature Boomers' craving for personal enhancement will fare well. These include travel providers, especially adventure travel modified for aging Boomers' health and fitness levels; health and beauty spas; and colleges and adult-education experiences, including training such as cooking or language schools."**
>
> Pamela N. Danziger, CEO
> Unity Marketing

30.2 Purchase Satisfaction

In their book *Happy Money: The Science of Smarter Spending* (2013, Simon & Schuster), authors Elizabeth Dunn and Michael Norton draw on years of quantitative and qualitative research to present five principles that can make spending a rewarding experience for consumers. The principle Buy Experiences shows material purchases being less satisfying than experiences such as vacations or concerts.

"One of the most common things people do with their money is get stuff. But we have shown ... in research that stuff isn't good for you. It doesn't make you unhappy, but it doesn't make you happy. But one thing that does make us happy is an experience."

Michael Norton, Ph.D.
Associate Professor of Marketing
Harvard Business School
HBS Working Knowledge, 8/5/13

30.3 Research Findings

Studies at Cornell University and Harvard University have found favorable consumer response to purchasing experiences versus material goods.

Research by Thomas D. Gilovich, Ph.D., a professor of psychology at Cornell University, and his colleagues suggests that when people spend for an experience such as a trip, they are likely to feel better about that purchase in the long run versus spending the same amount on clothes.

In one study, Dr. Gilovich examined the uniqueness of objects and experiences. He found that a major reason why people regret buying objects is that after they own the object, they can continue to compare it to other objects that are available. When they buy a computer, for instance, they may regret the purchase when they find another one that is faster, smaller, and cheaper. When they go on a vacation, though, that experience is relatively unique. It is hard to compare a particular trip with other trips they might have taken, so they spend less time comparing the experience to other things they might have done.

Research by Daniel Gilbert, Ph.D., a professor of psychology at Harvard University, has also found that spending on experiences is more rewarding than spending on goods. One of the reasons is that experiences can be shared.

While the memories of experiences can endure, objects generally wear out their welcome, according to Dr. Gilbert, who provides the following example: "If you really love a rug, you might buy it. The first few times you see, you might admire it, and feel happy. But over time, it will probably reveal itself to be just a rug." Psychologists call this habituation, economists call it declining marginal utility.

"We think that experiences can be fun but leave us with nothing to show for them. But that turns out to be a good thing. Happiness, for most people not named Sartre, is other people; and experiences are usually shared – first when they happen and then again and again when we tell our friends."

Prof. Daniel Gilbert, Ph.D.
Harvard University
The Atlantic, 6/11/13

PART IV: AFFLUENT CONSUMERS

31

LUXURY & AFFLUENT MARKETS

31.1 Luxury Market

The luxury market is composed of the wealthiest 1% of U.S. households. There are 1.1 million households in this category.

These luxury consumers, who are the most likely to be viewed as conspicuous consumers, have the following profile (source: American Affluence Research Center):

- With an average annual income of $982,000, they earn about 14% of the total income earned by all American households.
- They account for about 20% of all consumer spending.
- They have a minimum net worth of $6 million.
- With an average net worth of $15.3 million, they control 33% of the total net worth of all U.S. households.

31.2 Spending By High-Net-Worth Households

Luxury brand companies must take an entirely different approach when selling to the high-net-worth spender because they are a different breed from the general affluent consumer. They spend freely, and they spend frequently and extravagantly. They not only have the interest and the resources to purchase exclusive, expensive items, but their wealth – and often fame – adds a level of distinction to the luxury brands they are buying. It is becoming harder for the super-rich to differentiate themselves, and many of them go to greater lengths to make the statement that they are successful. Further, the 'massification' of luxury drives them to consume and splurge even more.

The New Jet Set, a report by *Elite Traveler*, included a survey of 661 high-net-worth individuals who own private jets. Participants in the survey, which was conducted by Prince & Associates (www.russalanprince.com), had an average income of $9.2 million and a net worth of $89.3 million. The following was average annual spending by this group for luxury goods:

- Fine art: $1.75 million
- Home improvement: $ 542,000
- Yacht rentals: $ 404,000
- Jewelry: $ 248,000
- Luxury cars: $ 226,000
- Events at hotels/resorts: $ 224,000
- Villa/chalet rentals: $ 168,000

- Hotels/resorts: $ 157,000
- Watches: $ 147,000
- Cruises: $ 138,000
- Fashion & accessories: $ 117,000
- Spas: $ 107,000
- Experiential travel: $ 98,000
- Wine and spirits: $ 29,000

"The thing that surprises me about the survey is the depth of their pockets. These folks don't make financial decisions when making a luxury purchase. For them, it's like me going to Starbucks."

Doug Golian, President
Elite Traveler

The New Jet Set reported holiday season spending by survey participants – either for themselves or gifts – as follows:

- Yacht charters: $367,000
- Jewelry: $ 74,600
- Gifts to charity: $ 62,100
- Villa and ski house rental: $ 61,700
- Hotel or resort stay: $ 54,600
- Watches: $ 44,900
- Holiday entertaining: $ 29,800
- Fashion accessories: $ 29,100
- Wines and spirits for entertaining: $ 14,200

The survey also found that 51% of the super-rich were planning to host an event or reception at a hotel, spending on average $36,300, and 75% were planning to send gifts to the tune of, on average, $29,200.

31.3 Affluent Market

The wealthiest 10% of U.S. households, as defined by net worth in the Federal Reserve Board research, have the following profile (source: American Affluence Research Center):

- With an average annual income of $256,000, they earn 36% of the total income earned by all American households.
- They account for almost half of all consumer spending and thus represent about a third of total GDP (gross domestic product).
- With an average net worth of $3.1 million, they control 70% of the total net worth of all U.S. households.
- The average value of their financial assets is $1.3 million. As a group, these 11.4 million households hold 89% of the value of all publicly traded stocks and stock mutual funds in the U.S.

Excluding the high-net-worth households, or the upper 1%, the affluent market is comprised primarily of people who are careful spenders and aggressive savers. They are generally not conspicuous or ostentatious consumers.

31.4 Media for Affluent Consumers

The *Robb Report*, a magazine about luxury life, features products of the lifestyle, including high-end cars, watches, and real estate. It was originally started as a magazine to complement the purchase of a Rolls-Royce automobile. The average income of subscribers is $1.2 million. *Worth, Vacation Homes, Luxury Home, Digital TV*, and *MotorCycling* are other publications of the Robb Report brand.

Elite Traveler, a bi-monthly luxury travel and lifestyle magazine published exclusively for elite-affluent consumers, has over 400,000 readers – who collectively have a $5.3 million average household income. The magazine is distributed exclusively through private jets, mega yachts, premier country clubs, first-class lounges, professional sports locker rooms, and its subscriber base. An annual subscription of six issues is $155.

Thousands of affluent travelers pay up to $500 a year for subscriptions to private travel guides and newsletters. The most popular are *Andrew Harper's Hideaway Report* (www.andrewharpertravel.com), which closes its circulation at 25,000 to maintain exclusivity, *Nota Bene* (www.nbreview.com), *Terra Firma* (www.terrafirma.com), and *Passport Newsletter* (www.passportnewsletter.com).

31.5 Market Resources

American Affluence Research Center, 2426 Loxford Lane, Alpharetta, GA 30009. (770) 740-2200. (www.affluenceresearch.org)

Ipsos Mendelsohn, 1271 Avenue of the Americas, 15th Floor, New York, NY 10020. (212) 265-3200. (https://www.ipsos-na.com/products-tools/media-content-technology/syndicated-studies/mendelsohn-affluent-barometer.aspx)

L2 Think Tank, 51 East 12th Street, 2nd Floor, New York, NY 10003. (www.l2thinktank.com)

Luxury Institute, 115 East 57th Street, 11th Floor, New York, NY 10022. (646) 792-2669. (www.luxuryinstitute.com)

Luxury Society, 231 rue Saint-Honoré, 75001 Paris, France. (www.luxurysociety.com)

Martini Media, 415 Brannan Street, San Francisco, CA 94107. (415) 913-7446. (www.martinimedianetwork.com)

Prince & Associates, 9 Sidecut Road, Redding, CT 06896. (203) 938-5557. (www.russalanprince.com)

The Affluence Collaborative (www.affluencecollaborative.com)

The Shullman Research Center, 8 Quintard Avenue, Old Greenwich, CT 06830. (203) 990-0541. (www.shullman.net)

Unity Marketing, 206 E. Church Street, Stevens, PA 17578. (717) 336-1600. (www.unitymarketingonline.com)

Wealth Engine, 4330 East West Highway, Bethesda, MD 20814. (301) 215-5980. (www.wealthengine.com)

32

POPULATION CENTERS OF U.S. AFFLUENCE

32.1 Most Affluent ZIP Codes

According to the Internal Revenue Service, 2011 tax returns (most recent data available) showed the highest income per return in the following ZIP codes:

	# Returns	Income Per Return
• New York, NY 10104	14	$2,976,929
• New York, NY 10112	294	$2,239,881
• Miami Beach, FL 33109	191	$2,180,105
• New York, NY 10004	1,336	$2,118,766
• New York, NY 10153	84	$1,567,452
• New York, NY 10167	97	$1,412,072
• New York, NY 10158	44	$1,399,205
• Wilmington, DE 19898	22	$1,356,182
• New York, NY 10111	505	$1,234,972
• New York, NY 10151	25	$ 995,480
• Fresno, CA 93778	29	$ 955,345
• Universal City, CA 91608	55	$ 908,418
• Chattanooga, TN 37450	19	$ 865,579
• Dayton, OH 45423	43	$ 841,674
• Jersey City, NJ 07399	82	$ 809,817
• Corpus Christi, TX 78471	31	$ 782,419
• New York, NY 10271	45	$ 779,333
• New York, NY 10154	124	$ 765,202
• Memphis, TN 38157	20	$ 758,000
• Tallahassee, FL 32306	53	$ 749,566
• Northbrook, IL 60065	132	$ 725,371
• New York, NY 10152	165	$ 712,818
• Houston, TX 77010	247	$ 670,198
• Henderson, NV 89011	68	$ 665,559
• Foster City, CA 94400	15	$ 659,333
• Pittsburgh, PA 15259	11	$ 589,273
• New York, NY 10106	108	$ 578,259
• Fort Lauderdale, FL 33394	35	$ 565,314
• Tulsa, OK 74121	27	$ 560,259
• New Hyde Park, NY 11042	176	$ 556,392
• Dallas, TX 75247	264	$ 548,640

- Medina, WA 98039 1,514 $ 546,770
- Los Angeles, CA 90067 3,141 $ 546,672
- New York, NY 10155 40 $ 545,500
- Mill Neck, NY 11765 360 $ 544,244
- New York, NY 10020 870 $ 543,366
- Atherton, CA 94027 3,738 $ 537,684
- New York, NY 10105 67 $ 533,687
- New York, NY 10110 573 $ 533,480
- Incline Village, NV 89451 1,362 $ 529,403
- Minneapolis, MN 55440 292 $ 523,034
- Glenbrook, NV 89413 261 $ 507,318
- New York, NY 10165 381 $ 499,273
- New Vernon, NJ 07976 761 $ 497,928
- Chicago, IL 60604 409 $ 479,396
- Morristown, NJ 07962 267 $ 465,648
- Ross, CA 94957 1,215 $ 461,347
- Palm Beach, FL 33480 6,564 $ 457,517
- Memphis, TN 38124 140 $ 454,929
- Chicago, IL 60606 1,064 $ 452,781
- Oldwick, NJ 08858 471 $ 452,749
- Gibson Island, MD 21056 173 $ 450,012
- Lexington, KY 40580 16 $ 424,750
- Pensacola, FL 32581 25 $ 421,040
- Hunt Valley, MD 21031 44 $ 420,909
- Acton, ME 04000 16 $ 418,188
- New York, NY 10055 127 $ 417,795
- Greenwich, CT 06831 7,465 $ 414,686
- Kentfield, CA 94914 195 $ 410,995
- Greens Farms, CT 06436 181 $ 410,950
- San Francisco, CA 94111 2,459 $ 408,623
- Far Hills, NJ 07931 1,564 $ 401,311
- Weston, MA 02193 3,316 $ 400,922
- Old Westbury, NY 11568 1,785 $ 398,473
- New York, NY 10169 232 $ 395,897
- Boston, MA 02110 2,111 $ 395,215
- Roanoke, VA 24005 10 $ 394,400
- Wilson, WY 83014 997 $ 392,598
- New York, NY 10286 38 $ 388,447
- Dallas, TX 75270 27 $ 382,037
- Salt Lake City, UT 84133 10 $ 378,200
- New York, NY 10166 190 $ 375,511
- Boston, MA 02205 221 $ 374,597
- Jackson, MS 39272 51 $ 374,216
- Salt Lake City, UT 84145 16 $ 374,188

- Springfield, MO 65800 17 $ 372,353
- Minneapolis, MN 55415 438 $ 372,311
- Dallas, TX 75201 2,364 $ 372,255
- Rancho Santa Fe, CA 92067 4,912 $ 372,108
- Dumont, TX 79232 18 $ 368,611
- Charlottesville, VA 22905 327 $ 367,875
- Glenview, KY 40025 90 $ 367,022
- Portola Valley, CA 94028 3,572 $ 365,873
- Beaverton, OR 97076 29 $ 364,034
- Springfield, MA 01115 50 $ 362,480
- Minneapolis, MN 55402 842 $ 359,827
- Hartford, CT 06156 20 $ 358,050
- Purchase, NY 10577 1,620 $ 354,473
- Sea Island, GA 31561 241 $ 351,178
- Kenilworth, IL 60043 1,315 $ 348,016
- Lexington, KY 40583 178 $ 346,640
- Earth City, MO 63045 15 $ 345,800
- New York, NY 10175 74 $ 344,419
- Montchanin, DE 19710 217 $ 343,710
- Fort Wayne, IN 46866 57 $ 342,860
- Portland, OR 97291 97 $ 341,660
- Jacksonville, FL 32232 62 $ 339,145
- Boca Grande, FL 33921 653 $ 336,328
- New York, NY 10100 35 $ 334,200
- Indianapolis, IN 46282 12 $ 332,833

32.2 Most Expensive ZIP Codes

According to *Forbes* (November 2013), average home prices are highest in the following ZIP codes:

- Atherton, CA: $6.7 million
- Los Altos Hills, CA: $5.4 million
- New York, NY: $4.9 million
- Belvedere, CA: $4.8 million
- Sagaponack, NY: $4.8 million
- New York, NY: $4.6 million
- New York, NY: $4.6 million
- Alpine, NJ: $4.5 million
- Portola Valley, CA: $4.3 million
- New York, NY: $4.2 million

32.3 ZIP Codes With Highest Salaries

According to the Internal Revenue Service, 2011 tax returns (most recent data available) showed the highest salary per return in the following ZIP codes (only zip codes where more than 1,000 returns were filed are included):

- Los Angeles, CA 90067: $500,106
- Medina, WA 98039: $373,653
- Far Hills, NJ 07931: $321,171
- Greenwich, CT 06831: $298,370
- Ross, CA 94957: $290,555
- Atherton, CA 94027: $275,498
- New Canaan, CT 06840: $251,543
- Rancho Santa Fe, CA 92067: $242,282
- Darien, CT 06820: $240,794
- Short Hills, NJ 07078: $239,316
- New York, NY 10004: $234,831
- Old Westbury, NY 11568: $231,881
- Kenilworth, IL 60043: $219,120
- Weston, CT 06883: $216,909
- Portola Valley, CA 94028: $214,991
- St. Louis, MO 63124: $210,236
- Rye, NY 10580: $209,556
- Weston, MA 02193: $208,662
- Houston, TX 77210: $207,212
- Greenwich, CT 06830: $206,587
- Essex Fells, NJ 07021: $202,377
- Purchase, NY 10577: $202,354
- Wilmington, DE 19807: $194,791
- Beverly Hills, CA 90210: $193,425
- Los Angeles, CA 90077: $193,269
- Lake Forest, IL 60045: $191,022
- Chappaqua, NY 10514: $188,538
- Los Angeles, CA 90071: $188,522
- Bernardsville, NJ 07924: $184,757
- Los Altos, CA 94022: $183,289
- Villanova, PA 19085: $182,468
- Gladwyne, PA 19035: $180,834
- Westport, CT 06880: $179,422
- Austin, TX 78730: $176,711
- Bedford, NY 10506: $176,625
- Riverside, CT 06878: $176,060
- Mendham, NJ 07945: $174,763
- New York, NY 10022: $174,490
- Winnetka, IL 60093: $174,038
- Newport Coast, CA 92657: $168,721

- Saddle River, NJ 07458: $168,552
- Encino, CA 91436: $167,637
- Southport, CT 06490: $165,655
- Old Greenwich, CT 06870: $163,445
- Summit, NJ 07901: $162,180
- Armonk, NY 10504: $160,971
- Wilton, CT 06897: $160,749
- Wellesley, MA 02181: $160,724
- Belvedere Tiburon, CA 94920: $160,591
- Franklin Lakes, NJ 07417: $160,549
- Norwalk, CT 06853: $160,347
- Beverly Hills, CA 90212: $160,218
- Haverford, PA19041: $159,731
- Boston, MA 02108: $158,923
- Atlanta, GA 30327: $156,430
- Glencoe, IL 60022: $156,272
- Pacific Palisades, CA 90272: $155,856
- Great Falls, VA 22066: $155,749
- Stamford, CT 06903: $155,548
- Mountain Lakes, NJ 07046: $153,094
- San Jose, CA 95109: $152,076
- New York, NY 10280: $151,738
- Chicago, IL 60606: $151,236
- Houston, TX 77024: $149,854
- Briarcliff Manor, NY 10510: $148,590
- Skillman, NJ 08558: $148,574
- Weston, MA 02493: $147,536
- Dover, MA 02030: $147,366
- Larchmont, NY 10538: $146,654
- Saratoga, CA 95070: $146,482
- Shawnee Mission, KS 66211: $146,451
- Palm Beach, FL 33480: $145,612
- Manhasset, NY 11030: $145,115
- New York, NY 10021: $144,017
- Rumson, NJ 07760: $144,014
- New York, NY 10018: $143,543
- Santa Monica, CA 90402: $143,304
- Scarsdale, NY 10583: $141,772
- Dallas, TX 75225: $141,679
- Charlotte, NC 28207: $140,989
- Pound Ridge, NY 10576: $140,874
- Danville, CA 94506: $140,832
- San Francisco, CA 94104: $140,318
- Los Angeles, CA 90010: $139,130

- San Francisco, CA 94111: $138,431
- Cold Spring Harbor, NY 11724: $138,289
- San Antonio, TX 78257: $137,377
- Alamo, CA 94507: $137,203
- Houston, TX 77002: $136,067
- Dallas, TX 75205: $134,963
- Chester, NJ 07930: $134,372
- Longboat Key, FL 34228: $134,021
- Carlisle, MA 01741: $132,671
- New York, NY 10028: $130,688
- Houston, TX 77005: $129,915
- New York, NY 10005: $129,736
- Locust Valley, NY 11560: $129,590
- Los Altos, CA 94024: $127,273
- Palo Alto, CA 94301: $126,956

32.4 Millionaire Households By State

According to Phoenix Marketing International (www.phoenixmi.com), the number of millionaire households in each state and ratio of millionaire to total households is as follows:

	Total HH	$1MM+	Ratio
Alabama:	1,881,966	71,224	3.78%
Alaska:	248,009	14,805	5.97%
Arizona:	2,458,106	117,094	4.76%
Arkansas:	1,138,318	36,854	3.24%
California:	12,653,856	716,316	5.66%
Colorado:	1,949,583	98,085	5.03%
Connecticut:	1,347,693	89,647	6.65%
Delaware:	343,322	18,412	5.36%
District of Columbia:	262,976	14,533	5.53%
Florida:	7,455,767	362,285	4.86%
Georgia:	3,639,796	156,943	4.31%
Hawaii:	444,202	30,793	6.93%
Idaho:	575,621	22,917	3.98%
Illinois:	4,800,176	242,536	5.05%
Indiana:	2,501,280	99,440	3.98%
Iowa:	1,204,906	49,451	4.10%
Kansas:	1,096,736	47,226	4.31%
Kentucky:	1,743,587	61,315	3.52%
Louisiana:	1,701,745	65,382	3.84%
Maine:	553,493	22,191	4.01%
Maryland:	2,129,773	144,686	6.79%
Massachusetts:	2,521,928	150,844	5.98%

- Michigan: 3,846,728 166,611 4.33%
- Minnesota: 2,057,554 103,641 5.04%
- Mississippi: 1,113,217 35,847 3.22%
- Missouri: 2,364,933 95,312 4.03%
- Montana: 394,196 15,491 3.93%
- Nebraska: 704,049 29,272 4.16%
- Nevada: 990,855 48,220 4.87%
- New Hampshire: 514,667 29,790 5.79%
- New Jersey: 3,175,894 212,396 6.69%
- New Mexico: 766,050 31,145 4.07%
- New York: 7,263,927 381,197 5.25%
- North Carolina: 3,725,318 144,029 3.87%
- North Dakota: 265,786 9,907 3.73%
- Ohio: 4,566,369 188,908 4.14%
- Oklahoma: 1,442,985 53,910 3.74%
- Oregon: 1,513,336 66,839 4.42%
- Pennsylvania: 4,934,144 227,680 4.61%
- Rhode Island: 409,575 20,873 5.10%
- South Carolina: 1,802,904 71,114 3.94%
- South Dakota: 317,030 11,865 3.74%
- Tennessee: 2,519,914 94,560 3.75%
- Texas: 8,796,031 381,165 4.33%
- Utah: 891,901 42,238 4.74%
- Vermont: 252,584 11,806 4.67%
- Virginia: 3,043,091 180,638 5.94%
- Washington: 2,577,274 133,582 5.18%
- West Virginia: 761,493 26,090 3.43%
- Wisconsin: 2,252,664 97,266 4.32%
- Wyoming: 219,309 10,631 4.85%

32.5 Millionaires By Metropolitan Area

According to *2012 U.S. Metro Wealth Index*, by Capgemini (www.capgemini.com), the following metropolitan areas have the greatest number of individuals with assets of $1 million and more:

- New York, NY: 727,100
- Los Angeles, CA: 255,600
- Chicago, IL: 212,100
- Washington, DC: 166,200
- San Francisco, CA: 147,800
- Boston, MA: 110,200
- Philadelphia, PA: 109,200
- Houston, TX: 98,500
- San Jose, CA: 99,700
- Detroit, MI: 90,100

32.6 Market Resources

Capgemini, 623 Fifth Avenue, 33rd Floor, New York, NY 10022. (212) 314-8000. (www.capgemini.com)

Phoenix Marketing International, 6423 Montgomery Street, Suite 12, Rhinebeck, NY 12572. (845) 876-8228. (www.phoenixmi.com)

33

MARKET SURVEYS

33.1 Affluent Market Tracking Study

Since 2002, the American Affluence Research Center (www.affluenceresearch.org) has published the semiannual *Affluent Market Tracking Study*. The study tracks the 12-month outlook of the wealthiest 10% of U.S. households. The economy; the stock market; personal earnings, savings and investment objectives; and spending plans for 17 product categories and eight major expenditures are assessed.

The Fall 2013 assessment (index of 93) rose 22 percentage points from the Spring 2013 survey and 40 points above the Fall 2012 index. This was the highest reading for this index since Fall 2007 (108) and indicates good potential for increased spending by affluent and luxury consumers.

The index for future business conditions (105) and the index for change in the stock market (106) were both in positive territory in Fall 2013 and essentially unchanged from the Spring 2013 survey. This is contrary to the pattern in 2011 and 2012 when indexes were generally higher in the Spring than in the preceding and subsequent Fall surveys. The affluent seem to have a modestly better outlook for the future than the general public.

About 80% of affluent households expect their net worth to be the same or higher in the coming months. Two-thirds expect their income to be the same or better. Almost two-thirds say they do not plan to defer or reduce expenditures during the next 12 months, which represents an improvement of 7 percentage points from Spring 2013 survey.

For a selection of 17 brands, respondents were asked which ones they had owned or experienced during the prior five years, which ones they were familiar with or had knowledge of, and those which they considered to be overrated. Responses in the Fall 2013 tracking study were as follows:

	Owned/Experienced	Familiar With	Believe to be Overrated
• BMW:	17%	47%	27%
• Breitling:	4%	32%	28%
• Burberry:	21%	31%	28%
• Chanel:	17%	38%	29%
• Clinique:	33%	33%	14%
• Coach:	33%	27%	25%
• Four Seasons Hotels:	21%	41%	21%
• Gucci:	16%	36%	38%
• Hermès:	11%	33%	37%

• Lancôme:	26%	32%	15%
• Lexus:	21%	48%	17%
• Louis Vuitton:	18%	34%	44%
• Neiman Marcus:	33%	29%	28%
• Nordstrom's:	58%	20%	12%
• Prada:	14%	30%	37%
• Ritz-Carlton Hotels:	26%	39%	21%
• Rolex:	15%	40%	34%

33.2 Affluent Survey and Affluent Barometer

Ipsos (www.ipsos-na.com) has conducted the annual *Mendelsohn Affluent Survey* since 1977 and conducts monthly *Mendelsohn Affluent Barometer* surveys assessing specific topics related to the affluent market. The surveys are conducted among adults living in households with at least $100,000 in annual household income – approximately 20% of U.S. households are included in this group.

One of the *2013 Affluent Barometer* surveys found that luxury buyers used an average of 3.1 digital devices, compared with 2.9 devices for the general population. Ninety-six percent (96%) of affluents said they used a PC, laptop or notebook compared with 74% who used a smartphone and 62% using a tablet.

Another 2013 *Affluent Barometer* survey assessed media use by affluent consumers. Respondents of the survey said they used the following media on a daily basis:

- Internet: 98%
- TV: 85%
- Radio: 72%
- Newspapers: 54%
- Magazines: 37%

The *2013 Affluent Barometer* also reported that when they shop online, luxury shoppers primarily use the following types of e-commerce sites:

- Sites of specific brands: 39%
- Multibrand sites not solely focused on luxury goods: 36%
- Luxury sites that contain inventory from various brands: 22%

33.3 Affluent Online Shopper Index

Martini Media (www.martinimedianetwork.com) publishes quarterly the *Affluent Online Shopper Index*™ in conjunction with comScore (www.comscore.com). The assessment measures behaviors and engagement levels of the online affluent audience (annual household income > $100,000) by indexing affluent users against non-affluent online users (annual household income < $100,000). Indices are calculated to show the propensity of the affluent segment to buy or spend within various categories. Indices above 120 indicate a notable propensity, and those under 80 indicate the audience under-indexed relative to the lower income segment.

The October 2013 Index, which compared second quarters 2012 and 2013, found that affluent consumers were 90% more likely to make a purchase online, an increase of 5% over 2012. The increased spending was seen across a variety of categories, including video games and consoles (up 20% year-over-year), apparel, accessories and jewelry (up 16% y-o-y), flowers, greetings and gifts (up 15% y-o-y), and event and movie tickets (up 13% y-o-y). Among luxury retail sites (tiffany.com, coach.com, etc.), average Q2 2013 spending was up 20% from the previous year.

Affluent shoppers are increasingly more likely to visit auto sites compared to those earning under $100,000, with the gap in visitation growing 6% y-o-y. The gap in auto search reach also grew, with affluent shoppers posting an 11% higher index over those earning under $100,000.

33.4 Luxury and Affluence Monthly Pulse

The Shullman Research Center (www.shullman.net) publishes the results of surveys of affluent consumers in its *Luxury and Affluence Monthly Pulse*. Shullman surveys four groups of consumers: those making over $75,000, those making $250,000 or more, those making upward of $500,000, and, for comparison, the general population. The following are some 2013 findings:

Advertising Exposure

Consumers in households with incomes of $250,000 or more say they saw or heard adverting in the prior 30 days associated with the following media or venues:

	Total	Age <35	Age 35-to-54	Age 55+
• Television:	80%	64%	80%	91%
• Magazines:	73%	60%	74%	81%
• Radio:	66%	42%	74%	69%
• Websites:	66%	52%	67%	75%
• Newspapers:	64%	31%	71%	76%
• Mail sent to home:	58%	27%	59%	76%
• Billboards:	47%	27%	45%	64%
• Facebook/social sites:	41%	46%	40%	38%
• Movie theaters:	39%	46%	32%	44%
• Shopping malls:	35%	24%	40%	35%

Advertising Response

Consumers in households with incomes of $250,000 or more say they had interest in ads seen/heard in the prior 30 days associated with the following media or venues:

	Total	Age <35	Age 35-to-54	Age 55+
• Health clubs/gyms:	66%	85%	67%	50%
• Magazines:	59%	63%	61%	55%
• Newspapers:	55%	27%	61%	54%

• Television:	52%	43%	58%	49%
• Sports stadiums/arenas:	50%	46%	54%	43%
• Websites:	45%	36%	53%	39%
• Medical offices:	45%	72%	62%	21%
• Smartphones:	45%	84%	39%	22%
• Radio:	44%	41%	47%	40%
• Shopping malls:	43%	50%	45%	7%
• Subway/train stations:	41%	89%	34%	27%

"According to the Shullman *Luxury and Affluence Monthly Pulse* ... over 65% of very affluent consumers said health clubs and gyms are the places where they are most ad receptive – possibly because while one is jogging, biking, or rowing in a gym, one is not actually going anywhere and is therefore surrounded by messages that are not easily ignored. Eighty-five percent (85%) of 35-and-under very affluent people surveyed said they were interested in ads they saw in the gym or club. Sixty-seven percent (65%) of those 35-to-54 said they like ads at the gym, while 50% of those over 55 said they could be reached at the gym, too."

Marketing Daily, 4/12/13

E-Commerce

Fifty-one percent (51%) of affluent consumers purchase luxury items online. For comparison, 87% make such purchases in retail stores. Among those who make high-end purchases online, most do so using laptop or desktop computers; use of smartphones and tablets is cited by only 10% and 7%, respectively.

Approximately half of affluent consumers say they do not always feel comfortable shopping via the Internet. Forty percent (40%) say they do not like using smartphones to buy, 21% say they feel the same way about tablets, and 8% don't feel comfortable shopping by computer. For comparison, 25% do not like shopping by phone or by mail order, and 10% are uncomfortable buying in stores.

Among affluents who shop online, 40% say convenience is the primary reason they do so; 19% cite price as the primary reason.

Forty-three percent (43%) of adults with household incomes of $500,000 or above say they do not buy online at all.

Electronic Device Purchases

Consumers in households with incomes of $250,000 or more say they plan to purchase the following electronic devices within the next 12 months:

	Total	Age <35	Age 35-to-54	Age 55+
• Smartphone:	24%	27%	26%	20%
• Tablet:	18%	36%	16%	9%
• Digital media receiver:	15%	13%	16%	13%
• Internet-connected TV:	15%	36%	11%	8%
• e-Reader:	13%	15%	14%	10%
• Netbook:	12%	12%	11%	14%
• Video game system:	12%	16%	16%	4%
• Digital streaming device:	12%	18%	10%	11%

Spending

In 2013, major spending plans among those making $250,000 or more were as follows:

- Home-related investments: 96%
- Health-exercise equipment: 88%
- Leisure travel: 88%
- Financial investing, donations: 83%
- Luxury goods: 61%

33.5 Luxury Trend Reports

Unity Marketing (www.unitymarketingonline.com) publishes Luxury Trend Reports that provide an assessment of various aspects of spending by affluent households.

A March 2013 Luxury Trend Report assessed travel plans among affluent consumers based on a survey of over 1,300 affluent consumers (average income $267,800; 45.4 years). Forty-five percent (45%) of those surveyed planned to spend more on their travels in 2013 compared with the prior year. The typical luxury traveler took 2.8 separate four or more day vacations in 2012.

Travel plans for 2013 included increased visits among affluent travelers to Asia, Australia/New Zealand, and the Caribbean.

Unity Marketing also publishes the *Luxury Tracking Study*, a quarterly report about what products and brands luxury consumers are buying and how much they spend on luxuries.

33.6 WealthSurvey

Luxury Institute (www.luxuryinstitute.com) publishes the *WealthSurvey*™, which assesses behavioral characteristics of affluent consumers. The surveys focus on adults with gross incomes above $150,000.

The April 2013 *WealthSurvey* assessed shopping channels used by affluent consumers to make recent purchases. Responses by age were as follows:

	<50	50+
• Retail stores:	78%	78%
• Websites using a computer:	78%	76%
• Websites using a tablet:	26%	16%
• Catalogs/mailers:	13%	20%
• Telephone customer service rep:	15%	16%
• Websites using a mobile device:	25%	8%
• Mobile app:	20%	7%
• Tablet app:	15%	8%

M-commerce activities of affluent smartphone and tablet users are as follows:

	Smartphone	Tablet
• Search for store information:	49%	41%
• Look up product details while on-the-go:	33%	18%
• Compare prices while shopping in-store:	29%	13%
• View product images:	28%	42%
• Receive special deals or discounts:	28%	22%
• Compare prices while on-the-go:	27%	15%
• Look up product details while shopping in-store:	27%	11%
• Read user reviews and recommendations:	26%	42%
• Check status of an order:	23%	36%
• Check availability at other retailers:	20%	24%
• Opt-in to receive marketing messages:	11%	10%
• Watch product videos:	10%	21%

Even if affluent shoppers have sufficient financial resources at their disposal, that doesn't mean a deal won't help make a sale. With tablets, special deals or price discounts were the No. 1 reason respondents would purchase via these devices, with 43% indicating that would sway them. With smartphones, special deals tied with ease of use, at 45%, was the top reason to complete a purchase on the device.

33.7 Market Resources

American Affluence Research Center, 2426 Loxford Lane, Alpharetta, GA 30009. (770) 740-2200. (www.affluenceresearch.org)

Ipsos Mendelsohn, 1271 Avenue of the Americas, 15th Floor, New York, NY 10020. (212) 265-3200. (https://www.ipsos-na.com/products-tools/media-content-technology/syndicated-studies/mendelsohn-affluent-barometer.aspx)

Luxury Institute, 115 East 57th Street, 11th Floor, New York, NY 10022. (646) 792-2669. (www.luxuryinstitute.com)

Martini Media, 415 Brannan Street, San Francisco, CA 94107. (415) 913-7446. (www.martinimedianetwork.com)

The Shullman Research Center, 8 Quintard Avenue, Old Greenwich, CT 06830. (203) 990-0541. (www.shullman.net)

Unity Marketing, 206 E. Church Street, Stevens, PA 17578. (717) 336-1600. (www.unitymarketingonline.com)

PART V: CUSTOMER BRAND PREFERENCES

34

BRAND ATTRACTION

34.1 Overview

NewMediaMetrics (www.newmediametrics.com) uses Emotional Attachment (EA) as a predictive measure of consumer purchase behavior and media behavior. In an annual assessment called the Leap Index, NewMediaMetrics applies EA to assess consumers' relationship with brands in various categories. The Leap Index uses a 0-to-10 scale to measure Emotional Attachment to brands. The more attached consumers are to a brand, the more likely it is they will be buyers of the brand.

34.2 Leap Index

Ranked by the percentage of consumers rating their Emotional Attachment at 9 or 10, the 2013 Leap Index found consumers most attached to the following brands:

- iPhone 61.2%
- Lexus: 61.0%
- Disney Cruise Lines: 59.0%
- Disney Parks: 57.2%
- Apple: 55.1%
- Google Search: 55.0%
- Jaguar: 53.8%
- Audi: 53.6%
- Google: 53.2%
- Universal Studios: 52.7%
- BMW: 52.3%
- iPad: 52.0%
- I-Pod: 51.5%
- Cadillac: 51.4%
- Microsoft Office Suite: 51.0%
- Sea World: 50.8%
- Sony Play Station: 50.3%
- Ford Focus: 50.0%
- Uniqlo: 50.0%
- Android (phones w/Google software): 48.1%
- Volvo: 47.8%
- X-Box: 47.8%

• Franklin Templeton:	46.8%
• Samsung Galaxy:	49.8%
• E*Trade:	47.6%
• Always:	46.6%
• Lincoln Mercury:	46.2%
• Six Flags:	46.0%
• Microsoft Windows:	46.0%
• Microsoft:	45.8%
• Volkswagen:	45.0%
• Norwegian Cruise Lines:	44.2%
• Toyota:	44.1%
• Clinique:	44.1%
• Chevy Malibu:	44.0%
• Kindle Fire:	44.0%
• Chevy:	43.9%
• Windows Phones (MS software):	43.7%
• Infinity:	43.6%
• Excedrin:	43.4%
• In-N-Out Burger:	43.3%
• Honda:	42.9%
• Victoria's Secret:	42.8%
• Nike:	42.3%
• Jeep:	42.3%
• Verizon Droid:	41.9%
• Lancôme:	41.8%
• United States Postal Service (USPS):	41.8%
• Huggies:	41.8%
• GM:	41.3%
• Converse:	41.1%
• Sony:	41.0%
• Vault:	40.8%
• Ford Fusion:	40.6%
• New Castle:	40.5%
• Kotex:	40.4%
• Costco:	40.3%
• Mercedes Benz:	40.2%
• Suburu:	40.0%
• Visa:	39.9%
• Verizon Wireless:	39.8%
• Clorox:	39.7%
• Dr. Pepper:	39.6%
• Johnnie Walker:	39.3%
• Samsung:	39.2%
• Estee Lauder:	39.2%

- Embassy Suites: 39.2%
- Acura: 38.7%
- Febreeze: 38.4%
- BJ's: 38.4%
- Jet Blue: 38.4%
- Pull Ups: 38.3%
- State Farm: 38.2%
- Starbucks: 38.2%
- Walmart: 38.0%
- Guiness: 37.8%
- Southwest Airlines: 37.8%
- Ford: 37.8%
- Liberty Mutual: 37.7%
- Crest Pro-Health Mouth Rinse: 37.7%
- Hershey's Milk Chocolate: 37.7%
- Levi's: 37.3%
- AT&T: 37.3%
- Bombay Sapphire: 37.3%
- Gamestop: 37.0%
- Advil: 36.9%
- Sony Vaio: 36.8%
- Gillette Fusion Razors: 36.8%
- Athleta: 36.7%
- Oreo's: 36.6%
- Red Lobster: 36.6%
- Hellman's: 36.4%
- Mountain Dew: 36.4%
- Olay: 36.4%
- Patrón: 36.3%
- Neutrogena: 36.3%
- Coke: 36.2%
- Claritin: 36.2%
- Johnson & Johnson: 36.2%
- Tide: 36.1%

35

BRAND EQUITY

35.1 Overview

Harris Interactive (www.harrisinteractive.com) has assessed brand equity for consumer product and retail brands through EquiTrend ® surveys since 1989.

The 2013 EquiTrend assessment surveyed 37,000 U.S. consumers.

35.2 Top Brands Among Adults

The following brands ranked highest among adults in the 2013 EquiTrend study:

Airlines

Full Service Airlines
1. Alaska/Horizon
2. Hawaiian
3. Delta Airlines
4. United Airlines

Brands ranked below category average: Air Canada, American Airlines, US Airways

Value Airlines
1. Southwest

Brands ranked below category average: AirTran Airways, Frontier/Midwest Airlines, JetBlue Airways, Spirit Airlines

Apparel

Running Shoes
1. Merrell
2. New Balance
3. Nike
4. ASICS

Brands ranked below category average: Brooks, K-Swiss, Puma, Reebok, Saucony

Sporting Apparel
1. Under Armour
2. Nike
3. Columbia
4. Bauer
5. Champion

6. adidas

Brands ranked below category average: Head, Puma, Reebok, Russell, Wilson

Appliances

Coffee Makers

1. Keurig
2. Mr. Coffee
3. Bosch
4. DeLonghi
5. Cuisinart
6. Krups

Brands ranked below category average: Black & Decker, GE, Gevalia, Hamilton Beach, Kenmore, Proctor Silex, Waring

Major Appliances

1. Kenmore
2. KitchenAid
3. Whirlpool
4. Viking
5. GE
6. Samsung

Brands ranked below category average: Amana, Bosch, Electrolux, Frigidaire, Haier, Jenn-Air, LG, Maytag, Sub-Zero, Thermador

Small Kitchen Appliances

1. Crock-Pot
2. KitchenAid
3. Cuisinart
4. Black & Decker
5. Calphalon
6. GE

Brands ranked below category average: Hamilton Beach, Oster, Proctor-Silex, Rival, Sunbeam, Waring

Automotive

Full Line Automotive

1. Toyota
2. Honda
3. Chevrolet
4. Ford
5. Nissan

Brands ranked below category average: Buick, Chrysler, Dodge, Fiat, Hyundai, Kia, Mazda, Mini Cooper, Mitsubishi, Subaru, Volkswagen

Luxury Automotive
1. Mercedes-Benz
2. BMW
3. Lexus
4. Acura
5. Infiniti
6. Porsche
7. Audi

Brands ranked below category average: Cadillac, Jaguar, Land Rover, Lincoln, Tesla, Volvo

Recreational Vehicles
1. Jayco
2. Airstream
3. Coachmen

Brands ranked below category average: Fleetwood, Gulf Stream, Winnebago

Automotive Service Centers
1. Discount Tires
2. Napa AutoCare
3. Goodyear Tire and Service Network
4. Valvoline Instant Oil Change
5. National Tire and Battery
6. Penzoil 10 Minute Oil Change Center
7. WalMart Tire & Lube Express

Brands ranked below category average: AAMCO Transmission, Firestone Complete Auto Care, Havoline xpress Lube, Jiffy Lube Oil Change Centers, Meineke Car Care Center, Midas Auto Service Express, Mobil 1 Lube Express, PepBoys Automotive Service Centers, Precision Tune Auto Care, Sears Automotive Centers

Automotive Tires
1. Michelin
2. Goodyear
3. Pirelli
4. Yokohama
5. BF Goodrich

Brands ranked below category average: Bridgestone, Continental, Firestone, General, Hankook, Kelly Tires, Uniroyal

Motor Oil
1. Valvoline
2. Pennzoil
3. Mobil 1

4. Castrol

Brands ranked below category average: Havoline, Mobil, Quaker State, Shell

Beverages - Alcoholic

Beer

1. Yuengling Traditional Lager
2. Bass Ale
3. Sierra Nevada Pale Ale
4. Stella Artois
5. Newcastle Brown Ale
6. Blue Moon
7. Samuel Adams
8. Grolsch
9. Dos Equis Lager
10. Guinness
11. Modelo Especial
12. Negra Modelo
13. Becks
14. Heineken

Brands ranked below category average: Budweiser, Busch, Coors, Corona Extra, Fosters Lager, Labatt Blue, Michelob, Miller High Life, Milwaukee's Best, Pabst Blue Ribbon

Light Beer

1. Sam Adams Light
2. Amstel Light
3. Corona Light
4. Heineken Premium Light
5. Bud Light
6. Michelob Ultra
7. MGD 64 (Miller Genuine Draft)
8. Coors Light

Brands ranked below category average: Budweiser Select, Busch Light, Michelob Light, Miller High Life Light, Miller Light, Milwaukee's Best Light, Natural Light

Beverages - Coffee and Tea

Bottled Iced Teas

1. AriZona
2. Gold Peak
3. Snapple

Brands ranked below category average: Lipton, Luzianne, Nestea, Turkey Hill

Coffee

1. Folger's

2. Green Mountain
3. Seattle's Best
4. Dunkin' Donuts
5. Maxwell House
6. Eight O'clock

Brands ranked below category average: Caribou, Chock full O'Nuts, Millstone, Nescafe, Newman's Own, Starbucks

Hot Teas

1. Lipton
2. Twinnings

Brands ranked below category average: Bigelow, Celestial Seasonings, Red Rose, Salada, Stash, Tazo, Tetley

Beverages - Refreshment and Other Non-Alcoholic

Bottled Water

1. Deer Park
2. Poland Spring
3. Nestle Pure Life
4. Ice Mountain
5. Aquafina

Brands ranked below category average: Arrowhead, Crystal Geyser, DASANI, Evian, Fiji

Diet Soft Drinks

1. Sprite Zero
2. Coke Zero
3. Diet Coke
4. Diet Dr Pepper

Brands ranked below category average: Diet Mountain Dew, Diet Pepsi

Energy Drinks

1. Full Throttle
2. AMP
3. Rock Star
4. Red Bull

Brands ranked below category average: 5-Hour Energy Shot, Monster Energy Drink

Fruit Flavored Drinks

1. 5 Alive
2. Kool-Aid
3. Capri Sun

Brands ranked below category average: Hawaiian Punch, Hi-C, Sunny D

Fruit Juice
1. Ocean Spray
2. Tropicana
3. Florida Natural
4. Minute Maid
5. Welch's
6. Naked
7. Dole

Brands ranked below category average: Bolthouse Farms, Juicy Juice, Mott's, Northland, Odwalla Fruit and Smoothies, Pom Wonderful, Simply Juice, V8 V-Fusion

Soft Drink
1. Coca-Cola
2. Pepsi-Cola
3. Sprite
4. 7-Up
5. Dr Pepper

Brands ranked below category average: Mountain Dew, Sierra Mist

Car Rentals
1. Enterprise
2. Hertz
3. Budget

Brands ranked below category average: Advantage, Alamo, Dollar, Avis, National, Thrifty

Computers & Peripherals

PCs
1. Apple
2. Hewlett Packard
3. Dell
4. Sony

Brands ranked below category average: Acer, Asus, Compaq, Fujitsu, Gateway, Lenovo, Panasonic, Samsung, Toshiba

Tablets
1. Apple iPad
2. Kindle Fire
3. Google Nexus
4. Samsung Galaxy
5. HP Slate

Brands ranked below category average: BlackBerry PlayBook, Microsoft Surface, Motorola XOOM, Nook HD

Printing & Imaging
1. HP
2. Canon
3. Kodak
4. Xerox
5. Samsung
Brands ranked below category average: Brother, Dell, Epson, Konica, Minolta, Kyocera Mita, Lexmark, Panasonic, Ricoh, Sharp, Toshiba

Consumer Electronics
Car Audio
1. Bose
2. Harman/Kardon
Brands ranked below category average: Alpine, Infinity, JBL, Panasonic, Pioneer, Sony

Home Electronics
1. Sony
2. Samsung
3. LG
4. Vizio
5. Panasonic
Brands ranked below category average: Dynex, Insignia, JVC, Mitsubishi, Philips, Sanyo, Sharp, Sylvania, Toshiba

Digital Cameras
1. Canon
2. Nikon
3. Sony
Brands ranked below category average: Casio, FujiFilm, Kodak, Olympus, Panasonic, Pentax, Ricoh, Samsung

Gaming Consoles
1. Microsoft Xbox 360
2. Ninteno Wii
3. Sony PSP/PSP Vita
Brands ranked below category average: Nintendo 3DS/3DS XL, Sony PlayStation 3 (PS3), Wii U, from Nintendo

GPS Navigation Systems
1. Garmin Navigation System
Brands ranked below category average: Magellan, TomTom

Cruise Lines
1. Norwegian

2. Royal Caribbean International
3. Disney
4. Princess Cruises

Brands ranked below category average: Carnival Cruise Lines, Celebrity, Holland America

Entertainment/Recreation

Amusement Attractions

1. Disney Theme Parks
2. Sea World Theme Parks

Brands ranked below category average: Busch Garden, Hershey Theme Park, Six Flags, Universal Studios

Las Vegas Casinos

1. Bellagio
2. The Venetian
3. Caesars Palace
4. Wynn
5. Rio
6. The Palms
7. Mandelay Bay
8. The Mirage

Brands ranked below category average: Binion's, Circus-Circus, Excalibur, Hard Rock, Harrahs, Luxor, MGM Grand, Monte Carlo, New York-New York, Paris, Planet Hollywood, The Stratosphere, Treasure Island

Financial Services/Insurance

Health Insurance

1. Blue Cross and Blue Shield
2. UnitedHealthcare
3. Health Net

Brands ranked below category average: Aetna, Amerigroup, Cigna, Humana, Kaiser Permanente

Insurance

1. USAA Financial Services
2. State Farm
3. AAA
4. Allstate
5. Northwestern Mutual
6. Pacific Life
7. MetLife

Brands ranked below category average: Aflac, American Family, Esurance, Farmers, Geico, Guardian, Liberty Mutual, MassMutual, Nationwide, New York Life, Progressive,

The Hartford, Transamerica Life, Travelers

Investments
- Fidelity Investments
- AXA Equitable
- The Vanguard Group
- ShareBuilder
- Franklin Templeton Investments
- Edward Jones
- Ameriprise Financial
- UBS

Brands ranked below category average: Charles Schwab Financial Services, E*Trade, Merrill Lynch, T. Rowe Price, TD Ameritrade

Payment Networks
1. Visa
2. MasterCard

Brands ranked below category average: American Express, Discover Card

National Retail Banks
1. Chase Bank
2. Wells Fargo

Brands ranked below category average: Bank of America, Capital One, Citibank

Super Regional Retail Banks
1. Ally
2. Regions
3. PNC

Brands ranked below category average: BB&T, KeyBank, PNC, M&T, SunTrust, U.S. Bank

Food & Snacks

Chocolate Candy
1. Reese's Peanut Butter Cups
2. M&M's Peanut
3. M&M's Milk Chocolate
4. Hershey's Kisses
5. Hershey's Milk Chocolate Bars
6. Snickers
7. Kit Kat
8. Reese's Pieces

Brands ranked below category average: 3 Musketeers, Almond Joy, Baby Ruth, Butterfinger, Heath Toffee Bar, Junior Mints, Milk Duds, Milky Way, Nestle Crunch, Tootsie Roll, Twix, York Peppermint Pattie

Premium Chocolate Candy
1. Ghirardelli
2. Dove Milk
3. Godiva
4. Lindt

Brands ranked below category average: Cadbury, Ferrero Roche, Hershey Bliss, Russell Stover, Toblerone

Non-Chocolate Candy
1. Life Savers
2. Jolly Rancher
3. Starburst
4. Tootsie Pops
5. Skittles
6. Twizzlers
7. PayDay

Brands ranked below category average: Airheads, Good & Plenty, Haribo Gummi Bears, Laffy Taffy, Nerds, Red Vines, Sour Patch, Sour Punch Straws, SweeTARTS

Gum
1. Extra
2. Trident
3. Orbit
4. Stride
5. Dentyne

Brands ranked below category average: 5 Gum, BubbleYum, Bubblicious, Double Bubble, Juicy Fruit

Cookies
1. Oreo
2. Pepperidge Farm Milano
3. Chips Ahoy
4. Lofthouse Frosted Sugar Cookies
5. Keebler Chips Deluxe
6. Keebler Fudge Shoppe Fudge Stripes Original
7. Keebler Sandies Pecan Shortbread
8. Nilla Wafers

Brands ranked below category average: Archway, Famous Amos Chocolate Chip, Keebler Vanilla Wafers, Keebler Vienna Fingers, Mother's Cookies, Mrs Fields, Nabisco Newtons, Nabisco Nutter Butter Cookies, Nabisco SnackWells, Pepperidge Farms Soft Baked Cookies, Voortman

Energy Bars
1. Clif

2. Luna
3. Odwalla
4. Zone Perfect
5. Kashi GOLEAN
6. PROBAR

Brands ranked below category average: Atkins, Balance Bar, Power Bar

Popcorn
1. Orville Redenbacher
2. Pop Secret

Brands ranked below category average: ACT II, Jiffy Pop, Jolly Time, Newman's Own, Smart Balance

Salty Snacks
1. Lay's Chips
2. Doritos Chips
3. Tostitos Chips
4. Ruffles Chips
5. Fritos

Brands ranked below category average: Cape Cod Chips, Cheetos Snacks, Chex Mix, Combos, Jay's Chips, Kettle Chips, Pringles, Rold Gold Pretzels, Snyder's of Hanover Pretzels, Sun Chips, Utz Chips, Utz Pretzels

Yogurt
1. Yoplait
2. Chobani Greek Yogurt
3. Stonyfield Farm Oikos Greek Yogurt
4. Dannon
5. Stonyfield Farm

Brands ranked below category average: Danimals, Dannon Activia, Dannon DanActive, Go-Gurt, Trix Yogurt

Greeting Cards
1. Hallmark
2. Expressions from Hallmark
3. DaySpring
4. Shoebox

Brands ranked below category average: American Greeting, Carlton, Connections from Hallmark, Just for You from American Greetings, Mahogany, Papyrus, Recycled Paper

Health & Beauty

Mass-Market Cosmetics
1. Neutrogena
2. Physicians Formula

3. Olay
4. CoverGirl
5. L'Oreal

Brands ranked below category average: almay, MAX Factor, Maybelline New York, Revlon, Rimmel

Prestige Cosmetics
1. MAC Cosmetics
2. Clinique
3. Origins
4. Sephora
5. Bobbi Brown
6. Dior

Brands ranked below category average: Avon, Bare Escentuals, Chanel, Elizabeth Arden, Estee Lauder, Lancôme

Sun Screens
1. Neutrogena
2. Blue Frog

Brands ranked below category average: Banana Boat, Coppertone, Hawaiian Tropic, No-Ad

Weight-Loss Plans
1. Weight Watchers
2. Nutrisystem

Brands ranked below category average: Jenny Craig, LA Weight Loss

Hotels

Luxury Hotels
1. Starwood
2. The Ritz Carlton
3. W
4. Inter-Continental
5. Omni

Brands ranked below category average: Conrad, Four Seasons, Waldorf Astoria

Full Service Hotels
1. Hilton
2. Marriott
3. Sheraton
4. Courtyard Marriott
5. Wyndham

Brands ranked below category average: Crowne Plaza, Doubletree by Hilton, Embassy Suites, Hilton Garden Inn, Hyatt, Radisson, Renaissance Hotels, Springhill Suites,

Westin

Mid-Market Hotels
1. Holiday Inn
2. Hampton Inn & Suites
3. Holiday Inn Express
4. Fairfield Inns and Suites
5. Country Inns & Suites by Carlson

Brands ranked below category average: Best Western, Clarion, Comfort Inn, Comfort Suites, Howard Johnson, LaQuinta, Quality Inn, Ramada, Sleep Inn

Extended Stay Hotels
1. MainStay
2. Candlewood Suites
3. Homewood Suites by Hilton

Brands ranked below category average: Extended Stay America, Residence Inn

Economy Hotels
1. America's Best Value Inn
2. EconoLodge
3. Super 8
4. Red Roof Inns
5. Rodeway Inn

Brands ranked below category average: Motel 6

Household Products

Faucets
1. Moen
2. Kohler
3. Delta

Brands ranked below category average: American Standard, Glacier Bay, Peerless, Pfister

Gas Grills
1. Weber
2. Char•Broil

Brands ranked below category average: Brinkmann, Jenn-Air, Kenmore

Household Cleaners
1. Lysol All Purpose Cleaner
2. Clorox Clean-Up
3. Mr Clean
4. Pine-Sol

Brands ranked below category average: Clorox Green Works, fantastiK, Formula 409,

Green Works All Purpose, Murphy All Purpose, Pledge Multi-Surface, Seventh Generation, Spic and Span

Kitchen Cabinetry
1. KraftMaid
2. Thomasville
3. Armstrong

Brands ranked below category average: IKEA, Martha Stewart, Merillat

Lawn Mowers
1. John Deere
2. Craftsman
3. Honda
4. Toro

Brands ranked below category average: Black & Decker, Husqvarna, MTD, Simplicity, Snapper

Mattress
1. Tempur-Pedic
2. Sealy
3. Serta

Brands ranked below category average: King Koil, Simmons, Sleep Number, Spring Air. Stearns & Foster

Paint
1. KILZ
2. Sherman-Williams
3. Behr
4. Valspar

Brands ranked below category average: Benjamin Moore, Dutch Boy, Glidden Paint, Martha Stewart Living, Olympic, Pittsburgh, Pratt & Lambert, Sears Easy Living

Power Tools
1. Craftsman
2. DeWALT
3. RIDGID
4. Hilti
5. Black & Decker

Brands ranked below category average: Bosch, Campbell Hausfeld, Hitachi, Makita, Milwaukee, Porter-Cable, Ryobi, SKIL

Vacuum Cleaners
1. Dyson
2. Hoover

3. Kenmore
4. LG

Brands ranked below category average: Bissell, Black & Decker, Dirt Devil, Electrolux, Eureka, Oreck, Panasonic, Shark

Window Coverings

1. Hunter Douglas Blinds & Shades
2. Kirsch Blinds & Shades
3. Levolor Blinds & Shades

Brands ranked below category average: Bali Blinds & Shades, Hampton Bay Blind & Shades

Pet Food

Cat Food

1. Blue Buffalo
2. Purina
3. Eukanuba
4. Friskies
5. Iams
6. 9 Lives

Brands ranked below category average:, Fancy Feast, Hills Science Diet, Meow Mix, Newman's Own Organics, Whiskas

Dog Food

1. Blue Buffalo
2. Hills Science Diet
3. Purina
4. Iams
5. Beneful
6. Pedigree Dog Food

Brands ranked below category average: Alpo, Cesar Canine Cuisine, Eukanuba, Gravy Train, Kibbles 'n Bits, Mighty Dog, Neuwman's Own Organics

Media

Factual Entertainment TV

1. History Channel
2. Discovery Channel
3. National Geographic Channel
4. ID (Investigation Discovery)
5. H2
6. Food Network
7. Science
8. Animal Planet

Brands ranked below category average: Bio, Crime & Investigation, Disovery (en

Espanol), Discovery Fit & Health, HGTV, Military Channel, History Channel, Nat Geo WILD, TLC, Travel Channel, truTV

General Entertainment TV
1. A&E
2. USA
3. FX
4. TNT
5. Syfy
6. AMC
7. BBC America
8. TV Land
9. Lifetime
10. TBS
11. Comedy Central
12. Hallmark

Brands ranked below category average: BET, Bravo, E! Entertainment, G4, IFC, LMN, Logo, Nick at Nite, OWN, Oxygen, Spike, Sundance, Univision, WE

Business Magazines
1. *Forbes*
2. *Inc.*
3. *Money*

Brands ranked below category average: *Bloomberg BusinessWeek*, *Fortune*

General Interest Magazines
1. *Consumer Reports*
2. *National Geographic*
3. *Reader's Digest*

Brands ranked below category average: *AARP The Magazine*, *Atlantic Monthly*, *Ebony, Entertainment Weekly, People, Rolling Stone, The New Yorker, TV Guide*, *Wired*

Weekly News Magazines
1. *The Economist*
2. *Time*

Brands ranked below category average: *Newsweek*

Women's Magazines
1. *Real Simple*
2. *Better Homes and Gardens*
3. *Southern Living*
4. *Good Housekeeping*
5. *Prevention*
6. *Women's Day*

7. *Family Circle*

Brands ranked below category average: *Cosmopolitan, Glamour, Ladies Home Journal, Martha Stewart Living, O, The Oprah Magazine, Parents, Redbook, Vogue, Women's Health*

News Services
1. Google News
2. Yahoo! News
3. BBC News
4. Associated Press (AP)
5. Reuters
6. National Public Radio (NPR)
7. CNN Online
8. USA Today

Brands ranked below category average: Bloomberg, Fox News Online, *Los Angeles Times*, MSNBC Online, The Huffington Post, *The Wall Street Journal*, *The Washington Post*, United Press International (UPI)

Kids TV Programming
1. Boomerang
2. PBS KIDS Sprout
3. PBS Kids
4. Disney Channel
5. Disney Junior

Brands ranked below category average: Cartoon Network, Disney XD, Nick Jr, Nickelodeon, Nicktoons, TeenNick, The Hub

Broadcast Networks
1. PBS (Public Broadcasting Service)
2. ABC
3. CBS
4. NBC

Brands ranked below category average: Fox, The CW

Pay Cable Networks
1. HBO
2. Starz

Brands ranked below category average: Cinemax, Showtime

Sports TV
1. ESPN
2. CBS Sports
3. NFL Red Zone
4. NFL Television Network

5. NBC Sports

Brands ranked below category average: Fox Sports News Channel, MLB Televison Network, NHL Television Network, SPEED, Tennis, The Golf Channel

TV News Programming

1. The Weather Channel

Brands ranked below category average: CNBC, CNN, Fox News Channel, MSNBC News Channel

Motorcycles

- Yamaha Motorcycles
- Harley Davidson Motorcycles

Brands ranked below category average: Honda Motorcycles, Kawasaki Motorcycles, Suzuki Motorcycles

Non-Profits

Animal Welfare Non-Profits

- ASPCA
- The Humane Society

Brands ranked below category average: People for the Ethical Treatment of Animals (PETA)

Disability Non-Profits

1. Wounded Warrior Project
2. Goodwill
3. Special Olympics
4. National Autism Association
5. The American Association of People with Disabilities
6. Autism Society

Brands ranked below category average: Austism Speaks, Easter Seals, March of Dimes, National Down Syndrome Society, United Cerebral Palsy

Environmental Non-Profits

1. Nature Conservancy
2. Wildlife Conservation Society
3. National Wildlife Federation
4. Natural Resources Defense Council
5. Environmental Defense Fund
6. World Wildlife Fund

Brands ranked below category average: Audubon Society, Greenpeace USA, Sierra Club

Health Non-Profits

1. American Heart Association

2. Make-A-Wish Foundation
3. The Breast Cancer Research Foundation
4. Stand Up To Cancer
5. Children's Miracle Network
6. American Diabetes Association
7. American Cancer Society
8. Leukemia & Lymphoma Society
9. Juvenile Diabetes Research Foundation
10. National Kidney Foundation
11. American Stroke Association
12. Alzheimer's Association
13. Cystic Fibrosis Foundation
14. Susan G Komen for the Cure
15. American Lung Association
16. National Multiple Sclerosis Society

Brands ranked below category average: Arthritis Foundation, Avon Foundation for Women, Livestrong, Muscular Dystrophy Association, National Stroke Association, Planned Parenthood, World Health Organization

International Aid Non-Profits

1. Doctors Without Borders/MSF
2. Heifer International
3. Smile Train
4. Food for the Poor
5. World Visoin
6. Catholic Relief Charities

Brands ranked below category average: CARE, Catholic, Save the Children, UNICEF

Social Service Non-Profits

1. American Red Cross
2. Ronald McDonald House Charities
3. Habitat for Humanity
4. The Salvation Army
5. Feeding America

Brands ranked below category average: AARP Foundation, Catholic Charities USA, Children's Defense Fund, Dave Thomas Foundation, Feed The Children, United Way, United Service Organization, Volunteers of America

Youth Interest Non-Profits

1. Girl Scouts of the USA
2. Big Brothers Big Sisters
3. Reading is Fundamental (RIF)

Brands ranked below category average: 4-H, Boy Scouts of America, Boys & Girls Clubs of America, Junior Achievement, The Y-YMCA

Online Organizations

E-Retailers

1. Amazon.com
2. ebay.com

Brands ranked below category average: Craigslist.org, HSN.com, Land's End, Overstock.com, QVC.com, ShopNBC.com, Zappos.com

Health Information Websites

1. MayoClinic.com
2. WebMD

Brands ranked below category average: CNN Health, Drugs.com, Lifescript.com, MSN Health, NIH.com, RealAge.com, Yahoo! Health

Online Auto Shopping

1. Kelley Blue Book (KBB.com)
2. Edmunds.com

Brands ranked below category average: AutoTrader.com, Cars.com, eBay Motors

Online Computer Retailers

1. Newegg.com
2. Microsoft.com
3. Store.Apple.com
4. BestBuy.com

Brands ranked below category average: CDW.com, Dell.com, HPShopping.com, Store.Sony.com, TigerDirect.com

Online Daily Deals

1. Woot.com
2. CouponMom.com
3. LivingSocial
4. RetailMeNot.com
5. Coupons.com
6. CouponCabin.com
7. Groupon

Brands ranked below category average: Ebates.com, Google Offers

Online Department Stores

1. Kohls.com
2. Macys.com
3. JCP.com

Brands ranked below category average: NeimanMarcus.com, Nordstrom.com, Sears.com

Online Job Search
1. Indeed.com
2. CareerBuilder.com
Brands ranked below category average: Monster.com, USAJobs.com

Online Mass Merchandisers
1. Walmart.com
Brands ranked below category average: Costco.com, Target.com

Online Office Supply Retailers
1. Staples.com
Brands ranked below category average: OfficeDepot.com, OfficeMax.com

Online Travel Services
1. Expedia.com
2. Travelocity.com
3. Orbitz.com
Brands ranked below category average: Hotels.com, Kayak, priceline.com

Video Streaming Apps
1. YouTube
2. Redbox Instant
3. Netflix
4. HBO GO
5. Watch ESPN
Brands ranked below category average: Amazon Instant Video, Blockbuster On Demand, Crackle, Hulu Plus

Over-the-Counter Products
OTC Cold/Allergy Medications
1. Vicks Cold an Flu Products (DayQuil/NyQuil)
2. Benadryl
3. Tylenol Allergy and Cold Medications
4. Robitussin
5. Advil Cold & Sinus
Brands ranked below category average: Actifed, Alavert, Alka-Seltzer Plus Cold Medicine, Allegra-Allergy, Chlor-trimeton, Claritin Allergy, Comtrex, Corcidin HBP, Dimetapp, Sudafed, Triaminic Cold Medicine, Zicam, Zyrtec

OTC Digestive Aids
1. Tums
2. Pepto-Bismol Stomach Remedy
3. Prilosec OTC
4. Alka-Seltzer

Brands ranked below category average: Gaviscon, Maalox Antacids, Mylanta, Pepcid, Prevacid 24HR, Rolaids, Tagamet HB, Zantac

OTC Fiber Supplements
1. FiberCon
2. Benefiber
Brands ranked below category average: Citrucel, Metamucil

OTC Laxatives
1. Ducolax
2. MiraLax
3. Phillips Milk of Magnesia
Brands ranked below category average: Correctol, exLax, Fleet, Senocot

OTC Pain Relievers
1. Tylenol
2. Advil
3. Aleve
4. Bayer
Brands ranked below category average: Anacin, BC Powder, Bufferin, Excedrin, Motrin

OTC Sleep Aids
1. Tylenol PM
2. Advil PM
3. ZzzQuil SleepAid
4. Tylenol Simply Sleep
Brands ranked below category average: Nature Made, Nytol, Sominex, Unisom

Restaurants
Casual Dining
1. Panera Bread
2. Longhorn Steakhouse
3. IHOP (International House of Pancakes)
4. Outback Steakhouse
5. Red Loster Seafood
6. Chili's Grill & Bar
7. Applebee's
Brands ranked below category average: Bahama Breeze, Bonefish Grill, Denny's, Shoney's, TGI Friday's

Fast Casual Mexican
1. Chipotle Mexican Grill
2. Moe's Southwest Grill
Brands ranked below category average: Baja Fresh Mexican Grill, Qdoba Mexican Grill

Italian Dining
1. Olive Garden
Brands ranked below category average: Carrabba's Italian Grill, Maggiano's Little Italy, Romano's Macaroni Grill

Quick Service Restaurants
1. Subway
2. Dairy Queen
3. Five Guys Burgers and Fries
4. Wendy's
5. In-N-Out Burger
6. McDonald's
7. Chik-fil-A
8. Noodles & Company
9. Taco Bell

Brands ranked below category average: Arby's, Burger King, Church's Chicken, Hardee's, Jack in the Box, KFC (Kentucky Fried Chicken), Long John Silver's, Sonic, White Castle

Coffee & Quick Service
1. Dunkin' Donuts Stores
2. Einstein Bros. Bagels
3. Starbucks Coffee Shops

Brands ranked below category average: Bruegger's Bagels, Caribou, McCafe, Tim Hortons

Pizza Chains
1. Pizza Hut

Brands ranked below category average: Domino's, Little Caesar's, Papa John's Pizza

Retail

Convenience Stores
1. QuickTrip
2. Sheetz
3. WaWa
4. 7-Eleven
5. Speedway

Brands ranked below category average: Aplus Convenience Store at Sunoco, ARCO ampm, BP, Chevron Food Mart, Circle K, Shell

Department Stores
1. Kohl's
2. Macy's
3. JCPenney

Brands ranked below category average: Belk, Dillard's, Sears

Gasoline Retail
1. Costco
2. Murphy (Walmart)
3. Speedway
4. Shell
5. Sam's Club
6. Valero
7. Hess
8. ExxonMobil
9. Marathon
10. Chevron

Brands ranked below category average: ARCO, BP, CITGO, Conoco/Phillips 66/76, Gulf Oil, Sunoco, Texaco

Hardware & Home Stores
1. The Home Depot
2. Lowe's

Brands ranked below category average: Ace Hardware, Menard, True Value

Luxury Department Stores
1. Saks
2. Nordstrom
3. Bloomingdale's

Brands ranked below category average: Lord & Taylor, Neiman Marcus

Mass Merchandisers
1. Target
2. Walmart

Brands ranked below category average: Kmart

Off-Price Retailers
1. Marshalls
2. Ross
3. TJ Maxx

Brands ranked below category average: Burlington Coat Factory

Office Supply Stores
1. Staples Stores
2. Office Depot

Brands ranked below category average: Office Max

harmacies
1. Walgreen's
2. CVS
3. Rite Aid

Brands ranked below category average: Costco Pharmacy, Kmart Pharmacy, Target Pharmacy, Walmart Pharmacy

Sporting Goods Stores
1. Cabela's
2. REI
3. Dick's Sporting Goods
4. Gander Mountain
5. Sports Authority

Brands ranked below category average: Champs, Dunham's Sports, Finish Line, Foot Locker, Lady Foot Locker

Value Stores
1. Dollar Tree
2. Dollar General

Brands ranked below category average: 99 Cents Only Store, Big Lots, Family Dollar

Warehouse Clubs
1. Costco
2. Sam's Club

Brands ranked below category average: BJ's Wholesale Club, Inc.

Sports Leagues
1. NFL (National Football League)
2. NCAA Football (college football)
3. MLB (Major League Baseball)
4. NCAA Basketball (college basketball)

Brands ranked below category average: Formula 1 Racing, MLS (Major League Soccer), NASCAR (auto racing), NBA (National Basketball Association), NHL (National Hockey League), PGA Tour (Professional Golfers Association), UFC (Ultimate Fighting Championship), WWE (World Wrestling Entertainment)

Telecommunications

Mobile Networks
1. Verizon Mobile
2. AT&T Mobile

Brands ranked below category average: Alltel Mobile, CenturyLink, Cricket, Sprint, T-Mobile, Virgin, Vonage

Mobile Phones
- Apple iPhone
- HTC
- Samsung
- LG

Brands ranked below category average: Blackberry, Kyocera, Motorola, Nokia, Pantech, Sanyo, Sharp, Sony, T-Mobile

No-Contract Mobile Carriers
1. Verizon Wireless
2. AT&T GoPhone
3. TracFone

Brands ranked below category average: Boost Mobile, Cricket Wireless, MetroPCS, Net10, Virgin Mobile

35.3 Market Resources

Harris Interactive, 60 Corporate Woods, Rochester, NY 14623. (585) 272-8400. (www.harrisinteractive.com)

36

CUSTOMER EXPERIENCE

36.1 Overview

Temkin Group (www.temkingroup.com), a customer experience research and consulting company, publishes annual Temkin Ratings (www.temkinratings.com) in six categories, as follows:

- Overall experience
- Customer service
- Forgiveness
- Loyalty
- Trust
- Web experience

Temkin ranks over 100 companies in each category. This chapter presents a list of the top 20 in each category.

36.2 Temkin Ratings

The following are the 2013 Temkin Ratings:

Overall Experience

The Temkin Experience Ratings are based on three components of the customer experience: functional, accessible, and emotional. The 2013 ratings are as follows:

	Company	Segment
1.	Publix	Grocery
2.	Trader Joe's	Grocery
3. (tie)	Chick-fil-A	Fast food
3. (tie)	Aldi	Grocery
5. (tie)	Sam's Club	Retailer
5. (tie)	Amazon.com	Retailer
7. (tie)	Save-a-Lot	Grocery
7. (tie)	H.E.B.	Grocery
7. (tie)	Little Caesar's	Fast food
7. (tie)	Sonic Drive-In	Fast food
7. (tie)	Dunkin' Donuts	Fast food
7. (tie)	Ace Hardware	Retailer
13. (tie)	ShopRite	Grocery
13. (tie)	Hy-Vee	Grocery

13. (tie)	Arby's	Fast food
13. (tie)	Subway	Fast food
13. (tie)	Costco	Retailer
13. (tie)	Nordstrom	Retailer
13. (tie)	A credit union	Bank
20. (tie)	Kroger	Grocery

Customer Service

The Temkin Customer Service Ratings are based on feedback from consumers regarding companies they've recently interacted with. The 2013 ratings are as follows:

	Company	Segment
1.	USAA	Insurance carrier
2.	USAA	Bank
3.	A credit union	Bank
4. (tie)	Ace Hardware	Retailer
4. (tie)	Charles Schwab	Investment firm
6. (tie)	Dollar Tree	Retailer
6. (tie)	Chick-fil-A	Fast food
8. (tie)	Sonic Drive-In	Fast food
8. (tie)	Hy-Vee	Grocery
8. (tie)	Trader Joe's	Grocery
8. (tie)	Costco	Retailer
12. (tie)	Advantage	Rental car agency
12. (tie)	Publix	Grocery
12. (tie)	H.E.B.	Grocery
15. (tie)	Aldi	Grocery
15. (tie)	Alaska Airlines	Airline
15. (tie)	Amazon.com	Retailer
15. (tie)	Sam's Club	Retailer
15. (tie)	Lowe's	Retailer
20. (tie)	Marriott	Hotel chain

Forgiveness

The Temkin Forgiveness Ratings are based on consumers' likelihood to forgive companies if they deliver a bad experience. The 2013 ratings are as follows:

	Company	Segment
1.	Advantage	Rental car agency
2.	USAA	Bank
3.	USAA	Insurance carrier
4.	USAA	Credit card issuer
5.	H.E.B.	Grocery
6.	Blackboard	Software firm
7. (tie)	Aldi	Grocery
7. (tie)	Alaska Airlines	Airline

9. (tie)	A credit union	Bank
9. (tie)	Publix	Grocery
11. (tie)	Amazon.com	Retailer
11. (tie)	Ameriprise Financial	Investment firm
11. (tie)	Trader Joe's	Grocery
15. (tie)	Scottrade	Investment firm
15. (tie)	QVC	Retailer
15. (tie)	Electrolux	Appliance maker
18. (tie)	Courtyard Marriott	Hotel chain
18. (tie)	Chick-fil-A	Fast food
18. (tie)	TriCare	Health plan

Loyalty

The Temkin Loyalty Ratings are based on three elements of customer loyalty: willingness to buy more, reluctance to switch business away, and likelihood to recommend. The 2012 ratings are as follows:

	Company	**Segment**
1.	Sam's Club	Retailer
2.	Aldi	Grocery
3.	USAA	Bank
4.	Publix	Grocery
5. (tie)	Amazon.com	Retailer
5. (tie)	A credit union	Bank
7.	H.E.B.	Grocery
8. (tie)	Target	Retailer
8. (tie)	Chick-fil-A	Fast food
8. (tie)	Starbucks	Fast food
8. (tie)	USAA	Insurance carrier
12. (tie)	ShopRite	Grocery
12. (tie)	Hy-Vee	Grocery
12. (tie)	Lowe's	Retailer
12. (tie)	Subway	Fast food
16. (tie)	Winn-Dixie	Grocery
16. (tie)	Kroger	Grocery
16. (tie)	Home Depot	Retailer
16. (tie)	Southwest Airlines	Airline
16. (tie)	USAA	Credit card issuer

Trust

The Temkin Trust Ratings are based on customers' rating of their likelihood to trust companies they deal with. The 2013 ratings are as follows:

	Company	**Segment**
1. (tie)	USAA	Insurance carrier
1. (tie)	USAA	Bank

3.	A credit union	Bank
4.	Publix	Grocery
5.	H.E.B.	Grocery
6.	Amazon.com	Retailer
8. (tie)	Trader Joe's	Grocery
8. (tie)	Charles Schwab	Investment firm
8. (tie)	Sam's Club	Retailer
11.	Hy-Vee	Grocery
12. (tie)	State Farm	Insurance carrier
12. (tie)	Aldi	Grocery
12. (tie)	Advantage	Rental car agency
12. (tie)	Walgreens	Retailer
16. (tie)	Costco	Retailer
16. (tie)	Chick-fil-A	Fast food
16. (tie)	Marriott	Hotel chain
16. (tie)	Toyota	Auto dealer
20.	Save-a-Lot	Grocery

Web Experience

The Temkin Web Experience Ratings are based consumer satisfaction with recent online experiences. The 2013 ratings are as follows:

	Company	Segment
1.	Amazon.com	Retailer
2.	USAA	Bank
3.	USAA	Insurance carrier
4.	Regions	Bank
5. (tie)	Advantage	Rental car agency
5. (tie)	US Bank	Bank
5. (tie)	eBay	Retailer
8. (tie)	A credit union	Bank
8. (tie)	QVC	Retailer
10. (tie)	Charles Schwab	Investment firm
10. (tie)	Fidelity Investments	Investment firm
10. (tie)	ING Direct	Investment firm
14. (tie)	USAA	Credit card issuer
14. (tie)	Vanguard	Investment firm
16. (tie)	Hilton	Hotel chain
16. (tie)	PNC	Bank
16. (tie)	Marriott	Hotel chain
16. (tie)	Courtyard by Marriott	Hotel chain
16. (tie)	Sonic Drive-In	Fast food

36.3 Market Resources

Temkin Group, 48 White Oak Road, Waban, MA 02468. (617) 916-2075. (www.temkingroup.com)

37

CUSTOMER LOYALTY ENGAGEMENT

37.1 Overview

Brand Keys (www.brandkeys.com) produces an annual assessment of brand leaders in customer loyalty engagement. Initiated in 1997, the Brand Keys Customer Loyalty Engagement Index ranks brands based on their ability to engage consumers and create loyal customers.

The Brand Keys data paints a detailed picture of the category drivers that engage customers, engender loyalty, and drive real profits. The comparison is aimed to define how the consumer will view the category, compare offerings and, ultimately, buy.

37.2 Customer Loyalty Engagement Rankings

The 2013 assessment by Brand Keys examines customers' relationships with 375 brands in 54 categories.

The 2013 Customer Loyalty Engagement Index ranking is as follows:

Airlines

1. Southwest
2. JetBlue
3. Delta
4. United
5. American

Athletic Footwear

1. (tie) Nike
1. (tie) Asics
2. New Balance
3. Reebok
4. (tie) Adidas
4. (tie) Brooks

Automotive

1. (tie) Ford
1. (tie) Hyundai
3. (tie) Toyota
3. (tie) Honda

5. GM
6. (tie) Chrysler (Dodge)
6. (tie) Chrysler (Jeep)
8. (tie) BMW
8. (tie) Lexus
10. Mercedes
11. (tie) Suburu
11. (tie) Mazda
11. (tie) Kia
14. Mini
15. Volkswagen
16. Nissan

Banks
1. JPMorgan Chase
2. Wells Fargo
3. Bank of New York Mellon
4. PNC
5. (tie) Bank of America
5. (tie) Citi

Beer (Light)
1. Coors Light
2. Sam Adams Light
3. (tie) Amstel Light
3. (tie) Bud Light
4. Corona Light
5. Busch Light
6. Miller Light

Beer (Regular)
1. (tie) Sam Adams
1. (tie) Coors
3. (tie) Heineken
3. (tie) Miller
5. (tie) Busch
5. (tie) Budweiser
7. Corona
8. Michelob

Breakfast Cereals: Adults
1. Cheerios
2. Special K
3. (tie) Honey Nut Cheerios

3. (tie) Frosted Mini Wheats
5. (tie) Honey Bunches of Oats
5. (tie) Chex
7. Fiber One
8. Rice Krispies
9. Post Raisin Bran
10. Corn Flakes
11. Life
12. Grape Nuts
13. Post Raisin Bran
14. Kix

Breakfast Cereals: Kids
1. Cherrios
2. Frosted Flakes
3. Special K
4. (tie) Honey Nut Cheerios
4. (tie) Corn Flakes
6. Honey Bunches of Oats
7. Rice Krispies
8. (tie) Lucky Charms
8. (tie) Trix
8. (tie) Froot Loops
11. Cap'n Crunch

Car Insurance
1. Allstate
2. GEICO
3. Progressive
4. USAA
5. Liberty Mutual
6. Nationwide

Car Rental
1. Avis
2. (tie) Hertz
2. (tie) Enterprise
3. Budget
4. National
5. (tie) Dollar
5. (tie) Alamo

Cellphones
1. Samsung

2. LG
3. HTC
4. (tie) Motorola
4. (tie) Sanyo
6. Sony Ericsson
7. Panasonic
8. Nokia

Coffee
1. Dunkin' Donuts
2. Starbucks
3. McDonald's
4. Tim Hortons

Coffee (Packaged)
1. Dunkin'
2. Starbucks
3. (tie) Green Mountain
3. (tie) Allegro
5. (tie) Folgers
5. (tie) Chock Full O' Nuts
5. (tie) Peets
5. (tie) Eight O'Clock
9. (tie) Nescafé
9. (tie) Yuban
9. (tie) Peets
12. LavAzza
13. Maxwell House

Computers (Laptop)
1. (tie) Samsung
1. (tie) Apple
3. Asus
4. (tie) Toshiba
4. (tie) Sony VAIO
6. (tie) Acer
6. (tie) HP
8. (tie) Lenovo
8. (tie) Vizio
10. Dell

Cosmetics (Luxury)
1. Clinique
2. Lancôme

3. Chanel
4. Estée Lauder
5. Shiseido

Credit Cards

1. Discover
2. American Express
3. Chase
4. Visa
5. (tie) Capital One
5. (tie) MasterCard
7. (tie) Citibank
7. (tie) Wells Fargo
9. (tie) Bank of America
9. (tie) Barclaycard

Credit Cards (Bank)

1. Chase
2. Barclaycard
3. Wells Fargo
4. HSBC
5. Citibank
6. Bank of America

Diapers

1. Pampers
2. Huggies
3. 7th Generation
4. Luv's

Drug Stores

1. Walgreens
2. Duane Reade
3. CVS
4. Rite Aid

E-Readers

1. Kindle
2. Nook
3. iPad
4. Kobo
5. Sony

Evening News Show
1. ABC
2. NBC
3. FOX
4. CBS
5. (tie) MSNBC
5. (tie) CNN

Flat Screen TVs
1. Samsung
2. Vizio
3. Sony
4. LG
5. Toshiba
6. (tie) Panasonic
6. (tie) Hitachi

Gasoline
1. Shell
2. Chevron
3. (tie) Exxon
3. (tie) BP
5. Mobil
6. Sunoco
7. Citgo
8. Texaco

Hotels (Economy)
1. Days Inn
2. Econo Lodge
3. Travelodge
4. Motel 6

Hotels (Luxury)
1. Inter-Continental
2. Ritz-Carlton
3. W Hotels
4. Fairmont Hotels

Hotels (Midscale)
1. Best Western
2. Hampton Inn
3. Ramada
4. Holiday Inn

5. Comfort Inn

Hotels (Upscale)
1. Hilton
2. Marriott
3. Hyatt
4. Doubletree
5. (tie) Embassy Suites
5. (tie) Wyndham
7. Radisson
8. Sheraton
9. Westin

Insurance Companies
1. NY Life
2. MetLife
3. (tie) The Hartford
3. (tie) Liberty Mutual
5. Prudential
6. Travelers

Major League Sports
1. NFL
2. MLB
3. NBA
4. NHL

MFP Office Copiers
1. (tie) Konica Minolta
1. (tie) Canon
3. (tie) Sharp
3. (tie) Lexmark
5. Xerox
6. Epson
7. (tie) Ricoh
7. (tie) HP
9. Toshiba

Morning News Shows
1. Good Morning America (ABC)
2. Today (ABC)
3. This Morning (CBS)
4. Fox & Friends (FOX)
5. Starting Point (CNN)

Mutual Funds

1. American Funds
2. (tie) Vanguard
2. (tie) Fidelity
4. (tie) T. Rowe Price
4. (tie) Dreyfus
6. Putnam
7. Franklin
8. Janus

Natural Food Stores

1. Whole Foods
2. Trader Joe's
3. The Fresh Market
4. Sprouts Farmers Market

Online Brokerages

1. Fidelity.com
2. Scottrade.com
3. TDAmeritrade.com
4. (tie) Options Xpress
4. (tie) Etrade.com
6. (tie) Schwab.com
6. (tie) MerrillLynch.com
8. Vanguard.com

Online Retailers

1. Amazon.com
2. Ebay.com
3. Overstock.com
4. Zappos.com
5. Buy.com

Online Travel Services

1. Expedia
2. Orbitz
3. Travelocity
4. Kayak
5. Priceline
6. Hotwire
7. Hotels.com
8. CheapTickets

Parcel Delivery
1. UPS
2. FedEx
3. USPS

Pet Food - Canned (Cats)
1. Fancy Feast
2. Friskies
3. Purina
4. Iams
5. Hills
6. Whiskers
7. 9Lives

Pet Food - Canned (Dogs)
1. Cesar
2. Purina One
3. (tie) Pedigree
3. (tie) Iams
3. (tie) Mighty Dog
6. (tie) Gravy Train
6. (tie) Alpo
6. (tie) Hills

Pizza
1. Domino's
2. Pizza Hut
3. Papa John's
4. Little Caesars
5. Noble Roman's
6. Sbarro
7. Godfather's
8. Chuck E. Cheese

Printers
1. Canon
2. Samsung
3. (tie) HP
3. (tie) Lexmark
5. Brother
6. Epson
7. Dell

Restaurants (Casual Dining)

1. Olive Garden
2. Ruby Tuesday
3. (tie) Chili's
3. (tie) Red Lobster
5. (tie) IHOP
5. (tie) TGI Friday's
5. (tie) Applebee's
8. Arby's

Restaurants (Quick-Service)

1. Subway
2. Burger King
3. McDonald's
4. KFC
5. (tie) Wendy's
5. (tie) Taco Bell
7. Hardee's

Retail Stores (Apparel)

1. J. Crew
2. Victoria's Secret
3. L.L. Bean
4. Abercrombie & Fitch
5. GAP
6. H&M
7. PacSun
8. Aeropostale
9. Old Navy
10. American Eagle Outfitters

Retail Stores (Department)

1. Kohl's
2. Macy's
3. Marshall's
4. (tie) TJ Maxx
4. (tie) Dillard's
4. (tie) Sears
7. JCPenney

Retail Stores (Discount)

1. Walmart
2. Target
3. Kmart

Retail Stores (Home Improvement)

4. Home Depot
5. Lowe's
6. True Value
7. Ace

Retail Stores (Sporting/Recreation)

1. Dick's Sporting Goods
2. (tie) Sports Authority
2. (tie) REI
4. Cabela's
5. Modell's
6. Big 5 Sporting Goods

Search Engines

1. Google
2. Yahoo!
3. Bing
4. ASK
5. AOL
6. AltaVista

Smartphones

1. Samsung
2. Apple
3. LG
4. (tie) Nokia
4. (tie) Sony
6. Motorola
7. HTC
8. Blackberry

Social Networking Sites

1. Facebook
2. Twitter
3. YouTube
4. LinkedIn
5. Pinterest
6. Google+
7. MySpace
8. Yelp
9. Four Square
10. Flickr

11. Quora

Soft Drinks (Diet)

1. Diet Coke
2. Diet Mountain Dew
3. Diet Pepsi
4. Diet Dr. Pepper
5. Diet 7-UP

Soft Drinks (Regular)

1. Coca-Cola
2. Mountain Dew
3. 7-UP
4. (tie) Pepsi
4. (tie) Sprite
6. Dr. Pepper

Tablets

1. Amazon
2. (tie) Apple
2. (tie) Samsung
4. Barnes & Noble
5. (tie) Acer
5. (tie) Lenovo
5. (tie) Toshiba
8. (tie) Sony
8. (tie) Google
10. Asus

Toothpaste

1. Colgate
2. Crest
3. Arm & Hammer
4. (tie) Tom's of Maine
4. (tie) Listerine

Video Games

1. Call of Duty: Modern Warfare
2. Halo
3. (tie) Madden Football
3. (tie) NBA2K12
5. Battlefield
6. (tie) World of Warcraft
6. (tie) FIFA

8. Starcraft 2
9. Crysis

Vodka
1. Grey Goose
2. (tie) Smirnoff
2. (tie) Titos
4. (tie) Ketel One
4. (tie) Svedka
6. (tie) Chopin
6. (tie) Absolut
8. Ciroc
9. Stolichnaya
10. Finlandia

Wireless Phone Services
1. AT&T Wireless
2. Verizon Wireless
3. Sprint PCS
4. T-Mobile

37.3 Market Resources

Brand Keys, 9 West 29th Street, 5th Floor, New York, NY 10001. (212) 532-6028. (www.brandkeys.com)

38

CUSTOMER SATISFACTION

38.1 Overview

The American Customer Satisfaction Index (ACSI, www.theacsi.org) is a national economic indicator of satisfaction with the quality of products and services available to U.S. household consumers. Established in 1994, the ACSI produces indices of customer satisfaction on a 0-100 scale.

The ACSI is based on about 65,000 interviews conducted annually, with 250 to 260 interviews completed per company/agency. Industry sample sizes vary from 750 to 10,000, depending on the number of measured companies in each industry.

The ACSI is produced by the Stephen M. Ross Business School at the University of Michigan (www.bus.umich.edu) in partnership with the American Society for Quality (www.asq.org) and CFI Group (www.cfigroup.com), a consulting firm. ForeSee Results (www.foreseeresults.com) sponsors the e-commerce and e-business measurements.

This chapter presents 2013 ACSI scores for consumer brands in 46 categories.

38.2 ACSI Scores

ACSI scores from 2013 surveys and change from 2012 scores are as follows:

Airlines
- JetBlue: 83 (2.5%)
- Southwest: 81 (5.2%)
- Delta: 68 (4.6%)
- American: 65 (1.6%)
- US Airways: 64 (-1.5%)
- United: 62 (no change)
- All others: 72 (-2.7%)
- Sector average: 70 (3.0%)

Apparel
- Levi Strauss: 82 (no change)
- Hanesbrands: 81 (2.5%)
- V.F.: 81 (-1.2%)
- Jones Group: 80 (-2.4%)
- All others: 78 (-1.3%)
- Sector average: 79 (no change)

Athletic Shoes

- adidas: 80 (3.9%)
- Nike: 78 (-2.5%)
- All others: 83 (3.8%)
- Sector average: 81 (1.3%)

Automobiles and Light Vehicles

- Mercedes-Benz (Daimler): 88 (3.5%)
- Lexus (Toyota): 87 (-2.2%)
- Honda: 86 (3.6%)
- Toyota (Toyota): 86 (1.2%)
- Subaru: 86 (-1.1)
- Cadillac (GM): 85 (-1.2%)
- GMC (GM): 85 (6.3%)
- Volkswagen: 84 (-1.2%)
- Nissan: 83 (no change)
- Acura (Honda): 83 (n/a)
- Ford (Ford): 83 (no change)
- Chrysler (Chrysler): 83 (6.4%)
- Hyundai: 82 (-3.5%)
- BMW: 82 (-4.7%)
- Buick (GM): 82 (-5.7%)
- Kia: 82 (no change)
- Mazda: 82 (no change)
- Jeep (Chrysler): 80 (-3.6%)
- Dodge (Chrysler): 79 (2.5%)
- Chevrolet (GM): 79 (-6.0%)
- All others: 81 (-1.2%)
- Sector average: 83 (-1.2%)

Banks*

- JPMorgan Chase: 74 (5.7%)
- Wells Fargo: 71 (-2.7%)
- Citigroup: 70 (-4.1%)
- Bank of America: 66 (-2.9%)
- All others: 79 (no change)
- Sector average: 77 (2.7%)

Breweries

- MillerCoors: 82 (1.2%)
- Anheuser-Busch InBev: 81 (no change)
- All others: 80 (-3.6%)
- Sector average: 81 (no change)

Cellular Phones/Smartphones

- Apple: 81 (-2.4%)
- Motorola Mobility: 77 (5.5%)
- Samsung Electronics: 76 (7.0%)
- Nokia: 76 (1.3%)
- HTC: 72 (-4.0%)
- LG Electronics: 71 (-5.3)
- Blackberry: 69 (no change)
- All others: 76 (4.1%)
- Sector average: 76 (2.7%)

Computer Software

- Microsoft: 74 (-1.3%)
- All others: 76 (-1.3%)
- Sector average: 76 (-1.3%)

Department and Discount Stores*

- Nordstrom: 84 (no change)
- JCPenney: 81 (-1.2%)
- Kohl's: 81 (no change)
- Target: 81 (1.3%)
- Dillard's: 79 (-1.3%)
- Dollar General: 78 (no change)
- Macy's: 78 (1.3%)
- Sears: 75 (-1.3%)
- Exchange: 75 (-1.3%)
- Walmart: 71 (1.4%)
- All others: 78 (1.3%)
- Sector average: 77 (1.3%)

Fixed Line Telephone Service

- Cox Communications: 74 (4.2%)
- Verizon Communications: 74 (5.7%)
- AT&T: 73 (4.3%)
- Charter Communications: 72 (n/a)
- CenturyLink: 71 (7.6%)
- Comcast: 71 (6.0%)
- All others: 75 (1.3%)
- Sector average: 74 (5.7%)

Food Manufacturing

- Quaker (PepsiCo): 87 (1.2%)
- H.J. Heinz: 87 (-2.2%)

- General Mills: 87 (4.8%)
- Kraft: 86 (6.0%)
- Hershey: 86 (1.2%)
- Kellogg: 85 (2.4%)
- Campbell Soup: 84 (3.7%)
- Hillshire Brands: 84 (1.2%)
- Mars: 84 (-2.3%)
- Dole: 84 (1.2%)
- ConAgra: 83 (-1.2%)
- Néstle: 83 (-2.4%)
- Tyson Foods: 80 (-1.2%)
- All others: 80 (-2.4%)
- Sector average: 81 (-2.4)

Full-Service Restaurants
- Olive Garden (Darden): 83 (3.8%)
- Red Lobster (Darden): 83 (no change)
- Applebee's: 82 (6.5%)
- Outback Steakhouse: 81 (no change)
- Chili's: 78 (2.6%)
- All others: 81 (1.3%)
- Sector average: 81 (1.3%)

Health & Personal Care
- Rite Aid: 77 (2.7%)
- Walgreen: 76 (1.3%)
- CVS (Caremark): 75 (2.7%)
- All others: 79 (-3.7%)
- Sector average: 77 (1.3%)

Health Insurance*
- Blue Cross/Blue Shield: 73 (7.4%)
- UnitedHealth: 70 (-2.8%)
- WellPoint: 70 (-5.4%)
- Aetna: 67 (no change)
- All others: 71 (-5.3%)
- Sector average: 72 (no change)

Hotels
- Marriott: 82 (5.1%)
- Hilton: 80 (no change)
- Hyatt: 79 (3.9%)
- Best Western: 79 (3.9%)
- Starwood: 78 (4.0%)

- InterContinental: 78 (1.3%)
- Choice: 75 (-1.3%)
- Wyndham: 72 (2.9%)
- All others: 76 (-1.3%)
- Sector average: 77 (no change)

Household Appliances
- Whirlpool: 82 (-1.2%)
- General Electric: 80 (no change)
- Electrolux: 78 (-4.9%)
- All others: 80 (1.3%)
- Sector average: 80 (-1.2%)

Internet Brokerage*
- Fidelity Investments: 78 (-1.3%)
- Charles Schwab: 77 (-2.5%)
- TD Ameritrade: 77 (-1.3%)
- E*Trade Financial: 73 (-7.6%)
- All others: 78 (4.0%)
- Sector average: 78 (2.6%)

Internet News and Information
- FOXNews.com: 82 (-2.4%)
- ABCNews.com: 75 (-1.3%)
- NBCNews.com: 75 (2.7%)
- NYTimes.com: 74 (no change)
- CNN.com (Time Warner): 73 (-2.7%)
- USAToday.com: 73 (-2.7%)
- TheHuffingtonPost.com: 69 (no change)
- All others: 72 (no change)
- Sector average: 73 (no change)

Internet Portals and Search Engines
- Google: 77 (-6.1%)
- Bing.com (Microsoft): 76 (-6.2%)
- Yahoo!: 76 (-2.6%)
- MSN (Microsoft): 74 (-5.1%)
- AOL: 71 (-4.1%)
- All others: 70 (-12.5%)
- Sector average: 76 (-3.8%)

Internet Retail*
- Amazon.com: 85 (-1.2%)
- Newegg: 84 (-1.2%)

- eBay: 83 (2.5%)
- Overstock.com: 81 (-2.4%)
- Netflix: 75 (1.4%)
- All others: 82 (2.5%)
- Sector average: 82 (1.2%)

Internet Social Media

- Wikipedia: 78 (no change)
- Pinterest: 72 (4.3%)
- YouTube (Google): 71 (-2.7%)
- Google+: 71 (-9.0%)
- Twitter.com: 65 (1.6%)
- Facebook: 62 (1.6%)
- LinkedIn: 62 (-1.6%)
- Sector average: 68 (-1.4%)

Internet Travel*

- Expedia: 76 (-1.3%)
- Orbitz: 76 (no change)
- Travelocity.com: 75 (-5.1%)
- Priceline: 74 (-2.6%)
- All others: 76 (-3.8%)
- Sector average: 76 (-2.6%)

Limited-Service Restaurants

- Subway: 83 (1.2%)
- Papa John's: 82 (-1.2%)
- Little Caesar: 82 (no change)
- Domino's Pizza: 81 (5.2%)
- KFC (YUM! Brands): 81 (8.0%)
- Starbucks: 80 (5.3%)
- Pizza Hut (YUM! Brands): 80 (2.6%)
- Dunkin' Donuts: 80 (1.3%)
- Wendy's: 79 (1.3%)
- Burger King: 76 (1.3%)
- Taco Bell (YUM! Brands): 74 (-3.9%)
- McDonald's: 73 (no change)
- All others: 82 (no change)
- Sector average: 80 (no change)

Personal Care and Cleaning Products

- Clorox: 85 (-2.3%)
- Colgate-Palmolive: 85 (2.4%)
- Unilever: 85 (-1.2%)

- Procter & Gamble: 84 (2.4%)
- Dial: 84 (1.2%)
- All others: 82 (no change)
- Sector average: 83 (no change)

Personal Computers
- Apple: 87 (1.2%)
- Hewlett-Packard: 80 (1.3%)
- Dell: 79 (-2.5%)
- Toshiba: 78 (1.3%)
- Acer: 77 (-2.5%)
- All others: 79 (-5.0%)
- Sector average: 79 (-1.3%)

Pet Food*
- Néstle Purina PetCare: 83 (1.2%)
- Mars Petcare: 82 (2.5%)
- Iams (Proctor & Gamble): 83 (2.5%)
- Hill's Pet Nutrition: (Colgate-Palmolive) 83 (-1.2%)
- Del Monte: 86 (4.9%)
- All others: 84 (2.4%)
- Sector average: 83 (1.2%)

Property & Casualty Insurance*
- Progressive: 81 (2.5%)
- State Farm: 81 (-1.2%)
- Allstate: 79 (1.3%)
- Farmers: 79 (no change)
- GEICO: 79 (-2.5%)
- All others: 77 (-7.2%)
- Sector average: 78 (-6.0%)

Soft Drinks
- Dr. Pepper Snapple: 86 (-1.1%)
- PepsiCo: 85 (1.2%)
- Coca-Cola: 84 (no change)
- All others: 82 (-2.4%)
- Sector average: 84 (no change)

Specialty Retail Stores*
- Office Depot: 84 (6.3%)
- Costco: 83 (no change)
- Barnes & Noble: 82 (3.8%)

- Sam's Club: 80 (-1.2%)
- Staples: 79 (no change)
- Lowe's: 79 (no change)
- Best Buy: 78 (1.3%)
- OfficeMax: 78 (no change)
- Home Depot: 77 (-1.3%)
- Gap: 76 (-1.3%)
- TJX: 76 (-2.6%)
- All others: 77 (1.3%)
- Sector average: 78 (-1.3%)

Subscription Television Services
- Verizon Communications: 73 (-1.4%)
- DirecTV: 72 (5.9%)
- AT&T (U-verse): 71 (4.4%)
- DISH Network: 70 (1.4%)
- Cox Communications: 65 (3.2%)
- Charter Communications: 64 (8.5%)
- Comcast: 63 (3.3%)
- Time Warner Cable: 60 (-4.8%)
- All others: 69 (1.5%)
- Sector average: 68 (3.0%)

Supermarkets*
- Publix: 86 (2.4%)
- Whole Foods: 80 (no change)
- Kroger: 79 (no change)
- Winn-Dixie: 78 (4.0%)
- Supervalu: 76 (2.7%)
- Safeway: 75 (no change)
- Walmart: 72 (4.3%)
- All others: 78 (-1.3%)
- Sector average: 77 (1.3%)

Wireless Telephone Services
- Verizon Wireless: 73 (4.3%)
- Sprint Nextel: 71 (no change)
- AT&T Mobility: 70 (1.4%)
- T-Mobile: 68 (-1.4%)
- All others: 78 (2.6%)
- Sector average: 72 (2.9%)

* 2012 figures

38.3 Market Resources

American Customer Satisfaction Index (ACSI), 625 Avis Drive, Ann Arbor, MI 48108. (734) 913-0788. (www.theacsi.org)

ForeSee Results, 2500 Green Road, Suite 400, Ann Arbor, MI 48105. (800) 621-2850. (www.foreseeresults.com)

39

CUSTOMER SERVICE

39.1 Overview

J.D. Power and Associates (www.jdpower.com) identifies companies that excel in customer service based customer feedback, opinions, and perceptions of more than 800 companies in more than 20 industries annually. The assessment identifies 50 brands as Customer Service Champions. Brands that receive the Customer Service Champions designation are among the top 5% based on their performance in five key areas: people, presentation, price, process, and product.

39.2 Customer Service Champions

Brands named as J.D. Power Customer Service Champions for 2012 are as follows:

- ACE Rent A Car
- Amazon.com
- Amica
- Apple
- Auto-Owners Insurance
- Barnes & Noble
- Bass Pro Shops
- Boost Mobile
- Cadillac
- Clark Public Utilities
- David Weekley Homes
- Drury Inn & Suites
- Enterprise Rent-A-Car
- Erie Insurance
- First Federal
- Four Seasons Hotels and Resorts
- Frost Bank
- Good Neighbor Pharmacy
- Hampton Hotels
- Hancock Bank
- Health Mart Pharmacy
- Hotel Indigo

- ING Direct Home Loans
- Jackson EMC
- Jaguar
- JetBlue Airways
- Kohl's
- L.L. Bean
- Lexus
- MetroPCS
- MINI
- New Jersey Manufacturers
- Publix Pharmacy
- Quicken Loans
- Saks Fifth Avenue
- Salt River Project
- Sawnee EMC
- Scottrade, Inc.
- Shea Homes
- Southern Maryland Electric Cooperative
- Southwest Airlines
- Straight Talk
- The Ritz-Carlton
- U.S. Cellular
- U.S. Department of Veterans Affairs, Pharmacy Services
- USAA
- Virgin America
- Virgin Mobile
- Wegmans
- Wegmans Pharmacy

39.3 Market Resources

J.D. Power and Associates, 2625 Townsgate Road, Westlake Village, CA 91361. (805) 418-8000. (www.jdpower.com)

40

FACEBOOK FAN BRAND LOYALTY

40.1 Overview

LoudDoor (www.louddoor.com), a Facebook Insights preferred marketing developer, tracks every major brand on Facebook and how likely fans are to recommend those brands to friends or colleagues. Over one million monthly survey responses from Facebook fans of over 15,000 Facebook pages are used to determine the Top 20 brands with the most loyal fans.

40.2 Brand Satisfaction 2013

The top brands in the 2013 Brand Satisfaction survey are as follows:

1. St. Jude Children's Research Hospital
2. Facebook
3. Google
4. Walt Disney World
5. ALDI USA
6. Xbox
7. Starbucks Frappuccino
8. Google Chrome
9. Duncan Hines
10. Adobe Photoshop
11. Tim Hortons
12. Hershey's
13. In-N-Out Burger
14. Dove Chocolates
15. NFL
16. Portillo's
17. BRAVO
18. Disneyland
19. Dollar Tree
20. AMC Theatre

40.3 Market Resources

LoudDoor, 419 Lafayette Street, New York, NY 10003. (888) 782-0409. (www.louddoor.com)

41

ONLINE RETAILER SHOPPER SATISFACTION

41.1 Overview

Harris Interactive (www.harrisinteractive.com) conducts an annual Shopper Satisfaction Study Of Online Retailers. The study is based on a consumer poll which asks questions about selection of products, ease of shopping, perceived value, liklihood to recommend, and overall satisfaction.

This chapter presents the results of the Shopper Satisfaction Study Of Online Retailers conducted in November 2012.

41.2 Shopper Satisfaction Rankings

Mass Merchandisers

1. Amazon
2. Costco Wholesale
3. Target
4. Walmart

Department Stores

1. (tie) JCPenney
1. (tie) Kohl's
3. Macy's
4. Nordstrom

Apparel

1. L.L.Bean
2. (tie) Zappos
2. (tie) Victoria's Secret
4. Gap
5. (tie) Abercrombie & Fitch
5. (tie) Urban Outfitters

41.3 Market Resources

Harris Interactive, 60 Corporate Woods, Rochester, NY 14623. (585) 272-8400. (www.harrisinteractive.com)

PART VI: ETHNIC FOCUS

42

AFRICAN-AMERICAN CONSUMERS

42.1 Overview

African-Americans, also referred to as Black Americans, are Americans who have total or partial ancestry from any of the native populations of Sub-Saharan Africa, according to the U.S. Census Bureau (www.census.gov). Black Hispanics are generally not classified as African-Americans.

African-Americans constitute the third largest racial and ethnic group in the U.S., trailing Caucasians and Hispanic-Americans.

When asked in a 2012 survey by The Nielsen Company (www.nielsen.com) which term is preferable, 44% said they prefer Black, 43% prefer African-American, and 11% do not have a preference.

42.2 Profile

Census 2010 counted 38.9 million people, or 12.6% of the total U.S. population, of black- or African-American-only ancestry. An additional 1.0 million people reported black as well as one or more other races in that census. Combined, there were 42.0 million African Americans, representing 13.6% of the population.

Nielsen reports the number Black Americas in 2012 at 44 million, representing approximately 13.8% of the U.S. population.

Since 2000, the black population increased by 17.9%, a rate that is 1.6 times greater than overall growth. For comparison, the total U.S. population has increased by only 11.3% since 2000.

The age African-American population in the U.S. is distributed by age as follows (source: Nielsen):

- 0-to-17: 28%
- 18-to-34: 25%
- 35-to-44: 14%
- 45-to-64: 24%
- 65 and older: 9%

A majority of African Americans (55%) reside in the South; 72% live in the central areas of cities. A quarter (25%) of African-American households live in suburban areas.

According to Nielsen, African Americans live in the following housing locales:

- Big city urban: 29.4%
- Metropolitan suburban: 24.9%
- Mid-size cities/satellites: 21.8%
- Small towns and rural: 24.0%

42.3 Buying Power

According to the Census Bureau, the median income of African-American households in 2012 was $33,321; the median for all U.S. households was $51,017.

The Selig Center for Economic Growth at the University of Georgia (www.selig.uga.edu) estimates African-American buying power as follows:

		Pct. of Consumer Spending
1990:	$ 318 billion	7.4%
2000:	$ 590 billion	8.2%
2009:	$ 910 billion	8.5%
2014:	$1.14 trillion	8.7%
2015:	$1.20 trillion	8.8%

African-Americans controlled more disposable personal income than any other U.S. minority group until 2006, when it was equaled by Hispanic-American buying power in the United States. Hispanics actually surpassed blacks as the nation's largest minority group seven years before, based on population counts. But in terms of spending power, 2007 marked the first year that Hispanics' buying power led that of blacks.

The following are the largest African-American consumer markets:

- New York: $91 billion
- Texas: $72 billion
- Georgia: $66 billion
- California: $64 billion
- Florida: $63 billion
- Maryland: $57 billion
- Illinois: $46 billion
- North Carolina: $44 billion
- Virginia: $42 billion
- New Jersey: $36 billion

This ranking is largely based on overall populations, not on ethnic concentration. Only Maryland, North Carolina, and Virginia do not rank among the top ten markets for all consumers.

The largest percentage of buying power marketshare is as follows:

- District of Columbia: 29%
- Mississippi: 24%
- Maryland: 22%

- Georgia: 21%
- Louisiana: 20%
- South Carolina: 18%
- Alabama: 18%
- Delaware: 15%
- North Carolina: 14%
- Virginia: 13%

According to the Selig Center, African Americans spend more than non-black households on electricity, phone services, children's clothing, and footwear. They also spend a significantly higher proportion on groceries, housing, natural gas, women's and girls clothing, and gasoline. Blacks and non-blacks spend about the same proportion for housekeeping supplies, furniture, floor coverings, appliances, men's and boys' clothing, medical supplies, TVs, reading materials, education, tobacco products, and life insurance. Compared to non-blacks, blacks spend much less of their money on eating out, alcoholic beverages, household operations, vehicle purchases, health care, entertainment, and pensions.

Among affluent ethnic individuals – those with an annual income of at least $75,000 and households with an annual income of $150,000 or greater – African-Americans control $87.3 billion in purchasing power, according to *Black Is The New Green: Marketing To Affluent African Americans* (2010, MacMillan).

There are 2.4 billion African-American households in the U.S. with an annual income of $75,000 or higher. These households are more likely than other affluent consumers to spend money on fashionable dress, toiletries and cosmetics, and cruise vacations.

42.4 Population Centers

According to the 2010 Census, the following metropolitan areas have the highest African-American population:

- New York, NY: 3.36 million
- Atlanta, GA: 1.71 million
- Chicago, IL: 1.65 million
- Washington, DC: 1.44 million
- Philadelphia, PA: 1.24 million
- Miami, FL: 1.17 million
- Houston/Galveston, TX: 1.03 million
- Detroit, MI: 980,451
- Dallas/Ft. Worth, TX: 961,871
- Los Angeles, CA: 907,618
- Baltimore, MD: 778,879
- Memphis, TN: 601,043
- Virginia Beach, VA: 522,409
- St. Louis, MO: 516,446

- Charlotte, NC: 421,105
- Cleveland, OH: 416,528
- New Orleans, LA: 397,095
- Richmond, VA: 375,427
- San Francisco, CA: 363,905
- Orlando, FL: 344,820
- Boston, MA: 331,292
- Tampa, FL: 329,334
- Riverside, CA: 322,405
- Birmingham, AL: 318,373
- Jacksonville, FL: 292,881

42.5 Market Resources

Black Is The New Green: Marketing To Affluent African Americans, Macmillan, 2010. (http://us.macmillan.com/blackisthenewgreen)

The African-American Consumer: Resilient, Receptive, and Relevant - 2013 Report, Nielsen. (www.nielsen.com/us/en/reports/2013/resilient--receptive-and-relevant.html)

The Multicultural Economy, The Selig Center for Economic Growth at the University of Georgia, October 2013. (www.terry.uga.edu/selig/buying_power.html)

The State of the News Media: African-American, Pew Project for Excellence in Journalism. (www.stateofthemedia.org/2011/ethnic_african_american.php)

43

ARAB-AMERICAN CONSUMERS

43.1 Overview

Arab Americans constitute an ethnicity made up of several waves of immigrants from the Arabic-speaking countries of southwestern Asia and North Africa that have settled in the United States since the 1880s. Their Arab heritage reflects a culture that is thousands of years old and includes 23 Arab countries as diverse as Egypt, Lebanon, Morocco, Yemen, Tunisia, and Palestine.

The U.S. Census Bureau (www.census.gov) considers anyone who reported being Algerian, Bahraini, Egyptian, Emirati, Iraqi, Jordanian, Kuwaiti, Lebanese, Libyan, Moroccan, Omani, Palestinian, Qatari, Saudi Arabian, Syrian, Tunisian, and Yemeni to be of Arab ancestry.

While the majority of the population of the Arab World is composed of people of the Muslim faith, 63% of Arab Americans are Christian. Twenty-four percent (24%) of Arab-Americans are Muslim; 13% are of other faiths or claim no affiliation.

According to the Arab American Institute (www.aaiusa.org), 89% of Arab Americans over 25 have obtained at least a high school diploma. More than 45% have a bachelor's degree or higher, compared to 28% of Americans at large, and 18% of Arab Americans have a post-graduate degree, which is nearly twice the average (10%) of non-Arab Americans.

Similar to the national average, about 60% of Arab American adults are in the labor force; with 5% unemployed. Seventy-three percent (73%) percent of working Arab Americans are employed in managerial, professional, sales, or administrative fields. Twelve percent (12%) are government employees.

43.2 Profile

Census 2010 reported 1.52 million Arab Americans, a 27% increase from Census 2000. Between 1990 and 2000, the Arab-American population grew 38%, according to the Census Bureau.

By Arab ancestry, Census 2010 reported populations and number of households as follows:

	Population	Households
• Lebanese:	485,917	181,127
• Egyptian:	179,853	60,137
• Syrian:	147,426	56,040

• Palestinian:	83,241	25,679
• Moroccan:	74,908	23,365
• Iraqi:	73,896	22,979
• Jordanian:	60,056	18,134
• Yemeni:	29,358	6,812

In 2012, Zogby Poll International (www.zogby.com) reported that there are 3.5 million Americans of ancestry belonging to one of the 23 United Nations member countries of the Arab World, although they don't necessarily self-report as Arabs.

43.3 Buying Power

In May 2013, the Census Bureau reported the median household income for Arab households in 2010 at $56,433, about $4,500 higher than the median household income of $52,029 for all households in the United States. Lebanese households had the highest median income ($67,264), while Iraqi and Yemeni households had lower median incomes ($32,075 and $34,667).

43.4 Population Centers

The following states have the highest Arab-American populations:

- California: 272,485
- Michigan: 191,607
- New York: 149,627
- Florida: 100,627
- Texas: 91,568
- New Jersey: 85,956
- Illinois: 85,465
- Ohio: 65,813
- Massachusetts: 65,150
- Pennsylvania: 60,870

Ninety-four percent (94%) of Arab Americans live in metropolitan areas. Los Angeles, Detroit, New York City, Chicago, and Washington, DC, are the top five metropolitan areas of Arab-American concentration.

Among cities with 100,000 or more in population, the following have the highest percentages of Arabs:

- Sterling Heights, MI: 3.69%
- Jersey City, NJ: 2.81%
- Warren, MI: 2.51%
- Allentown, PA: 2.45%
- Burbank, CA: 2.39%
- Glendale, CA: 2.07%

- Livonia, MI: 1.94%
- Arlington, VA: 1.77%
- Paterson, NJ: 1.77%
- Daly City, CA: 1.69%

The 2010 Census reported an Arab-American population of 5.0% in Bayonne, New Jersey, a city of 63,000.

43.5 Market Resources

Arab American Institute, 1600 K Street NW, Suite 601, Washington, DC 20006. (202) 429-9210. (www.aaiusa.org)

Arab Households in the United States: 2006-2010, American Community Survey Briefs, U.S. Census Bureau, May 2013. (www.census.gov/prod/2013pubs/acsbr10-20.pdf)

Arab-American Media, Pew Research Journalism Project, November 2012. (www.journalism.org/2012/11/28/arabamerican-media/)

44

ASIAN-AMERICAN CONSUMERS

44.1 Overview

The U.S. Census Bureau (www.census.gov) refers to Asian-Americans as a person having ancestry from any of the original peoples of the Far East, Southeast Asia, or the Indian subcontinent. This includes people who indicate their race(s) as "Asian" or report entries such as 'Chinese', 'Filipino', 'Indian', 'Vietnamese', 'Korean', 'Japanese', and 'Other Asian.'

44.2 Profile

Census 2010 counted 14.7 million people, or 4.8% of the total U.S. population, of Asian-only ancestry. An additional 2.6 million people reported their ethnicity as Asian as well as one or more other race. Combined, 17.3 million Asian-Americans were counted, representing 5.6% of the population.

The relative youth and affluence of the Asian-American community is attractive to marketers. With a median age of 32, the Asian-American population is five years younger than the overall U.S. median age.

The Asian population includes many groups, who differ in language, culture, and length of residence in the United States. Some of the Asian groups, such as the Chinese and Japanese, have been in the U.S. for several generations. Other groups, such as the Hmong, Vietnamese, Laotians, and Cambodians, are comparatively recent immigrants. The following were the largest Asian groups counted in the U.S. census (including those with one or more other race):

- Chinese: 4.0 million
- Asian Indian: 3.8 million
- Filipino: 3.4 million
- Vietnamese: 1.7 million
- Korean: 1.7 million
- Japanese: 1.3 million
- Pakistani: 409,000
- Cambodian: 277,000
- Hmong: 260,000
- Thai: 238,000
- Laotian: 232,000
- Bangladeshi: 147,000

The Asian population in the U.S. is distributed by age as follows (source: U.S. Census Bureau):

- Under 15 years: 19.2%
- Under 21 years: 27.0%
- Over 21 years: 73.0%
- 55 years and over: 17.6%
- 65 years and over: 8.9%

44.3 Buying Power

According to the Census Bureau, the median income of Asian-American households in 2012 was $68,636; the median for all U.S. households was $51,017. Median household income differs greatly by Asian group. For Asian Indians, for example, the median income in 2011 was $92,418; for Bangladeshi, it was $45,185.

The Selig Center for Economic Growth at the University of Georgia (www.selig.uga.edu) estimates Asian-American buying power as follows:

		Pct. of Consumer Spending
• 1990:	$116 billion	2.7%
• 2000:	$269 billion	3.7%
• 2009:	$509 billion	4.7%
• 2014:	$696 billion	5.3%
• 2015:	$775 billion	5.6%

The following are the largest Asian-American consumer markets:

- California: $172 billion
- New York: $ 54 billion
- Texas: $ 34 billion
- New Jersey: $ 34 billion
- Illinois: $ 24 billion
- Hawaii: $ 23 billion
- Washington: $ 18 billion
- Florida: $ 17 billion
- Virginia: $ 17 billion
- Massachusetts: $ 14 billion

Compared to the overall consumer market, Asian-American spending is much more focused geographically. The five and the ten states with the largest Asian consumer markets account for 59% and 75% of Asian buying power, respectively. By contrast, the five and the ten largest total consumer markets account for 39% and 56% of U.S. buying power, respectively.

The ten states with the largest shares of total Asian buying power are as follows:

- Hawaii: 46.5%
- California: 11.8%

- New Jersey: 8.3%
- Washington: 6.6%
- Nevada: 6.5%
- New York: 6.4%
- Maryland: 5.1%
- Virginia: 5.1%
- Illinois: 4.8%
- Massachusetts: 4.5%

According to the Selig Center, Asian-American households spend nearly 22% more than the average U.S. household on homes, furniture, clothing, footwear, vehicle purchases, public transportation, education, cash contributions, and pensions and Social Security. They also spend more on food (groceries and dining out) and insurance. Asian households spend less than average on utilities, healthcare, tobacco products, entertainment, floor coverings, major appliances, personal care products and services, housekeeping supplies, and alcoholic beverages.

According to *Asian-American Market in the U.S.*, a report from Packaged Facts (www.packagedfacts.com), Asian-American households represent 40% of all multicultural households with income between $150,000 and $200,000 and account for nearly half of those with income of $200,000 or more. Asian-American households are more affluent than any other population group in the country, including non-Hispanic whites.

The *American Community Survey* reported that 61% of Asians are homeowners, compared to 67% for the total population. According to a June 2013 report by International Demographics (www.themediaaudit.com), the average home value for the Asian-American population is $460,373, a figure that is nearly 50% higher when compared to the general U.S. population.

International Demographics reports that more than one in five luxury car owners of BMW, Mercedes, Lexus, Infinity, Jaguar, or Porsche brands are Asian. The figure compares to 9.4% for all U.S. consumers who own a luxury car.

The poverty rate for the Asian-alone population in 2011 was 12.8%. For the nation as a whole, the poverty rate was 15.9%.

44.4 Population Centers

The following are the states with the highest Asian populations (including those of mixed race) and the percentages of the total population within these areas:

	Population	Percentage
• California:	4.15 million	10.9%
• New York:	1.17 million	6.2%
• Hawaii:	703,000	58.0%
• Texas:	644,000	3.1%
• New Jersey:	524,000	6.2%
• Illinois:	474,000	3.8%

• Washington:	396,000	6.7%
• Florida:	333,000	2.1%
• Virginia:	305,000	4.3%
• Massachusetts:	265,000	4.2%

The following are the cities with the highest Asian populations (including those of mixed race) and the percentages of the total population within these states:

	Population	Percentage
• New York, NY:	873,000	10.9%
• Los Angeles, CA:	407,000	11.0%
• San Jose, CA:	258,000	28.8%
• San Francisco, CA:	253,000	32.6%
• Honolulu, HI:	252,000	67.7%
• San Diego, CA:	189,000	15.5%
• Chicago, IL:	141,000	4.9%
• Houston, TX:	114,000	5.8%
• Seattle, WA:	85,000	15.0%
• Fremont, CA:	81,000	39.8%

The following cities have the highest concentration of Asian-Americans:

• Honolulu, HI:	67.7%
• Daly City, CA:	53.6%
• Fremont, CA:	39.8%
• Sunnyvale, CA:	34.2%
• San Francisco, CA:	32.6%
• Irvine, CA:	32.3%
• Garden Grove, CA:	32.2%
• Santa Clara, CA:	31.4%
• Torrance, CA:	31.1%
• San Jose, CA:	28.8%

The following counties have the most Asian-American-owned businesses:

• Los Angeles, CA:	140,411
• Queens, NY:	48,241
• Orange, CA:	46,015
• Honolulu, HI:	35,376
• Santa Clara, CA:	30,007
• New York, NY:	29,020
• Cook, IL:	27,779
• Kings, NY:	25,989
• Harris, TX:	24,922
• Alameda, CA:	24,908

44.5 Market Resources

Asian-American Studies Center at the University of California, Los Angeles. (www.aasc.ucla.edu)

Demographics Of Asian Americans, Pew Research Social & Demographic Trends, April 2013. (www.pewsocialtrends.org/2013/04/04/asian-groups-in-the-u-s/)

Facts For Features: Asian/Pacific American Heritage, Census Bureau, March 2013. (www.census.gov/newsroom/releases/archives/facts_for_features_special_editions/cb13-ff09.html)

The Multicultural Economy, The Selig Center for Economic Growth at the University of Georgia, October 2013. (www.terry.uga.edu/selig/buying_power.html)

The Rise of Asian Americans, Pew Research Center, June 2012. (www.pewsocialtrends.org/2012/06/19/the-rise-of-asian-americans)

Asian American State of the Media, Pew Research Journalism Project. (http://stateofthemedia.org/2009/ethnic-intro/asian-american/)

45

HISPANIC- & LATINO-AMERICAN CONSUMERS

45.1 Overview

Hispanic-Americans and Latino-Americans are residents of the United States with origins in the countries of Latin America or the Iberian peninsula.

The terms 'Hispanic-American' and 'Latino-American' are typically used interchangeably. Technically, however, Hispanic is a narrower term which mostly refers to persons of Spanish-speaking origin or ancestry. Latino is more frequently used to refer more generally to anyone of Latin American origin or ancestry, including Brazilians.

Hispanic-/Latino-Americans are very racially diverse and as a result form an ethnic category, rather than a race.

45.2 Profile

According to Census 2010, 308.7 million people resided in the United States in April 2010, of which 50.5 million (or 16%) were of Hispanic or Latino origin. The Hispanic population increased from 35.3 million in 2000, when this group made up 13% of the total population. The Hispanic population increased 43.0% between Census 2000 and Census 2010, while the non-Hispanic population increased 4.9% during that period.

According to a September 2012 report by the Pew Research Hispanic Trends Project (www.pewhispanic.org), Hispanic-Americans are distributed by nationality as follows:

	Population	Pct. of Total
• Mexican:	33.54 million	64.6%
• Puerto Rican:	4.92 million	9.5%
• Salvadoran:	1.95 million	3.8%
• Cuban:	1.89 million	3.6%
• Dominican:	1.53 million	2.9%
• Guatemalan:	1.22 million	2.3%
• Columbian:	989,000	1.9%
• Spaniard:	707,000	1.4%
• Honduran:	702,000	1.4%
• Equadorian:	645,000	1.2%
• Peruvian:	556,000	1.1%
• Nicaraguan:	395,000	0.8%

- Venezuelan: 259,000 0.5%
- Argentinean: 242,000 0.5%

The Census Bureau projects that by 2050 there will be 102.6 million Hispanics living in the U.S., constituting 24% of the population.

45.3 Buying Power

According to the Census Bureau, the median income of Hispanic-American households in 2012 was $39,005; the median for all U.S. households was $51,017.

The Selig Center for Economic Growth at the University of Georgia (www.selig.uga.edu) estimates Hispanic-American buying power and percentage of total U.S. consumer spending as follows:

	Buying Power	Pct. of Spending
• 1990:	$ 212 billion	5.0%
• 2000:	$ 489 billion	6.8%
• 2009:	$ 978 billion	9.1%
• 2014:	$1.33 trillion	10.2%
• 2015:	$1.50 trillion	11.0%

The following are the largest Hispanic consumer markets:

- California: $265 billion
- Texas: $176 billion
- Florida: $107 billion
- New York: $ 81 billion
- Illinois: $ 44 billion
- New Jersey: $ 39 billion
- Arizona: $ 34 billion
- Colorado: $ 22 billion
- New Mexico: $ 20 billion
- Georgia: $ 17 billion

Hispanics and their buying power are much more geographically concentrated than non-Hispanics. California alone accounts for 26% of Hispanic buying power. The five states and the ten states with the largest Hispanic markets account for 66% and 80% of Hispanic buying power, respectively. In contrast, the five states with the largest non-Hispanic markets account for only 39% of total buying power, and the ten largest non-Hispanic markets account for only 54% of total buying power.

The ten states with the largest share of Hispanic buying power are as follows:

- New Mexico: 30.9%
- Texas: 20.4%
- California: 18.4%
- Arizona: 16.2%
- Florida: 15.8%

- Nevada: 15.3%
- Colorado: 11.5%
- New York: 9.6%
- New Jersey: 9.6%
- Illinois: 8.9%

Because of differences in per capita income, wealth, demographics, and culture, the spending habits of Hispanics as a group are not the same as those of the average U.S. consumer. Among Hispanics, income levels are, on average, lower than the general population.

The most recent *Consumer Expenditure Survey* indicates that Hispanic households spend in only about 82% as much as the average non-Hispanic household. Hispanic households spend more on telephone services, men's and boys' clothing, children's clothing, and footwear. Also, Hispanics spend a higher proportion of their money on food (groceries and restaurants), housing, utilities, and transportation. Hispanics spend about the same as non-Hispanics on housekeeping supplies, furniture, appliances, women's and girls clothing, and personal care products and services. Compared to non-Hispanics, they spend substantially less on alcoholic beverages, healthcare, entertainment, reading materials, education, tobacco products, cash contributions, and personal insurance and pensions.

45.4 Population Centers

Census 2010 reported Hispanic or Latino populations by state, percentages of total state populations, and population changes from Census 2000 as follows:

	Population	Pct.	Change
• Alabama:	185,000	3.9%	144.8%
• Alaska:	39,000	5.5%	51.8%
• Arizona:	1.89 million	29.6%	46.3%
• Arkansas:	186,000	6.4%	114.2%
• California:	14.01 million	37.6%	27.8%
• Colorado:	1.04 million	20.7%	41.2%
• Connecticut:	479,000	13.4%	41.6%
• Delaware:	73,000	8.2%	96.4%
• District of Columbia:	54,000	9.1%	21.8%
• Florida:	4.22 million	22.5%	57.4%
• Georgia:	854,000	8.8%	96.1%
• Hawaii:	120,000	8.9%	37.8%
• Idaho:	176,000	11.2%	73.0%
• Illinois:	2.03 million	15.8%	32.5%
• Indiana:	390,000	6.0%	81.7%
• Iowa:	151,000	5.0%	83.7%
• Kansas:	300,000	10.5%	59.4%
• Kentucky:	132,000	3.1%	121.6%

• Louisiana:	193,000	4.2%	78.7%
• Maine:	17,000	1.3%	80.9%
• Maryland:	471,000	8.2%	106.5%
• Massachusetts:	628,000	9.6%	46.4%
• Michigan:	436,000	4.4%	34.7%
• Minnesota:	250,000	4.7%	74.5%
• Mississippi:	81,000	2.7%	105.9%
• Missouri:	212,000	3.5%	79.2%
• Montana:	28,000	2.9%	58.0%
• Nebraska:	167,000	9.2%	77.3%
• Nevada:	716,000	26.5%	81.9%
• New Hampshire:	36,000	2.8%	79.1%
• New Jersey:	1.56 million	17.7%	39.2%
• New Mexico:	953,000	46.3%	24.6%
• New York:	3.42 million	17.6%	19.2%
• North Carolina:	800,000	8.4%	111.1%
• North Dakota:	13,000	2.0%	73.0%
• Ohio:	355,000	3.1%	63.4%
• Oklahoma:	332,000	8.9%	85.2%
• Oregon:	450,000	11.7%	63.5%
• Pennsylvania:	719,000	5.7%	82.6%
• Rhode Island:	131,000	12.4%	43.9%
• South Carolina:	236,000	5.1%	147.9%
• South Dakota:	22,000	2.7%	102.9%
• Tennessee:	290,000	4.6%	134.2%
• Texas:	9.46 million	37.6%	41.8%
• Utah:	358,000	13.0%	77.8%
• Vermont:	9,000	1.5%	67.3%
• Virginia:	632,000	7.9%	91.7%
• Washington:	756,000	11.2%	71.2%
• West Virginia:	22,000	1.2%	81.4%
• Wisconsin:	336,000	5.9%	74.2%
• Wyoming:	50,000	8.9%	58.6%

According to a September 2012 report by the Pew Research Hispanic Trends Project, the largest metropolitan areas by Hispanic or Latino population are as follows:

	Hispanic Population	**Pct. of Total**
1. Los Angeles-Long Beach, CA:	5,724,000	44.5%
2. New York-Northeastern NJ:	4,243,000	23.9%
3. Houston-Brazoria, TX:	2,044,000	36.3%
4. Riverside-San Bernardino,CA:	2,012,000	47.4%
5. Chicago, IL:	1,934,000	21.1%
6. Dallas-Fort Worth, TX:	1,746,000	27.9%
7. Miami-Hialeah, FL:	1,610,000	65.7%

8.	Phoenix, AZ:	1,136,000	29.7%
9.	San Antonio, TX:	1,090,000	55.5%
10.	San Francisco-Oakland-Vallejo, CA:	1,088,000	22.2%
11.	San Diego, CA:	1,000,000	32.2%
12.	Washington, DC/MD/VA:	774,000	14.0%
13.	McAllen-Edinburg-Pharr-Mission, TX:	707,000	90.7%
14.	El Paso, TX:	662,000	82.3%
15.	Denver-Boulder, CO:	596,000	23.1%
16.	Las Vegas, NV:	571,000	29.2%
17.	Fresno, CA:	552,000	50.9%
18.	Orlando, FL:	543,000	25.4%
19.	Atlanta, GA:	530,000	10.8%
20.	Austin, TX:	502,000	31.0%
21.	San Jose, CA:	482,000	27.0%
22.	Tampa-St. Petersburg-Clearwater, FL:	456,000	16.4%
23.	Fort Lauderdale-Hollywood-Pompano Beach, FL:	442,000	25.2%
24.	Philadelphia, PA/NJ/NJ:	420,000	7.9%
25.	Bakersfield, CA:	416,000	49.4%
26.	Albuquerque, NM:	411,000	47.0%
27.	Boston, MA-NH:	403,000	9.9%
28.	Sacramento, CA:	375,000	19.2%
29.	Brownsville-Harlingen-San Benito, TX:	359,000	88.1%
30.	Tucson, AZ:	341,000	34.7%
31.	Ventura-Oxnard-Simi Valley, CA:	333,712	40.4%
32.	Visalia-Tulare-Porterville, CA:	269,611	60.8%
33.	Stockton, CA:	268,103	39.0%
34.	West Palm Beach-Boca Raton-Delray Beach, FL:	253,108	19.1%
35.	Salt Lake City-Ogden, UT:	242,681	15.4%
36.	Laredo, TX:	240,864	95.7%
37.	Seattle-Everett, WA:	238,560	9.0%
38.	Portland, OR-WA:	226,356	10.9%
39.	Modesto, CA:	216,473	42.0%
40.	Charlotte-Gastonia-Rock Hill, NC-SC:	189,279	9.7%
41.	Santa Barbara-Santa Maria-Lompoc, CA:	182,941	43.1%
42.	Minneapolis-St. Paul, MN:	175,426	5.6%
43.	Raleigh-Durham, NC:	171,551	10.7%
44.	Detroit, MI:	167,569	3.9%
45.	Kansas City, MO-KS:	161,062	8.6%
46.	Corpus Christi, TX:	157,275	54.1%
47.	Milwaukee, WI:	147,510	9.5%
48.	Merced, CA:	141,097	55.1%
49.	Salinas-Sea Side-Monterey, CA:	139,394	51.5%
50.	Las Cruces, NM:	138,829	65.9%
51.	Providence-Fall River-Pawtucket, MA/RI:	134,815	13.0%

52.	Oklahoma City, OK:	130,397	12.8%
53.	Hartford-Bristol-Middleton-New Britain, CT:	127,897	17.3%
54.	Greensboro-Winston Salem-High Point, NC:	126,593	8.9%
55.	Odessa, TX:	124,633	45.5%
56.	Baltimore, MD:	123,029	4.6%
57.	Santa Rosa-Petaluma, CA:	121,330	25.0%
58.	Yuma, AZ:	117,471	59.8%
59.	Fort Myers-Cape Coral, FL:	113,839	18.4%
60.	Indianapolis, IN:	112,857	6.1%

Census 2010 reported the places with the highest percentage of Hispanics or Latinos as follows:

- East Los Angeles, CA: 97.1%
- Laredo, TX: 95.6%
- Hialeah, FL: 94.7%
- Brownsville, TX: 93.2%
- McAllen, TX: 84.6%
- El Paso, TX: 80.7%
- Santa Ana, CA: 78.2%
- Salinas, CA: 75.0%
- Oxnard, CA: 73.5%
- Downey, CA: 70.7%

45.5 Market Resources

Characteristics Of The 60 Largest Metropolitan Areas By Hispanic Population, Pew Research Hispanic Trends Project, September 2012. (www.pewhispanic.org/2012/09/19/characteristics-of-the-60-largest-metropolitan-areas-by-hispanic-population/)

Diverse Origins: The Nation's 14 Largest Hispanic Origins Groups, Pew Research Hispanic Trends Project, June 2013. (www.pewhispanic.org/files/2013/06/summary_report_final.pdf)

Hispanic Fact Pack - 2013 Edition, *Advertising Age*, July 2013. (http://adage.com/trend-reports/report.php?id=78)

Pew Research Hispanic Trends Project. (www.pewhispanic.org)

State Of The Hispanic Consumer, Nielsen, April 2012. (http://nielsen.com/content/dam/corporate/us/en/reports-downloads/2012-Reports/State-of-the-Hispanic-Consumer.pdf)

The Multicultural Economy, The Selig Center for Economic Growth at the University of Georgia, October 2013. (www.terry.uga.edu/selig/buying_power.html)

The State of the News Media: Hispanic, Pew Project for Excellence in Journalism. (www.stateofthemedia.org/2011/ethnic_hispanic.php)

Upscale Latinos: America's New Baby Boomers, Nielsen, June 2013. (www.nielsen.com/us/en/newswire/2013/upscale-latinos--americas-new-baby-boomers.html)

46

JEWISH-AMERICAN CONSUMERS

46.1 Overview

Jewish-Americans, also called American Jews, include both those of Jewish faith and people of Jewish ethnicity.

The American-Jewish population is composed predominantly of Ashkenazi Jews and their U.S.-born descendants, comprising about 90% of the American Jewish population.

"Secularism has a long tradition in Jewish life in America, and most U.S. Jews seem to recognize this: 62% say being Jewish is mainly a matter of ancestry and culture, while just 15% say it is mainly a matter of religion. Even among Jews by religion, more than half (55%) say being Jewish is mainly a matter of ancestry and culture, and two-thirds say it is not necessary to believe in God to be Jewish."

A Portrait Of Jewish Americans
Pew Research, 10/1/13

46.2 Profile

American Jewish Year Book 2013, by Sergio DellaPergola (2013, Springer Publishing) puts the core American Jewish population at 5,425,000.

The community self-identifying as Jewish by birth, irrespective of halakhic (unbroken maternal line of Jewish descent or formal Jewish conversion) status, numbers about 7 million, or 2.5% of the U.S. population.

The nature of Jewish identity is changing in America. According to *A Portrait Of Jewish Americans*, an October 2013 report by the Religion & Public Life Project at the

Pew Research Center (www.pewresearch.org), the percentage of U.S. adults who say they are Jewish when asked about their religion has declined by about half since the late 1950s and currently is a little less than 2%. Meanwhile, the number of Americans with direct Jewish ancestry or upbringing who consider themselves Jewish, yet describe themselves as atheist, agnostic or having no particular religion, appears to be rising and is now about 0.5% of the U.S. adult population. Twenty-two percent (22%) of American Jews now describe themselves as having no religion.

The changing nature of Jewish identity stands out sharply among generations. Among Senior Jewish-Americans, 93% identify as Jewish on the basis of religion; only 7% describe themselves as having no religion. Among Millennial Jewish-Americans, 68% identify as Jews by religion, while 32% describe themselves as having no religion as well as identify as Jewish on the basis of ancestry, ethnicity or culture.

Within the community, intermarriage rates seem to have risen substantially. Among Jewish-Americans who have gotten married since 2000, 58% have a non-Jewish spouse. Among those who got married in the 1980s, that figure was 42%.

Despite the changes in Jewish identity, 94% of American Jews say they are proud to be Jewish.

46.3 Buying Power

According to the Pew Project on Religion and Public Life, 25% of Jewish-Americans report household incomes of over $150,000, compared to 8% of all U.S. households. The higher incomes are, in part, because Jewish-Americans are generally better educated. While 27% of Americans have had college or postgraduate education, 59% of American Jews and 66% of Reform Jews have. Twenty-five percent (25%) of American Jews hold a graduate degree, compared with 6% of the general American population who do so.

46.4 Population Centers

According to the Glenmary Research Center (www.glenmary.org), the following are the metropolitan areas with the highest Jewish populations:

- New York, NY: 3,750,000
- Miami, FL: 535,000
- Los Angeles, CA: 490,000
- Philadelphia, PA: 285,000
- Chicago, IL: 265,000
- San Francisco, CA: 210,000
- Boston, MA: 208,000
- Washington, DC-Baltimore, MD: 165,000

The counties with the largest Jewish population are as follows (Jewish as a percentage of total population also given):

	Total	Percentage
• Los Angeles County, CA:	564,700	5.9%
• Kings County, NY:	379,000	15.4%
• New York County, NY:	314,500	20.5%
• Queens County, NY:	238,000	10.7%
• Cook County, IL:	234,400	4.4%
• Broward County, FL:	213,000	13.1%
• Nassau County, NY:	207,000	15.5%
• Palm Beach County, FL:	167,000	14.8%
• Miami-Dade County, FL:	124,000	5.5%
• Middlesex County, MA:	113,700	7.8%
• Suffolk County, NY:	100,000	7.0%
• Baltimore/Baltimore County, MD:	94,500	7.7%
• Westchester County, NY:	94,000	10.2%
• Rockland County, NY:	90,000	31.4%
• Philadelphia County, PA:	86,600	5.7%
• Montgomery County, MD:	83,800	9.1%
• Bergen County, NJ:	83,700	9.5%
• Bronx County, NY:	83,700	6.3%
• Cuyahoga County, OH:	79,000	5.7%
• Oakland County, MI:	77,200	6.5%
• Essex County, NJ:	76,200	9.6%
• Clark County, NV:	75,000	5.5%
• San Diego County, CA:	70,000	2.5%
• Fulton County, GA:	65,900	8.1%
• Monmouth County, NJ:	65,000	10.6%
• Montgomery County, PA:	59,550	7.9%
• Santa Clara County, CA:	54,000	3.2%
• San Francisco County, CA:	49,500	6.4%
• St. Louis County, MO:	47,100	4.6%
• Middlesex County, NJ:	45,000	6.0%
• Norfolk County, MA:	38,300	5.9%
• Denver County, CO:	38,100	6.6%
• Camden County, NJ:	38,000	7.1%
• Bucks County, PA:	34,800	5.8%
• Allegheny County, PA:	34,600	2.7%
• Richmond County, NY:	33,700	7.6%
• Morris County, NJ:	33,500	7.1%
• Alameda County, CA:	32,500	2.3%
• Hennepin County, MN:	31,600	2.8%
• Union County, NJ:	30,100	5.8%
• Hartford County, CT:	30,000	3.5%
• New Haven County, CT:	28,900	3.5%

46.5 Market Resources

A Portrait Of Jewish Americans, Pew Research Religion & Public Life Project, October 2013. (www.pewforum.org/2013/10/01/jewish-american-beliefs-attitudes-culture-survey/)

American Jewish Year Book 2013, Springer Publishing, 2013. (www.springer.com/social+sciences/population+studies/book/978-3-319-01657-3)

The Jewish Center, 131 West 86th Street, New York, NY 10024. (212) 724-2700. (www.jewishcenter.org)

47

MUSLIM-AMERICAN CONSUMERS

47.1 Overview

Because the United States does not track population by religion in its Census, there is no recognized source of data on the U.S. Muslim population.

According to the Gallup Organization (www.gallup.com), American Muslims are one of the most racially diverse religious groups in the United States.

Twenty-four percent (24%) of Arab-Americans are Muslim. Census 2010 reported 1.52 million Arab Americans.

Native-born American Muslims are mainly African Americans who make up about a quarter of the total Muslim population. Many have converted to Islam during the last seventy years.

47.2 Profile

Self-Described Religious Identification of Adult Population, published by the Census Bureau in 2012, listed 2.6 million Americans of Muslim faith in 2008 (most recent data available).

A 2011 assessment by Pew Research Center (www.pewresearch.org) placed the number at 2.8 million.

According to the study *Muslim Americans: Middle Class and Mostly Mainstream*, by Pew Research Center, of all Muslim-Americans, 65% are foreign-born, with about 34% of Pakistani or South Asian origin and 26% of Arab origin. Of U.S.-born Muslims, 25% are African-American. Of all U.S.-born Muslims, 21% converted to Islam, 14% were raised Muslim.

The percentage of foreign-born U.S. Muslims by country of origin is as follows:

- Iran: 12%
- Pakistan: 12%
- India: 7%
- Lebanon: 6%
- Bangladesh: 5%
- Afghanistan: 4%
- Bosnia & Herzegovina: 4%
- Iraq: 4%
- Jordan: 3%
- Palestinian territories: 3%

- Morocco: 3%
- Africa (unspecified): 2%
- Egypt: 2%
- Israel: 2%
- Saudi Arabia: 2%
- Somalia: 2%
- Sudan: 2%
- Other: 19%

The makeup of the Muslim-American population is as follows:

Gender
- Male: 54%
- Female: 46%

Age
- 18-to-29: 29%
- 30-to-49: 48%
- 50-to-64: 18%
- 65 and older: 5%

Muslim Americans, a 2011 report by Pew Research Center, provides the following profile of Muslim Americans:

- A majority of Muslim Americans (56%) say that most Muslims who come to the U.S. want to adopt American customs and ways of life; just 20% say that Muslims in this country want to be distinct from the larger American society.

> **"When it comes to many aspects of American life, Muslim Americans look similar to the rest of the public. Comparable percentages say they watch entertainment television, follow professional or college sports, recycle household materials, and play video games."**
>
> Pew Research Center

- U.S. Muslims are about as likely as other Americans to report household incomes of $100,000 or more (14% of Muslims, compared with 16% of all adults).

- Overall, 46% say they are in excellent or good shape financially; among the general public, 38% say this.
- Muslim Americans are as likely as the public overall to have graduated from college (26% of Muslims vs. 28% among the general public).
- Because as a group Muslim Americans are younger than the general public, twice as many report being currently enrolled in a college or university class (26% vs. 13%). Similar numbers of Muslim Americans and members of the general public report being self-employed or owning a small business (20% for Muslim Americans, 17% for the general public).

47.3 Buying Power

The buying power of Muslim-Americans is more than $170 billion a year, according to JWT (www.jwt.com).

47.4 Population Centers

According to Pew Research Center, the following are the most populous U.S. regions with Muslim-Americans residents:

- South: 32%
- Northeast: 29%
- Midwest: 22%
- West: 18%

About half of the Arab-American population live in five states: California, New York, Michigan, Florida, and New Jersey.

Detroit, Michigan, has the largest percentage of Arab-Americans in its population. Other communities with significant Arab-American populations include Paterson, New Jersey; Clifton, New Jersey; Brooklyn, New York; and Glendale, California.

According to the *2010 U.S. Religious Census*, by the Association of Statisticians of American Religious Bodies (www.asarb.org), the counties with the largest Muslim populations are as follows:

- Cook (Illinois): 201,152
- Harris (Texas): 117,148
- Kings (New York): 95,126
- Dallas (Texas): 84,256
- Queens (New York): 81,456
- Los Angeles (California): 69,080
- Warren (Michigan): 67,775
- DuPage (Illinois): 59,821
- Fairfax (Virginia): 50,108
- New York (New York): 42,545

47.5 Market Resources

American Muslim Consumer Conference. (www.americanmuslimconsumer.com)

Muslim American Outreach, Allied Media Corporation. (www.allied-media.com/muslim_americans/Public_Relations_Muslim_American_Community_Outreach.html)

Muslim Americans, Pew Research Center, August 2011. (http://people-press.org/2011/08/30/muslim-americans-no-signs-of-growth-in-alienation-or-support-for-extremism/)

The Muslim Journal (www.muslimjournal.com)

48

NATIVE-AMERICAN CONSUMERS

48.1 Overview

According to Office of Management and Budget (www.omb.gov), American Indian or Alaska Native refers to a person as having ethnic origin from any of the original peoples of North and South America (including Central America) and who maintains tribal affiliation or community attachment.

Native Americans are the indigenous peoples within the boundaries of the present-day United States, including those in Alaska and Hawaii. They are composed of numerous distinct tribes and ethnic groups, many of which survive as intact political communities. According to interviews conducted by the Census Bureau, most with an expressed preference refer to themselves as 'American Indians' or simply 'Indians'; this term has been adopted by major media and some academic groups, but does not traditionally include Native Hawaiians or certain Alaska Natives, such as Aleut, Yup'ik, or Inuit peoples.

48.2 Profile

Census 2010 counted 2.9 million people, or 0.9% of the total U.S. population, of American-Indian or Alaska-Native-only ancestry. An additional 2.3 million people reported their ethnicity as American Indian or Alaska Native as well as one or more other race. Combined, 5.3 million American Indians or Alaska Natives were counted, representing 1.7% of the population.

The Census Bureau projects the population of American Indians and Alaska Natives, alone or in combination, at 11.2 million, or 2.7% of the total U.S. population.

According to the 2012 American Community Survey, there are 1,122,043 American Indian and Alaska Native family households. Of these, 54.7 percent were married-couple families, including those with children.

The median age of the American Indian and Alaska Native population is 31.0 years; 437,339 are age 65 and over. This compares with a median age of 37.4 for the U.S. population as a whole.

Seventy-eight percent (78%) of single-race American Indians and Alaska Natives 25 and older have at least a high school diploma, GED certificate, or alternative credential; 14% have obtained a bachelor's degree or higher. For the overall U.S. population, these figures are 86% and 29%, respectively.

The Bureau of Indian Affairs (www.bia.gov) recognizes 566 Indian tribes. The

Cherokee is the largest tribe, with 819,000 individuals; it has 284,000 full-blood individuals. The Navajo, with 286,000 full-blood individuals, is the largest tribe if only full-blood individuals are counted; the Navajo are the tribe with the highest proportion of full-blood individuals, 86.3%.

48.3 Buying Power

In 2012, the median household income of single-race American Indian and Alaska Native households was $35,310. This compares with $51,371 for all U.S. households.

The Selig Center for Economic Growth at the University of Georgia (www.selig.uga.edu) estimates Native-American buying power as follows:

	Spending	Pct. of Consumer Spending
• 1990:	$20 billion	0.5%
• 2000:	$39 billion	0.5%
• 2009:	$65 billion	0.6%
• 2014:	$83 billion	0.6%

The Selig Center notes that the growth in Native American buying power is supported by rapid population growth and growth in the number of Native-American-owned businesses.

The following states have the largest marketshare of Native-American buying power:

- California: $9.4 billion
- Oklahoma: $6.5 billion
- Texas: $4.9 billion
- Arizona: $3.9 billion
- New Mexico: $2.6 billion
- Washington: $2.5 billion
- Florida: $2.5 billion
- Alaska: $2.4 billion
- North Carolina: $2.3 billion
- New York: $2.3 billion

The states with the largest Native-American shares of total buying power are as follows:

- Alaska: 8.6%
- Oklahoma: 5.3%
- New Mexico: 4.5%
- Montana: 3.4%
- South Dakota: 3.3%
- North Dakota: 2.7%
- Arizona: 2.0%
- Wyoming: 1.3%

- Nevada: 1.0%
- Washington: 1.0%

In 2012, 29.1% of single-race American Indians and Alaska Natives lived in poverty. For the nation as a whole, the poverty rate was 15.9%.

48.4 Population Centers

By state, Census 2010 reported the proportion of residents citing American Indian or Alaska Native ancestry and total Native-American population as follows:

	Pct.	Population
• California:	1.0%	362,801
• Oklahoma:	8.6%	321,687
• Arizona:	4.6%	296,529
• New Mexico:	9.4%	193,222
• Texas:	0.7%	170,972
• North Carolina:	1.3%	122,110
• New York:	0.6%	106,906
• Alaska:	14.8%	104,871
• Washington:	1.5%	103,869
• South Dakota:	8.8%	71,817
• Florida:	0.4%	71,458
• Montana:	6.3%	62,555
• Michigan:	0.6%	62,007
• Minnesota:	1.1%	60,916
• Colorado:	1.1%	56,010
• Wisconsin:	1.0%	54,526
• Oregon:	1.4%	53,203
• Illinois:	0.3%	43,963
• North Dakota:	5.4%	36,591
• Utah:	1.2%	32,927
• Georgia:	0.3%	32,151
• Nevada:	1.2%	32,062
• Louisiana:	0.7%	30,579
• Virginia:	0.4%	29,225
• New Jersey:	0.3%	29,026
• Alabama:	0.6%	28,218
• Kansas:	1.0%	28,150
• Missouri:	0.5%	27,376
• Pennsylvania:	0.2%	26,843
• Ohio:	0.2%	25,292
• Arkansas:	0.8%	22,248
• Idaho:	1.4%	21,441
• Maryland:	0.4%	20,420

- Tennessee: 0.3% 19,994
- South Carolina: 0.4% 19,524
- Massachusetts: 0.3% 18,850
- Indiana: 0.3% 18,462
- Nebraska: 1.2% 18,427
- Mississippi: 0.5% 15,030
- Wyoming: 2.4% 13,336
- Connecticut: 0.3% 11,256
- Iowa: 0.4% 11,084
- Kentucky: 0.2% 10,120
- Maine: 0.6% 8,568
- Rhode Island: 0.6% 6,058
- Delaware: 0.5% 4,181
- Hawaii: 0.3% 4,164
- West Virginia: 0.2% 3,787
- New Hampshire: 0.2% 3,150
- Vermont: 0.4% 2,207
- District of Columbia: 0.3% 2,079

Seventy percent (70%) of Native Americans lived in urban areas 2012, an increase from 45% in 1970. Metropolitan areas with significant Native-American populations include Minneapolis, Denver, Phoenix, Tucson, Chicago, Oklahoma City, Houston, New York City, and Rapid City.

There are 325 federally recognized American Indian reservations 2012. There are 618 American Indian and Alaska Native legal and statistical areas for which the Census Bureau provides statistics. Census 2010 reported that 22% of American Indians and Alaska Natives, alone or in combination, lived in American Indian areas or Alaska Native Village Statistical Areas. These American Indian areas include federal American Indian reservations or off-reservation trust lands, Oklahoma tribal statistical areas, tribal designated statistical areas, state American Indian reservations, and state designated American Indian statistical areas.

48.5 Market Resources

Facts for Features: American Indian and Alaska Native Heritage, U.S. Census Bureau, October 2013.
(www.census.gov/newsroom/releases/archives/facts_for_features_special_editions/cb13-ff26.html)

Indian Americans, Pew Research Social & Demographic Trends, 2013.
(www.pewsocialtrends.org/asianamericans-graphics/indians/)

National Congress of American Indians (www.ncai.org)

Native American State of the News Media, Pew Research Journalism Project. (http://stateofthemedia.org/2010/ethnic-summary-essay/native-american/)

The Multicultural Economy, The Selig Center for Economic Growth at the University of Georgia, October 2013. (www.terry.uga.edu/selig/buying_power.html)

The State of the News Media: Native American, Pew Project for Excellence in Journalism, 2011. (www.stateofthemedia.org/2011/ethnic_native_american.php)

U.S. Department of Interior, Bureau of Indian Affairs (www.bia.gov)

PART VII: GENDER FOCUS

49

FEMALE CONSUMERS

49.1 Profile

According to the Census Bureau (www.census.gov), the U.S. female population in 2012 was an estimated 159.42 million, which represents 50.8% of the population. Distribution by age was as follows:

- Under 18: 36.04 million
- 18-to-64: 99.05 million
- 65 and older: 24.33 million

Census 2010 counted 156.96 million females.

Educational attainment is an important consumer metric because adults with higher education typically have higher incomes and spend more. *Educational Attainment in the United States*, a 2012 report from the U.S. Census Bureau, counted 31.4 million women ages 25 and older with a bachelor's degree or more education, higher than the corresponding number for men (30.0 million). Women have a larger share of high school diplomas as well as associate's, bachelor's, and master's degrees. Fewer women than men have a professional or doctoral degree.

According to *School Enrollment in the United States*, published in October 2013 by the U.S. Census Bureau, 55% of college students are women.

49.2 Working Women

According to the U.S. Bureau of Labor Statistics (www.bls.gov), 59% of adult women work or are actively seeking employment.

Among women who don't work, 27% do not because of family responsibilities; 14% don't because their family doesn't want them to work. Only 6% of men do not work because of either of these reasons.

Women are found to have higher career aspirations than men. According to a 2012 study by the Pew Research Center (www.pewresearch.org), 66% of women ages 18-to-34 say that being successful in a high-paying career or profession is very important in their lives; 59% of men in that age group feel the same way.

Women now hold the majority of professional positions in several occupations, including journalism, law, marketing, and communications. These are, in general, among the highest paying occupations. In 47 of the 50 largest U.S. metro areas, single women in their 20s and without children earn more money than their male peers.

Overall career outlooks appear bright for women. Of the 15.3 million new jobs projected for the next decade, the vast majority will be in fields that currently attract more women than men. Of the 12 job titles projected by the Bureau of Labor Statistics to grow the most through 2018, women dominate ten categories.

According to *Profile America*, from the Census Bureau, women own 29% of all non-farm businesses; women are also equal partners with men in the ownership of another 17% of businesses. Women own 52% of all businesses operating in the healthcare and social assistance sector.

49.3 Mothers

Profile America provides the following profile of mothers:

Overall

- Estimated number of mothers in the United States: 85.4 million
- Percentage of 15-to-44-year-old women who are mothers: 54%
- Percentage of women 40-to-44 who have given birth: 82%
- Total fertility rate, or number of births per woman: 2.0
- Average age of women when they give birth for the first time: 25.1

Moms Who Have Recently Given Birth

- Number of births registered in the United States in 2010 (most recent data available): 4.01 million
- Births to teens ages 15-to-19: 409,840
- Births to mothers ages 45-to-54: 7,934
- Rate of twin births per 1,000 total births: 32.6

Stay-at-Home and Working Mothers

- Number of stay-at-home moms: 5.0 million
- Proportion of married-couple family groups with children under 15 with a stay-at-home mother: 23%
- Proportion of mothers with a recent birth who were in the labor force: 61%

Single Moms

- Number of single mothers living with children younger than 18: 9.9 million

The following are other facts provided by *Profile America*:

- Among the 37.8 million mothers with children younger than 18 living at home, 94% live with their biological children only; 3% live with stepchildren, 2% with adopted children, and less than 1% with foster children.
- Of the four million women ages 15-to-44 who had a birth in the last year, 1.5 million, or 38%, were to women who were not married, who were separated, or married but

with an absent spouse. Of those 1.5 million mothers, 425,000, or 28%, were living with a cohabiting partner.

According to *The U.S. Fertility Forecast*, from Demographic Intelligence (www.demographicintel.com), the total fertility rate in the United States rose from 1.93 children per woman in 2010 to 1.98 children per woman in 2012. The United States registered 3,958,000 births in 2012.

49.4 Working Mothers

Sixty-six percent (66%) of women with children ages 17 or younger are working women. Among those working mothers, 74% work full time and 26% work part time.

According to the Pew Research Center's Social & Demographic Trends Project (www.pewsocialtrends.org), 62% of working mothers would prefer to work part time.

According to Scarborough Research (www.scarborough.com), working mothers comprise the highest percentage of the adult population in the following cities:

- Des Moines, IA: 12%
- Honolulu, HI: 12%
- New Orleans, LA: 12%
- Kansas City, MO: 11%
- San Antonio, TX: 11%

The cities with the lowest percentage of working moms are as follows:

- Pittsburgh, PA: 6%
- Greenville, SC: 7%
- Knoxville, TN: 7%

According to another study by Pew, 40% of all households with children under the age of 18 include mothers who are either the sole or primary source of income for the family. The share was just 11% in 1960.

Of these breadwinner moms, 5.1 million (37%) are married mothers who earn more than their husbands; 8.6 million (63%) are single mothers. In households where women out-earn their spouses, median family income is $80,000 – compared to the national median of $57,100.

49.5 Engaging Moms

With influence over $2.4 trillion in annual household spending, mothers are an important market for brands. Determining the preferences of moms and keeping this cohort engaged is critical for businesses.

A recent study by PunchTab (www.punchtab.com) found that 81% of moms will engage more with a brand when offered some type of reward. The following is an assessment of engagement motivators:

- Moms will engage more with a brand when some type of reward is in place: 81%
- Would sign up for regular mail updates when reward is offered: 59%
- Would share content on Facebook when offered reward: 50%
- Would share personal details and purchase behavior if offered incentive: 41%
- Would be interested in receiving perks associated with elite status (e.g., free shipping or branded merchandise) as reward: 67%
- Would like free products and services from the brand: 83%
- Would be interested in a loyalty program for a parent company: 73%

A study by Babycenter (www.babycenter.com) found that moms are great at engaging other moms, with 59% of moms saying they've responded to a recommendation from other moms on parenting sites.

A survey by Burst Media (www.burstmedia.com) found the following are digital channels where mothers post about products/services:

	18-34	**35-54**	**55+**
• Social network and sharing sites:	69.6%	55.4%	61.6%
• Shopping/retail and e-commerce sites:	56.8%	51.7%	48.2%
• Independent sites and blogs:	36.1%	29.8%	40.1%
• Portals and news sites:	23.3%	10.5%	9.0%
• Other:	22.9%	22.0%	20.5%

49.6 Mobile Moms

Today's moms have integrated mobile devices almost seamlessly into their lives. Referring to their smartphone as their 'backup brain,' most use this technology to stay organized.

According to eMarketer (www.emarketer.com), 87% of moms were smartphone users in 2013, up from 65% in 2012 and 59% in 2011. And moms are pretty attached to these devices.

> **"One third of moms tell us they'd return home for their forgotten smartphone but not for their wallet."**
>
> Mike Fogarty, SVP
> BabyCenter, 9/24/2013

BabyCenter's *Profile of 2013 Mobile Mom* found that from it's previous survey, conducted in 2011, mom's activities have migrated from leisure to productivity. A whopping 81% of moms reported using their smartphone to help manage the day, an increase of 212% since 2011. In 2011, mom's top activities were mostly about personal enjoyment: social media (72%), gaming (72%), weather (69%), listening to music and podcasts (53%), and shopping (42%). Now, her activities are about getting the job done; the following are the top activities by mobile moms:

- Texting: 96%
- Emailing: 91%
- Searching for information: 88%
- Checking the weather: 87%
- Social networking: 86%
- Directions/maps/GPS: 83%
- Productivity (calendar, notes): 81%
- Posting or viewing photos/videos: 79%
- Voice calling: 78%
- Music/podcasts: 69%
- Reading news: 67%
- Parenting social media: 64%
- Shopping: 63%
- Banking/finance: 60%
- Watching online videos: 58%
- Gaming: 53%
- Children's apps: 52%
- Health information/advice: 51%
- Reading blogs: 42%
- Planning travel: 28%
- Reading books: 27%
- Business: 25%
- Sports: 14%

49.7 Social Moms

According to BabyCenter's *2013 Social Mom Report*, moms are 20% more likely to use social media than the general population. Ninety-one percent (91%) of moms now use social media regularly, a 20% increase since 2010. And they expect their friends and family to use it, too. In fact, 22% of moms say that if friends or family don't participate in social media, they are not as much a part of their lives.

"Today's mom is the most influential and social consumer you'll meet. Before she clicks to buy, she's posted, pinned, tweeted, and shared. In fact, social media is so much a part of mom's life that checking her various social platforms comes before enjoying her first cup of coffee in the morning. In the three short years since our last report on the topic, social media has become so pervasive, it's now fundamental to the way today's moms live their lives."

Mike Fogarty, SVP
BabyCenter, 9/24/2013

The study found moms to be the top users among various social platforms, as follows:

	Moms	General Population
• YouTube:	77%	61%
• Instagram:	27%	15%
• Twitter:	25%	19%
• Pinerest:	24%	15%
• Google+:	20%	17%

Social moms shop online more than other moms; and moms, in general, spend more than the general population. The following is the percentages of online spending over the general population spent by moms and social moms:

	Social Moms	Moms
• Mobile phones:	124%	51%
• Photo printing:	102%	51%
• Food & beverage:	96%	47%
• Toys & games:	82%	21%
• Movies & videos:	73%	14%
• Home & garden:	65%	9%
• Baby supplies:	63%	46%
• Apparel:	61%	22%
• Health & beauty:	43%	24%

Social media drives mom's purchases as follows:

- A mom recommended it on a parenting site: 59%
- A brand posted a coupon or other offer on a social network: 59%
- A friend liked or posted about the brand on a social network: 44%
- The brand posted information on a social network: 38%
- You saw a picture on Pinterest: 32%
- You saw a sponsored ad on a social network: 23%
- You saw someone following the brand on a social network: 21%

Overall, moms are responsible for 32% of total online spending, despite making up only 18% of the total Internet audience.

Saving money and keeping up with her favorite brands is important to mothers. Seventy-eight percent (78%) of moms follow a brand for coupons and discounts, compared to only 55% of the general population. To learn about which brands and products to buy, 73% of moms rely on recommendations from parenting social media. Moms report that posts from a friend are 16% more influential than posts from a brand, and posts from another mom are 55% more influential than posts from a brand.

49.8 Affluent Women

According to *Affluent Working Women*, a report by International Demographics (www.themediaaudit.com), affluent working women with family incomes of $75,000 or more comprise 10.1% of the 80 largest metropolitan areas. The following are the markets with the highest percentages of affluent working women:

- Washington, DC: 14.7%
- Southern New Hampshire: 13.0%
- San Jose, CA: 12.5%
- Hartford, CT: 12.3%
- Minneapolis-Saint Paul, MN: 11.9%
- Little Rock, AR: 11.7%
- Omaha-Council Bluffs, NE: 11.7%
- San Francisco, CA: 11.6%
- Baltimore, MD: 11.4%
- Madison, WI: 11.3%

According to Ipsos (www.ipsos.com), there are 15.6 million affluent (annual household incomes of $100,000 or more) female heads of household ages 18-to-54.

According to the Luxury Institute (www.luxuryinstitute.com), 72% of women in households with incomes of $150,000 or higher work; 54% work full time. Affluent women are most likely to control the food and clothing purchase decisions for their household. In households above this income level, women make the decisions about the following:

- Home appliance purchases: 68%
- Family vacations: 61%

- Electronics purchases: 40%
- Vehicle purchases: 40%
- Real estate purchases: 31%

Overall, this group makes approximately 68% of the purchases on behalf of their household. When purchasing, these women have a decided preference for products that are made by established and well-known brands.

49.9 Purchase Decision Making

Eighty-five percent (85%) of purchasing decisions are made or influenced by women, according to The 85% Niche (www.85percentniche.com). Frank About Women (www.frankaboutwomen.com) puts the figure at 80%.

Findings of a study by Fleishman-Hillard (www.fleishman.com) reveal that women consider themselves the primary decision-maker in their home. Seventy-nine percent (79%) say their opinion determines family financial decisions, 74% are primarily responsible for buying groceries and basic supplies, and 55% are primarily responsible for paying the bills.

49.10 Purchasing Power

Various market assessments put female purchasing power at anywhere from $5 trillion to $15 trillion annually. Fleishman-Hillard estimates that women will control two-thirds of the consumer wealth in the U.S. over the next decade. Boston Consulting Group (www.bcg.com) notes in a recent study that women are forecast to add $6 trillion in additional earned income over the next five years.

49.11 Market Resources

All About Women Consumers, EPM Communications, February 2012. (www.epmcom.com/products/item10.cfm)

Frank About Women, 101 North Cherry Street, Winston-Salem, NC 27101. (336) 774-9378. (www.frankaboutwomen.com)

The 85% Niche, 21 Royal James Drive, Hilton Head Island, SC 29926. (843) 681-7878. (www.85percentniche.com)

50

MALE CONSUMERS

50.1 Profile

According to the Census Bureau (www.census.gov), the U.S. male population in 2012 was an estimated 154.49 million, which represents 49.2% of the population. Distribution by age was as follows:

- Under 18: 37.69 million
- 18-to-64: 97.99 million
- 65 and older: 18.82 million

The median age for men was 36.1 years.

Census 2010 counted 151.78 million males. The median age for men was 35.8 years.

Educational Attainment in the United States, a 2012 report from the U.S. Census Bureau, counted 30.0 million men ages 25 and older with a bachelor's degree or more education, lower than the corresponding number for women (31.4 million). More men than women have a professional or doctoral degree but they have a lower share of high school diplomas as well as associate's, bachelor's, and master's degrees.

According to *School Enrollment in the United States*, published in October 2013, 45% of college students are men.

50.2 Fathers

Profile America, a report from the Census Bureau, estimated there are 70.1 million fathers in the United States. Among these, 25.3 million fathers are part of married-couple families with children younger than 18. Twenty-two percent (22%) are raising three or more children younger than 18.

There are 1.8 million single fathers; 15% of single parents are men. Forty-six percent (46%) of single fathers are divorced, 30% have never been married, 19% are separated, and 6% are widowed. Nine percent (9%) of single fathers are raising three or more children younger than 18.

America's Families and Living Arrangements, an annual report by the Census Bureau, estimates there are 189,000 stay-at-home dads. These married fathers with children younger than 15 have remained out of the labor force for at least one year primarily so they can care for the family while their wives work outside the home. Collectively, stay-at-home dads care for 287,000 children. Approximately 16% of preschoolers are regularly cared for by their father during their mother's working hours.

A Tale Of Two Fathers, by the Pew Research Center (www.pewresearch.org), reported that an increasing number of fathers live apart from their children. But, those living with their children are more involved in their lives than in the past.

> **"The role of fathers in the modern American family is changing in important and countervailing ways. Fathers who live with their children have become more intensely involved in their lives, spending more time with them and taking part in a greater variety of activities. However, the share of fathers who are residing with their children has fallen significantly in the past half century."**
>
> Pew Research Center

In 1960, only 11% of children in the U.S. lived apart from their fathers. That share has risen to 27%. The share of minor children living apart from their mothers increased only modestly, from 4% in 1960 to 8%.

More than one-in-four fathers with children ages 18 or younger now live apart from their children – with 11% living apart from some of their children and 16% living apart from all of their children. One-in-five absent fathers say they visit their children more than once a week, but an even greater share (27%) say they have not seen their children at all in the past year.

Almost all fathers who live with their children take an active role in their children's day-to-day lives through activities such as sharing meals, helping with homework, and playing.

In 1965, married fathers with children younger than age 18 living in their household spent an average of 2.6 hours per week caring for those children. Fathers' time spent caring for their children rose gradually over the past two decades, to 2.7 hours per week in 1975 and 3 hours per week in 1985. From 1985 to 2000, the amount of time married fathers spent with their children more than doubled, to 6.5 hours.

50.3 Gender Roles Are Blurring

While women still do the majority of work in the home, studies have found that men are more involved domestically than in past decades.

According to Prof. Scott Coltrane, Ph.D., a sociologist and dean of the College of Arts & Sciences at University of Oregon, compared with the 1960s, the portion of housework done by men in couple households has doubled, with men now doing 30% of housework compared with 15%. Men have also tripled the amount of childcare they do.

According to *Meet The Modern Dad*, a 2012 study by The Parenting Group (www.parenting.com), fathers say the following tasks are mostly their responsibility:

Task	%
• Grocery shopping:	49%
• Cooking:	43%
• Driving kids to/from school, activities and appointments:	39%
• Getting kids ready for school or daycare:	36%

A survey by Yahoo! (www.yahoo.com) found that 51% of men are primarily responsible in their household for grocery shopping. For laundry and cooking the percentages are 41% and 39%, respectively.

"Dads today are more involved in raising their kids and managing the household than most typical dads of earlier generations."

eMarketer, 9/18/12

Despite the increase in their roles in the household, the vast majority of men still take a secondary role in household chores and childcare. Less than 3% of men are stay-at-home dads.

50.4 Purchasing Decision Making

Marketing to Men, a study by Jacobs Media (www.jacobsmedia.com), reported that men and women share purchase decision-making for big ticket items as follows:

	Male	**Female**
• Sole decision maker:	24.4%	27.9%
• Play a key role but share in decision:	34.7%	27.8%
• Share decision equally:	36.7%	37.6%
• Have some, but not primary, influence:	2.8%	4.8%
• No role in decision:	0.5%	0.6%

In a survey by Yahoo!, men reported that they had become more involved in decision-making related to the following household purchases (percentage of respondents):

- Consumer packaged goods: 60%
- Apparel: 54%
- Housewares and household goods: 54%
- Personal care products: 53%
- Baby and child care products: 50%
- Toys: 50%

A survey by eMarketer (www.emarketer.com) found that 65% of men search for online products in the CPG category. For comparison, only 49% of women do so.

The report also found that men spend less time on a product page before making an online purchase.

The survey *Beauty Online* by Mintel (www.mintel.com) found that increasingly men are deciding to go online to make purchases. In particular the report found that 60% of men 18-to-34 years old buy grooming products online, saying doing so is more convenient than going into a store for such purchases. Among men ages 55 and older, 41% purchase grooming products online.

50.5 Market Resources

A Tale Of Two Fathers, Pew Research Center, June 2011. (http://pewresearch.org/pubs/2026/survey-role-of-fathers-fatherhood-american-family-living-apart-from-children)

PART VIII: GENERATIONAL FOCUS

51

GENERATIONAL COMPARISONS

51.1 Unique Characteristics

A recent survey by The Pew Research Center (www.pewresearch.org) asked people of all ages what makes their generation unique. Responses were as follows (percentage of respondents):

Seniors

• Experienced World War II:	14%
• Experienced the Great Depression:	14%
• Smarter:	13%
• Honest:	12%
• Work ethic:	10%
• Values/morals:	10%

Baby Boomers

• Work ethic:	17%
• Respectful:	14%
• Values/morals:	8%
• Largest generation:	6%
• Smarter:	5%

Generation X

• Technology:	12%
• Work ethic:	11%
• Conservative/traditional:	7%
• Smarter:	6%
• Respectful:	5%

Millennials

• Technology:	24%
• Music and pop culture:	11%
• Liberal/tolerant:	7%
• Smarter:	6%
• Clothes:	5%

WJSchroer Company (www.socialmarketing.org) provides the following assessment of the various generations:

The Depression Era: Born 1912-1921

- Coming of Age: 1930-1939
- Current population: 11 million to12 million (and declining rapidly)
- Depression era individuals are conservative, compulsive savers, maintain low debt, and value financial security. They tend to be patriotic, oriented toward work before pleasure, have respect for authority, and have a sense of moral obligation.

World War II: Born 1922-1927

- Coming of Age: 1940-1945
- Current population: 11 million (in quickening decline)
- People in this cohort shared in a common goal of defeating the Axis powers. There was an accepted sense of "deferment" among this group, contrasted with the emphasis on "me" in more recent cohorts.

Post-War Cohort: Born 1928-1945

- Coming of Age: 1946-1963
- Current population: 41 million (declining)
- This generation had significant opportunities in jobs and education as the War ended and post-war economic boom struck America. The growth in Cold War tensions, the potential for nuclear war and never before seen threats, led to levels of discomfort and uncertainty throughout the generation. Members of this group value security, comfort, and familiar, known activities and environments.

Boomers I: Born 1946-1954

- Coming of Age: 1963-1972
- Current population: 33 million
- Baby Boomers were defined as those born between 1946 and 1964. That generation encompassed 71 million people 20 years apart in age. Attitudes, behaviors, and society were vastly different for those born in 1964 compared with those born in 1946. All the elements that help to define a cohort were violated by the broad span of years originally included in the concept of the Baby Boomers. The first Boomer segment is bound by the John F. Kennedy and Martin Luther King assassinations, the Civil Rights movements, and the Vietnam War. Boomers I were in or protested the war. Boomers I had good economic opportunities and were largely optimistic about the potential for America and their own lives.

Boomers II: Born 1956-1965

- Coming of Age: 1973-1983
- Current population: 49 million
- The first post-Watergate generation lost much of its trust in government and optimistic views the Boomers I maintained. Economic struggles including the oil embargo of 1979 reinforced a sense of "I'm out for me" and narcissism and a focus on self-help and skepticism over media and institutions is representative of attitudes of this cohort. While Boomers I had Vietnam, Booomers II had AIDS as part of their rites of passage.

Generation X: Born 1966-1976

- Coming of Age: 1988-1994
- Current population: 41 million
- Sometimes referred to as the "lost" generation, this was the first generation of "latchkey" kids, exposed to lots of daycare and divorce. Known as the generation with the lowest voting participation rate of any generation, Gen Xers were quoted by *Newsweek* as "the generation that dropped out without ever turning on the news or tuning in to the social issues around them."
  Gen X is often characterized by high levels of skepticism, "what's in it for me" attitudes, and a reputation for some of the worst music to ever gain popularity. William Morrow cited the childhood divorce of many Gen Xers as "one of the most decisive experiences influencing how Gen Xers will shape their own families".
  Gen Xers are the best educated generation, with 29% obtaining a bachelor's degree or higher. With that education and a growing maturity, they are forming families with a higher level of caution and pragmatism than their parents. Concerns run high over avoiding broken homes, kids growing up without a parent around, and financial planning.

Generation Y, Echo Boomers or Millenniums: Born 1977-1994

- Coming of Age: 1998-2006
- Current Population: 71 million
- The largest cohort since the Baby Boomers. Gen Y kids are known as incredibly sophisticated, technology wise, immune to most traditional marketing and sales pitches...as they not only grew up with it all, they've seen it all and been exposed to it all since early childhood.
  Gen Y members are more racially and ethnically diverse and more segmented as an audience, aided by the rapid expansion in Cable TV channels, satellite radio, the Internet, e-zines, etc. Gen Y are less brand loyal and the speed of the Internet has led the cohort to be flexible and changing in its fashion, style consciousness and where and how it is communicated with. One in nine Gen Yers has a credit card co-signed by a parent.

Generation Z: Born 1995-2012

- Coming of Age: 2013-2020
- Current Population: 23 million and growing rapidly
- While not much is known about Gen Z yet, there is a lot known about the environment in which they are growing up. Their highly diverse environment will make the grade schools of the next generation the most diverse ever. Higher levels of technology will make significant inroads in academics, allowing for customized instruction, data mining of student histories to enable pinpoint diagnostics, and re-mediation or accelerated achievement opportunities.
  Gen Z kids will grow up with a highly sophisticated media and computer environment and will be more Internet savvy and expert than their Gen Y forerunners.

51.2 Shopping

Mining the U.S. Generation Gaps, a study by The Nielsen Company (www.nielsen.com), provides the following assessment of shopping frequency and spending:

Annual Shopping Trips Per Household
- Millennials: 140
- Generation X: 155
- Baby Boomers: 175
- Seniors: 185

Amount Spent Per Shopping Trip
- Millennials: $55
- Generation X: $54
- Baby Boomers: $45
- Seniors: $34

Percent of Spending On Promotional Deals
- Millennials: 18%
- Generation X: 20%
- Baby Boomers: 22%
- Seniors: 26%

Spending Per Household
- Millennials: $6,500
- Generation X: $7,000
- Baby Boomers: $7,200
- Seniors: $6,000

Spending per shopping trip to various retail channels is as follows:

Drug Stores
- Millennials: $24
- Generation X: $27
- Baby Boomers: $25
- Seniors: $22

Grocery Stores
- Millennials: $50
- Generation X: $49
- Baby Boomers: $41
- Seniors: $30

Mass Merchandisers

- Millennials: $54
- Generation X: $57
- Baby Boomers: $47
- Seniors: $35

Supercenters

- Millennials: $75
- Generation X: $70
- Baby Boomers: $64
- Seniors: $49

51.3 Use Of The Internet

The Pew Research Center found Internet usage among adults as follows:

	Internet	Broadband	Mobile Internet
• Millennials:	97%	75%	88%
• Generation X:	91%	77%	76%
• Baby Boomers:	77%	62%	53%
• Seniors:	53%	39%	21%

Digital Differences, a report by the Pew Research Center, found online activities by demographic is as follows:

	Search	Email	Buy Products	Social Networking	Banking
• Millennials:	96%	91%	70%	87%	61%
• Generation X:	91%	93%	73%	68%	68%
• Baby Boomers:	91%	90%	76%	49%	59%
• Seniors:	87%	86%	56%	29%	44%

51.4 Use Of Social Media

According to a 2012 survey by the Pew Research Center, the following percentages of consumers use social networks:

- Millennials: 86%
- Generation X: 72%
- Baby Boomers: 50%
- Seniors: 34%

Social site usage is as follows:

	Facebook	Instagram	LinkedIn	Pinterest	Tumblr	Twitter
• Millennials:	83%	27%	16%	16%	11%	27%
• Generation X:	72%	8%	25%	12%	4%	15%
• Baby Boomers:	56%	6%	22%	13%	2%	12%
• Seniors:	40%	4%	11%	4%	1%	17%

51.5 Use Of Cellphones and Mobile Devices

According to *Mobile Access*, a report by the Pew Internet & American Life Project (www.pewinternet.org), consumer use of cellphones and mobile devices is as follows:

	Millennials	Gen-X	Boomers	Seniors
• Own a cellphone:	90%	88%	82%	57%
• Text message:	95%	82%	57%	19%
• Access Internet:*	65%	43%	18%	10%
• Watch video:*	40%	20%	6%	4%

* Access by smartphone or other mobile device

Ownership of smartphones is as follows (source: Pew Internet: Mobile):

- Millennials: 66%
- Generation X: 59%
- Baby Boomers: 34%
- Seniors: 13%

51.6 Market Resources

Digital Differences, Pew Research Center's Internet & American Life Project, April 2012. (www.pewinternet.org/reports/2012/digital-differences.aspx)

Older Adults And Internet Use, Pew Internet & American Life Project, June 2012. (www.pewinternet.org/Reports/2012/older-adults-and-internet-use.aspx)

Photos and Videos as Social Currency Online, Pew Internet & American Life Project, September 2012. (www.pewinternet.org/reports/2012/online-pictures.aspx)

52

SENIOR CONSUMERS

52.1 Profile

Those born before 1946 have been tagged with various monikers, the most common being simply 'Seniors.' The youngest Seniors turned 68 in 2013.

Census 2010 counted 40.27 million Americans ages 65 or older, representing 13.0% of the population. The senior population increased 15.1% from Census 2000, when 34.99 million people in that age demographic represented 12.4% of the population.

It should be noted that there is a slight overlap between the youngest 'Seniors' and the oldest 'Baby Boomers,' who are assessed in Chapter 53.

52.2 General Characteristics

According to the Pew Research Center's Social & Demographic Trends Project (www.pewsocialtrends.org), daily activities among those ages 65 or older are as follows:

- Talk with family or friends: 90%
- Read a book, magazine, or newspaper: 83%
- Take a prescription medication: 83%
- Watch one hour or more of television: 77%
- Pray: 76%
- Drive a car: 65%
- Spend time on a hobby: 43%
- Take a nap: 40%
- Go shopping: 39%
- Use the Internet: 28%
- Get some type of vigorous exercise: 22%

Seniors say the benefits of growing older are as follows (percentage of respondents):

- More time with family: 70%
- Not working: 66%
- More times for hobbies/interests: 65%
- More financial security: 64%
- Less stress: 59%
- More respect: 59%
- More travel: 52%

- Volunteer work: 52%
- Second career: 14%

Seniors' living arrangements are as follows (source: Pew Research Center):

	65-74	75-84	85+	All
• Own home or apartment:	95%	90%	80%	92%
• Child's/family member's home:	2%	4%	5%	3%
• Assisted living facility:	2%	4%	15%	4%

Characteristics among those living independently are as follows:

	65-74	75-84	85+	All
• Live in age-restricted community:	6%	11%	20%	10%
• Live alone:	30%	47%	66%	41%

Aging in America, by Prince Market Research (www.pmresearch.com), reports that 89% of Seniors feel that the ability to live independently and remain in their home is very important. More than half (53%), however, are concerned with their ability to do so. Seniors cited three primary concerns that could jeopardize their ability to live independently: health problems (53%), memory problems (26%), and the inability to drive/get around (23%).

The majority of Seniors (55%) view themselves as very independent in that they receive no assistance from their children – and seem content with that fact; 75% said their children are involved enough in their life. Seniors who do require help from others receive assistance with household maintenance (20%), transportation (13%), and healthcare (8%). Only 1% reported receiving any financial support.

According to the Pew Research Center's Social & Demographic Trends Project, 63% of those ages 65 or older feel they are in excellent or good health. For those living in the west, that figure rises to 72%.

By region, those that say they don't feel old are as follows:

- West: 79%
- Northeast: 72%
- South: 71%
- Midwest: 66%

"If a latter-day Ponce de Leon were to search for a modern fountain of youth, he'd do well to explore America's West. There he'd find the highest concentration of older adults in the United States who don't think of themselves as old."

Pew Research Center

52.3 Buying Power

There are 13.40 million households headed by a person age 65 or older. According to the *Annual Social and Economic Supplement* (2010), by the Census Bureau, total income of these households is as follows:

- $20,000 or more: 11.74 million
- $100,000 or more: 1.93 million
- $200,000 or more: 377,000

"Seniors – most of whom have already retired and downsized their lifestyles – have been far better insulated from the current storm than those who need to worry about keeping their jobs and building up diminished retirement accounts."

Pew Research Center's Social & Demographic Trends Project

52.4 Media Activities

According to the Pew Internet & American Life Project (www.pewinternet.org), 53% of Seniors use the Internet. Once online, the Internet becomes a part of daily life for the majority of seniors.

Overall, 82% of all adult Internet users go online on an average day. Among adults age 65 and older, 70% use the Internet on a typical day.

Focalyst (www.focalyst.com) provides the following assessment of online Seniors and, for comparison, those that do not go online:

	Internet Users	Not Online
• Annual household income:	$55,000	$27,000
• Average monthly household expenditures:	$ 1,754	$ 1,059
• Married/partnered:	70%	48%
• Employed:	26%	13%
• Attended college:	75%	42%

The Cable & Telecommunications Association for Marketing (www.ctam.org) reports the following activities among online Seniors:

- Use email: 94%
- Shop online: 77%
- Access health and medical information: 71%
- Read news: 70%
- Manage finances and banking: 59%
- Play free online games: 47%

According to the Pew Research Center, Senior ownership of media and technology devices is as follows:

- Cellphone: 69%
- Desktop: 48%
- Laptop: 32%
- eReader: 11%
- Tablet: 8%

52.5 Market Resources

AARP Research, 601 E Street NW, Washington DC 20049. (888) 687-2277. (www.aarp.org/research/)

Demographic Profile - Seniors, eMarketer, January 2011. (www.emarketer.com/Report.aspx?code=emarketer_2000738)

Growing Old In America: Expectations Vs. Reality, Pew Research Center, June 2009. (http://pewsocialtrends.org/assets/pdf/Getting-Old-in-America.pdf)

Older Adults and Social Media, Pew Internet & American Life Project, August 2010. (www.pewinternet.org/Reports/2010/Older-Adults-and-Social-Media.aspx)

53

BABY BOOMER CONSUMERS

53.1 Profile

The oldest of the Baby Boomers – born in 1946 and 2.8 million in number – turned 67 in 2013; the youngest Boomers – born in 1964 – turned 49.

Census 2010 counted 76.94 million Americans born between 1946 and 1964, representing 24.9% of the population.

53.2 Generational Characteristics

AARP (www.aarp.org) provides the following insight into Baby Boomer households:

- Contrary to popular perception, few Baby Boomers are downsizing. Only 6% expect to be living in a smaller home within five years.
- Thirty-seven percent (37%) of Baby Boomers have a child age 18 or younger living in the household.
- Over five million Baby Boomer parents have recently had an adult child move back into the home, partially due to the rise of "adultolescents" who've boomeranged back into the parental household.
- Four million Baby Boomers have a parent living with them.
- Eighty-two percent (82%) of Boomers use the Internet, engaging in activities such as instant messaging, downloading music or movies, financial transactions, and online gaming.
- Just 11% of Baby Boomers plan to stop working altogether when they reach retirement age.

According to the Pew Research Center's Social & Demographic Trends Project (www.pewsocialtrends.org), 52% of Baby Boomers say they are considering delaying retirement because of the recession.

The Nielsen Company (www.nielsen.com) provides the following facts about Boomers:

- They dominate 1,023 out of 1,083 consumer packaged goods categories.
- They watch the most video among demographic groups: 9:34 hours per day.
- They comprise ⅓ of all TV viewers, online users, and social media users.
- They watch time-shift TV more than 18-to-24 year olds (2:32 vs. 1:32).

According to Nielsen, while Baby Boomers account for 38.5% of spending on consumer packaged goods, less than 5% of advertising spending targets them.

> **"You'll find that people over age 50 drive today's economy, whether up or down. Ninety million people with full wallets and low-balance credit cards are a lot of consumers to ignore. The 50+ cohort controls 75% of the wealth in this country, earns $2.3 trillion annually compared to $1 trillion for the 18-to-34 group, and they stand to inherit between $14 trillion and $20 trillion over the next 20 years."**
>
> *Brandweek*

53.3 Spending Power

By 2017, the Boomer generation is expected to account for 50% of the U.S. population and control 70% of the country's disposable income, according to *Introducing Boomers: Marketing's Most Valuable Generation*, a report by Nielsen. Moreover, Boomers stand to inherit $15 trillion over the next 20 years.

Now some 80 million strong, Boomers constitute 44% of the U.S. population, with 49% of CPG (consumer packaged goods) sales in the U.S. (roughly $230 billion annually).

In spite of being the wealthiest generation in U.S. history, the recent wave of job losses has hit working Baby Boomers particularly hard. Though the unemployment rate for older workers is lower than the overall average, once they become unemployed older workers find it harder to land a job; and they tend to remain out of work longer than younger workers, according to the Bureau of Labor Statistics (www.bls.gov).

Among those Boomers at or near retirement age, many have decided to continue working – most in order to shore up their shrunken retirement accounts.

53.4 Media Activities

According to the Pew Internet & American Life Project (www.pewinternet.org), 81% of younger Baby Boomers and 76% of older Baby Boomers use the Internet. Top online activities are as follows:

	Younger Boomers (45-54)	Older Boomers (55-64)
• Email:	91%	93%
• Search engines:	86%	87%
• News:	84%	85%
• Buy products:	73%	75%
• Book travel:	70%	67%
• Watch videos:	62%	55%
• Bank online:	58%	56%
• Social networks:	50%	43%

Social networks use by Baby Boomers is as follows:

	Younger Boomers (45-54)	Older Boomers (55-64)
• Facebook:	32%	9%
• LinkedIn:	31%	12%
• Twitter:	24%	6%
• Pinterest:	25%	8%
• Google+:	5%	6%

A recent study by Ipsos (www.ipsos.com) found Boomers rely heavily on the Internet to gain access to information. Among those who use the Internet at home, 14.8 hours weekly is spent; 4.8 hours are spent online away from home.

53.5 Market Resources

Introducing Boomers: Marketing's Most Valuable Generation, The Nielsen Company, 2013. (www.nielsen.com)

Reaching Today's Boomers And Seniors Online, Google & Ipsos MediaCT, May 2013.

The Baby Boom Americans, 7th Edition, New Strategist, June 2012. (www.newstrategist.com)

54

GENERATION X CONSUMERS

54.1 Profile

Most analysts classify those born 1965 thru 1979, a span of 15 years, as Generation X. With no major event providing a marker for the boundaries of this generation – as the end of World War II did for the Baby Boom Generation – some analysts classify only those born 1965 thru 1975 as Gen X. Whatever definition is used, analysts agree that consumers now in their 30s and 40s differ in many ways from Baby Boomers that proceeded them and Millennials that followed.

Census 2010 counted 61.03 million Americans born between 1965 and 1979, representing 19.8% of the population.

The ethnic makeup of Generation X is as follows (source: U.S. Census Bureau):

- Caucasian: 62.8%
- Hispanic: 16.8%
- African-American: 13.2%
- Asian: 1.6%
- Other: 5.6%

Generation X is significantly smaller in number than either the Baby Boomer or the Millennial generations – and, it seems, often overshadowed by these generations.

"It's so annoying. First, it was always the Baby Boomers overshadowing everything. Then there was this brief period in the mid-'90s when Gen X was cool. Now it's, 'What are the new kids doing?'"

Lisa Chamberlain, Author
Slackonomics: Generation X in the Age of Creative Destruction

---

54.2 Generational Characteristics

What Generation X is, perhaps foremost in importance, is the best-educated generation in U.S. history. Almost half of Gen Xers have a 2- or 4-year college degree, and more than 10% have a graduate degree. Gen X households typically include two income earning spouses; 68% have dual incomes.

Several recent surveys have shown that younger workers, especially those in Generation X, hold a work/life balance, opportunities for growth, and good work relationships higher in importance than generations before them. Gen X employees view work as secondary to their lives outside the office, which may mean more time with their children or time to pursue a hobby.

According to Ann A. Fishman, president of Generational-Targeted Marketing Corp. (www.annfishman.com), Gen Xers have different values from Boomers, especially related to their careers. They want to enjoy their jobs as well as have time for their own lives. So Gen Xers are often willing to trade off less money for more freedom.

A survey of employees by Deloitte (www.deloitte.com) found that about 37% of Gen Xers said they planned to stay in their current jobs after the recession ends, compared with 44% of Millennials, 50% of Baby Boomers, and 52% of Seniors who said the same. According to Robin Erickson, a manager with Deloitte's Human Capital Division, a lack of career advancement was by far the biggest gripe from Gen Xers, with 40% giving that as a reason for planning to change jobs, compared with 30% of Millennials, 20% of Baby Boomers, and 14% of Senior workers.

54.3 Spending Behaviors

Generation X has often been characterized as being non-materialistic, shunning fashion, brand names, and technological advancements. The values, to some extent, were the generations's effort to distinguish itself from the Baby Boomer's preppy era of the early 1980s. However, while they may not yet have the affluence of Baby Boomers, Gen Xers have plenty of style and a desire to show it off. This segment initially affected fashion and style, then music and movies, and now is influencing the marketing of furniture and housewares.

For all its individuality and the promise that might have been for marketers as Generation X approached its peak earning years, Gen X reached the height of its earnings power during the Great Recession. Now holding mortgages on homes worth less than when they bought, saddled with tens of thousands of dollars in student loans, on average, and raising children under age 18 who are dependent upon them, the timing of the Great Recession could not have been worse for this generation.

54.4 Media Activities

According to recent estimates by eMarketer (www.emarketer.com), nearly 95% of Gen Xers are using mobile phones, and 60% of that group use smartphones.

Among Gen Xers, 62.2% use the mobile Internet at least monthly.

Gen X Internet users also are avid consumers of online content. They typically use social networking sites on at least a monthly basis (74.5% of Gen X web users), and nearly two-thirds used Facebook in particular (65.6%). Growth in these areas, as in Internet usage as a whole, is relatively flat due to market saturation. Twitter, however, reached only 14.7% of Gen X Internet users, eMarketer estimates, and usage is growing quickly, expected to reach 19.5% of this audience by 2017.

Digital video is even more popular among Gen X Internet users than social networking, with 78.7% downloading or streaming video online at least once per month.

Generation X bridges traditional and digital media usage and its members are virtually always connected, thanks to mobile devices. Born before the digital revolution, Gen X is the first generation to come of age with PCs and the Internet. Its members are fully comfortable using both traditional and digital media channels.

54.5 Market Resources

Generation X, 6th Edition, New Strategist, June 2012. (www.newstrategist.com)

How Digital Behavior Differs Among Millennials, Gen Xers and Boomers, eMarketer, March 2013.

55

MILLENNIAL CONSUMERS

55.1 Profile

Most analysts classify those born from 1980 thru 2000, a span of 20 years, as the Millennial generation (also known as Generation Y or Echo Boomers). In 2013, Millennials spanned ages 13 through 33.

Census 2010 counted 93.40 million Americans born between 1980 and 2000, representing 30.3% of the population.

Already the largest generation in the U.S., immigration will further boost the number of Millennials by 2020, according to the Census Bureau (www.census.gov).

The ethnic makeup of the Millennials is as follows (source: U.S. Census Bureau):

- Caucasian: 61.0%
- Hispanic: 17.0%
- African-American: 15.0%
- Asian: 3.4%
- Other: 3.6%

> **"Today's teens and young adults are quite the multi-cultural bunch. The 12-to-17, 18-to-24 and 25-to-34 groups are almost identically multi-cultural, as 42% of each comprises Hispanics, African-Americans, and Asian-Americans. This is only the tip of the iceberg – U.S. Census data shows that African-Americans, Asian-Americans, and Hispanics will generate the vast majority of the U.S. population growth over the next few decades."**
>
> Nielsen, 4/16/13

According to a May 2013 study by the Urban Land Institute (www.uri.org), Millennial residency is as follows:

• City neighborhood outside downtown:	34%
• Small city/town (Population under 50,000):	19%
• Downtown/near downtown:	14%
• Dense, older suburb:	13%
• Newer, outlying suburb:	11%
• Rural community:	10%

Estimates of Millennial buying power range between $170 billion and $200 billion. By 2017, their buying power is projected to eclipse that of Baby Boomers.

In addition to the assessment of Millennials in this chapter, an assessment of college students is presented in Chapter 56.

55.2 Generational Characteristics

Analysts agree that Millennials differ in many ways from the Baby Boomers and Generation X that proceeded them: They were raised with the Internet and digital technologies and they multitask well. Millennials don't just embrace technology, for them it's a way of life.

Advertising Age provides the following characteristics of Millennials:

- Millennials spend almost 15 hours a day interacting with various media and communications technologies.
- More than one-half of Millennials talk on the phone regularly while watching television.
- Twenty percent (20%) of adult Millennials (ages 18-to-31) have at least 25 friends in their social network.
- Fifty-nine percent (59%) of Millennials spend at least an hour a day talking on their cellphones.
- Console gaming is, by far, the leading leisure activity for Millennial males. Watching television and talking on cellphones are most popular with Millennial females.
- Approximately 11 million Millennials are married – two-thirds of those who are married have children.
- Forty-five percent (45%) of Millennials refer to themselves as non-white.
- Eighty-four percent (84%) of Millennials believe that getting a college degree is important.
- Fifty-one percent (51%) of Millennials say it's important to volunteer for community service, and 48% have done so.

55.3 Impact of the Great Recession

Many of the young adult Millennials who expected to be in the early stage of a career saw their plans derailed by the Great Recession.

As of March 2013, only 34% of Millennials headed up their own household, according to the Pew Research Center (www.pewresearch.org). This rate was unchanged from March 2012 and even lower than the level observed in the depths of the Great Recession.

> **"Though the nation is officially four years into economic recovery ... most Millennials are still not setting out on their own."**
>
> Pew Research Social & Demographic Trends, 10/18/13

The term Boomerang Generation has been coined to reflect those young adults who have returned to their parents' home, many overburdened with student loan debt as well as unemployment. According to the Pew Research Center, 24% of Millennials have moved back home at least once.

According to the 2012 Clark University *Poll Of Emerging Adults*, more people ages 18-to-29 live with their parents than with a spouse.

55.4 Affluent Millennials

While many Millennials are struggling with their careers and personal finances, others are achieving financial success.

International Demographics (www.themediaaudit.com) reported in an August 2013 assessment that 7.3 million households headed by an 18-to-34 year-old in the 81 largest metropolitan areas had an annual income in excess of $100,000.

The Nielsen Company (www.nielsen.com) assesses that younger Millennials (i.e., teens) tend to be more affluent than older Millennials (i.e., young adults). In 2012, 29% of U.S. teens lived in high-income homes ($100k+), while only 25% of young adults lived in households within this same income bracket. There were also more teen households with middle incomes ($30k-$100k) than those of young adults. And fewer teens lived in lower-income homes ($30k) than their slightly older counterparts.

Many in this cohort are also focused on savings. In its May 2013 study of 'mass affluents,' Merrill Edge (www.merrilledge.com) reported that young adults (ages 18-to-34) in households with investable assets of between $50,000 and $250,000 began their retirement savings at an average age of 22. For comparison, Baby Boomers began saving, on average, at age 35. These Millennials say they plan to save an average of $2.5 million by retirement, considerably more ambitious than affluents ages 51-to-64, who anticipate saving $260,000. Among all adults in affluent households, the average retirement savings goal is $860,000.

The Merrill Edge survey found that 47% of affluent Millennial households with children are willing to cut back on family vacations in order to contribute to a college fund for their kids; 45% would forego purchasing a new car.

55.5 Shopping Attitudes

In a May 2013 study by the Urban Land Institute, Millennials expressed their attitude toward shopping as follows:

	Female	Male
• Love to shop:	44%	29%
• Shop when necessary and enjoy it:	45%	51%
• Shopping is a necessary chore; I can deal with it:	9%	15%
• Hate shopping:	3%	5%

Ninety-one percent (91%) of Gen Yers made online purchases during the first six months of 2013, and 45% spend more than an hour per day looking at retail-oriented websites. They are researching products, comparing prices, envisioning how clothing or accessories would look on them, or responding to flash sales or coupon offers.

Still, shopping at bricks-and-mortar stores dominates among Millennials. The following percentages say they go to retail formats at least once a month (source: Urban Land Institute):

- Discount department stores: 91%
- Neighborhood and community shopping centers: 74%
- Enclosed malls: 64%
- Full-line department stores: 64%
- Big-box power centers: 63%
- Chain apparel stores: 58%
- Neighborhood business districts: 54%

In an April 2013 survey by DDB Worldwide (www.ddb.com), adults ages 18-to-24 profiled their e-commerce activities as follows:

	Female	Male
• Ideally would buy everything online:	33%	40%
• Typically shop on auction sites:	31%	43%
• Typically use shopping apps on mobile phone:	28%	30%
• Typically use retail store apps:	24%	27%
• An extreme couponer:	23%	22%
• Have requested a price match using mobile phone:	21%	25%
• Typically use mobile phone to scan and find the best price in town for a specific item:	20%	25%
• Typically shop for and buy items on mobile phone:	19%	24%

55.6 Media Activities

An April 2013 report by Nielsen segments Millennials into three age groups: 12-to-17, 18-to-24, and 25-to-34. Device ownership in households with teens and young adults is as follows:

	12-to-17	18-to-24	25-to-34
• DVD Player:	86%	80%	80%
• Game console:	79%	68%	68%
• Laptop:	71%	75%	71%
• Smartphone:	61%	74%	78%
• DVR:	51%	46%	53%
• Tablet:	27%	20%	24%

Time spent monthly watching video is as follows:

	12-to-17	18-to-24	25-to-34
• Television:	98.43 hrs	110.33 hrs	136.17 hrs
• Internet:	5.43 hrs	15.13 hrs	11.07 hrs
• Mobile:	7.80 hrs	6.60 hrs	5.33 hrs

"While everyone under 34 is spending less time in front of the TV, viewing preferences aren't consistent across [age] groups. For example, teens like to watch on mobile more than anyone else. They watched 18% more video on their mobile phones than persons 18-to-24 and 46% more than persons 25-to-34. While teens are watching more content on mobile devices, they watch less video online than young adults. Persons 18-to-24 spent almost 3 times more time watching video on the Internet than teens."

Nielsen, 4/16/13

As of September 2013, smartphone user penetration was 71.8% among females ages 18-to-34 and 70.0% for males in that age group, according to eMarketer (www.emarketer.com). Among all adults, smartphone ownership was 52.6%.

55.7 Market Resources

Generation Y: Shopping and Entertainment In The Digital Age, Urban Land Institute, May 2013.

Marketing To Millennials: Reach the Largest and Most Influential Generation of Consumers Ever, American Management Association, 2013.

Millennials, 5th Edition, New Strategist, June 2012. (www.newstrategist.com)

Teenage Research Unlimited, 707 Skokie Boulevard, Northbrook, IL 60062. (847) 564-3440. (www.teenresearch.com)

PART IX: SEGMENTATION

56

COLLEGE STUDENTS

56.1 Student Population

According to the *2013 Digest of Education Statistics*, by the National Center for Education Statistics (www.nces.ed.gov), the collegiate population in the U.S. numbers 21.59 million. Sixty-two percent (62%) are enrolled at four-year institutions.

According to the U.S. Census Bureau (www.census.gov), 62% of college students are age 24 or under, 22% are under age 20.

College students' residency for the 2013-2014 school year was as follows (source: Prosper Business Development [www.goprosper.com]):

- At home: 47.7%
- Off campus apartment or housing: 24.0%
- Dorm room or college housing: 22.5%
- Fraternity or sorority house: 4.0%

The Institute of International Education (www.iie.org) reports that about 260,000 U.S. students study abroad.

Enrollments of foreign students at U.S. institutions is approximately 690,000. An estimated $20 billion is pumped into the U.S. economy as a result.

56.2 Spending

The *2013 College Explorer Study*, conducted by Crux Research (www.cruxresearch.com) for re:fuel (www.refuelnow.com) estimated that the nearly-22 million students that began classes in Fall 2013 had $404 billion in total spending power. This spending includes $117 billion in discretionary spending and $287 billion in non-discretionary spending (on items such as tuition, room & board and books & supplies). Per-student academic spending was $13,178 for the school year.

Food expenditures topped discretionary outlays among students, with spending at roughly $42.1 billion, distributed as follows:

- Grocery stores: $21.1 billion
- Restaurants: $13.6 billion
- Convenience stores: $ 7.9 billion

The second largest category for discretionary spending among college students is for automotive needs (car payments, insurance, maintenance, and gas), with an estimated $17.5 billion in spending. Spending for apparel follows with $13.1 billion.

56.3 Use Of Technology

On average, college students own 6.9 devices, with laptop computers topping ownership at 85%. Tech devices are owned by college students as follow (source: re:Fuel):

- Laptop computer: 85%
- Smartphone: 69%
- Videogame console: 68%
- MP3 player: 67%
- Printer: 62%
- Digital camera: 61%
- Flat screen TV: 60%
- Desktop computer: 48%
- Tablet computer: 36%
- Handheld gaming system: 35%
- Feature phone: 33%
- Camcorder/video recorder: 25%
- E-Reader: 21%
- TiVo/DVR: 18%

These wired students mostly use their devices for in-class note-taking and studying, but with 14.4 daily hours of multitasking across devices, entertainment runs a close second in usage. From downloading content to playing games to interacting on social networks, usage of a second screen is also popular with this demographic.

Nearly half (49%) of college students report daily usage of a second screen while watching television, with 63% using Facebook or Twitter, 58% surfing other online sites, 50% playing games, and 37% doing school work.

56.4 The Millennial Mindset

In August 2013, Concentric Marketing (www.getconcentric.com) published a comprehensive assessment of college students' views on topics ranging from brand preferences to eating habits. The following are some findings of the study:

- Although college students are digitally adept and show a bias for convenience, they still prefer a traditional bricks-and-mortar shopping experience over e-commerce for the majority of their regular purchases. When asked for the type of store they prefer to shop the most, 60% cited the traditional grocery store and mass merchants such as Target and Walmart.
- Forty-nine percent (49%) of college students said they stick with brands that they know and trust. Over 40% of those surveyed buy brands that were recommendations by friends and family. Only 30% said that brands meant little and their purchase decisions were price driven. In terms of brand categories, survey participants reported feeling the most connections with clothing/apparel brands,

followed closely by technology. They feel the strongest connections to Apple, Nike, Coke, and Adidas. Interestingly, these are all brands that predate Millennials themselves. It is likely that they have interacted with these branded products in some way their entire lives and their loyalty to products introduced to them by their parents remains as they transition into making independent purchasing decisions.

"In the face of being dubbed a 'brand agnostic' generation by some studies, Millennials are surprisingly pragmatic in forming their perceptions around brands and are heavily influenced and loyal to brands introduced to them by their parents."

Concentric Marketing, 8/13

- Despite studies showing that more than one-third of Millennials are considered obese, college students are knowledgeable about nutrition. Sixty percent (60%) cited the importance of monitoring caloric intake, protein, fat grams, and sugar grams in their diets. They are also eating out less and cooking at home five or more times per week.
- Nearly half of the 96% of college students with a Facebook account said they don't believe brands should be on social media. Seventy percent (70%) report following three or fewer brands across all social media channels.

"The takeaway for brands is that the key to using social media effectively with this generation takes a lot more prowess than simply posting marketing messages or launching clever promotions."

Concentric Marketing, 8/13

- When asked about their careers and employment, The highest number of responders (36%) indicated they would be willing to work for less in a job that they love while only 22% were focused on finding the highest paying job. Nearly 25% wanted to work to make the world a better place.

56.5 Market Resources

2013 College Explorer Study, 13th Edition, re:fuel and Crux Research, June 2013.

National Center for Education Statistics, 1990 K Street NW, Washington, DC 20006, (202) 502-7300. (www.nces.ed.gov)

57

CONSUMERS WITH DISABILITIES

57.1 Profile

According to *Profile America*, from the U.S. Census Bureau (www.census.gov), 36 million people, or 12% of the U.S. population, have disabilities. By demographic, those with disabilities are as follows:

Gender

- Females: 12.3%
- Males: 11.6%

Age

- 5-to-17: 5.0%
- 18-to-64: 10.0%
- 65 and older: 37.0%

The percentage of people with various types of disabilities is as follows:

- Difficulty walking or climbing stairs: 19.4%
- Difficulty concentrating, remembering or making decisions: 13.5%
- Hearing: 10.2%
- Vision: 6.5%

Among those ages 16 and older with a disability, 72% are not in the workforce; 27% of the overall adult population is not in the workforce.

The National Data Program for the Sciences (www.norc.org) at the University of Chicago puts the number of people with a disability higher, estimating that 29% of adult Americans suffer from some disability; 8% have three or more conditions that restrict their ability to function. The most common limitation among the disabled is not being able to carry out basic physical activities like walking, lifting, or carrying things, which affects 16% of adults. This is followed by not being able to participate fully in regular daily activities and other physical disabilities (both 10%), difficulty remembering things (9%), a serious hearing loss (6%), a serious vision problem (5%), and a mental-health disability (5%).

WE Media (www.wemedia.com) estimates that 23 million parents in the U.S. have at least one child between the ages of 5 and 16 with special needs.

57.2 Market Assessment

The special needs community has nearly $200 billion in discretionary spending, according to the U.S. Department of Labor, two times the spending power of teens and more than 17 times the spending power of tweens. Other estimates are even higher. Americans with physical disabilities have combined discretionary income of more than $250 billion annually, and the 20 million families with at least one member with a disability represent additional annual disposable income of approximately $258 billion, according to W.C. Duke Associates (www.wcduke.com). *Fortune* estimated that people with disabilities command approximately $1 trillion in household purchasing power.

> **"Handicapitalism. It's a brand new term that describes what's behind a dawning realization in business: People with disabilities shouldn't be viewed as charity cases or regulatory burdens, but rather as profitable marketing targets. Now, mainstream companies, from financial services to cellphone makers, are going beyond what's mandated by law and rapidly tailoring products to attract them."**
>
> *The Wall Street Journal*

According to Open Doors Organization (ODO, www.opendoorsnfp.org) and the U.S. Travel Association (www.ustravel.org), people with disabilities spend $13.6 billion on 31.7 million trips annually. The airline industry sees $3.3 billion in annual spending by travelers with disabilities; spending in the lodging sector is $4.2 billion.

Seventy-one percent (71%) of adults with disabilities dine out at least once a week.

57.3 Marketing to People With Disabilities

Many large companies are raising their profile among people with disabilities. MetLife, for example, is reaching out to this community with a division dedicated to assisting families with special needs in planning for their futures. The company's integrated program includes a comprehensive website, strategic alliances with national non-profit organizations, and TV ads aired during prime time that feature individuals with special needs. The program has won awards from the National Business &

Disability Council (www.nbdc.com).

Still, while some 100 companies have aired commercials featuring people with disabilities, such ads are relatively rare.

The most recent Paralympic Games offered a marketing opportunity for companies. Official Sponsors and Partners included Adidas, Budweiser, Coca-Cola, Haier, Johnson & Johnson, McDonald's, Samsung, UPS, Visa, and Volkswagen.

Disability Matters, an annual conference hosted by Springboard Consulting (www.consultspringboard.com), brings together marketers that focus on marketing to people with disabilities. The 2014 Disability Matters conference is scheduled for April 8-10 in San Antonio, TX.

57.4 Market Resources

Open Doors Organization, 8623 W Bryn Mawr, Suite 508, Chicago, IL, 60631. (773) 388-8839. (www.opendoorsnfp.org)

Springboard Consulting, 14 Glenbrook Drive, Mendham, NJ 07945. (973) 813-7260. (www.consultspringboard.com)

58

FAMILIES WITH CHILDREN

58.1 Profile

According to the U.S. Census Bureau (www.census.gov), the are 35.7 million families (46%) with children under 18 living at home. At peak, 57% of families had children under 18 living at home – in 1953.

Among families with children under 18 at home, there are 5.0 million stay-at-home moms and 154,000 stay-at-home dads.

There are 11.0 million households consisting of an unmarried parent with children under 18. These households have the following characteristics:

- Mother working: 62%
- Father working: 21%
- Mother not working: 15%
- Father not working: 2%

Analysts estimate that more than 18 million adults between the ages of 20 and 34 live with their parents, representing about one-third of that age group.

Some five million American grandparents live with one of their grandchildren, according to the Census Bureau. Dubbed 'grandfamilies,' these households represent nearly 7% of American families.

For a great number of families now, the economy may be a factor in deciding family size, including whether to have children at all. The U.S. recorded 4.25 million live births in 2008, the first full year of the recession, down about 68,000 from the prior year and the first annual decline in births since the start of the decade, according to the National Center for Health Statistics (NCHS, www.cdc.gov/nchs). The number of births declined further in 2009 to 4.13 million and to 3.95 million in 2012.

For comparison, the following number of U.S. women are projected to remain child free:

- 1 in 8 with high income
- 1 in 14 with middle income
- 1 in 20 with low income

In 1976, one in ten women had no children; in 2012 that figure was one in five.

58.2 Cost of Raising Children

Since 1960, the U.S. Department of Agriculture (www.usda.gov) has provided estimates of expenditures for raising children. According to the department, it will cost an estimated $241,080 for a middle-income couple to raise a child born in 2012 for 18 years, an increase of almost 3% from 2011 and not including the cost of college. Spending is distributed as follows:

- Housing: 30%
- Child care and education: 18%
- Food: 16%
- Transportation: 14%
- Healthcare: 8%
- Clothing: 6%
- Miscellaneous: 8%

Child-rearing expenses vary considerably by household income level. For a child in a two-child, husband-wife family, average annual expenses range from $8,990 to $10,230 (depending on age of the child) for households with before-tax income less than 60,640; from $12,600 to $14,770 for households with before-tax income between $60,640 and $105,000; and from $20,930 to $25,180 for households with before-tax income more than $105,000.

On average, households in the lowest income group spend 25% of their before-tax income on a child; those in the middle-income group spend 16%; and those in the highest group spend 12%.

Single-parent families typically spend less for child-rearing than married families because with one less potential income earner their average income is lower. For comparison, the expenses of a single parent are $161,220, compared to $173,490 for a husband-wife household. Child-rearing expenses consume a greater percentage of income for single-parent families.

Annual expenditures for raising one, two, or three children, by age of the youngest child, are as follows:

	Married Family	Single-Parent Family
One-child Household		
• Age 2:	$15,890	$10,260
• Age 5:	$15,900	$11,390
• Age 8:	$15,750	$11,170
• Age 11:	$16,810	$11,930
• Age 14:	$17,730	$12,460
• Age 17:	$18,380	$12,110
Two-child Household*		
• Age 2:	$27,410	$17,060
• Age 5:	$27,420	$17,940
• Age 8:	$27,300	$17,770
• Age 11:	$28,150	$18,360

• Age 14:	$28,880	$18,770
• Age 15:	$29,400	$18,500

* Age of older child: 16

Three-child Household*

• Age 2:	$32,440	$20,350
• Age 5:	$34,450	$21,030
• Age 8:	$32,350	$20,900
• Age 11:	$33,020	$21,350
• Age 12:	$35,590	$21,670

* Age of older children: 13, 16

58.3 Shopping and Spending Characteristics

A survey by The Nielsen Company (www.nielsen.com) found that children accompany parents on about 13% of food shopping trips, and their presence makes adult shoppers 150% more likely to buy seasonal items, like pumpkins and turkey.

According to *Parental Attitudes Toward Family-Friendly Establishments*, 75% of parents with young children deliberately seek out establishments that have child-accommodating amenities. Such amenities might include the availability of high chairs, child-friendly restrooms, or child activity centers.

Though birthrates have dropped to their lowest levels, the baby-product industry saw record high spending of $49 billion in 2013.

58.4 Intergenerational Households

According to *The Return of the Multi-Generational Family Household*, a report by the Social & Demographic Trends Project at The Pew Research Center (www.pewsocialtrends.com), U.S. family households are distributed by generational category as follows:

• Two generations (parent and minor child/children):	47%
• One generation:	34%
• Multi-generational:	16%
• Other:	1%

According to the U.S. Census Bureau, the number of households with family and relatives other than children living in the household, and the increase since 2000, is as follows:

	Households	Increase
• Parents living in adult children's household:	3.6 million	62.7%
• Live-in brothers or sisters:	3.5 million	24.0%
• Other relatives in household:	3.3 million	65.0%
• Grandchildren in household:	5.8 million	10.6%

According to Amy Gover, a multigenerational issues expert at AARP (www.aarp.org), the most common multigenerational household is one with a grandparent as head of household with adult children that have moved in with their children, an arrangement usually spurred by the needs of one or both to combine resources and save money. The second most popular arrangement is a grandparent moving in with an adult child's family, usually for caregiving reasons.

Census 2010 counted 3.1 million children in the U.S. living without a parent in the household; 59% were living with grandparents.

The Pew Research Center found that grandparents who are primary caregivers of grandchildren are relatively young: 67% are under age 60 and 13% are under 45.

There were also 6.2 million households in 2010 with non-relatives, including unmarried partners and roommates, an 8% increase from 2000.

According to Stephanie Coontz, Ph.D., a family history professor at Evergreen State College, a host of factors – among them higher housing costs and the struggling economy – is prompting families to combine expenses. Also, inter-generational households are common among the country's growing number of immigrants.

58.5 Stepfamilies

According to *A Portrait Of Stepfamilies*, a report by Pew Social & Demographic Trends Project, 42% of American adults have at least one step relative in their family. Three-in-10 have a step- or half-sibling, 18% have a stepparent, and 13% have at least one stepchild.

> **"Several sweeping changes in the demography of American family life in the past half century – including increases in divorce and in the share of babies born out of wedlock – have contributed to the prevalence of step relatives."**
>
> Pew Research Center

Seventy percent (70%) of adults who have at least one step-relative say they are very satisfied with their family life. Those who don't have any step-relatives register slightly higher levels of family satisfaction (78% very satisfied).

People with step-relatives are just as likely as others to say that family is the most important element of their life. However, they typically feel a stronger sense of obligation to their biological family members (be it a parent, a child or a sibling) than to their step-relatives, according to Pew surveys.

58.6 Market Trends: Adult Children At Home

According to an analysis of Census Bureau data by Pew Research Center, a record 21.6 million Millennials (those ages 18 to 31) lived in their parents' home in 2012, an increase from 18.5 million for youth of the same age in 2007. It should be noted that between one-third and half of this group are college students, and some students reside in dormitories during the academic year. Nonetheless, this is the highest share in at least four decades for this age group.

Compared with those in this age group in 2007, fewer in this group today have a job, more are enrolled in college, and more have delayed marriage.

58.7 Market Resources

Center for Economic Research On The Family, Clemson University, Sirrine Hall, Clemson, SC 29634, (www.clemson.edu/economics/cerf/index.html)

Center for Family & Demographic Research, Bowling Green State University, Five Williams Hall, Bowling Green, OH 43403. (419) 372-7279. (www.bgsu.edu/organizations/cfdr/)

Center for Family Research, University of Georgia, 1095 College Station Road, Athens, GA 30602. (706) 425-2992. (www.cfr.uga.edu)

Center for Family Studies, University of California Riverside, Olmstead Hall, 3rd Floor, Riverside CA, 92521. (http://familystudies.ucr.edu/)

Center for Marital and Family Studies, University of Denver, 2155 S. Race Street, Denver, CO 80208. (303) 871-3062. (www.du.edu/psychology/marriage/)

Center for Research on Families, University of Massachusetts, 135 Hicks Way, 622 Tobin Hall, Amherst, MA 01003. (413) 545-4631. (www.umass.edu/family/)

Expenditures on Children By Families, 2012, Center for Nutrition Policy and Promotion, U.S. Department of Agriculture, August 2013. (www.cnpp.usda.gov/Publications/CRC/crc2012.pdf)

Family Research Center, University of North Carolina Greensboro, 536 Highland Avenue, Greensboro, NC 27402. (336) 334-3601. (www.uncg.edu/frc/)

59

FAMILY CAREGIVERS

59.1 Profile

According to a June 2013 report by the Pew Internet & American Life Project (www.pewinternet.org), 39% of U.S. adults provide care for a child or adult with significant health issues, an increase from 30% who did so in 2010.

According to Gallup (www.gallup.com), 35% of caregivers say the person receiving care lives with them. The ailments of the person receiving care are as follows:

- Non-specific age-related: 19%
- Alzheimer's disease/dementia: 15%
- Heart disease: 8%
- Type 2 diabetes: 7%
- Cancer: 7%
- Stroke/aneurysm: 5%
- Arthritis: 4%
- Memory decline: 3%
- COPD: 2%
- Eye disease: 2%
- Parkinson's disease: 2%
- Other: 17%

"More than one in six Americans who work a full- or part-time job also report assisting with care for an elderly or disabled family member, relative, or friend."

Gallup

The Alzheimer's Association (www.alz.org) estimates that over 10 million family members, friends, and neighbors provide unpaid care for a person with Alzheimer's disease or other dementia. Combined, they provide 8.4 billion hours of unpaid care annually, a contribution estimated at $89 billion.

A survey by the Health Resources and Services Administration (www.hrsa.gov), part of the U.S. Department of Health and Human Services, found that more than one-fifth of U.S. households with children have at least one child with special needs. For many of these families, much of the care the children receive is at-home family care.

59.2 Eldercare

According to a September 2013 report by the Bureau of Labor Statistics (www.bls.gov), 16% of the U.S. population age 15 and over, or 39.6 million people, provide unpaid eldercare to someone age 65 or older who needs help because of a condition related to aging. One-fourth of eldercare providers engage in unpaid eldercare on a given day, spending an average of 3.2 hours providing this care. Eldercare can involve a range of care activities, such as assisting with grooming, preparing meals, and providing transportation. Eldercare also can involve providing companionship or being available to assist when help is needed, and thus it can be associated with nearly any activity.

Seventy percent (70%) of eldercare providers care for only one person, 22% care for two persons, and 7% care for three or more persons.

Among those providing eldercare, 50% have done so for 2 years or less; 15% have provided care for 10 years or more.

59.3 Demographics of Caregivers

Caring for a loved one is an activity that cuts across most demographic groups, but is especially prevalent among adults ages 30-to-64, a group traditionally still in the workforce. The percentages of adults who are caregivers are as follows (source: Pew Internet & American Life Project):

Gender

- Female: 40%
- Male: 37%

Age

- 18-to-29: 36%
- 30-to-49: 42%
- 50-to-64: 44%
- 65 and older: 30%

Race/Ethnicity

- Black: 40%
- Caucasian: 39%
- Hispanic: 32%

Annual Household Income

- Less than $30,000: 36%
- $30,000 to $49,999: 38%
- $50,000 to $74,999: 46%
- $75,000 and higher: 43%

The percentages of adults who provide eldercare are as follows (source: Bureau of Labor Statistics):

Gender

- Female: 18%
- Male: 16%

Age

- 15-to-24: 12%
- 25-to-34: 10%
- 35-to-44: 13%
- 45-to-54: 23%
- 55-to-64: 22%
- 65 and older: 16%

Race/Ethnicity

- Black: 16%
- Caucasian: 17%
- Hispanic: 10%

Employment Status

- Full-time worker: 16%
- Part-time worker: 18%
- Not employed: 15%

59.4 The Cost Of Caregiving

AARP (www.aarp.org) estimates that unpaid caregivers provide the equivalent of $350 billion in elder care annually, more than total annual Medicare spending.

According to Gallup, caregiving costs the U.S. economy about $25.2 billion per year in lost productivity. Caregivers report missing an average of 6.6 workdays per year because of caregiving responsibilities.

According to *Caregiving In The U.S. - Needs, Issues and Insights*, a report by the Caregivers Advisory Panel, 96% of caregivers influence decisions regarding the purchase of caregiving health products, and 79% of caregivers purchase all or nearly all of those products.

59.5 Support for Caregivers

There is evidence that caregivers experience considerable health issues as a result of their focus on caring for others. In the National Caregiver Survey by AARP and the National Alliance for Caregiving (www.caregiving.org), 31% of adult caregivers reported stress, anxiety, or depression.

A four-year study at University of Pittsburgh found caregiver mortality rates are 63% above those of non-caregivers. According to Prof. David W. Coon, Ph.D., at Arizona State University, the depression rate among caregivers is 23%.

Researchers at New York University School of Medicine reported that even a short period of counseling can have a long-term beneficial impact on the emotional well-being of caregivers.

Some employers are now offering elder-care programs aimed at the health and well-being of workers who also are caregivers. Raytheon, for example, offers employee caregiver seminars on self-care and emotional support. At Nike and Intel, Powerful Tools for Caregivers, a program developed by Legacy Health Systems (www.legacyhealth.org), is offered. IBM, Exxon Mobil, and Texas Instruments have funded development of an online version of Powerful Tools. Similarly, companies like PepsiCo, KPMG, and Northrop Grumman are offering services to caregivers that range from parent networks to Web seminars to financial planning. By encouraging workers who also have elder-care duties to take better care of themselves, employers hope not only to raise productivity, but also to scale down healthcare costs.

Retailers are also beginning to provide support. Kmart, for example, offers The Caregivers Marketplace, a cash-back program for the purchase of brand-name healthcare products commonly purchased by caregivers. It is the first program to assist family caregivers in managing everyday healthcare product expenses.

Some assisted-living facilities are also offering services for elder-caregiving families through "respite stay" programs, where the senior family member is signed up for a short-term stay. This allows caregivers time off for, say, vacation, or even for caring for their own major personal needs, like surgery, for example. Costs typically range from $150-$200 daily and include meals, snacks, housekeeping, laundry, personal care assistance, and basic clinical care.

A specialized media sector also has evolved to serve this demographic – from publications like *Today's Caregiver*, with approximately 50,000 subscribers who pay $18 a year for the periodical, to *Exceptional Parents*, a publication for parents of special needs children, to a host of online resources.

59.6 Market Resources

Caregivers Advisory Panel, 3949 Old Post Road, Suite 200C, Charlestown, RI 02813. (401) 364-9100. (www.caregiversadvisorypanel.com)

Caregiving Costs to Working Caregivers, MetLife Mature Market Institute, June 2011. (www.caregiving.org/wp-content/uploads/2011/06/mmi-caregiving-costs-working-caregivers.pdf)

Family Caregiver Alliance, 785 Market Street, Suite 750, San Francisco, CA 94103. (415) 434.3388. (www.caregiver.org)

Family Caregivers Are Wired For Health, Pew Internet & American Life Project, June 2013. (http://pewinternet.org/Reports/2013/Family-Caregivers.aspx)

National Alliance for Caregiving, 4720 Montgomery Lane, 2nd Floor, Bethesda, MD 20814. (www.caregiving.org)

Unpaid Eldercare In The United States, Bureau of Labor Statistics, September 2013. (www.bls.gov/news.release/pdf/elcare.pdf)

60

GAY & LESBIAN CONSUMERS

60.1 Profile

Between 6% and 7% of the adult U.S. population self-identifies as lesbian, gay, bisexual, and transgender (LGBT), suggesting that there is a LGBT adult population of 15 million to 16 million in the U.S. Some estimates, however, place the number of LGBTs at up to 30 million. Unlike estimates of other populations, the LGBT population generally includes adults over the age of 18 – the age when a person is more likely to be fully aware and able to define sexual orientation or gender identity.

A study directed by Prof. Amy Falkner, an associate dean at the S.I. Newhouse School of Public Communications at Syracuse University, provides the following facts about LGBT households:

- Twenty-one percent (21%) of females and nearly 5% of males have a child under age 18 living at home.
- Eleven percent (11%) of males and 8% of females have a child or children ages 18 and older.
- Four percent (4%) of males and 8% of females are grandparents.
- Seventy-seven percent (77%) of males and 73% of females are employed full-time.
- Twelve percent (12%) of males and 15% of females work for a government entity.
- Thirty-seven percent (37%) are employed at a company providing domestic-partner health benefits.
- Twelve percent (12%) of male and 9% of female households own a second home.
- Ninety-seven percent (97%) of gay Americans are out to their families, friends, or at work; 85% are out to family, 95% to friends, and 74% at the workplace.
- Fifty-three percent (53%) of females are partnered, as are 42% of males, with the largest percentage together four to seven years.
- Thirty-two percent (32%) of males and 66% of females plan on adding children to their family in the next three years.
- Fifty-seven percent (57%) of males and 45% of females live in cities.

A study by Gary J. Gates, Ph.D., of the Williams Institute at the University of California at Los Angeles (www.law.ucla.edu/williamsinstitute/), based on the Census Bureau's *American Community Survey*, found that 31% of same-sex households who identify themselves as spouses are raising children, compared with 43% of hetrosexual households.

60.2 Coming Out

According to a poll by Harris Interactive (www.harrisinteractive.com) in conjunction with Witeck-Combs Communications (www.witeckcombs.com), a large majority of gay and lesbian adults are "out" and honest with others about their sexual orientation. The survey showed that four out of five (80%) gay and lesbian adults consider themselves "out" as a gay or lesbian person. In terms of their relationships, 95% of gay and lesbian adults consider themselves open about their sexual orientation to their close friends. Seventy-nine percent (79%) of gay and lesbian adults consider themselves open about their sexual orientation with their acquaintances/ casual friends. When it comes to the workplace, a significant majority (67%) of gay and lesbian adults reported being open about their sexual orientation with their co-workers/ colleagues.

Among heterosexuals, 87% said that if someone were to come out to them as gay, lesbian, bisexual, or transgender, it would have a positive impact or no impact on how they would view gay, lesbian, bisexual, or transgender people. Also, 67% agree that if someone they knew was gay or lesbian, they'd want that individual to be open and honest with them about it, rather than feel the need to hide who he or she really is.

60.3 Same-Sex Marriage

In 2003, Massachusetts became the first state to legalize same-sex marriage. At year-end 2013, the District of Columbia plus 16 states – California, Connecticut, Delaware, Hawaii, Illinois Iowa, Maine, Maryland, Massachusetts, Minnesota, New Hampshire, New Jersey, New York, Rhode Island, Vermont, Washington – had enacted legislation allowing same-sex marriage.

Anyone who had reported being married to someone of the same gender in the 2000 Census was reclassified as an "unmarried partner." The Bureau changed its survey and Census 2010 reported 131,729 married same-sex couples. Of the 646,454 reporting same-sex households, 514,735 consider themselves partnered rather than married.

Public opinion polls about gay marriage skew toward increased support for legalization of gay marriage. A May 2013 *Washington Post*-ABC News poll found that 55% of American adults support gay marriage while 40% do not. A July 2013 poll by Gallup found support for gay marriage at 54%, a record high, and double the support of 27% Gallup first measured when the question was asked in 1996. A September 2013 Quinnipiac University poll found that 56% of American adults and 57% of registered voters supported same-sex marriage; only 36% of both groups were opposed.

60.4 Buying Power

Witeck-Combs Communications estimates adult LGBT buying power at $830 billion for 2013.

Although past studies have portrayed the LGBT community as an affluent sub-group, more recent findings suggest they are probably no better off than heterosexual consumers. Research at the University of Maryland found that, on average, partnered gay males earn $10,000 less annually than straight married men. Partnered lesbians, however, generally earn $7,000 a year more than straight married women. But one key difference influencing disposable income is that gays and lesbians collectively have fewer children.

> **"Buying power is not the same as wealth. There is no evidence that same-sex households are more affluent or, on average, earn more than others, which is little more than a stereotype. We recognize economic research that strongly suggests that gay men appear likely to earn slightly less than their heterosexual counterparts, for instance and that LGBT populations of color particularly face many job and earnings barriers."**
>
> Bob Witeck, CEO
> Witeck-Combs Communications, 11/18/13

A recent survey conducted by The Nielsen Company (www.nielsen.com) found that spending power aside, U.S. same-sex partnered households make 16% more shopping trips than the average U.S. household (173 average shopping trips vs. 149 average shopping trips for total U.S. households).

These additional trips result in CPG spending of $8,651 vs. $6,898, with m/m households making 182 shopping trips compared to f/f households making 163 trips.

Buy rates for same-sex households for select CPG products are as follows:

Female/Female Purchase Index

- Pet care: 132
- Butter and margarine: 128
- Coffee: 125
- Cat food: 125
- Frozen novelties: 123
- Gum: 123
- Yogurt: 122
- Paper products: 121
- Frozen baked goods: 121
- Fresh produce: 121
- Vitamins: 119

- Flour: 119
- Salad dressing: 119
- Nuts: 119

Male/Male Purchase Index
- Liquor/beer/wine: 222
- Men's toiletries: 190
- Refrigerated meal starters: 173
- Coffee: 173
- Fresheners and deodorizers: 164
- Dog Food 163
- Oral Hygiene: 156
- Medications and remedies: 152
- Pet Care: 150
- Yogurt: 149
- Shaving needs: 147
- Nuts: 146
- Vitamins: 145
- Frozen novelties: 144
- Dairy snacks and spreads: 141

60.5 Population Centers

According to real-estate site Trulia (www.trulia.com), the following are the ZIP codes with the most gay residents:

Same-sex Female Couples
- 02657 (Provincetown, Cape Cod, MA)
- 01062 (Northhampton, MA)
- 01060 (Northhampton, MA)
- 02160 (Jamaica Plain, Boston, MA)
- 19971 (Rehoboth Beach, DE)
- 95446 (Guernville, north of San Francisco, CA)
- 02667 (Wellfleet, Cape Cod, MA)
- 94619 (Redwood Heights/Skyline, Oakland, CA)
- 30002 (Avondale Estates, suburban Atlanta, GA)
- 94114 (Castro, San Francisco, CA)

Same-sex Male Couples
- 94114 (Castro, San Francisco, CA)
- 92264 (Palm Springs, CA)
- 02657 (Provincetown, Cape Cod, MA)
- 92262 (Palm Springs, CA)
- 33305 (Wilton Manors, Fort Lauderdale, FL)

- 90069 (West Hollywood, Los Angeles, CA)
- 75219 (Oak Lawn, Dallas, TX)
- 19971 (Rehoboth Beach, DE)
- 48069 (Pleasant Ridge, suburban Detroit, MI)

"The best available Census data on same-sex couples supports the understanding that LGBT households skew into major metro and suburban areas."

Bob Witeck, CEO
Witeck-Combs Communications

Of all same-sex households, 51% are female couples and 49% are male couples, which means that of all U.S. households 0.3% are male couples and 0.3% of are female couples.

Some neighborhoods are found to have a concentration of same-sex couples more than ten times that national average.

For those 55 and over, living in an LGBT-retirement communities is an option. According to Services & Advocacy for GLBT Elders (SAGE, www.sageusa.org), there are currently between 1.75 million and 4 million gays and lesbians over age 65, numbers that are expected to double by 2030.

Conceived of by Bonnie McGowan in 1999, Birds of a Feather, in Pecos, New Mexico, which opened in 2004, is the first retirement community to open that was specifically developed for LGBT older adults. The community plans to double in size before 2014. There are communities in Portland, Oregon, and Fort Myers, Florida, and similar projects are underway in Philadelphia, Chicago, San Francisco, and Minneapolis.

About 49% of Americans older than 65 considered poor or low-income, and this includes LGBT seniors. As such, the issue of affordable housing is critical to this demographic. Developers of Fountaingrove Lodge in Santa Rosa, California, however, have decided to build high-end, with entrances fees as high as $1 million and monthly dues ranging from $3,395 to upward of $6,000. It's most expensive luxury residences are priced at just under $1 million and amenities include wine cages and an upscale restaurant on site.

"I thought we'd struggle with selling more expensive homes, but it's been the opposite. We have more higher-end homes reserved."

Gena Jacobs, Sr. Marketing Director
Fountaingrove Lodge
Bloomberg Businessweek, 5/20/13

60.6 Activities

According to Community Marketing, Inc. (CMI, www.communitymarketing.com), the following are percentages of gay and lesbian consumers who regularly engage in various activities:

	Lesbians	Gay Men
• Dine out with friends:	90%	88%
• Attend a concert:	32%	24%
• Go to a club or bar:	31%	50%
• Go to the movies:	28%	40%
• Attend live theater:	26%	39%
• Visit a museum:	18%	24%

One major area recognized as an outlet for the discretionary income spent by the LGBT community is travel. According to the *17th Annual LGBT Tourism Study 2012-2013*, by Community Marketing, the annual economic impact of LGBT travelers is approximately $65 billion, about 10% of the U.S. travel market.

Approximately 85% of the LGBT community take annual vacations, compared with a national average of 64%. Annually, more than one-third take three or more trips. Almost 50% travel abroad, compared with the national average of 9%.

Similar to all travelers, location and price are key factors when LGBT travelers select a hotel, but an "LGBT friendly" reputation is also an important motivator.

Further, the CMI survey estimates that 79% of LGBTs in the United States hold a valid passport, which translates into a significant amount of potential international travel, and compares to about 39% of the U.S. population overall holding a passport, according to a January 2013 U.S. State Department report.

60.7 Internet Usage

According to eMarketer, the following are the leading media activities of U.S. gay and lesbian Internet users (June 2013):

	Gay males	Lesbians
• LGBT sites/blogs:	67%	58%
• Network/cable TV:	68%	57%
• Mainstream sites/blogs:	57%	46%
• Mainstream general newspapers:	55%	46%
• LGBT email newsletters:	41%	45%
• LGBT pubs for my city or region:	50%	42%
• Mainstream radio:	41%	39%
• Mainstream magazines:	43%	34%
• LGBT national magazines(s):	38%	30%
• Streaming video on computer:	38%	30%
• Alternative newspapers:	29%	26%
• Mainstream email newsletters:	24%	21%
• Satellite radio:	23%	17%
• LGBT-dedicated TV shows:	23%	16%
• Podcasts:	14%	13%
• LGBT radio:	11%	8%
• LGBT mobile apps:	25%	6%

A recent Harris Interactive poll found that gay and lesbian Internet users are more likely than heterosexuals to use social networks and blogs. The following is a comparison of use by each group:

	Gays & Lesbians	Heterosexuals
Social Networks		
• Facebook:	73%	65%
• MySpace:	32%	22%
• LinkedIn:	22%	16%
Blogs		
• Any type:	54%	40%
• News/current issues blogs:	36%	25%
• Personal blogs:	28%	19%
• Entertainment blogs:	25%	16%
• Political blogs:	22%	14%
• Travel blogs:	16%	8%
• Music blogs:	16%	6%
• Gay and lesbian blogs:	35%	n/a

60.8 Market Resources

17th Annual Gay & Lesbian Tourism Report, Community Marketing, October 2012. (www.communitymarketinginc.com/documents/temp/CMI_17thLGBTTourismStudy.pdf)

Community Marketing Inc., 584 Castro Street, Suite 834, San Francisco, CA 94114. (415) 437-3800. (www.communitymarketing.com)

Witeck-Combs Communications, 2120 L Street NW, Suite 850, Washington, DC 20037. (202) 887-0500. (www.witeckcombs.com)

61

IMMIGRANT CONSUMERS

61.1 Profile

More than one million immigrants are granted residency in the United States each year. The U.S. Census Bureau (www.census.gov) reports that 12.5% of the population (38.52 million people) in 2010 was foreign-born (most recent data available). This count does not include undocumented immigrants, of which there is an estimated 12 million living in the United States.

The immigrant population in the U.S. peaked in 2007, when 12.7% of the total population was foreign-born. Prior to 2007, the foreign-born population of the United States had continuously increased in size and as a percentage of the total population for almost five decades: from 9.6 million or 4.7% in 1970 to 14.1 million or 6.2% in 1980, 19.8 million or 7.9% in 1990, and 31.1 million or 11.1% in 2000.

The nativity region of the U.S. foreign-born population is distributed as follows:

- Latin America: 53.1%
- Asia: 27.7%
- Europe: 12.7%
- Africa: 3.9%
- Other regions: 2.7%

The foreign-born population is distributed by country of birth as follows:

- Mexico: 29.8%
- China: 5.2%
- Phillippines: 4.5%
- India: 4.3%
- El Salvador: 3.0%
- Vietnam: 3.0%
- Korea: 2.6%
- Cuba: 2.6%
- Canada: 2.1%
- Guatemala: 2.1%
- Dominican Republic: 2.1%
- All other countries: 38.8%

Residency of the foreign-born population in 2010, by state, was as follows:

- Alabama: 147,000
- Alaska: 49,000
- Arizona: 925,000
- Arkansas: 120,000
- California: 9.95 million
- Colorado: 487,000

- Connecticut: 460,000
- Delaware: 74,000
- District of Columbia: 72,000
- Florida: 3.48 million
- Georgia: 920,000
- Hawaii: 224,000
- Idaho: 98,000
- Illinois: 1.74 million
- Indiana: 281,000
- Iowa: 116,000
- Kansas: 171,000
- Kentucky: 128,000
- Louisiana: 152,000
- Maine: 44,000
- Maryland: 730,000
- Massachusetts: 943,000
- Michigan: 614,000
- Minnesota: 358,000
- Mississippi: 60,000
- Missouri: 213,000
- Montana: 19,000
- Nebraska: 106,000
- Nevada: 507,000
- New Hampshire: 68,000
- New Jersey: 1.76 million
- New Mexico: 196,000
- New York: 4.18 million
- North Carolina: 665,000
- North Dakota: 15,000
- Ohio: 433,000
- Oklahoma: 190,000
- Oregon: 367,000
- Pennsylvania: 691,000
- Rhode Island: 133,000
- South Carolina: 205,000
- South Dakota: 22,000
- Tennessee: 266,000
- Texas: 3.98 million
- Utah: 218,000
- Vermont: 21,000
- Virginia: 806,000
- Washington: 811,000
- West Virginia: 23,000
- Wisconsin: 256,000
- Wyoming: 17,000

In 2010, the following states had the highest percentages of foreign-born population:

- California: 25.8%
- New York: 10.8%
- Texas: 10.3%
- Florida: 9.0%
- New Jersey: 4.6%
- Illinois: 4.5%
- Massachusetts: 2.4%
- Arizona: 2.4%
- Georgia: 2.4%
- Washington: 2.1%
- Virginia: 2.1%
- All other states: 23.4%

61.2 Second-Generation Americans

According to *Second-Generation Americans: A Portrait of the Adult Children of Immigrants*, a 2013 report by the Pew Research Social & Demographic Trends Project (www.pewsocialtrends.org), there are 20 million adults born in the U.S. who have at least one immigrant parent. The adult second generation is young (median age 38, compared with 46 for U.S. adults overall) and has no racial or ethnic majority group.

> **"Among the key measures on which the second generation U.S.-born adults are better off than immigrant adults: Their median adjusted annual household income and homeownership rates are higher. They are more likely to hold a college degree. The share in poverty is lower. On all these measures, second generation adults are at least as well off as the overall adult population."**
>
> Pew Research Center, 2/7/13

61.3 U.S.-Born Children

The 14th Amendment to the U.S. Constitution grants an automatic right to citizenship to anyone born in the U.S.

The Pew Research Hispanic Trends Project (www.pewhispanic.org) estimated 340,000 of the 4.3 million babies born in the United States are the offspring of unauthorized immigrants.

Unauthorized immigrants comprise slightly more than 4% of the adult population of the U.S., but because they are relatively young and have high birthrates, their children make up a much larger share of both the newborn population (8%) and the child population (7% of those younger than age 18) in the U.S.

Of the 5.1 million children (younger than age 18) of unauthorized immigrants, 79% were born in this country and therefore are U.S. citizens. In total, four million U.S.-born children of unauthorized immigrant parents reside in the U.S.; there are 1.1 million foreign-born children of unauthorized immigrant parents.

61.4 Life In The U.S.

A Place to Call Home: What Immigrants Say Now About Life in America, a study by Public Agenda (www.publicagenda.org), asked immigrants their feelings about their lives in the United States. Responses were as follows:

- Somewhat happy: 53%

- Extremely happy: 34%
- Generally disappointed: 10%

When asked if they could do it over again, or what would be their choice, responses were as follows:

- Come to the United States: 71%
- Stay in birth country: 19%
- Pick a different country: 6%
- Don't know: 3%

There are an estimated 1.5 million immigrant-owned U.S. businesses, according to a study for the Small Business Association (www.sba.gov). In all, immigrants own 12.5% of U.S. businesses and account for 11.6% of all small business income.

61.5 Assimilation

Measuring assimilation is challenging because it is difficult to define. For some, it's the ability to speak English or the willingness to become a U.S. citizen. With others, it may be as superficial as appearance or style of dress. Others, still, maintain aspects of their native culture in private while displaying traits of American culture in public.

More than 80% of immigrants say they have tried to learn English. Among Spanish-speaking immigrants residing in the U.S. for more than 15 years, 75% speak English regularly; and 91% of their children and 97% of their grandchildren can speak English well, according to the Anti-Defamation League (www.adl.org).

A study by the Manhattan Institute for Policy Research (MIRP, www.manhattan-institute.org) assessed how well immigrants fit in with native-born Americans in three areas: economic, cultural, and civic. The assessment, which was directed by Prof. Jacob L. Vigdor, Ph.D., Public Policy Studies and Economics at Duke University, found that the nation's immigrants are adopting American ways just as quickly as they were in 1990, despite a doubling in their numbers. This contrasts with the historical trend that the level of assimilation typically drops during times of high immigration because there are more newcomers who are different from native-born Americans. This happened, for example, between 1900 and 1920, when the immigrant population grew by 40% and assimilation occurred more slowly. The MIRP study found, however, that Mexicans, the largest immigrant group, are making slower progress at assimilating than others. While assimilating well culturally, Mexicans have a low civic assimilation.

61.6 Future Growth

According to the Pew Research Center (www.pewresearch.org), if current trends continue, the population of the United States will rise to 438 million in 2050, from 296 million in 2005, with 82% of the increase from new immigrants and their U.S.-born descendants. Of the 117 million people added to the population during this period, 67 million will be first-generation immigrants, and 50 million will be their U.S.-born children or grandchildren.

The following are other projections:

- Nearly one in five Americans (19%) will be an immigrant in 2050, compared with one in eight (12%) in 2005. By 2025, the immigrant, or foreign-born, share of the population will surpass the peak of the last great wave of immigration a century before.
- The major role of immigration in national growth builds on the pattern of recent decades, during which immigrants and their U.S.-born children and grandchildren accounted for most of the population increase.
- The Latino population, already the nation's largest minority group, will triple in size and will account for most of the nation's population growth from 2005 through 2050. Hispanics will make up 29% of the U.S. population in 2050, compared with 14% in 2005.
- Births in the United States will play a growing role in Hispanic and Asian population growth; as a result, a smaller proportion of both groups will be foreign-born in 2050 than now.

61.7 Market Resources

Center for Immigration Studies, 1522 K Street NW, Suite 820, Washington, DC 20005. (202) 466-8185. (www.cis.org)

Pew Research Hispanic Trends Project, 1615 L Street NW, Suite 700, Washington, DC 20036. (202) 419-3600. (www.pewhispanic.org)

Place Of Birth Of The Foreign-Born Population, U.S. Census Bureau, October 2010. (www.census.gov/prod/2010pubs/acsbr09-15.pdf)

Second-Generation Americans, By The Numbers, Pew Research Social & Demographic Trends, February 2013. (www.pewsocialtrends.org/2013/02/07/second-generation-americans-by-the-numbers/)

62

MARRIED COUPLES

62.1 Profile

Among the total U.S. population age 18 and older, the share of men and women who were married fell from 57% in 2000 to 51% in 2010, the lowest percentage since the government began collecting marital status data more than 100 years ago.

The median age of their first marriage is 28.4 for men and 26.5 and for women. In 1970, the ages were 22.5 and 20.6, respectively, according to the U.S. Census Bureau (www.census.gov).

"The age at first marriage is continuing to rise. Cohabitation is continuing to rise in popularity. Marriage is something that is more optional now and it's also something increasingly people do later in the life course."

Susan Brown, Ph.D., Co-Director
Center for Family & Demographic Research
Bowling Green State University

62.2 Buying Power

According to the U.S. Census Bureau, the median income for married-couple households was $64,053 in 2012. This was 26% above the overall median household income of $51,017.

There were 55.52 million married-couple households in 2011, or 48% of all U.S. households. Their combined income was over $4 trillion.

62.3 Trends

The long-term decline in marriage accelerated during the recession.

Interestingly, divorce rates also fell during the economic downturn, suggesting that the challenges of job losses, foreclosures, and depleted retirement accounts may be driving some couples to stick together. The divorce rate fell from 17.0 divorces per 1,000 married women in 2007 to 16.9 in 2008 (and from a rate of 17.3 in 2005).

While divorce rates are down, the Great Recession took a toll on marriages. Research at the National Marriage Project, University of Virginia, found that men are 61% less likely to be happy in a marriage if they work fewer hours than their wives. Since men, particularly working class and poor men, have absorbed 75% of job losses since 2007, researchers foresee that economic conditions will ultimately undercut marriage in working class communities, furthering a "divorce divide" that has been growing since the 1980s between couples with college degrees and those with less education.

Research by Jeffrey Dew, Ph.D., a professor of family studies at Utah State University, indicates that financial conflict is a top predictor of divorce. Couples who report disagreeing over finances once a week are over 30% more likely to divorce than couples who disagree about finances a few times per month. Prof. Dew also found that couples who had no assets were 70% more likely to divorce than couples with at least $10,000 in assets.

According to *Women, Men and the New Economics of Marriage*, a report by Pew Research Center's Social & Demographic Trends Project (www.pewsocialtrends.org), 28% of married women have more education than their husbands, while 19% of married men are more educated that their wives; couples are equally educated in 53% of marriages. This is a reversal of this statistic in 1970, when 28% of husbands were more educated and 20% of wives had a higher level of education.

62.4 Market Resources

Center for Marital and Family Studies, University of Denver, 2155 S. Race Street, Denver, CO 80208. (303) 871-3062. (www.du.edu/psychology/marriage/)

National Center for Marriage & Research, Bowling Green State University, 005 Williams Hall, Bowling Green, OH 43403. (419) 372-4910. (http://ncfmr.bgsu.edu)

National Marriage Project, University of Virginia, P.O. Box 400766, Charlottesville, VA 22904. (434) 982-4509. (www.virginia.edu/marriageproject/)

Women, Men and the New Economics of Marriage, Pew Research Center, January 2010. (http://pewsocialtrends.org/pubs/750/new-economics-of-marriage)

The State Of Our Unions: Marriage In America 2012, National Marriage Project, 2012. (http://nationalmarriageproject.org/wp-content/uploads/2012/12/SOOU2012.pdf)

63

MILITARY CONSUMERS

63.1 Overview

The United States Armed Forces consists of the Army, Navy, Marine Corps, Air Force, and Coast Guard. At year-end 2012, there were 1,427,490 active personnel in the U.S. military.

63.2 Buying Power

Soldiers, sailors, and Marines received average compensation of $122,263 per person in 2009 (most recent data available), up from $58,545 in 2000. Military compensation – an average of $70,168 in pay and $52,095 in benefits – includes the value of housing, medical care, pensions, hazardous-duty incentives, enlistment bonuses, and combat pay in war zones.

The U.S. military provides housing, medical care, schools, and other social services to the spouses and children of active duty service members.

Military spending has helped boost cities and towns across the U.S. Of the 18 metros with the highest income gains during the past decade, 13 are military towns. They are as follows:

- Cheyenne, WY: Warren Air Force Base
- Clarksville, TN: Fort Campbell (Army)
- Columbus, GA: Fort Benning (Army)
- Crestview-Fort Walton Beach-Destin, FL: Eglin Air Force Base
- El Paso, TX: Fort Bliss (Army)
- Fayetteville, NC: Fort Bragg (Army)
Pope Air Force Base
- Hanford-Corcoran, CA: Lemoore Naval Air Station
- Hinesville-Fort Stewart, GA: Fort Stewart (Army)
- Jacksonville, NC: Camp Lejeune (Marines)
- Killeen-Temple-Fort Hood, TX: Fort Hood (Army)
- Las Cruces, NM: Fort Bliss (Army)
Holloman Air Force Base
- Lawton, OK: Fort Sill (Army)
- Manhattan, KS: Fort Riley (Army)

63.3 The Military Exchange System

The Military Exchange System (MES) serves all of the U.S. Armed Forces with a combined 4,028 stores. MES annual retail sales are approximately $13 billion.

The largest component of the MES is the Army and Air Force Exchange Service (AAFES), with $8.8 billion in annual sales. During its 111 years of operation, AAFES has evolved from a purveyor of discounted basic necessities to a multichannel retailer with over 3,000 stores and restaurants and movie theaters, as well as catalogs and a growing Internet site. A survey found its prices are just 2.5% higher than Walmart's, but shoppers get the added benefit of forgoing sales taxes.

Within the U.S., AAFES stores, also called the PX for 'post exchange,' serve as de facto community centers for 11.5 million active or retired military service members and their families. Overseas, AAFES stores give troops the chance to connect with American culture and commerce through their broad selection of DVDs and electronics in addition to basic drugstore goods.

For grocery shopping, military personnel, including retirees, turn to a network of 281 stores (including about 95 overseas) operated by the Defense Commissary Agency (DeCA, www.commissaries.com). With annual sales of about $5 billion, DeCA generates revenues roughly equivalent to a conventional supermarket chain. Federal law does not allow the agency to make a profit, however, and products are sold at only a 5% markup from cost.

64

PET OWNERS

64.1 Overview

According to *2013-2014 National Pet Owners Survey*, by the American Pet Products Association (APPA, www.americanpetproducts.org), 82.5 million U.S. households (68% of all households) own pets. For comparison, in 1988, 56% of U.S. households owned a pet. Some 46% of all households today own more than one pet.

Topping the list of most-owned pets, there are 145 million freshwater fish in 14.3 million U.S. homes. Cats, with 95.6 million felines owned by 45.3 million household, are the second-most-popular pets in the U.S. Owned by more households than any other pet, 83.3 million pet dogs are owned by 56.7 million households.

64.2 Pets Owner Demographics

The following percentages of adults have pets (source: Harris Interactive [www.harrisinteractive.com]):

Gender
- Female: 64%
- Male: 56%

Age
- 18-to-35: 62%
- 35-to-47: 66%
- 48-to-66: 64%
- 67 and older: 19%

Race/Ethnicity
- Hispanic: 68%
- White: 63%
- African-American: 40%

Income
- $34,999 or less: 56%
- $35,000 to $49,999: 65%
- $50,000 to $74,999: 60%
- $75,000 to $99,999: 66%
- $100,000 or more: 68%

Education

- High school or less: 59%
- Some college: 63%
- College graduate: 61%
- Post graduate: 54%

Region

- West: 68%
- Midwest: 61%
- South: 57%
- East: 56%

64.3 Spending On Pets

According to the APPA, spending on pets has been as follows:

- 2004: $34.4 billion
- 2005: $36.3 billion
- 2006: $38.5 billion
- 2007: $41.2 billion
- 2008: $43.2 billion
- 2009: $45.5 billion
- 2010: $48.4 billion
- 2011: $50.8 billion
- 2012: $53.3 billion
- 2013*: $55.3 billion

*estimated

The distribution of spending on pets in 2013 is estimated as follows:

- Food: $21.3 billion
- Veterinarian care: $14.2 billion
- Supplies and over-the-counter medicines: $13.2 billion
- Pet services, boarding, and grooming: $ 4.5 billion
- Live animal purchases: $ 2.3 billion

The yearly cost of buying, feeding, and caring for pets tops what Americans spend on movies, video games, and recorded music combined. This is understandable considering one in ten pet owners (91%) say they consider their pet to be a member of the family.

Pet owners spend a combined $2.6 billion on holiday gifts for their pets, according to the APPA. One quarter of pet-related expenditures occur between Thanksgiving and Christmas.

64.4 Market Resources

American Pet Products Association, 255 Glenville Road, Greenwich, CT 06831. (203) 532-0000. (www.appa.org)

65

RETIREES

65.1 Profile

According to International Demographics (www.themediaaudit.com), 18% of all U.S. adults are retired, a figure that has increased by 6% in the last five years and will further increase as Baby Boomers exit the workforce over the next few decades.

According to the Employee Benefit Research Institute (EBRI, www.ebri.org), about 72% of Americans expect to remain engaged in some type of work after they officially retire. Almost half (47%) said they left their jobs sooner than they had planned.

65.2 Retiree Consumers

International Demographics provides the following characteristics of retirees:

- Eighty-three percent (83%) of retired adults in the U.S. own their own home.
- Thirty percent (30%) of retired adults have stocks and CDs.
- Thirteen percent (13%) of new automobile purchasers are retired, compared with 11% five years ago. Eight percent (8%) of adults who have a car loan are retired, compared to 6% five years ago.
- Sixteen percent (16%) of adults who frequently stay in hotels are retired, compared to 14% five years ago.
- Adults who are retired are 6% more likely than the average U.S. adult to frequently dine out at a full-service restaurant; retirees now make up nearly 20% of all adults who frequently dine out.
- Fourteen percent (14%) of adults taking an ocean cruise are retired.
- Compared with the average U.S. adult, those who are retired spend nearly 30% more time watching broadcast television, 14% more time watching cable television, and 25% more time reading a daily newspaper.
- Retired adults spend only 89 minutes per day online, 26% less than the average U.S. adult.

Ranked by retirees as a percentage of community population, the largest retiree markets are as follows:

- Ocala, FL: 36%
- Fort Myers-Naples, FL: 34%
- Daytona Beach, FL: 33%

- West Palm Beach, FL: 31%
- Melbourne-Titusville-Cocoa, FL: 29%

The most affluent retirees can be found in larger markets such as Washington, D.C., where the average retired adult earns $64,000 in household income and investment returns. San Jose, Fort Myers-Naples, San Francisco, and Long Island follow with household incomes of more than $50,000.

65.3 Financial Security

Household incomes of retirees are distributed as follows (percent with such income, source: International Demographics):

- Under $50,000: 72%
- $50,000 and above: 28%
- $75,000 and above: 14%
- $100,000 and above: 7%

Social security provides, on average, about 40% of retirement income.

The percentage of retirees by amount of liquid assets is as follows:

- Less than $100,000: 70%
- $100,000 and above: 30%
- $250,000 and above: 14%

The Employee Benefit Research Institute put the gap between what Americans need for retirement and what they have saved at $4.6 trillion. If Social Security benefits were to be eliminated, the deficit would rise to $8.5 trillion.

65.4 Trends in Retirement and Semi-retirement

Unlike earlier generations, the milestone of turning 65 will have little significance for most Baby Boomers. Few plan to retire completely, and by age 65 many Boomers will have already transitioned into semi-retirement. Many surveys suggest work will be routine during Baby Boomers' older years. An AARP (www.aarp.org) national poll of Boomers found that 80% intend to work at least part time during their 'retirement' years.

According to the Social & Demographic Trends Project at the Pew Research Center (www.pewsocialtrends.com), 52% of working adults ages 40-to-64 say they may delay their retirement; an additional 16% say they expect never to stop working.

Most who choose to continue working after age 60, or even 65, will likely find a new source of income; relatively few will remain in their current jobs. In fact, many have either already left their career jobs. According to the Bureau of Labor Statistics (www.bls.gov), just 60% of 60 year-olds are currently employed. But according to the AARP, 16% of older Baby Boomers are self-employed, compared with 10% of the overall workforce.

Aside from a desire to stay active, there will be a wide variation in the lifestyles of retiring Boomers. According to Nancy Schlossberg, Ph.D., a professor emeritus of education at the University of Maryland and author of *Retire Smart, Retire Happy: Finding Your True Path in Life* (2005, APA Life Tools), most retirees fall into one of a half-dozen distinct categories. There are 'continuers,' who maintain work ties in their chosen fields; 'adventurers,' who strike out in entirely different career paths; and 'searchers,' who try one organization after another until they find their niche. A lesser number may become 'easy gliders,' who take each day as it comes, or 'retreaters,' who would rather sit on the couch and watch television.

"I believe the word 'retirement' in a decade will be a quaint, charming term that people used to use."

Larry Minnix, President
American Association of Homes and Services for the Aging

65.5 Market Resources

AARP, 601 E Street NW, Washington DC 20049. (888) 687-2277. (www.aarp.org)

Employee Benefit Research Institute, 1100 13th Street NW, Suite 878, Washington, DC 20005. (202) 659-0670. (www.ebri.org)

66

SINGLE CONSUMERS

66.1 Overview

According to the U.S. Census Bureau, in 2012 there were 112 million unmarried people over age 18 in the U.S., representing nearly 47% of the adult population.

America's Families and Living Arrangements: 2012, a report from the U.S. Census Bureau (www.census.gov), assesses single U.S. households by type as follows:

	Men living alone	Women living alone
• 2000:	10.7%	14.8%
• 2005:	11.3%	15.3%
• 2010:	11.9%	14.8%
• 2012:	12.3%	15.2%

Overall, the number of single-dwellers increased 78.7% since 1970 to 33.3 million households in 2012, more than one-third of all U.S. households.

Profile America, a 2013 report from the Census Bureau, provides the following profile of unmarried and single Americans:

- Among unmarried adults, 45% are women; 55% are men.
- Among unmarried adults, 62% have never been married, 24% are divorced, and 14% are widowed.
- There are 17 million unmarried U.S. residents ages 65 and older. The elderly comprise 16% of all unmarried and single people 18 and older.
- There are 87 unmarried men ages 18 and older for every 100 unmarried women in the United States.
- There are 56 million households maintained by unmarried adults. These households comprise 46% of households nationwide.
- Thirty-three million people live alone, comprising 27% of all households; in 1970, this figure was 17%.

> **"Never-married single people ages 25-to-34 now outnumber the married crowd by 46%, a stark reversal from just a decade ago when couples held a 20-point edge in that age group."**
>
> *Advertising Age*

66.2 Growth of Singles Demographics

According to the U.S. Census Bureau, almost three-quarters of men and almost two-thirds of women in their 20s reported that they had never been married, a sharp increase in never-married 20-somethings in just six years. Among men ages 20-to-29, 73% reported in 2006 that they had never been married, compared with 64% in 2000. For women, 62.2% had never married, compared with 53.4% six years earlier.

The Census Bureau data also shows that the percentage of those marrying in their 20s continues to decline. Just 23.5% of men and 31.5% of women ages 20-to-29 were married in 2006, excluding those married but separated. For comparison, in 2000, 31.5% of men and 39.5% of women were married.

Driven by several factors, the trend toward delaying marriage has emerged over several decades. Financial burdens, such as large college loan debt, have made it more difficult for those in their 20s to reach independence, forcing some to move back in with their parents. Also, an increasing number of young adults are preoccupied with their careers, and there are increasing numbers of cohabiting couples.

While almost a quarter of single-person households are made up of young people under the age of 35 who have never been married, many are financially independent singles.

66.3 Cohabitation

According to the U.S. Census Bureau, the estimated number of unmarried couples living together is as follows:

- Opposite-sex couples: 7.5 million
- Same-sex couples: 620,000
- Total: 8.1 million

Couples who choose cohabitation over marriage cite several advantages to the arrangement. Studies show that never-married couples with the intention of living together permanently are just as likely to stay together as married couples.

"The question," says Andrew J. Cherlin, Ph.D., a professor of sociology at Johns Hopkins University and author of *The Marriage-Go-Round* (2009, Random House), "is not why fewer people are getting married, but why are so many still getting married?"

"It's a mistake to think of all unmarried people as single. Lots are living with partners."

Prof. Andrew J. Cherlin, Ph.D.
Johns Hopkins University
The New York Times

A trend that is increasing among singles is that of "committed unmarrieds," so dubbed by one sociologist. More than five million such couples cohabit in the U.S., nearly eight times the number in 1970, according to *Time*. The family dynamic of committed unmarried with children is also on the rise. Households such as these challenge the perceptions of family, and the greater majority of marketers don't even identify the market.

For comparison, 56 million households were maintained by unmarried men and women in 2012, accounting for 46% of households nationwide. The number of people living alone in 2012 topped 33 million, comprising 27% of all households.

66.4 Spending Power

According to the Bureau of Labor Statistics (www.bls.gov), singles spend $2.2 trillion annually, which is 35% of all consumer spending.

The average single-household income is approximately $1,400 greater than the average income of two-person households divided by two; the average one-person household has over $1,300 in discretionary income.

Despite their spending clout, singles are seldom targeted by advertisers.

"Some marketers are taking notice: More ads are featuring singles and some companies are reaching out to them. But for the most part marketers are only slowly adjusting to the new normal."

Advertising Age

A study from Packaged Facts (www.packagedfacts.com) points out that singles are more receptive to ad pitches than the general population.

Diamond company De Beers got attention in 2004 when it debuted its "Right-hand Ring" campaign that targeted women who were single *or* married. Recent pitches by Honda and by Chevrolet focused specifically on singles hanging out with their friends.

66.5 Market Resources

Alternatives to Marriage Project, PMB 131, 358 7th Avenue, Brooklyn NY 11215. (347) 987-1068. (www.unmarried.org)

Profile America: Unmarried and Single Americans, U.S. Census Bureau, July 2013. (www.census.gov/newsroom/releases/archives/facts_for_features_special_editions/cb13-ff21.html)

PART X: GEODEMOGRAPHICS

67

MEGAPOLITAN REGIONS

67.1 Overview

Megapolitan regions, also called megaregions, are clustered networks of American cities characterized by high density populations, high growth, and, in some instances, blurring boundaries between cities.

Eleven (11) megapolitans have been defined by Metropolitan Institute at Virginia Tech (www.mi.vt.edu) and the America 2050 project at the Regional Plan Association (RPA, www.rpa.org).

A map of the megapolitan regions, as defined by the America 2050 project, is presented online at www.america2050.org/pdf/2050_Map_Megaregions2008.pdf.

67.2 Megapolitan Regions Defined

Eighty-three (83) of the top 100 primary census statistical areas are included in the 11 megapolitan areas. Major cities in the regions are as follows:

Arizona Sun Corridor
- Phoenix, Tucson

Cascadia
- Portland, Seattle, Tacoma, Vancouver, Victoria

Florida
- Daytona Beach, Fort Lauderdale, Jacksonville, Miami, Orlando, St. Petersburg, Tampa, West Palm Beach

Front Range
- Albuquerque, Colorado Springs, Denver, Pueblo, Santa Fe

Great Lakes
- Akron, Buffalo, Chicago, Cincinnati, Cleveland, Columbus, Dayton, Detroit, Fort Wayne, Grand Rapids, Green Bay, Hamilton, Indianapolis, Kansas City, Louisville, Milwaukee, Pittsburgh, Rochester, St. Louis, Toledo, Toronto, Twin Cities (Minneapolis-Saint Paul)

Gulf Coast

- Baton Rouge, Corpus Christi, Houston, Mobile, New Orleans, Pensacola

Northeast

- Baltimore, Boston, Hampton Roads (Virginia Beach-Norfolk), Harrisburg, Hartford, Lehigh Valley (Allentown-Bethlehem), New York City, Philadelphia, Portland, Providence, Richmond, Washington, Worcester

Northern California

- Fresno, Modesto, Reno, Sacramento, San Francisco Bay Area (San Francisco-Oakland-San Jose), Stockton

Piedmont Atlantic

- Atlanta, Birmingham, Charlotte, Chattanooga, Columbia, Huntsville, Knoxville, Montgomery, Nashville, Piedmont Triad (Greensboro-Winston-Salem), Research Triangle (Raleigh-Durham), Upstate South Carolina (Greenville-Spartanburg)

Southern California

- Anaheim, Las Vegas, Long Beach, Los Angeles, Riverside, San Bernardino, San Diego

Texas Triangle

- Austin, Dallas-Fort Worth Metroplex (Dallas-Fort Worth-Arlington), Houston, Oklahoma City, San Antonio, Tulsa, Wichita

67.3 Regional GDP

Megapolitan regions were first defined in 2005. The 11 regions account for 74% of the total U.S. GDP, or $11.60 in 2012. The GDP of each region was as follows:

- Northeast: $3.27 trillion
- Gulf Coast: $2.61 trillion
- Southern California: $1.31 trillion
- Texas Triangle: $1.03 trillion
- Northern California: $ 786 billion
- Florida: $ 767 billion
- Great Lakes: $ 661 billion
- Piedmont Atlantic: $ 613 billion
- Cascadia: $ 425 billion
- Front Range: $ 289 billion
- Arizona Sun Corridor: $ 241 billion

67.4 Population Projections

Seventy four percent (75%) of the U.S. population resides in the 11 megapolitan regions. The population of the megaregions is projected by the RPA to increase 18% from the 2010 Census through 2025; the rest of the U.S. is expected to rise 14% during that period.

Population projections for 2025 are as follows:

- Arizona Sun Corridor: 7,362,613
- Cascadia: 10,209,826
- Florida: 21,358,829
- Front Range: 6,817,462
- Gulf Coast: 15,832,117
- Great Lakes: 62,894,147
- Northeast: 58,124,740
- Northern California: 17,290,363
- Piedmont Atlantic: 30,351,698
- Southern California: 28,692,923
- Texas Triangle: 23,586,856

*Megapolitan America (*2011, APA Planners Press), by Arthur C. Nelson, Professor of City and Metropolitan Planning at the University of Utah, and Robert E. Lang, Professor of Sociology and the Director of Brookings Mountain West at the University of Nevada Las Vegas, predicts that by 2040 there will be ten distinct clusters composed of 23 megapolitan areas that will work together to dominate the U.S. economy.

"The threat of global competition has made these regions seek each other out for competitive advantage. These regions are now merging, and that's the geography by which America accesses the global economy."

Prof. Robert E. Lang
University of Nevada Las Vegas

67.5 Market Resources

Regional Plan Association, 4 Irving Place, 7th Floor, New York, NY 10003. (212) 253-2727. (www.rpa.org)

Metropolitan Institute at Virginia Tech, 1021 Prince Street, Suite 100, Alexandria, VA 22314. (703) 706-8100. (www.mi.vt.edu)

68

METROPOLITAN PROFILES

68.1 Overview

This chapter presents a demographic profile of major metropolitan areas based on data provided by The Nielsen Company (www.nielsen.com), Scarborough Research (www.scarborough.com), and Arbitron (www.arbitron.com).

For comparison with metro data, these statistics for the overall U.S. population are as follows:

Gender

- Men: 49%
- Women: 51%

Marital Status

- Married: 58%
- Never married: 25%
- Divorced/separated/widowed: 17%

Ethnicity*

- White: 83%
- African-American: 12%
- Hispanic: 14%
- Other: 4%

* does not add to 100% because of mixed- race persons

Employment Status

- Employed full-time*: 46%
- Employed part-time: 16%
- Not employed: 38%

* 35 hours or more

Children in Household

- None: 59%
- One or more: 42%
- Two or more: 25%
- Three or more: 10%

Age

- 18-to-24: 12%
- 25-to-34: 18%
- 35-to-44: 19%
- 45-to-54: 19%
- 55-to-64: 15%
- 65 or older: 17%

Household Income

- Less than $29,999: 21%
- $30,000 to $49,999: 14%
- $40,000 to $59,999: 11%
- $50,000 to $74,999: 18%
- $75,000 to $99,999: 15%
- $100,000 or more: 21%

68.2 Atlanta

- Population (age two and older): 6.37 million

Gender

- Men: 49%
- Women: 51%

Marital Status

- Married: 58%
- Never married: 26%
- Divorced/separated/widowed: 16%

Ethnicity

- White: 69%
- African-American: 26%
- Hispanic: 9%
- Other: 4%

Employment Status

- Employed full-time: 49%
- Employed part-time: 18%
- Not employed: 33%

Children in Household

- None: 59%
- One or more: 42%

- Two or more: 25%
- Three or more: 11%

Age
- 18-to-24: 13%
- 25-to-34: 19%
- 35-to-44: 21%
- 45-to-54: 20%
- 55-to-64: 14%
- 65 or older: 13%

Household Income
- Less than $29,999: 17%
- $30,000 to $49,999: 12%
- $40,000 to $59,999: 12%
- $50,000 to $74,999: 17%
- $75,000 to $99,999: 15%
- $100,000 or more: 27%

68.3 Baltimore

- Population (age two and older): 7.73 million

Gender
- Men: 47%
- Women: 53%

Marital Status
- Married: 54%
- Never married: 28%
- Divorced/separated/widowed: 18%

Ethnicity
- White: 69%
- African-American: 26%
- Hispanic: 5%
- Other: 3%

Employment Status
- Employed full-time: 53%
- Employed part-time: 15%
- Not employed: 32%

Children in Household

- None: 60%
- One or more: 40%
- Two or more: 20%
- Three or more: 7%

Age

- 18-to-24: 12%
- 25-to-34: 17%
- 35-to-44: 19%
- 45-to-54: 20%
- 55-to-64: 15%
- 65 or older: 17%

Household Income

- Less than $29,999: 13%
- $30,000 to $49,999: 11%
- $40,000 to $59,999: 10%
- $50,000 to $74,999: 19%
- $75,000 to $99,999: 19%
- $100,000 or more: 29%

68.4 Birmingham

- Population (age two and older): 1.76 million

Gender

- Men: 48%
- Women: 52%

Marital Status

- Married: 57%
- Never married: 23%
- Divorced/separated/widowed: 20%

Ethnicity

- White: 74%
- African-American: 24%
- Hispanic: 2%
- Other: 3%

Employment Status

- Employed full-time: 42%

- Employed part-time: 14%
- Not employed: 44%

Children in Household
- None: 61%
- One or more: 39%
- Two or more: 22%
- Three or more: 7%

Age
- 18-to-24: 12%
- 25-to-34: 17%
- 35-to-44: 18%
- 45-to-54: 19%
- 55-to-64: 16%
- 65 or older: 18%

Household Income
- Less than $29,999: 27%
- $30,000 to $49,999: 13%
- $40,000 to $59,999: 12%
- $50,000 to $74,999: 20%
- $75,000 to $99,999: 14%
- $100,000 or more: 15%

68.5 Boston

- Population (age two and older): 5.98 million

Gender
- Men: 49%
- Women: 51%

Marital Status
- Married: 56%
- Never married: 28%
- Divorced/separated/widowed: 16%

Ethnicity
- White: 90%
- African-American: 6%
- Hispanic: 6%
- Other: 5%

Employment Status

- Employed full-time: 48%
- Employed part-time: 18%
- Not employed: 34%

Children in Household

- None: 62%
- One or more: 38%
- Two or more: 23%
- Three or more: 8%

Age

- 18-to-24: 11%
- 25-to-34: 17%
- 35-to-44: 20%
- 45-to-54: 20%
- 55-to-64: 15%
- 65 or older: 17%

Household Income

- Less than $29,999: 13%
- $30,000 to $49,999: 11%
- $40,000 to $59,999: 10%
- $50,000 to $74,999: 17%
- $75,000 to $99,999: 18%
- $100,000 or more: 31%

68.6 Charlotte

- Population (age two and older): 2.76 million

Gender

- Men: 49%
- Women: 51%

Marital Status

- Married: 59%
- Never married: 24%
- Divorced/separated/widowed: 17%

Ethnicity

- White: 79%

- African-American: 18%
- Hispanic: 6%
- Other: 1%

Employment Status
- Employed full-time: 54%
- Employed part-time: 13%
- Not employed: 34%

Children in Household
- None: 60%
- One or more: 40%
- Two or more: 24%
- Three or more: 8%

Age
- 18-to-24: 12%
- 25-to-34: 19%
- 35-to-44: 20%
- 45-to-54: 19%
- 55-to-64: 15%
- 65 or older: 16%

Household Income
- Less than $29,999: 23%
- $30,000 to $49,999: 13%
- $40,000 to $59,999: 13%
- $50,000 to $74,999: 19%
- $75,000 to $99,999: 15%
- $100,000 or more: 18%

68.7 Chicago
- Population (age two and older): 9.38 million

Gender
- Men: 49%
- Women: 51%

Marital Status
- Married: 59%
- Never married: 24%
- Divorced/separated/widowed: 17%

Ethnicity

- White: 88%
- African-American: 8%
- Hispanic: 8%
- Other: 4%

Employment Status

- Employed full-time: 50%
- Employed part-time: 13%
- Not employed: 37%

Children in Household

- None: 58%
- One or more: 40%
- Two or more: 26%
- Three or more: 11%

Age

- 18-to-24: 11%
- 25-to-34: 29%
- 35-to-44: 19%
- 45-to-54: 19%
- 55-to-64: 16%
- 65 or older: 18%

Household Income

- Less than $29,999: 22%
- $30,000 to $49,999: 15%
- $40,000 to $59,999: 10%
- $50,000 to $74,999: 17%
- $75,000 to $99,999: 14%
- $100,000 or more: 24%

68.8 Cleveland

- Population (age two and older): 3.67 million

Gender

- Men: 48%
- Women: 52%

Marital Status

- Married: 56%
- Never married: 25%
- Divorced/separated/widowed: 19%

Ethnicity

- White: 85%
- African-American: 13%
- Hispanic: n/a
- Other: n/a

Employment Status

- Employed full-time: 48%
- Employed part-time: 16%
- Not employed: 36%

Children in Household

- None: 64%
- One or more: 36%
- Two or more: 22%
- Three or more: 9%

Age

- 18-to-24: 17%
- 25-to-34: 20%
- 35-to-44: 16%
- 45-to-54: 19%
- 55-to-64: 16%
- 65 or older: 21%

Household Income

- Less than $29,999: 13%
- $30,000 to $49,999: 19%
- $40,000 to $59,999: 16%
- $50,000 to $74,999: 16%
- $75,000 to $99,999: 17%
- $100,000 or more: 28%

68.9 Columbus

- Population (age two and older): 2.22 million

Gender

- Men: 49%
- Women: 51%

Marital Status

- Married: 55%
- Never married: 27%
- Divorced/separated/widowed: 18%

Ethnicity

- White: 87%
- African-American: 10%
- Hispanic: 4%
- Other: 2%

Employment Status

- Employed full-time: 53%
- Employed part-time: 13%
- Not employed: 34%

Children in Household

- None: 60%
- One or more: 41%
- Two or more: 24%
- Three or more: 9%

Age

- 18-to-24: 14%
- 25-to-34: 19%
- 35-to-44: 20%
- 45-to-54: 19%
- 55-to-64: 14%
- 65 or older: 15%

Household Income

- Less than $29,999: 20%
- $30,000 to $49,999: 15%
- $40,000 to $59,999: 13%
- $50,000 to $74,999: 20%
- $75,000 to $99,999: 16%
- $100,000 or more: 16%

68.10 Dallas/Fort Worth

- Population (age two and older): 6.78 million

Gender

- Men: 50%
- Women: 50%

Marital Status

- Married: 61%
- Never married: 24%
- Divorced/separated/widowed: 15%

Ethnicity

- White: 83%
- African-American: 13%
- Hispanic: 23%
- Other: 2%

Employment Status

- Employed full-time: 51%
- Employed part-time: 15%
- Not employed: 34%

Children in Household

- None: 53%
- One or more: 47%
- Two or more: 29%
- Three or more: 11%

Age

- 18-to-24: 13%
- 25-to-34: 21%
- 35-to-44: 21%
- 45-to-54: 19%
- 55-to-64: 13%
- 65 or older: 13%

Household Income

- Less than $29,999: 18%
- $30,000 to $49,999: 13%
- $40,000 to $59,999: 10%
- $50,000 to $74,999: 15%
- $75,000 to $99,999: 17%
- $100,000 or more: 27%

68.11 Denver

- Population (age two and older): 3.77 million

Gender
- Men: 50%
- Women: 50%

Marital Status
- Married: 61%
- Never married: 25%
- Divorced/separated/widowed: 15%

Ethnicity
- White: 92%
- African-American: 4%
- Hispanic: 18%
- Other: 3%

Employment Status
- Employed full-time: 51%
- Employed part-time: 18%
- Not employed: 31%

Children in Household
- None: 58%
- One or more: 42%
- Two or more: 28%
- Three or more: 11%

Age
- 18-to-24: 12%
- 25-to-34: 20%
- 35-to-44: 20%
- 45-to-54: 20%
- 55-to-64: 15%
- 65 or older: 14%

Household Income
- Less than $29,999: 17%
- $30,000 to $49,999: 12%
- $40,000 to $59,999: 12%
- $50,000 to $74,999: 19%
- $75,000 to $99,999: 18%
- $100,000 or more: 23%

68.12 Detroit

- Population (age two and older): 4.78 million

Gender

- Men: 48%
- Women: 52%

Marital Status

- Married: 54%
- Never married: 27%
- Divorced/separated/widowed: 19%

Ethnicity

- White: 74%
- African-American: 20%
- Hispanic: 3%
- Other: 4%

Employment Status

- Employed full-time: 44%
- Employed part-time: 16%
- Not employed: 40%

Children in Household

- None: 60%
- One or more: 40%
- Two or more: 24%
- Three or more: 8%

Age

- 18-to-24: 12%
- 25-to-34: 17%
- 35-to-44: 19%
- 45-to-54: 20%
- 55-to-64: 16%
- 65 or older: 16%

Household Income

- Less than $29,999: 17%
- $30,000 to $49,999: 15%
- $40,000 to $59,999: 11%
- $50,000 to $74,999: 17%
- $75,000 to $99,999: 16%
- $100,000 or more: 25%

68.13 Greenville/Spartanburg/Asheville

- Population (age two and older): 1.32 million

Gender

- Men: 48%
- Women: 52%

Marital Status

- Married: 56%
- Never married: 23%
- Divorced/separated/widowed: 20%

Ethnicity

- White: 83%
- African-American: 13%
- Hispanic: n/a
- Other: n/a

Employment Status

- Employed full-time: 43%
- Employed part-time: 14%
- Not employed: 42%

Children in Household

- None: 63%
- One or more: 37%
- Two or more: 21%
- Three or more: 7%

Age

- 18-to-24: 12%
- 25-to-34: 17%
- 35-to-44: 18%
- 45-to-54: 18%
- 55-to-64: 16%
- 65 or older: 20%

Household Income

- Less than $29,999: 28%
- $30,000 to $49,999: 16%
- $40,000 to $59,999: 12%
- $50,000 to $74,999: 18%
- $75,000 to $99,999: 13%
- $100,000 or more: 13%

68.14 Hartford/New Haven

- Population (age two and older): 2.47 million

Gender

- Men: 48%
- Women: 52%

Marital Status

- Married: 55%
- Never married: 28%
- Divorced/separated/widowed: 17%

Ethnicity

- White: 87%
- African-American: 9%
- Hispanic: 9%
- Other: 5%

Employment Status

- Employed full-time: 50%
- Employed part-time: 18%
- Not employed: 33%

Children in Household

- None: 61%
- One or more: 39%
- Two or more: 22%
- Three or more: 9%

Age

- 18-to-24: 12%
- 25-to-34: 15%
- 35-to-44: 18%
- 45-to-54: 20%
- 55-to-64: 16%
- 65 or older: 18%

Household Income

- Less than $29,999: 15%
- $30,000 to $49,999: 13%
- $40,000 to $59,999: 8%
- $50,000 to $74,999: 18%
- $75,000 to $99,999: 18%
- $100,000 or more: 28%

68.15 Houston

- Population (age two and older): 5.82 million

Gender

- Men: 50%
- Women: 50%

Marital Status

- Married: 59%
- Never married: 26%
- Divorced/separated/widowed: 15%

Ethnicity

- White: 78%
- African-American: 16%
- Hispanic: 31%
- Other: 6%

Employment Status

- Employed full-time: 52%
- Employed part-time: 16%
- Not employed: 33%

Children in Household

- None: 51%
- One or more: 49%
- Two or more: 31%
- Three or more: 13%

Age

- 18-to-24: 13%
- 25-to-34: 20%
- 35-to-44: 20%
- 45-to-54: 20%
- 55-to-64: 14%
- 65 or older: 12%

Household Income

- Less than $29,999: 19%
- $30,000 to $49,999: 12%
- $40,000 to $59,999: 11%
- $50,000 to $74,999: 13%
- $75,000 to $99,999: 16%
- $100,000 or more: 29%

68.16 Kansas City

- Population (age two and older): 2.30 million

Gender

- Men: 49%
- Women: 52%

Marital Status

- Married: 60%
- Never married: 22%
- Divorced/separated/widowed: 18%

Ethnicity

- White: 86%
- African-American: 9%
- Hispanic: 5%
- Other: 3%

Employment Status

- Employed full-time: 51%
- Employed part-time: 16%
- Not employed: 34%

Children in Household

- None: 57%
- One or more: 43%
- Two or more: 26%
- Three or more: 10%

Age

- 18-to-24: 12%
- 25-to-34: 19%
- 35-to-44: 19%
- 45-to-54: 20%
- 55-to-64: 15%
- 65 or older: 16%

Household Income

- Less than $29,999: 19%
- $30,000 to $49,999: 13%
- $40,000 to $59,999: 11%
- $50,000 to $74,999: 19%
- $75,000 to $99,999: 16%
- $100,000 or more: 23%

68.17 Las Vegas

- Population (age two and older): 1.89 million

Gender

- Men: 50%
- Women: 50%

Marital Status

- Married: 54%
- Never married: 27%
- Divorced/separated/widowed: 19%

Ethnicity

- White: 83%
- African-American: 9%
- Hispanic: 24%
- Other: 8%

Employment Status

- Employed full-time: 47%
- Employed part-time: 13%
- Not employed: 40%

Children in Household

- None: 55%
- One or more: 45%
- Two or more: 27%
- Three or more: 13%

Age

- 18-to-24: 12%
- 25-to-34: 20%
- 35-to-44: 20%
- 45-to-54: 18%
- 55-to-64: 15%
- 65 or older: 15%

Household Income

- Less than $29,999: 19%
- $30,000 to $49,999: 16%
- $40,000 to $59,999: 13%
- $50,000 to $74,999: 17%
- $75,000 to $99,999: 16%
- $100,000 or more: 20%

68.18 Los Angeles

- Population (age two and older): 16.97 million

Gender

- Men: 49%
- Women: 51%

Marital Status

- Married: 54%
- Never married: 31%
- Divorced/separated/widowed: 16%

Ethnicity

- White: 83%
- African-American: 7%
- Hispanic: 40%
- Other: 10%

Employment Status

- Employed full-time: 43%
- Employed part-time: 19%
- Not employed: 38%

Children in Household

- None: 52%
- One or more: 48%
- Two or more: 31%
- Three or more: 13%

Age

- 18-to-24: 14%
- 25-to-34: 19%
- 35-to-44: 20%
- 45-to-54: 19%
- 55-to-64: 13%
- 65 or older: 14%

Household Income

- Less than $29,999: 21%
- $30,000 to $49,999: 14%
- $40,000 to $59,999: 12%
- $50,000 to $74,999: 14%
- $75,000 to $99,999: 13%
- $100,000 or more: 26%

68.19 Miami/Fort Lauderdale

- Population (age two and older): 4.10 million

Gender

- Men: 48%
- Women: 52%

Marital Status

- Married: 50%
- Never married: 29%
- Divorced/separated/widowed: 21%

Ethnicity

- White: 77%
- African-American: 19%
- Hispanic: 47%
- Other: 3%

Employment Status

- Employed full-time: 47%
- Employed part-time: 15%
- Not employed: 37%

Children in Household

- None: 63%
- One or more: 37%
- Two or more: 21%
- Three or more: 7%

Age

- 18-to-24: 12%
- 25-to-34: 16%
- 35-to-44: 19%
- 45-to-54: 20%
- 55-to-64: 15%
- 65 or older: 19%

Household Income

- Less than $29,999: 21%
- $30,000 to $49,999: 15%
- $40,000 to $59,999: 13%
- $50,000 to $74,999: 16%
- $75,000 to $99,999: 14%
- $100,000 or more: 23%

68.20 Milwaukee

- Population (age two and older): 2.18 million

Gender

- Men: 49%
- Women: 51%

Marital Status

- Married: 56%
- Never married: 29%
- Divorced/separated/widowed: 16%

Ethnicity

- White: 86%
- African-American: 11%
- Hispanic: 6%
- Other: 2%

Employment Status

- Employed full-time: 50%
- Employed part-time: 19%
- Not employed: 32%

Children in Household

- None: 60%
- One or more: 40%
- Two or more: 25%
- Three or more: 11%

Age

- 18-to-24: 12%
- 25-to-34: 17%
- 35-to-44: 19%
- 45-to-54: 20%
- 55-to-64: 15%
- 65 or older: 17%

Household Income

- Less than $29,999: 18%
- $30,000 to $49,999: 12%
- $40,000 to $59,999: 11%
- $50,000 to $74,999: 22%
- $75,000 to $99,999: 18%
- $100,000 or more: 20%

68.21 Minneapolis/Saint Paul

- Population (age two and older): 4.28 million

Gender

- Men: 49%
- Women: 51%

Marital Status

- Married: 62%
- Never married: 24%
- Divorced/separated/widowed: 14%

Ethnicity

- White: 93%
- African-American: n/a
- Hispanic: n/a
- Other: n/a

Employment Status

- Employed full-time: 52%
- Employed part-time: 17%
- Not employed: 30%

Children in Household

- None: 59%
- One or more: 41%
- Two or more: 27%
- Three or more: 10%

Age

- 18-to-24: n/a
- 25-to-34: 18%
- 35-to-44: 19%
- 45-to-54: 20%
- 55-to-64: 15%
- 65 or older: 16%

Household Income

- Less than $29,999: 14%
- $30,000 to $49,999: 14%
- $40,000 to $59,999: 13%
- $50,000 to $74,999: 19%
- $75,000 to $99,999: 19%
- $100,000 or more: 22%

68.22 Nashville

- Population (age two and older): 2.46 million

Gender

- Men: 49%
- Women: 51%

Marital Status

- Married: 60%
- Never married: 21%
- Divorced/separated/widowed: 19%

Ethnicity

- White: 85%
- African-American: 12%
- Hispanic: 4%
- Other: 2%

Employment Status

- Employed full-time: 50%
- Employed part-time: 13%
- Not employed: 37%

Children in Household

- None: 58%
- One or more: 42%
- Two or more: 23%
- Three or more: 9%

Age

- 18-to-24: 13%
- 25-to-34: 18%
- 35-to-44: 19%
- 45-to-54: 19%
- 55-to-64: 15%
- 65 or older: 16%

Household Income

- Less than $29,999: 25%
- $30,000 to $49,999: 15%
- $40,000 to $59,999: 11%
- $50,000 to $74,999: 17%
- $75,000 to $99,999: 17%
- $100,000 or more: 15%

68.23 New York City

- Population (age two and older): 20.09 million

Gender

- Men: 48%
- Women: 52%

Marital Status

- Married: 53%
- Never married: 30%
- Divorced/separated/widowed: 16%

Ethnicity

- White: 77%
- African-American: 16%
- Hispanic: 19%
- Other: 8%

Employment Status

- Employed full-time: 46%
- Employed part-time: 17%
- Not employed: 37%

Children in Household

- None: 60%
- One or more: 40%
- Two or more: 24%
- Three or more: 9%

Age

- 18-to-24: 12%
- 25-to-34: 17%
- 35-to-44: 20%
- 45-to-54: 20%
- 55-to-64: 15%
- 65 or older: 17%

Household Income

- Less than $29,999: 17%
- $30,000 to $49,999: 12%
- $40,000 to $59,999: 9%
- $50,000 to $74,999: 14%
- $75,000 to $99,999: 14%
- $100,000 or more: 34%

68.24 Orlando

- Population (age two and older): 3.56 million

Gender

- Men: 49%
- Women: 51%

Marital Status

- Married: 58%
- Never married: 23%
- Divorced/separated/widowed: 20%

Ethnicity

- White: 84%
- African-American: 12%
- Hispanic: 15%
- Other: n/a

Employment Status

- Employed full-time: 44%
- Employed part-time: 15%
- Not employed: 40%

Children in Household

- None: 61%
- One or more: 39%
- Two or more: 24%
- Three or more: 9%

Age

- 18-to-24: 18%
- 25-to-34: 18%
- 35-to-44: 18%
- 45-to-54: 18%
- 55-to-64: 15%
- 65 or older: 22%

Household Income

- Less than $29,999: 19%
- $30,000 to $49,999: 17%
- $40,000 to $59,999: 13%
- $50,000 to $74,999: 18%
- $75,000 to $99,999: 16%
- $100,000 or more: 17%

68.25 Philadelphia

- Population (age two and older): 7.43 million

Gender

- Men: 48%
- Women: 52%

Marital Status

- Married: 56%
- Never married: 28%
- Divorced/separated/widowed: 17%

Ethnicity

- White: 79%
- African-American: 17%
- Hispanic: 7%
- Other: 2%

Employment Status

- Employed full-time: 51%
- Employed part-time: 15%
- Not employed: 34%

Children in Household

- None: 61%
- One or more: 39%
- Two or more: 23%
- Three or more: 8%

Age

- 18-to-24: 13%
- 25-to-34: 16%
- 35-to-44: 19%
- 45-to-54: 20%
- 55-to-64: 15%
- 65 or older: 18%

Household Income

- Less than $29,999: 14%
- $30,000 to $49,999: 13%
- $40,000 to $59,999: 12%
- $50,000 to $74,999: 17%
- $75,000 to $99,999: 18%
- $100,000 or more: 26%

68.26 Phoenix

- Population (age two and older): 4.98 million

Gender

- Men: 50%
- Women: 50%

Marital Status

- Married: 61%
- Never married: 25%
- Divorced/separated/widowed: 14%

Ethnicity

- White: 89%
- African-American: 5%
- Hispanic: 25%
- Other: 6%

Employment Status

- Employed full-time: 47%
- Employed part-time: 15%
- Not employed: 38%

Children in Household

- None: 57%
- One or more: 43%
- Two or more: 27%
- Three or more: 13%

Age

- 18-to-24: 12%
- 25-to-34: 20%
- 35-to-44: 19%
- 45-to-54: 18%
- 55-to-64: 14%
- 65 or older: 17%

Household Income

- Less than $29,999: 20%
- $30,000 to $49,999: 14%
- $40,000 to $59,999: 11%
- $50,000 to $74,999: 17%
- $75,000 to $99,999: 17%
- $100,000 or more: 22%

68.27 Pittsburgh

- Population (age two and older): 2.66 million

Gender

- Men: 48%
- Women: 52%

Marital Status

- Married: 56%
- Never married: 26%
- Divorced/separated/widowed: 19%

Ethnicity

- White: 92%
- African-American: 6%
- Hispanic: 1%
- Other: 2%

Employment Status

- Employed full-time: 42%
- Employed part-time: 16%
- Not employed: 42%

Children in Household

- None: 68%
- One or more: 32%
- Two or more: 17%
- Three or more: 5%

Age

- 18-to-24: 12%
- 25-to-34: 14%
- 35-to-44: 16%
- 45-to-54: 20%
- 55-to-64: 16%
- 65 or older: 22%

Household Income

- Less than $29,999: 23%
- $30,000 to $49,999: 15%
- $40,000 to $59,999: 13%
- $50,000 to $74,999: 17%
- $75,000 to $99,999: 14%
- $100,000 or more: 19%

68.28 Portland, Oregon

- Population (age two and older): 2.99 million

Gender

• Men:	49%
• Women:	51%

Marital Status

• Married:	60%
• Never married:	24%
• Divorced/separated/widowed:	16%

Ethnicity

• White:	90%
• African-American:	4%
• Hispanic:	10%
• Other:	6%

Employment Status

• Employed full-time:	45%
• Employed part-time:	16%
• Not employed:	39%

Children in Household

• None:	56%
• One or more:	44%
• Two or more:	28%
• Three or more:	10%

Age

• 18-to-24:	11%
• 25-to-34:	19%
• 35-to-44:	19%
• 45-to-54:	19%
• 55-to-64:	16%
• 65 or older:	16%

Household Income

• Less than $29,999:	20%
• $30,000 to $49,999:	11%
• $40,000 to $59,999:	12%
• $50,000 to $74,999:	21%
• $75,000 to $99,999:	16%
• $100,000 or more:	20%

68.29 Raleigh-Durham

• Population (age two and older):	2.65 million

Gender

• Men:	49%
• Women:	51%

Marital Status

• Married:	59%
• Never married:	25%
• Divorced/separated/widowed:	16%

Ethnicity

• White:	69%
• African-American:	26%
• Hispanic:	9%
• Other:	3%

Employment Status

• Employed full-time:	54%
• Employed part-time:	14%
• Not employed:	33%

Children in Household

• None:	57%
• One or more:	43%
• Two or more:	26%
• Three or more:	8%

Age

• 18-to-24:	14%
• 25-to-34:	19%
• 35-to-44:	20%
• 45-to-54:	19%
• 55-to-64:	14%
• 65 or older:	15%

Household Income

• Less than $29,999:	21%
• $30,000 to $49,999:	16%
• $40,000 to $59,999:	12%
• $50,000 to $74,999:	18%
• $75,000 to $99,999:	15%
• $100,000 or more:	18%

68.30 Sacramento

- Population (age two and older): 3.84 million

Gender

• Men:	49%
• Women:	51%

Marital Status

• Married:	59%
• Never married:	26%
• Divorced/separated/widowed:	16%

Ethnicity

• White:	83%
• African-American:	7%
• Hispanic:	22%
• Other:	6%

Employment Status

• Employed full-time:	47%
• Employed part-time:	16%
• Not employed:	37%

Children in Household

• None:	55%
• One or more:	45%
• Two or more:	22%
• Three or more:	12%

Age

• 18-to-24:	13%
• 25-to-34:	20%
• 35-to-44:	19%
• 45-to-54:	19%
• 55-to-64:	14%
• 65 or older:	16%

Household Income

• Less than $29,999:	19%
• $30,000 to $49,999:	13%
• $40,000 to $59,999:	10%
• $50,000 to $74,999:	17%
• $75,000 to $99,999:	19%
• $100,000 or more:	23%

68.31 San Francisco

- Population (age two and older): 6.72 million

Gender

- Men: 50%
- Women: 50%

Marital Status

- Married: 56%
- Never married: 29%
- Divorced/separated/widowed: 16%

Ethnicity

- White: 75%
- African-American: 6%
- Hispanic: 19%
- Other: 19%

Employment Status

- Employed full-time: 46%
- Employed part-time: 19%
- Not employed: 35%

Children in Household

- None: 59%
- One or more: 41%
- Two or more: 25%
- Three or more: 8%

Age

- 18-to-24: 11%
- 25-to-34: 17%
- 35-to-44: 20%
- 45-to-54: 20%
- 55-to-64: 16%
- 65 or older: 16%

Household Income

- Less than $29,999: 13%
- $30,000 to $49,999: 11%
- $40,000 to $59,999: 8%
- $50,000 to $74,999: 14%
- $75,000 to $99,999: 15%
- $100,000 or more: 39%

68.32 Seattle

- Population (age two and older): 4.44 million

Gender

- Men: 50%
- Women: 50%

Marital Status

- Married: 60%
- Never married: 25%
- Divorced/separated/widowed: 15%

Ethnicity

- White: 86%
- African-American: 5%
- Hispanic: 8%
- Other: 5%

Employment Status

- Employed full-time: 49%
- Employed part-time: 16%
- Not employed: 35%

Children in Household

- None: 61%
- One or more: 39%
- Two or more: 24%
- Three or more: 9%

Age

- 18-to-24: 12%
- 25-to-34: 17%
- 35-to-44: 20%
- 45-to-54: 20%
- 55-to-64: 15%
- 65 or older: 16%

Household Income

- Less than $29,999: 15%
- $30,000 to $49,999: 12%
- $40,000 to $59,999: 11%
- $50,000 to $74,999: 20%
- $75,000 to $99,999: 18%
- $100,000 or more: 25%

68.33 St. Louis

- Population (age two and older): 3.05 million

Gender

- Men: 48%
- Women: 52%

Marital Status

- Married: 56%
- Never married: 26%
- Divorced/separated/widowed: 18%

Ethnicity

- White: 82%
- African-American: 15%
- Hispanic: n/a
- Other: n/a

Employment Status

- Employed full-time: 47%
- Employed part-time: 17%
- Not employed: 36%

Children in Household

- None: 61%
- One or more: 39%
- Two or more: 23%
- Three or more: 10%

Age

- 18-to-24: 12%
- 25-to-34: 17%
- 35-to-44: 18%
- 45-to-54: 20%
- 55-to-64: 15%
- 65 or older: 18%

Household Income

- Less than $29,999: 18%
- $30,000 to $49,999: 15%
- $40,000 to $59,999: 13%
- $50,000 to $74,999: 19%
- $75,000 to $99,999: 17%
- $100,000 or more: 19%

68.34 Washington, D.C.

- Population (age two and older): 5.89 million

Gender

• Men:	48%
• Women:	52%

Marital Status

• Married:	58%
• Never married:	28%
• Divorced/separated/widowed:	14%

Ethnicity

• White:	71%
• African-American:	23%
• Hispanic:	10%
• Other:	3%

Employment Status

• Employed full-time:	57%
• Employed part-time:	14%
• Not employed:	29%

Children in Household

• None:	59%
• One or more:	41%
• Two or more:	24%
• Three or more:	8%

Age

• 18-to-24:	11%
• 25-to-34:	19%
• 35-to-44:	21%
• 45-to-54:	20%
• 55-to-64:	15%
• 65 or older:	14%

Household Income

• Less than $29,999:	10%
• $30,000 to $49,999:	8%
• $40,000 to $59,999:	8%
• $50,000 to $74,999:	15%
• $75,000 to $99,999:	16%
• $100,000 or more:	43%

69

METROPOLITAN STATISTICAL AREAS

69.1 Overview

The United States Office of Management and Budget (OMB, www.omb.gov) defines a Metropolitan Statistical Area (MSA) as one or more adjacent counties or county equivalents that have at least one urban core area with a population of at least 50,000, plus adjacent territory that has a high degree of social and economic integration with the core as measured by commuting ties.

There are 381 MSAs. A description of the regions included in each MSA is available at www.census.gov/population/www/metroareas/metrodef.html.

Population data is available from the U.S. Census Bureau (www.census.gov) at www.census.gov/popest/data/metro/totals/2012/.

69.2 MSA Populations

The July 2012 population in each MSA, as estimated by the U.S. Census Bureau, and change from the 2010 Census, is as follows:

		2012 Estimate	2010 Census	Change
1.	New York-Newark-Jersey City, NY-NJ-PA:	19,831,858	19,567,410	1.35%
2.	Los Angeles-Long Beach-Anaheim, CA:	13,052,921	12,828,837	1.75%
3.	Chicago-Naperville-Elgin, IL-IN-WI:	9,522,434	9,461,105	0.65%
4.	Dallas-Fort Worth-Arlington, TX:	6,700,991	6,426,214	4.28%
5.	Houston-The Woodlands-Sugar Land, TX:	6,177,035	5,920,416	4.33%
6.	Philadelphia-Camden-Wilmington, PA-NJ-DE-MD:	6,018,800	5,965,343	0.90%
7.	Washington-Arlington-Alexandria, DC-VA-MD-WV:	5,860,342	5,636,232	3.98%
8.	Miami-Fort Lauderdale-West Palm Beach, FL:	5,762,717	5,564,635	3.56%
9.	Atlanta-Sandy Springs-Roswell, GA:	5,457,831	5,286,728	3.24%
10.	Boston-Cambridge-Newton, MA-NH:	4,640,802	4,552,402	1.94%
11.	San Francisco-Oakland-Fremont, CA:	4,455,560	4,335,391	2.77%
12.	Riverside-San Bernardino-Ontario, CA:	4,350,096	4,224,851	2.96%
13.	Phoenix-Mesa-Scottsdale, AZ:	4,329,534	4,192,887	3.26%
14.	Detroit-Warren-Dearborn, MI:	4,292,060	4,296,250	-0.10%
15.	Seattle-Tacoma-Bellevue, WA:	3,552,157	3,439,809	3.27%
16.	Minneapolis-St. Paul-Bloomington, MN-WI:	3,422,264	3,348,859	2.19%
17.	San Diego-Carlsbad, CA:	3,177,063	3,095,313	2.64%
18.	Tampa-St. Petersburg-Clearwater, FL:	2,842,878	2,783,243	2.14%
19.	St. Louis, MO-IL:	2,795,794	2,787,701	0.29%

20.	Baltimore-Columbia-Towson, MD:	2,753,149	2,710,489	1.57%
21.	Denver-Aurora-Lakewood, CO:	2,645,209	2,543,482	4.00%
22.	Pittsburgh, PA:	2,360,733	2,356,285	0.19%
23.	Charlotte-Concord-Gastonia, NC-SC:	2,296,569	2,217,012	3.59%
24.	Portland-Vancouver-Hillsboro, OR-WA:	2,289,800	2,226,009	2.87%
25.	San Antonio-New Braunfels, TX:	2,234,003	2,142,508	4.27%
26.	Orlando-Kissimmee-Sanford, FL:	2,223,674	2,134,411	4.18%
27.	Sacramento–Roseville–Arden-Arcade, CA:	2,196,482	2,149,127	2.20%
28.	Cincinnati, OH-KY-IN:	2,128,603	2,114,580	0.66%
29.	Cleveland-Elyria, OH:	2,063,535	2,077,240	-0.66%
30.	Kansas City, MO-KS:	2,038,724	2,009,342	1.46%
31.	Las Vegas-Henderson-Paradise, NV:	2,000,759	1,951,269	2.54%
32.	Columbus, OH:	1,944,002	1,901,974	2.21%
33.	Indianapolis-Carmel-Anderson, IN:	1,928,982	1,887,877	2.18%
34.	San Jose-Sunnyvale-Santa Clara, CA:	1,894,388	1,836,911	3.13%
35.	Austin-Round Rock, TX:	1,834,303	1,716,289	6.88%
36.	Nashville-Davidson–Murfreesboro–Franklin, TN:	1,726,693	1,670,890	3.34%
37.	Virginia Beach-Norfolk-Newport News, VA-NC:	1,699,925	1,676,822	1.38%
38.	Providence-Warwick, RI-MA:	1,601,374	1,600,852	0.03%
39.	Milwaukee-Waukesha-West Allis, WI:	1,566,981	1,555,908	0.71%
40.	Jacksonville, FL:	1,377,850	1,345,596	2.40%
41.	Memphis, TN-MS-AR:	1,341,690	1,324,829	1.27%
42.	Oklahoma City, OK:	1,296,565	1,252,987	3.48%
43.	Louisville/Jefferson County, KY-IN:	1,251,351	1,235,708	1.27%
44.	Richmond, VA:	1,231,980	1,208,101	1.98%
45.	New Orleans-Metairie, LA:	1,227,096	1,189,866	3.13%
46.	Hartford-West Hartford-East Hartford, CT:	1,214,400	1,212,381	0.17%
47.	Raleigh, NC:	1,188,564	1,130,490	5.14%
48.	Birmingham-Hoover, AL:	1,136,650	1,128,047	0.76%
49.	Buffalo-Cheektowaga-Niagara Falls, NY:	1,134,210	1,135,509	-0.11%
50.	Salt Lake City, UT:	1,123,712	1,087,873	3.29%
51.	Rochester, NY:	1,082,284	1,079,671	0.24%
52.	Grand Rapids-Wyoming, MI:	1,005,648	988,938	1.69%
53.	Tucson, AZ:	992,394	980,263	1.24%
54.	Honolulu (Urban), HI:	976,372	953,207	2.43%
55.	Tulsa, OK:	951,880	937,478	1.54%
56.	Fresno, CA:	947,895	930,450	1.87%
57.	Bridgeport-Stamford-Norwalk, CT:	933,835	916,829	1.85%
58.	Worcester, MA-CT:	923,762	916,980	0.74%
59.	Albuquerque, NM:	901,700	887,077	1.65%
60.	Omaha-Council Bluffs, NE-IA:	885,624	865,350	2.34%
61.	Albany-Schenectady-Troy, NY:	874,646	870,716	0.45%
62.	New Haven-Milford, CT:	862,813	862,477	0.04%
63.	Bakersfield, CA:	856,158	839,631	1.97%

64.	Knoxville, TN:	848,350	837,571	1.29%
65.	Greenville-Anderson-Mauldin, SC:	842,853	824,112	2.27%
66.	Oxnard-Thousand Oaks-Ventura, CA:	835,981	823,318	1.54%
67.	El Paso, TX:	830,735	804,123	3.31%
68.	Allentown-Bethlehem-Easton, PA-NJ:	827,171	821,173	0.73%
69.	Baton Rouge, LA:	815,298	802,484	1.60%
70.	McAllen-Edinburg-Mission, TX:	806,552	774,769	4.10%
71.	Dayton, OH:	800,972	799,232	0.22%
72.	Columbia, SC:	784,745	767,598	2.23%
73.	Greensboro-High Point, NC:	736,065	723,801	1.69%
74.	North Port-Sarasota-Bradenton, FL:	720,042	702,281	2.53%
75.	Little Rock-North Little Rock-Conway, AR:	717,666	699,757	2.56%
76.	Stockton-Lodi, CA:	702,612	685,306	2.53%
77.	Akron, OH:	702,262	703,200	-0.13%
78.	Charleston-North Charleston, SC:	697,439	664,607	4.94%
79.	Colorado Springs, CO:	668,353	645,613	3.52%
80.	Syracuse, NY:	660,934	662,577	-0.25%
81.	Winston-Salem, NC:	647,697	640,595	1.11%
82.	Cape Coral-Fort Myers, FL:	645,293	618,754	4.29%
83.	Boise City, ID:	637,896	616,561	3.46%
84.	Wichita, KS:	636,105	630,919	0.82%
85.	Springfield, MA:	625,718	621,570	0.67%
86.	Madison, WI:	620,778	605,435	2.53%
87.	Lakeland-Winter Haven, FL:	616,158	602,095	2.34%
88.	Ogden-Clearfield, UT:	612,441	597,159	2.56%
89.	Toledo, OH:	608,711	610,001	-0.21%
90.	Deltona-Daytona Beach-Ormond Beach, FL:	595,309	590,289	0.85%
91.	Des Moines-West Des Moines, IA:	588,999	569,633	3.40%
92.	Jackson, MS:	576,800	567,122	1.71%
93.	Augusta-Richmond County, GA-SC:	575,898	564,873	1.95%
94.	Scranton–Wilkes-Barre–Hazleton, PA:	563,629	563,631	0.00%
95.	Youngstown-Warren-Boardman, OH-PA:	558,206	565,773	-1.34%
96.	Harrisburg-Carlisle, PA:	553,980	549,475	0.82%
97.	Provo-Orem, UT:	550,845	526,810	4.56%
98.	Palm Bay-Melbourne-Titusville, FL:	547,307	543,376	0.72%
99.	Chattanooga, TN-GA:	537,889	528,143	1.85%
100.	Spokane-Spokane Valley, WA:	532,253	527,753	0.85%
101.	Lancaster, PA:	526,823	519,445	1.42%
102.	Durham-Chapel Hill, NC:	522,826	504,357	3.66%
103.	Modesto, CA:	521,726	514,453	1.41%
104.	Portland-South Portland, ME:	518,117	514,098	0.78%
105.	Santa Rosa, CA:	491,829	483,878	1.64%
106.	Lexington-Fayette, KY:	485,023	472,099	2.74%
107.	Fayetteville-Springdale-Rogers, AR-MO:	482,200	463,204	4.10%

108.	Lafayette, LA:	474,415	466,750	1.64%
109.	Lansing-East Lansing, MI:	465,732	464,036	0.37%
110.	Pensacola-Ferry Pass-Brent, FL:	461,227	448,991	2.73%
111.	Visalia-Porterville, CA:	451,977	442,179	2.22%
112.	Shreveport-Bossier City, LA:	447,193	439,811	1.68%
113.	Springfield, MO:	444,617	436,712	1.81%
114.	York-Hanover, PA:	437,846	434,972	0.66%
115.	Corpus Christi, TX:	437,109	428,185	2.08%
116.	Reno, NV:	433,843	425,417	1.98%
117.	Port St. Lucie, FL:	432,683	424,107	2.02%
118.	Asheville, NC:	432,406	424,858	1.78%
119.	Santa Maria-Santa Barbara, CA:	431,249	423,895	1.73%
120.	Huntsville, AL:	430,734	417,593	3.15%
121.	Salinas, CA:	426,762	415,057	2.82%
122.	Fort Wayne, IN:	421,406	416,257	1.24%
123.	Vallejo-Fairfield, CA:	420,757	413,344	1.79%
124.	Killeen-Temple, TX:	420,375	405,300	3.72%
125.	Flint, MI:	418,408	425,790	-1.73%
126.	Brownsville-Harlingen, TX:	415,557	406,220	2.30%
127.	Mobile, AL:	413,936	412,992	0.23%
128.	Reading, PA:	413,491	411,442	0.50%
129.	Beaumont-Port Arthur, TX:	404,180	403,190	0.25%
130.	Canton-Massillon, OH:	403,455	404,422	-0.24%
131.	Manchester-Nashua, NH:	402,922	400,721	0.55%
132.	Salem, OR:	396,338	390,738	1.43%
133.	Myrtle Beach-Conway-N. Myrtle Beach, SC-NC:	394,542	376,722	4.73%
134.	Anchorage, AK:	392,535	380,821	3.08%
135.	Davenport-Moline-Rock Island, IA-IL:	382,630	379,690	0.77%
136.	Salisbury, MD-DE:	381,868	373,802	2.16%
137.	Peoria, IL:	380,447	379,186	0.33%
138.	Gulfport-Biloxi-Pascagoula, MS:	379,582	370,702	2.40%
139.	Montgomery, AL:	377,149	374,536	0.70%
140.	Tallahassee, FL:	375,371	367,413	2.17%
141.	Fayetteville, NC:	374,585	366,383	2.24%
142.	Trenton, NJ:	368,303	366,513	0.49%
143.	Huntington-Ashland, WV-KY-OH:	364,665	364,908	-0.07%
144.	Hickory-Lenoir-Morganton, NC:	363,627	365,497	-0.51%
145.	Savannah, GA:	361,941	347,611	4.12%
146.	Eugene, OR:	354,542	351,715	0.80%
147.	Ann Arbor, MI:	350,946	344,791	1.79%
148.	Rockford, IL:	346,009	349,431	-0.98%
149.	Ocala, FL:	335,125	331,298	1.16%
150.	Naples-Immokalee-Marco Island, FL:	332,427	321,520	3.39%
151.	Kalamazoo-Portage, MI:	330,034	326,589	1.05%

152.	South Bend-Mishawaka, IN-MI:	318,586	319,224	-0.20%
153.	Spartanburg, SC:	316,997	313,268	1.19%
154.	Evansville, IN-KY:	313,433	311,552	0.60%
155.	Green Bay, WI:	311,098	306,241	1.59%
156.	Columbus, GA-AL:	310,531	294,865	5.31%
157.	Fort Collins, CO:	310,487	299,630	3.62%
158.	Lincoln, NE:	310,342	302,157	2.71%
159.	Roanoke, VA:	310,118	308,707	0.46%
160.	Kingsport-Bristol-Bristol, TN-VA:	309,006	309,544	-0.17%
161.	Boulder, CO:	305,318	294,567	3.65%
162.	Utica-Rome, NY:	298,064	299,397	-0.45%
163.	Lubbock, TX:	297,669	290,805	2.36%
164.	Erie, PA:	280,646	280,566	0.03%
165.	Fort Smith, AR-OK:	280,521	280,467	0.02%
166.	Duluth, MN-WI:	279,452	279,771	-0.11%
167.	Atlantic City-Hammonton, NJ:	275,422	274,549	0.32%
168.	San Luis Obispo-Paso Robles-Arroyo Grande, CA:	274,804	269,637	1.92%
169.	Clarksville, TN-KY:	274,342	260,625	5.26%
170.	Norwich-New London, CT:	274,170	274,055	0.04%
171.	Kennewick-Richland, WA:	268,243	253,340	5.88%
172.	Gainesville, FL:	268,232	264,275	1.50%
173.	Santa Cruz-Watsonville, CA:	266,776	262,382	1.67%
174.	Greeley, CO:	263,691	252,825	4.30%
175.	Wilmington, NC:	263,429	254,884	3.35%
176.	Merced, CA:	262,305	255,793	2.55%
177.	Cedar Rapids, IA:	261,761	257,940	1.48%
178.	Laredo, TX:	259,172	250,304	3.54%
179.	Olympia-Tumwater, WA:	258,332	252,264	2.41%
180.	Amarillo, TX:	257,578	251,933	2.24%
181.	Waco, TX:	256,317	252,772	1.40%
182.	Hagerstown-Martinsburg, MD-WV:	256,278	251,599	1.86%
183.	Lynchburg, VA:	255,342	252,634	1.07%
184.	Bremerton-Silverdale, WA:	254,991	251,133	1.54%
185.	Binghamton, NY:	248,538	251,725	-1.27%
186.	Crestview-Fort Walton Beach-Destin, FL:	247,665	235,865	5.00%
187.	Yakima, WA:	246,977	243,231	1.54%
188.	Sioux Falls, SD:	237,251	228,261	3.94%
189.	Topeka, KS:	234,566	233,870	0.30%
190.	College Station-Bryan, TX:	234,501	228,660	2.55%
191.	Champaign-Urbana, IL:	233,788	231,891	0.82%
192.	Tuscaloosa, AL:	233,389	230,162	1.40%
193.	Macon, GA:	232,723	232,293	0.19%
194.	Appleton, WI:	228,450	225,666	1.23%
195.	Charleston, WV:	225,954	227,078	-0.49%

196.	Charlottesville, VA:	222,860	218,705	1.90%
197.	Chico, CA:	221,539	220,000	0.70%
198.	Longview, TX:	216,679	214,369	1.08%
199.	Fargo, ND-MN:	216,312	208,777	3.61%
200.	Barnstable Town, MA:	215,423	215,888	-0.22%
201.	Tyler, TX:	214,821	209,714	2.44%
202.	Las Cruces, NM:	214,445	209,233	2.49%
203.	Burlington-South Burlington, VT:	213,701	211,261	1.15%
204.	Prescott, AZ:	212,637	211,033	0.76%
205.	Springfield, IL:	211,993	210,170	0.87%
206.	Rochester, MN:	209,607	206,877	1.32%
207.	Houma-Thibodaux, LA:	208,922	208,178	0.36%
208.	Medford, OR:	206,412	203,206	1.58%
208.	Lafayette-West Lafayette, IN:	206,412	201,789	2.29%
210.	Florence, SC:	206,087	205,566	0.25%
211.	Bellingham, WA:	205,262	201,140	2.05%
212.	Lake Havasu City-Kingman, AZ:	203,334	200,186	1.57%
213.	Lake Charles, LA:	201,195	199,607	0.80%
214.	Johnson City, TN:	200,684	198,716	0.99%
215.	Yuma, AZ:	200,022	195,751	2.18%
216.	Elkhart-Goshen, IN:	199,619	197,559	1.04%
217.	Saginaw, MI:	198,353	200,169	-0.91%
218.	Athens-Clarke County, GA:	196,425	192,541	2.02%
219.	Racine, WI:	194,797	195,408	-0.31%
220.	Hilton Head Island-Bluffton-Beaufort, SC:	193,882	187,010	3.67%
221.	Daphne-Fairhope-Foley, AL:	190,790	182,265	4.68%
222.	St. Cloud, MN:	190,471	189,093	0.73%
223.	Bloomington, IL:	188,715	186,133	1.39%
224.	Panama City, FL:	187,621	184,715	1.57%
225.	Warner Robins, GA:	185,478	179,605	3.27%
226.	Gainesville, GA:	185,416	179,684	3.19%
227.	Jacksonville, NC:	183,263	177,772	3.09%
228.	Kingston, NY:	181,791	182,493	-0.38%
229.	Blacksburg-Christiansburg-Radford, VA:	178,933	178,237	0.39%
230.	Redding, CA:	178,586	177,223	0.77%
231.	Monroe, LA:	177,782	176,441	0.76%
232.	El Centro, CA:	176,948	174,528	1.39%
233.	Joplin, MO:	174,327	175,518	-0.68%
234.	Greenville, NC:	172,554	168,148	2.62%
235.	Terre Haute, IN:	172,493	172,425	0.04%
236.	Muskegon, MI:	170,182	172,188	-1.17%
237.	Sioux City, IA-NE-SD:	168,921	168,563	0.21%
238.	East Stroudsburg, PA:	168,798	169,842	-0.61%
239.	Oshkosh-Neenah, WI:	168,794	166,994	1.08%

240.	Waterloo-Cedar Falls, IA:	168,747	167,819	0.55%
241.	Columbia, MO:	168,535	162,642	3.62%
242.	Yuba City, CA:	167,948	166,892	0.63%
243.	Dover, DE:	167,626	162,310	3.28%
244.	Abilene, TX:	166,963	165,252	1.04%
245.	Eau Claire, WI:	163,599	161,151	1.52%
246.	Billings, MT:	162,848	158,934	2.46%
247.	Punta Gorda, FL:	162,449	159,978	1.54%
248.	Bloomington, IN:	162,399	159,549	1.79%
249.	Bend-Redmond, OR:	162,277	157,733	2.88%
250.	Bowling Green, KY:	162,231	158,599	2.29%
251.	Pueblo, CO:	160,852	159,063	1.12%
252.	Janesville-Beloit, WI:	160,418	160,331	0.05%
253.	Jackson, MI:	160,309	160,248	0.04%
254.	Kahului-Wailuku-Lahaina, HI:	158,316	154,924	2.19%
255.	Iowa City, IA:	158,231	152,586	3.70%
256.	Vineland-Bridgeton, NJ:	157,785	156,898	0.57%
257.	Albany, GA:	157,399	157,308	0.06%
258.	Niles-Benton Harbor, MI:	156,067	156,813	-0.48%
259.	State College, PA:	155,171	153,990	0.77%
260.	Alexandria, LA:	154,441	153,922	0.34%
261.	Decatur, AL:	154,233	153,829	0.26%
262.	Burlington, NC:	153,920	151,131	1.85%
263.	Bangor, ME:	153,746	153,923	-0.11%
264.	Madera, CA:	152,218	150,865	0.90%
265.	Rocky Mount, NC:	151,662	152,392	-0.48%
265.	Midland, TX:	151,662	141,671	7.05%
267.	Hanford-Corcoran, CA:	151,364	152,982	-1.06%
268.	Chambersburg-Waynesboro, PA:	151,275	149,618	1.11%
269.	Monroe, MI:	151,048	152,021	-0.64%
270.	Wichita Falls, TX:	150,829	151,306	-0.32%
271.	Elizabethtown-Fort Knox, KY:	150,413	148,338	1.40%
272.	Jefferson City, MO:	150,151	149,807	0.23%
273.	Texarkana, TX-AR:	149,701	149,198	0.34%
274.	Grand Junction, CO:	147,848	146,723	0.77%
275.	Dothan, AL:	147,620	145,639	1.36%
276.	Auburn-Opelika, AL:	147,257	140,247	5.00%
277.	Florence-Muscle Shoals, AL:	146,988	147,137	-0.10%
278.	Hattiesburg, MS:	146,766	142,842	2.75%
279.	Wheeling, WV-OH:	146,420	147,950	-1.03%
280.	Santa Fe, NM:	146,375	144,170	1.53%
281.	St. George, UT:	144,809	138,115	4.85%
282.	Valdosta, GA:	144,343	139,588	3.41%
283.	Odessa, TX:	144,325	137,130	5.25%

284.	Dalton, GA:	142,751	142,227	0.37%
285.	Coeur d'Alene, ID:	142,357	138,494	2.79%
286.	Johnstown, PA:	141,584	143,679	-1.46%
287.	Sebastian-Vero Beach, FL:	140,567	138,028	1.84%
288.	Homosassa Springs, FL:	139,360	141,236	-1.33%
289.	Napa, CA:	139,045	136,484	1.88%
290.	Rapid City, SD:	138,738	134,598	3.08%
291.	Springfield, OH:	137,206	138,333	-0.81%
292.	Idaho Falls, ID:	136,108	133,265	2.13%
293.	Flagstaff, AZ:	136,011	134,421	1.18%
294.	La Crosse-Onalaska, WI-MN:	135,298	133,665	1.22%
295.	Lebanon, PA:	135,251	133,568	1.26%
296.	Battle Creek, MI:	135,099	136,146	-0.77%
297.	Wausau, WI:	134,735	134,063	0.50%
298.	Morgantown, WV:	134,164	129,709	3.43%
299.	Lawton, OK:	132,545	130,291	1.73%
300.	Sierra Vista-Douglas, AZ:	132,088	131,346	0.56%
301.	Winchester, VA-WV:	130,907	128,472	1.90%
302.	Jackson, TN:	130,450	130,011	0.34%
303.	Pittsfield, MA:	130,016	131,219	-0.92%
304.	Farmington, NM:	128,529	130,044	-1.16%
305.	Glens Falls, NY:	128,472	128,923	-0.35%
306.	Harrisonburg, VA:	128,372	125,228	2.51%
307.	Logan, UT-ID:	128,306	125,442	2.28%
308.	New Bern, NC:	128,119	126,802	1.04%
309.	St. Joseph, MO-KS:	127,927	127,329	0.47%
310.	Altoona, PA:	127,121	127,089	0.03%
311.	Carbondale-Marion, IL:	126,745	126,575	0.13%
312.	Beckley, WV:	124,890	124,898	-0.01%
313.	Goldsboro, NC:	124,246	122,623	1.32%
314.	Jonesboro, AR:	124,042	121,026	2.49%
315.	Hammond, LA:	123,441	121,097	1.94%
316.	Mansfield, OH:	122,673	124,475	-1.45%
317.	Weirton-Steubenville, WV-OH:	122,547	124,454	-1.53%
318.	Sherman-Denison, TX:	121,935	120,877	0.88%
319.	Watertown-Fort Drum, NY:	120,262	116,229	3.47%
320.	Bismarck, ND:	120,060	114,778	4.60%
321.	Staunton-Waynesboro, VA:	118,686	118,502	0.16%
322.	Albany, OR:	118,360	116,672	1.45%
323.	Mount Vernon-Anacortes, WA:	118,222	116,901	1.13%
324.	Cleveland, TN:	117,820	115,788	1.75%
325.	Muncie, IN:	117,364	117,671	-0.26%
326.	Anniston-Oxford-Jacksonville, AL:	117,296	118,572	-1.08%
327.	Williamsport, PA:	117,168	116,111	0.91%

328. Owensboro, KY:	116,030	114,752	1.11%
329. Sheboygan, WI:	115,009	115,507	-0.43%
330. Morristown, TN:	114,937	113,951	0.87%
331. San Angelo, TX:	114,854	111,823	2.71%
332. Brunswick, GA:	113,448	112,370	0.96%
333. Kankakee, IL:	113,040	113,449	-0.36%
334. Wenatchee, WA:	113,037	110,884	1.94%
335. Lawrence, KS:	112,864	110,826	1.84%
336. Michigan City-La Porte, IN:	111,246	111,467	-0.20%
337. Missoula, MT:	110,977	109,299	1.54%
338. Decatur, IL:	110,122	110,768	-0.58%
339. California-Lexington Park, MD:	108,987	105,151	3.65%
340. Sumter, SC:	108,052	107,456	0.55%
341. Lewiston-Auburn, ME:	107,609	107,702	-0.09%
342. Bay City, MI:	106,935	107,771	-0.78%
343. Lima, OH:	105,141	106,331	-1.12%
344. Gadsden, AL:	104,392	104,430	-0.04%
345. Ithaca, NY:	102,554	101,564	0.97%
346. Longview, WA:	101,996	102,410	-0.40%
347. Cumberland, MD-WV:	101,968	103,299	-1.29%
348. Fond du Lac, WI:	101,843	101,633	0.21%
349. The Villages, FL:	101,620	93,420	8.78%
350. Gettysburg, PA:	101,482	101,407	0.07%
351. Fairbanks, AK:	100,272	97,581	2.76%
352. Grand Forks, ND-MN:	98,888	98,461	0.43%
353. Sebring, FL:	98,128	98,786	-0.67%
354. Mankato-North Mankato, MN:	98,020	96,740	1.32%
355. Manhattan, KS:	97,810	92,719	5.49%
356. Pine Bluff, AR:	97,451	100,258	-2.80%
357. Cape Girardeau, MO-IL:	97,080	96,275	0.84%
358. Hot Springs, AR:	96,903	96,024	0.92%
359. Victoria, TX:	96,620	94,003	2.78%
360. Ocean City, NJ:	96,304	97,265	-0.99%
361. Rome, GA:	96,177	96,317	-0.15%
362. Dubuque, IA:	95,097	93,653	1.54%
363. Cheyenne, WY:	94,483	91,738	2.99%
364. Parkersburg-Vienna, WV:	92,548	92,673	-0.13%
365. Ames, IA:	91,140	89,542	1.78%
366. Elmira, NY:	88,911	88,830	0.09%
367. Corvallis, OR:	86,430	85,579	0.99%
368. Bloomsburg-Berwick, PA:	85,243	85,562	-0.37%
369. Midland, MI:	83,822	83,629	0.23%
370. Pocatello, ID:	83,800	82,839	1.16%
371. Grand Island, NE:	83,472	81,850	1.98%

372.	Grants Pass, OR:	82,930	82,713	0.26%
373.	Kokomo, IN:	82,849	82,752	0.12%
374.	Great Falls, MT:	81,723	81,327	0.49%
375.	Hinesville, GA:	81,519	77,917	4.62%
376.	Danville, IL:	80,727	81,625	-1.10%
377.	Columbus, IN:	79,129	76,794	3.04%
378.	Casper, WY:	78,621	75,450	4.20%
379.	Walla Walla, WA:	63,399	62,859	0.86%
380.	Lewiston, ID-WA:	61,419	60,888	0.87%
381.	Carson City, NV:	54,838	55,274	-0.79%

70

MICROPOLITAN STATISTICAL AREAS

70.1 Overview

The United States Office of Management and Budget (OMB, www.omb.gov) defines a Micropolitan Statistical Area (µSA) as an urban area based around a core city or town with a population of 10,000 to 49,999.

There are 536 µSAs. The Census Bureau's description of the regions included in each µSA is available at www.census.gov/population/www/metroareas/metrodef.html.

Population data is available from the U.S. Census Bureau (www.census.gov) at www.census.gov/popest/data/metro/totals/2012/.

70.2 µSA Populations

The 2012 population in each µSA, as estimated by the U.S. Census Bureau, and change from the 2010 Census, is as follows:

		2012 Estimate	2010 Census	Change
1.	Claremont-Lebanon, NH-VT:	217,390	218,466	-0.49%
2.	Hilo, HI:	189,191	185,079	2.22%
3.	Torrington, CT:	187,530	189,927	-1.26%
4.	Ottawa-Peru, IL:	153,182	154,908	-1.11%
5.	Pottsville, PA:	147,063	148,289	-0.83%
6.	Concord, NH:	146,761	146,445	0.22%
7.	Traverse City, MI:	145,283	143,372	1.33%
8.	Tupelo, MS:	138,976	136,268	1.99%
9.	Lumberton, NC:	135,496	134,168	0.99%
10.	Eureka-Arcata-Fortuna, CA:	134,827	134,623	0.15%
11.	Jamestown-Dunkirk-Fredonia, NY:	133,539	134,905	-1.01%
12.	London, KY:	126,696	126,369	0.26%
13.	Dunn, NC:	122,135	114,678	6.50%
14.	Augusta-Waterville, ME:	121,853	122,151	-0.24%
15.	Wooster, OH:	114,848	114,520	0.29%
16.	Ogdensburg-Massena, NY:	112,232	111,944	0.26%
17.	Holland, MI:	112,039	111,408	0.57%
18.	Roseburg, OR:	107,164	107,667	-0.47%
19.	Meridian, MS:	107,111	107,449	-0.31%
20.	Show Low, AZ:	107,094	107,449	-0.33%
21.	Cookeville, TN:	106,860	106,042	0.77%

22.	Bluefield, WV-VA:	106,791	107,342	-0.51%
23.	East Liverpool-Salem, OH:	106,507	107,841	-1.24%
24.	Danville, VA:	105,803	106,561	-0.71%
25.	Whitewater-Elkhorn, WI:	102,851	102,228	0.61%
26.	Richmond-Berea, KY:	101,792	99,972	1.82%
27.	Twin Falls, ID:	101,094	99,604	1.50%
28.	Ashtabula, OH:	100,389	101,497	-1.09%
29.	Tullahoma-Manchester, TN:	100,333	100,210	0.12%
30.	Corning, NY:	99,063	98,990	0.07%
31.	Adrian, MI:	98,987	99,892	-0.91%
32.	Paducah, KY-IL:	98,539	98,762	-0.23%
33.	Truckee-Grass Valley, CA:	98,292	98,764	-0.48%
34.	Shelby, NC:	97,474	98,078	-0.62%
35.	Greenwood, SC:	94,857	95,078	-0.23%
36.	Albertville, AL:	94,776	93,019	1.89%
37.	Sunbury, PA:	94,428	94,528	-0.11%
38.	Clarksburg, WV:	94,310	94,196	0.12%
39.	Talladega-Sylacauga, AL:	92,728	93,830	-1.17%
40.	Bozeman, MT:	92,614	89,513	3.46%
41.	Sevierville, TN:	92,512	89,889	2.92%
42.	New Philadelphia-Dover, OH:	92,392	92,582	-0.21%
43.	Moses Lake, WA:	91,723	89,120	2.92%
44.	Kalispell, MT:	91,633	90,928	0.78%
45.	Orangeburg, SC:	91,476	92,501	-1.11%
46.	Brainerd, MN:	91,239	91,067	0.19%
47.	Pinehurst-Southern Pines, NC:	90,302	88,247	2.33%
48.	New Castle, PA:	89,871	91,108	-1.36%
49.	Beaver Dam, WI:	88,415	88,759	-0.39%
50.	Indiana, PA:	88,218	88,880	-0.74%
51.	Hermiston-Pendleton, OR:	88,064	87,062	1.15%
52.	Meadville, PA:	87,598	88,765	-1.31%
53.	Lufkin, TX:	87,597	86,771	0.95%
54.	Ukiah, CA:	87,428	87,841	-0.47%
55.	Zanesville, OH:	85,950	86,074	-0.14%
56.	Laurel, MS:	85,164	84,823	0.40%
57.	Russellville, AR:	84,697	83,939	0.90%
58.	Branson, MO:	84,524	83,877	0.77%
59.	Watertown-Fort Atkinson, WI:	84,498	83,686	0.97%
60.	Opelousas, LA:	83,662	83,384	0.33%
61.	Huntsville, TX:	82,717	82,446	0.33%
62.	Wilson, NC:	81,867	81,234	0.78%
63.	Plattsburgh, NY:	81,654	82,128	-0.58%
64.	DuBois, PA:	81,184	81,642	-0.56%
65.	Manitowoc, WI:	80,671	81,442	-0.95%

66.	Cullman, AL:	80,440	80,406	0.04%
67.	Auburn, NY:	79,552	80,026	-0.59%
68.	Olean, NY:	79,458	80,317	-1.07%
69.	Oak Harbor, WA:	79,177	78,506	0.85%
70.	Athens, TX:	79,094	78,532	0.72%
71.	Searcy, AR:	78,493	77,076	1.84%
72.	Portsmouth, OH:	78,477	79,499	-1.29%
73.	Stillwater, OK:	78,399	77,350	1.36%
74.	Warsaw, IN:	77,609	77,358	0.32%
75.	Chillicothe, OH:	77,429	78,064	-0.81%
76.	Quincy, IL-MO:	77,371	77,314	0.07%
77.	Somerset, PA:	76,957	77,742	-1.01%
78.	Keene, NH:	76,851	77,117	-0.34%
79.	Sandusky, OH:	76,398	77,079	-0.88%
80.	Helena, MT:	76,277	74,801	1.97%
81.	Findlay, OH:	75,671	74,782	1.19%
82.	Centralia, WA:	75,621	75,455	0.22%
83.	Roanoke Rapids, NC:	75,434	76,790	-1.77%
84.	Key West, FL:	74,809	73,090	2.35%
85.	Seneca, SC:	74,627	74,273	0.48%
86.	Wisconsin Rapids-Marshfield, WI:	74,424	74,749	-0.43%
87.	Glenwood Springs, CO:	74,216	73,537	0.92%
88.	Mount Airy, NC:	73,561	73,673	-0.15%
89.	Palatka, FL:	73,263	74,364	-1.48%
90.	Minot, ND:	73,146	69,540	5.19%
91.	Gallup, NM:	73,016	71,492	2.13%
92.	Statesboro, GA:	72,694	70,217	3.53%
93.	Port Angeles, WA:	71,863	71,404	0.64%
94.	Aberdeen, WA:	71,692	72,797	-1.52%
95.	Greenfield Town, MA:	71,540	71,372	0.24%
96.	Frankfort, KY:	71,532	70,706	1.17%
97.	Shawnee, OK:	70,760	69,442	1.90%
98.	Mount Pleasant, MI:	70,617	70,311	0.44%
99.	Muskogee, OK:	70,596	70,990	-0.56%
100.	Stevens Point, WI:	70,433	70,019	0.59%
101.	Marion, IN:	69,330	70,061	-1.04%
102.	North Wilkesboro, NC:	69,306	69,340	-0.05%
103.	Owosso, MI:	69,232	70,648	-2.00%
104.	Greeneville, TN:	68,819	68,831	-0.02%
105.	LaGrange, GA:	68,468	67,044	2.12%
106.	Kapaa, HI:	68,434	67,091	2.00%
107.	Richmond, IN:	68,346	68,917	-0.83%
108.	Lake City, FL:	67,966	67,531	0.64%
109.	Marquette, MI:	67,906	67,077	1.24%

110.	Morehead City, NC:	67,632	66,469	1.75%
111.	Marshall, TX:	67,450	65,631	2.77%
112.	Forest City, NC:	67,323	67,810	-0.72%
113.	Martinsville, VA:	66,702	67,972	-1.87%
114.	Hobbs, NM:	66,338	64,727	2.49%
115.	Marion, OH:	66,238	66,501	-0.40%
116.	Alamogordo, NM:	66,041	63,797	3.52%
117.	Nacogdoches, TX:	66,034	64,524	2.34%
118.	Farmington, MO:	65,917	65,359	0.85%
119.	Klamath Falls, OR:	65,912	66,380	-0.71%
120.	Roswell, NM:	65,784	65,645	0.21%
121.	Marinette, WI-MI:	65,378	65,778	-0.61%
122.	Faribault-Northfield, MN:	64,854	64,142	1.11%
123.	Charleston-Mattoon, IL:	64,623	64,921	-0.46%
124.	Hutchinson, KS:	64,438	64,511	-0.11%
125.	Athens, OH:	64,304	64,757	-0.70%
126.	Elizabeth City, NC:	64,244	64,094	0.23%
127.	Clearlake, CA:	63,983	64,665	-1.05%
128.	Ionia, MI:	63,941	63,905	0.06%
129.	Somerset, KY:	63,593	63,063	0.84%
130.	Red Bluff, CA:	63,406	63,463	-0.09%
131.	Sayre, PA:	62,792	62,622	0.27%
132.	Baraboo, WI:	62,597	61,976	1.00%
133.	Coos Bay, OR:	62,534	63,043	-0.81%
134.	Hudson, NY:	62,499	63,096	-0.95%
135.	Salina, KS:	62,060	61,697	0.59%
136.	Oneonta, NY:	61,709	62,259	-0.88%
137.	Rio Grande City, TX:	61,615	60,968	1.06%
138.	Fort Madison-Keokuk, IA-IL-MO:	61,477	62,105	-1.01%
139.	Marietta, OH:	61,475	61,778	-0.49%
140.	Enid, OK:	61,189	60,580	1.01%
141.	Rutland, VT:	60,869	61,642	-1.25%
142.	Shelton, WA:	60,832	60,699	0.22%
143.	Sturgis, MI:	60,796	61,295	-0.81%
144.	Mount Vernon, OH:	60,705	60,921	-0.35%
145.	Big Stone Gap, VA:	60,676	61,313	-1.04%
146.	Albemarle, NC:	60,576	60,585	-0.01%
147.	Jefferson, GA:	60,571	60,485	0.14%
148.	Fremont, OH:	60,510	60,944	-0.71%
149.	Oxford, NC:	60,436	59,916	0.87%
150.	Laconia, NH:	60,327	60,088	0.40%
151.	Georgetown, SC:	60,189	60,158	0.05%
152.	Batavia, NY:	59,977	60,079	-0.17%
153.	Sanford, NC:	59,715	57,866	3.20%

154.	Columbus, MS:	59,670	59,779	-0.18%
155.	Barre, VT:	59,465	59,534	-0.12%
156.	Norwalk, OH:	59,280	59,626	-0.58%
157.	Kinston, NC:	59,227	59,495	-0.45%
158.	Palestine, TX:	58,190	58,458	-0.46%
159.	Dublin, GA:	57,938	58,414	-0.81%
160.	Point Pleasant, WV-OH:	57,887	58,258	-0.64%
161.	Sterling, IL:	57,846	58,498	-1.11%
162.	Vicksburg, MS:	57,433	58,377	-1.62%
163.	Fergus Falls, MN:	57,288	57,303	-0.03%
164.	Crossville, TN:	57,029	56,053	1.74%
165.	Fairmont, WV:	56,678	56,418	0.46%
166.	Tiffin, OH:	56,018	56,745	-1.28%
167.	Calhoun, GA:	55,766	55,186	1.05%
168.	Gaffney, SC:	55,662	55,342	0.58%
169.	Eagle Pass, TX:	55,365	54,258	2.04%
170.	Milledgeville, GA:	55,363	55,149	0.39%
171.	Picayune, MS:	55,295	55,834	-0.97%
172.	Gloversville, NY:	54,925	55,531	-1.09%
173.	Jasper, IN:	54,837	54,734	0.19%
174.	Waycross, GA:	54,665	55,070	-0.74%
175.	Carlsbad-Artesia, NM:	54,419	53,829	1.10%
176.	Warrensburg, MO:	54,397	52,595	3.43%
177.	Oil City, PA:	54,272	54,984	-1.29%
178.	Sonora, CA:	54,008	55,365	-2.45%
179.	Kearney, NE:	53,948	52,591	2.58%
180.	Fort Polk South, LA:	53,869	52,334	2.93%
181.	Morgan City, LA:	53,697	54,650	-1.74%
182.	Ontario, OR-ID:	53,269	53,936	-1.24%
183.	Fort Leonard Wood, MO:	53,259	52,274	1.88%
184.	Elko, NV:	53,217	50,805	4.75%
185.	Payson, AZ:	53,144	53,597	-0.85%
186.	Danville, KY:	53,119	53,174	-0.10%
187.	McComb, MS:	53,057	53,535	-0.89%
188.	Scottsboro, AL:	53,019	53,227	-0.39%
189.	Ashland, OH:	52,962	53,139	-0.33%
190.	Rochelle, IL:	52,848	53,497	-1.21%
191.	Glasgow, KY:	52,600	52,272	0.63%
192.	Greenville, OH:	52,507	52,959	-0.85%
193.	Natchez, MS-LA:	52,487	53,119	-1.19%
194.	Athens, TN:	52,416	52,266	0.29%
195.	Durango, CO:	52,401	51,334	2.08%
196.	Galesburg, IL:	52,247	52,919	-1.27%
197.	Edwards, CO:	51,874	52,197	-0.62%

198.	Boone, NC:	51,871	51,079	1.55%
199.	Malone, NY:	51,795	51,599	0.38%
200.	Bartlesville, OK:	51,633	50,976	1.29%
201.	Winona, MN:	51,629	51,461	0.33%
202.	St. Marys, GA:	51,402	50,513	1.76%
203.	Fernley, NV:	51,327	51,980	-1.26%
204.	Mason City, IA:	51,307	51,749	-0.85%
205.	Enterprise, AL:	51,252	49,948	2.61%
206.	Jacksonville, TX:	51,206	50,845	0.71%
207.	Platteville, WI:	51,087	51,208	-0.24%
208.	Ozark, AL:	50,444	50,251	0.38%
209.	Rexburg, ID:	50,413	50,778	-0.72%
210.	Amsterdam, NY:	49,941	50,219	-0.55%
211.	Clovis, NM:	49,938	48,376	3.23%
212.	Paris, TX:	49,811	49,793	0.04%
213.	Kerrville, TX:	49,786	49,625	0.32%
214.	Greenville, MS:	49,750	51,137	-2.71%
215.	Oxford, MS:	49,495	47,351	4.53%
216.	Cortland, NY:	49,474	49,336	0.28%
217.	New Castle, IN:	49,345	49,462	-0.24%
218.	Sidney, OH:	49,167	49,423	-0.52%
219.	Clinton, IA:	48,717	49,116	-0.81%
220.	Del Rio, TX:	48,705	48,879	-0.36%
221.	Norfolk, NE:	48,286	48,271	0.03%
222.	Starkville, MS:	48,192	47,671	1.09%
223.	Tahlequah, OK:	48,150	46,987	2.48%
224.	Ardmore, OK:	48,085	47,557	1.11%
225.	Corsicana, TX:	47,979	47,735	0.51%
226.	Gillette, WY:	47,874	46,133	3.77%
227.	Cadillac, MI:	47,639	47,584	0.12%
228.	Kendallville, IN:	47,582	47,536	0.10%
229.	Washington, NC:	47,507	47,759	-0.53%
230.	Burlington, IA-IL:	47,383	47,656	-0.57%
231.	Nogales, AZ:	47,303	47,420	-0.25%
232.	Plymouth, IN:	47,024	47,051	-0.06%
233.	Gardnerville Ranchos, NV:	46,996	46,997	0.00%
234.	Freeport, IL:	46,959	47,711	-1.58%
235.	Ruston, LA:	46,953	46,735	0.47%
236.	Cañon City, CO:	46,788	46,824	-0.08%
237.	Lewistown, PA:	46,773	46,682	0.19%
238.	Cedar City, UT:	46,750	46,163	1.27%
239.	Madisonville, KY:	46,718	46,920	-0.43%
240.	Bogalusa, LA:	46,670	47,168	-1.06%
241.	Rockingham, NC:	46,627	46,639	-0.03%

242.	Pullman, WA:	46,606	44,776	4.09%
243.	Red Wing, MN:	46,336	46,183	0.33%
244.	Hillsdale, MI:	46,229	46,688	-0.98%
245.	Newport, OR:	46,151	46,034	0.25%
246.	Moultrie, GA:	46,137	45,498	1.40%
247.	Bedford, IN:	46,078	46,134	-0.12%
248.	Shawano, WI:	45,947	46,181	-0.51%
249.	Huntingdon, PA:	45,943	45,913	0.07%
250.	Ponca City, OK:	45,831	46,562	-1.57%
250.	Wapakoneta, OH:	45,831	45,949	-0.26%
252.	Shelbyville, TN:	45,573	45,058	1.14%
253.	Blytheville, AR:	45,562	46,480	-1.98%
254.	Bellefontaine, OH:	45,474	45,858	-0.84%
254.	Blackfoot, ID:	45,474	45,607	-0.29%
256.	Harrison, AR:	45,413	45,233	0.40%
257.	Bemidji, MN:	45,375	44,442	2.10%
258.	Rock Springs, WY:	45,267	43,806	3.34%
259.	Henderson, NC:	45,132	45,422	-0.64%
260.	McAlester, OK:	45,048	45,837	-1.72%
261.	Marion, NC:	44,998	44,996	0.00%
262.	Rolla, MO:	44,987	45,156	-0.37%
263.	Lewisburg, PA:	44,952	44,947	0.01%
264.	Mount Sterling, KY:	44,924	44,396	1.19%
265.	Duncan, OK:	44,779	45,048	-0.60%
266.	Thomasville, GA:	44,724	44,720	0.01%
267.	Bardstown, KY:	44,319	43,437	2.03%
268.	Menomonie, WI:	44,072	43,857	0.49%
269.	Ottumwa, IA:	44,055	44,378	-0.73%
270.	Coldwater, MI:	43,868	45,248	-3.05%
271.	Cornelia, GA:	43,520	43,041	1.11%
272.	Durant, OK:	43,399	42,416	2.32%
273.	Big Rapids, MI:	43,318	42,798	1.22%
274.	Burley, ID:	43,286	43,021	0.62%
275.	Douglas, GA:	43,170	42,356	1.92%
276.	Paragould, AR:	43,163	42,090	2.55%
277.	Bradford, PA:	43,127	43,450	-0.74%
278.	Seymour, IN:	43,083	42,376	1.67%
279.	Poplar Bluff, MO:	43,053	42,794	0.61%
280.	Pahrump, NV:	42,963	43,946	-2.24%
281.	Muscatine, IA:	42,879	42,745	0.31%
282.	Selma, AL:	42,864	43,820	-2.18%
283.	Bucyrus, OH:	42,849	43,784	-2.14%
284.	Willmar, MN:	42,379	42,239	0.33%
285.	Auburn, IN:	42,321	42,223	0.23%

286.	Sedalia, MO:	42,319	42,201	0.28%
287.	Lawrenceburg, TN:	42,086	41,869	0.52%
288.	Alma, MI:	42,063	42,476	-0.97%
289.	Wilmington, OH:	41,886	42,040	-0.37%
290.	Alice, TX:	41,754	40,838	2.24%
291.	Ellensburg, WA:	41,672	40,915	1.85%
292.	Greenwood, MS:	41,371	42,914	-3.60%
293.	Aberdeen, SD:	41,357	40,602	1.86%
294.	Port Clinton, OH:	41,339	41,428	-0.21%
295.	El Campo, TX:	41,285	41,280	0.01%
296.	Cedartown, GA:	41,188	41,475	-0.69%
297.	Garden City, KS:	41,168	40,753	1.02%
298.	Warren, PA:	41,146	41,815	-1.60%
299.	Riverton, WY:	41,110	40,123	2.46%
300.	Tifton, GA:	41,064	40,118	2.36%
301.	Mountain Home, AR:	41,048	41,513	-1.12%
302.	Celina, OH:	40,875	40,814	0.15%
303.	El Dorado, AR:	40,867	41,639	-1.85%
304.	Marshalltown, IA:	40,857	40,648	0.51%
305.	Montrose, CO:	40,725	41,276	-1.33%
306.	West Plains, MO:	40,629	40,400	0.57%
307.	Jacksonville, IL:	40,562	40,902	-0.83%
308.	Sandpoint, ID:	40,476	40,877	-0.98%
309.	Cullowhee, NC:	40,448	40,271	0.44%
310.	Española, NM:	40,318	40,246	0.18%
311.	McMinnville, TN:	39,839	39,839	0.00%
312.	Cambridge, OH:	39,817	40,087	-0.67%
313.	Selinsgrove, PA:	39,672	39,702	-0.08%
314.	Urbana, OH:	39,565	40,097	-1.33%
315.	Lock Haven, PA:	39,517	39,238	0.71%
316.	Okeechobee, FL:	39,467	39,996	-1.32%
317.	Natchitoches, LA:	39,436	39,566	-0.33%
318.	Austin, MN:	39,372	39,163	0.53%
319.	Pittsburg, KS:	39,361	39,134	0.58%
320.	Stephenville, TX:	39,321	37,890	3.78%
321.	Sikeston, MO:	39,139	39,191	-0.13%
322.	Scottsbluff, NE:	39,039	38,971	0.17%
323.	Hannibal, MO:	39,022	38,948	0.19%
324.	Sault Ste. Marie, MI:	38,917	38,520	1.03%
325.	Kill Devil Hills, NC:	38,911	38,327	1.52%
326.	Centralia, IL:	38,894	39,437	-1.38%
327.	Houghton, MI:	38,735	38,784	-0.13%
328.	Mount Vernon, IL:	38,720	38,827	-0.28%
329.	Gainesville, TX:	38,688	38,437	0.65%

330.	Defiance, OH:	38,677	39,037	-0.92%
331.	Pontiac, IL:	38,647	38,950	-0.78%
332.	Logansport, IN:	38,581	38,966	-0.99%
333.	Berlin, NH-VT:	38,322	39,361	-2.64%
334.	Dyersburg, TN:	38,255	38,335	-0.21%
335.	Crawfordsville, IN:	38,254	38,124	0.34%
336.	Moscow, ID:	38,184	37,244	2.52%
337.	Vincennes, IN:	38,122	38,440	-0.83%
338.	Easton, MD:	38,098	37,782	0.84%
339.	Junction City, KS:	38,013	34,362	10.63%
340.	Summit Park, UT:	38,003	36,324	4.62%
341.	Ada, OK:	37,958	37,492	1.24%
342.	Union City, TN-KY:	37,865	38,620	-1.95%
343.	Brownwood, TX:	37,825	38,106	-0.74%
344.	Murray, KY:	37,655	37,191	1.25%
345.	Newberry, SC:	37,576	37,508	0.18%
346.	Mayfield, KY:	37,544	37,121	1.14%
347.	Clewiston, FL:	37,447	39,140	-4.33%
348.	Safford, AZ:	37,416	37,220	0.53%
349.	North Platte, NE:	37,373	37,590	-0.58%
350.	Astoria, OR:	37,301	37,039	0.71%
351.	Laramie, WY:	37,276	36,299	2.69%
352.	Fort Dodge, IA:	37,273	38,013	-1.95%
353.	Corinth, MS:	37,164	37,057	0.29%
354.	Batesville, AR:	37,025	36,647	1.03%
355.	Huntington, IN:	36,987	37,124	-0.37%
356.	Escanaba, MI:	36,884	37,069	-0.50%
357.	Coshocton, OH:	36,779	36,901	-0.33%
358.	Bennington, VT:	36,697	37,125	-1.15%
359.	Big Spring, TX:	36,667	36,238	1.18%
360.	Canton, IL:	36,651	37,069	-1.13%
361.	Newton, IA:	36,602	36,842	-0.65%
362.	Bay City, TX:	36,547	36,702	-0.42%
363.	Americus, GA:	36,544	37,829	-3.40%
364.	Peru, IN:	36,486	36,903	-1.13%
365.	Fremont, NE:	36,427	36,691	-0.72%
366.	Alexandria, MN:	36,415	36,009	1.13%
367.	Plainview, TX:	36,385	36,273	0.31%
368.	Owatonna, MN:	36,322	36,576	-0.69%
369.	Arkansas City-Winfield, KS:	36,288	36,311	-0.06%
370.	DeRidder, LA:	36,281	35,654	1.76%
371.	Vidalia, GA:	36,228	36,346	-0.32%
372.	Logan, WV:	36,168	36,743	-1.56%
373.	Laurinburg, NC:	36,094	36,157	-0.17%

374.	Hutchinson, MN:	36,053	36,651	-1.63%
375.	Newport, TN:	35,571	35,662	-0.26%
376.	Sulphur Springs, TX:	35,469	35,161	0.88%
377.	Lebanon, MO:	35,417	35,571	-0.43%
378.	Seneca Falls, NY:	35,305	35,251	0.15%
379.	Dixon, IL:	35,037	36,031	-2.76%
380.	Brookhaven, MS:	34,900	34,869	0.09%
381.	Martin, TN:	34,793	35,021	-0.65%
382.	Dodge City, KS:	34,752	33,848	2.67%
383.	Arcadia, FL:	34,712	34,862	-0.43%
384.	Taylorville, IL:	34,638	34,800	-0.47%
385.	Vernal, UT:	34,524	32,588	5.94%
386.	Coffeyville, KS:	34,459	35,471	-2.85%
387.	Butte-Silver Bow, MT:	34,403	34,200	0.59%
388.	Decatur, IN:	34,365	34,387	-0.06%
389.	Effingham, IL:	34,353	34,242	0.32%
390.	Angola, IN:	34,124	34,185	-0.18%
391.	Brenham, TX:	34,093	33,718	1.11%
392.	Valley, AL:	34,064	34,215	-0.44%
393.	Cleveland, MS:	33,904	34,145	-0.71%
394.	Emporia, KS:	33,748	33,690	0.17%
395.	Susanville, CA:	33,658	34,895	-3.54%
396.	Malvern, AR:	33,394	32,923	1.43%
397.	Troy, AL:	33,182	32,899	0.86%
398.	Frankfort, IN:	33,022	33,224	-0.61%
399.	Jackson, OH:	32,954	33,225	-0.82%
400.	Brevard, NC:	32,849	33,090	-0.73%
401.	Taos, NM:	32,779	32,937	-0.48%
402.	Columbus, NE:	32,681	32,237	1.38%
403.	Mount Pleasant, TX:	32,663	32,334	1.02%
404.	Brookings, SD:	32,629	31,965	2.08%
405.	Juneau, AK:	32,556	31,275	4.10%
406.	Madison, IN:	32,554	32,428	0.39%
407.	Cambridge, MD:	32,551	32,618	-0.21%
408.	Macomb, IL:	32,537	32,612	-0.23%
409.	Beeville, TX:	32,527	31,861	2.09%
410.	Kingsville, TX:	32,456	32,477	-0.06%
411.	Wabash, IN:	32,361	32,888	-1.60%
412.	Paris, TN:	32,341	32,330	0.03%
413.	Dayton, TN:	32,247	31,809	1.38%
414.	Miami, OK:	32,236	31,848	1.22%
415.	Washington, IN:	32,064	31,648	1.31%
416.	Kennett, MO:	31,826	31,953	-0.40%
417.	Jackson, WY-ID:	31,727	31,464	0.84%

418.	Hastings, NE:	31,459	31,364	0.30%
419.	Albert Lea, MN:	31,054	31,255	-0.64%
420.	Lewisburg, TN:	30,883	30,617	0.87%
421.	Camden, AR:	30,703	31,488	-2.49%
422.	Iron Mountain, MI-WI:	30,702	30,591	0.36%
423.	Jesup, GA:	30,305	30,099	0.68%
424.	Lincoln, IL:	30,013	30,305	-0.96%
425.	Kirksville, MO:	29,951	30,038	-0.29%
426.	Sheridan, WY:	29,596	29,116	1.65%
427.	Silver City, NM:	29,388	29,514	-0.43%
428.	Elkins, WV:	29,384	29,405	-0.07%
429.	McPherson, KS:	29,356	29,180	0.60%
430.	Alpena, MI:	29,234	29,598	-1.23%
431.	Hays, KS:	29,053	28,452	2.11%
432.	Las Vegas, NM:	28,891	29,393	-1.71%
433.	Washington Court House, OH:	28,880	29,030	-0.52%
434.	Van Wert, OH:	28,744	28,744	0.00%
435.	Ludington, MI:	28,680	28,705	-0.09%
436.	Weatherford, OK:	28,536	27,469	3.88%
437.	Fort Morgan, CO:	28,472	28,159	1.11%
438.	Indianola, MS:	28,431	29,450	-3.46%
439.	Merrill, WI:	28,392	28,743	-1.22%
440.	Crescent City, CA:	28,290	28,610	-1.12%
441.	Middlesborough, KY:	28,183	28,691	-1.77%
442.	North Vernon, IN:	28,161	28,525	-1.28%
443.	Bennettsville, SC:	28,145	28,933	-2.72%
444.	Breckenridge, CO:	28,044	27,994	0.18%
445.	Forrest City, AR:	27,858	28,258	-1.42%
446.	Mineral Wells, TX:	27,856	28,111	-0.91%
447.	Watertown, SD:	27,606	27,227	1.39%
448.	Bastrop, LA:	27,559	27,979	-1.50%
449.	Great Bend, KS:	27,557	27,674	-0.42%
450.	Wauchula, FL:	27,514	27,731	-0.78%
451.	Bainbridge, GA:	27,509	27,842	-1.20%
452.	Hailey, ID:	27,500	27,701	-0.73%
453.	Grants, NM:	27,334	27,213	0.44%
454.	Dickinson, ND:	26,771	24,199	10.63%
455.	Uvalde, TX:	26,752	26,405	1.31%
456.	Williston, ND:	26,697	22,398	19.19%
457.	Thomaston, GA:	26,630	27,153	-1.93%
458.	Lexington, NE:	26,249	26,370	-0.46%
459.	Altus, OK:	26,237	26,446	-0.79%
460.	Mountain Home, ID:	26,223	27,038	-3.01%
461.	Boone, IA:	26,195	26,306	-0.42%

462.	Greensburg, IN:	26,042	25,740	1.17%
463.	Ottawa, KS:	25,906	25,992	-0.33%
464.	Toccoa, GA:	25,891	26,175	-1.09%
465.	La Grande, OR:	25,759	25,748	0.04%
466.	Summerville, GA:	25,725	26,015	-1.11%
467.	Clarksdale, MS:	25,709	26,151	-1.69%
468.	Mexico, MO:	25,621	25,529	0.36%
469.	Marshall, MN:	25,543	25,857	-1.21%
470.	The Dalles, OR:	25,487	25,213	1.09%
471.	New Ulm, MN:	25,425	25,893	-1.81%
472.	Moberly, MO:	25,330	25,414	-0.33%
473.	Heber, UT:	25,273	23,530	7.41%
474.	Fredericksburg, TX:	25,153	24,837	1.27%
475.	Deming, NM:	25,041	25,095	-0.22%
476.	Campbellsville, KY:	24,691	24,512	0.73%
477.	Magnolia, AR:	24,473	24,552	-0.32%
478.	Spearfish, SD:	24,397	24,097	1.24%
479.	Fallon, NV:	24,375	24,877	-2.02%
480.	Connersville, IN:	24,029	24,277	-1.02%
481.	Cordele, GA:	23,606	23,439	0.71%
482.	Liberal, KS:	23,547	22,952	2.59%
483.	Maryville, MO:	23,419	23,370	0.21%
484.	Marshall, MO:	23,339	23,370	-0.13%
485.	Steamboat Springs, CO:	23,334	23,509	-0.74%
486.	Mitchell, SD:	23,146	22,835	1.36%
487.	Elk City, OK:	23,081	22,119	4.35%
488.	Levelland, TX:	23,072	22,935	0.60%
489.	Pampa, TX:	22,978	22,535	1.97%
490.	Arkadelphia, AR:	22,936	22,995	-0.26%
491.	Wahpeton, ND-MN:	22,802	22,897	-0.41%
492.	Sterling, CO:	22,631	22,709	-0.34%
493.	Yankton, SD:	22,603	22,438	0.74%
494.	Hood River, OR:	22,584	22,346	1.07%
495.	Oskaloosa, IA:	22,443	22,381	0.28%
496.	Dumas, TX:	22,313	21,904	1.87%
497.	Brookings, OR:	22,248	22,364	-0.52%
498.	Raymondville, TX:	22,058	22,134	-0.34%
499.	Borger, TX:	21,922	22,150	-1.03%
500.	Pierre, SD:	21,846	21,361	2.27%
501.	Beatrice, NE:	21,806	22,311	-2.26%
502.	Grenada, MS:	21,682	21,906	-1.02%
503.	Port Lavaca, TX:	21,609	21,381	1.07%
504.	Guymon, OK:	21,498	20,640	4.16%
505.	Worthington, MN:	21,487	21,378	0.51%

506.	Parsons, KS:	21,284	21,607	-1.49%
507.	Price, UT:	21,246	21,403	-0.73%
508.	Evanston, WY:	21,025	21,118	-0.44%
509.	Jamestown, ND:	20,934	21,100	-0.79%
510.	Helena-West Helena, AR:	20,784	21,757	-4.47%
511.	Prineville, OR:	20,729	20,978	-1.19%
512.	Storm Lake, IA:	20,592	20,260	1.64%
513.	Woodward, OK:	20,548	20,081	2.33%
514.	Portales, NM:	20,419	19,846	2.89%
515.	Hereford, TX:	19,360	19,372	-0.06%
516.	Othello, WA:	19,005	18,728	1.48%
517.	Los Alamos, NM:	18,159	17,950	1.16%
518.	Huron, SD:	17,753	17,398	2.04%
519.	Fitzgerald, GA:	17,538	17,634	-0.54%
520.	Maysville, KY:	17,512	17,490	0.13%
521.	Snyder, TX:	17,126	16,921	1.21%
522.	Winnemucca, NV:	17,048	16,528	3.15%
523.	Vineyard Haven, MA:	17,041	16,535	3.06%
524.	Spirit Lake, IA:	16,972	16,667	1.83%
525.	Fairfield, IA:	16,867	16,843	0.14%
526.	Atchison, KS:	16,813	16,924	-0.66%
527.	Spencer, IA:	16,599	16,667	-0.41%
528.	Andrews, TX:	16,117	14,786	9.00%
529.	Sweetwater, TX:	14,924	15,216	-1.92%
530.	Zapata, TX:	14,290	14,018	1.94%
531.	Vermillion, SD:	14,131	13,864	1.93%
532.	Pecos, TX:	13,798	13,783	0.11%
533.	Ketchikan, AK:	13,779	13,477	2.24%
534.	Lamesa, TX:	13,640	13,833	-1.40%
535.	Vernon, TX:	13,258	13,535	-2.05%
536.	Craig, CO:	13,200	13,795	-4.31%

71

STATE POPULATION PROFILES

71.1 Overview

The population of the United States was counted in the 2010 Census at 308,745,538, an increase of 27,323,632, or 9.7%, from the 2000 census.

The racial and ethnic distribution of the U.S. population is presented in section 1.1 of this handbook. Median age was 37.2.

This chapter provides the population counts, median age, and racial/ethnic distributions for each state.

71.2 State Populations

Populations of the states and the District of Columbia, as counted in the 2000 and 2010 censuses, and the population change during the decade, are as follows:

		2000	2010	Change
1.	California:	33,871,648	37,253,956	3,382,308 (10.0%)
2.	Texas:	20,851,820	25,145,561	4,293,741 (20.6%)
3.	New York:	18,976,457	19,378,102	401,645 (2.1%)
4.	Florida:	15,982,378	18,801,310	2,818,932 (16.6%)
5.	Illinois:	12,419,293	12,830,632	411,339 (3.3%)
6.	Pennsylvania:	12,281,054	12,702,379	421,325 (3.4%)
7.	Ohio:	11,353,140	11,536,504	183,364 (1.6%)
8.	Michigan:	9,938,444	9,883,640	<54,804> (-0.6%)
9.	Georgia:	8,186,453	9,687,653	1,501,200 (18.3%)
10.	North Carolina:	8,049,313	9,535,483	1,486,170 (18.5%)
11.	New Jersey:	8,414,350	8,791,894	377,544 (4.5%)
12.	Virginia:	7,078,515	8,001,024	922,509 (13.0%)
13.	Washington:	5,894,121	6,724,540	830,419 (14.1%)
14.	Massachusetts:	6,349,097	6,547,629	198,532 (3.1%)
15.	Indiana:	6,080,485	6,483,802	403,317 (6.6%)
16.	Arizona:	5,130,632	6,392,017	1,261,385 (24.6%)
17.	Tennessee:	5,689,283	6,346,105	656,822 (11.5%)
18.	Missouri:	5,595,211	5,988,927	393,716 (7.0%)
19.	Maryland:	5,296,486	5,773,552	477,066 (9.0%)
20.	Wisconsin:	5,363,675	5,686,986	323,311 (6.0%)
21.	Minnesota:	4,919,479	5,303,925	384,446 (7.8%)
22.	Colorado:	4,301,261	5,029,196	727,935 (16.9%)

23.	Alabama:	4,447,100	4,779,736	332,636 (7.5%)
24.	South Carolina:	4,012,012	4,625,364	613,352 (15.3%)
25.	Louisiana:	4,468,976	4,533,372	64,396 (1.4%)
26.	Kentucky:	4,041,769	4,339,367	297,598 (7.4%)
27.	Oregon:	3,421,399	3,831,074	409,675 (12.0%)
28.	Oklahoma:	3,450,654	3,751,351	300,697 (8.7%)
29.	Connecticut:	3,405,565	3,574,097	168,532 (4.9%)
30.	Iowa:	2,926,324	3,046,355	120,031 (4.1%)
31.	Mississippi:	2,844,658	2,967,297	122,639 (4.3%)
32.	Arkansas:	2,673,400	2,915,918	242,518 (9.1%)
33.	Kansas:	2,688,418	2,853,118	164,700 (6.1%)
34.	Utah:	2,233,169	2,763,885	530,716 (23.8%)
35.	Nevada:	1,998,257	2,700,551	702,294 (35.1%)
36.	New Mexico:	1,819,046	2,059,179	240,133 (13.2%)
37.	West Virginia:	1,808,344	1,852,994	44,650 (2.5%)
38.	Nebraska:	1,711,263	1,826,341	115,078 (6.7%)
39.	Idaho:	1,293,953	1,567,582	273,629 (21.1%)
40.	Hawaii:	1,211,537	1,360,301	148,764 (12.3%)
41.	Maine:	1,274,923	1,328,361	53,438 (4.2%)
42.	New Hampshire:	1,235,786	1,316,470	80,684 (6.5%)
43.	Rhode Island:	1,048,319	1,052,567	4,248 (0.4%)
44.	Montana:	902,195	989,415	87,220 (9.7%)
45.	Delaware:	783,600	897,934	114,334 (14.6%)
46.	South Dakota:	754,844	814,180	59,336 (7.9%)
47.	Alaska:	626,932	710,231	83,299 (13.3%)
48.	North Dakota:	642,200	672,591	30,391 (4.7%)
49.	Vermont:	608,827	625,741	16,914 (2.8%)
50.	District of Columbia:	572,059	601,723	29,664 (5.2%)
51.	Wyoming:	493,782	563,626	69,844 (14.1%)

71.3 Median Age

The median age for each state and the District of Columbia is as follows:

- Alabama: 37.9
- Alaska: 33.8
- Arizona: 35.9
- Arkansas: 37.4
- California: 35.2
- Colorado: 36.1
- Connecticut: 40.0
- Delaware: 38.8
- District of Columbia: 33.3
- Florida: 40.7
- Georgia: 35.3
- Hawaii: 38.6
- Idaho: 34.6
- Illinois: 36.6
- Indiana: 37.0
- Iowa: 38.1
- Kansas: 36.0
- Kentucky: 38.1
- Louisiana: 35.8
- Maine: 42.7
- Maryland: 38.0
- Massachusetts: 39.1

- Michigan: 38.9
- Minnesota: 37.4
- Mississippi: 36.0
- Missouri: 37.9
- Montana: 39.8
- Nebraska: 36.2
- Nevada: 36.3
- New Hampshire: 41.1
- New Jersey: 39.0
- New Mexico: 36.7
- New York: 38.0
- North Carolina: 37.4
- North Dakota: 37.0
- Ohio: 38.8
- Oklahoma: 36.2
- Oregon: 38.4
- Pennsylvania: 40.1
- Rhode Island: 39.7
- South Carolina: 37.9
- South Dakota: 36.9
- Tennessee: 38.0
- Texas: 33.6
- Utah: 29.2
- Vermont: 41.5
- Virginia: 37.5
- Washington: 37.3
- West Virginia: 41.3
- Wisconsin: 38.5
- Wyoming: 36.8

71.4 Racial and Ethnic Distributions

Census 2010 reported distributions by race and ethnicity as follows:

Alabama

Race

- White: 68.5%
- Black: 26.2%
- Asian: 1.1%
- American Indian: 0.6%
- Native Hawaiian: 0.1%
- Two or more: 1.5%
- Other: 2.0%

Ethnicity

- Non-Hispanic: 96.1%
- Hispanic: 3.9%

Alaska

Race

- White: 66.7%
- American Indian: 14.8%
- Asian: 5.4%
- Black: 3.3%
- Native Hawaiian: 1.0%
- Two or more: 7.3%
- Other: 1.6%

Ethnicity

- Non-Hispanic: 94.5%
- Hispanic: 5.5%

Arizona

Race

- White: 73.0%
- American Indian: 4.6%
- Black: 4.1%
- Asian: 2.8%
- Native Hawaiian: 0.2%
- Two or more: 3.4%
- Other: 11.9%

Ethnicity

- Non-Hispanic: 70.4%
- Hispanic: 29.6%

Arkansas

Race

- White: 77.0%
- Black: 15.4%
- Asian: 1.2%
- American Indian: 0.8%
- Native Hawaiian: 0.2%
- Two or more: 2.0%
- Other: 3.4%

Ethnicity

- Non-Hispanic: 93.6%
- Hispanic: 6.4%

California

Race

- White: 57.6%
- Asian: 13.0%
- Black: 6.2%
- American Indian: 1.0%
- Native Hawaiian: 0.4%
- Two or more: 4.9%
- Other: 17.0%

Ethnicity

- Non-Hispanic: 62.4%
- Hispanic: 37.6%

Colorado

Race

- White: 81.3%
- Black: 4.0%
- Asian: 2.8%
- American Indian: 1.1%
- Native Hawaiian: 0.1%
- Two or more: 3.4%
- Other: 7.2%

Ethnicity

- Non-Hispanic: 79.3%
- Hispanic: 20.7%

Connecticut

Race

- White: 77.6%
- Black: 10.1%
- Asian: 3.8%
- American Indian: 0.3%
- Native Hawaiian: 0.0%
- Two or more: 2.6%
- Other: 5.6%

Ethnicity

- Non-Hispanic: 86.6%
- Hispanic: 13.4%

Delaware

Race

- White: 68.9%
- Black: 21.4%
- Asian: 3.2%
- American Indian: 0.5%
- Native Hawaiian: 0.0%
- Two or more: 2.7%
- Other: 3.4%

Ethnicity

- Non-Hispanic: 91.8%
- Hispanic: 8.2%

District of Columbia

Race

- White: 38.5%
- Black: 50.7%
- Asian: 3.5%
- American Indian: 0.3%
- Native Hawaiian: 0.1%
- Two or more: 2.9%
- Other: 4.1%

Ethnicity

- Non-Hispanic: 90.9%
- Hispanic: 9.1%

Florida

Race

• White:	75.0%
• Black:	16.0%
• Asian:	2.4%
• American Indian:	0.4%
• Native Hawaiian:	0.1%
• Two or more:	2.5%
• Other:	3.8%

Ethnicity

• Non-Hispanic:	77.5%
• Hispanic:	22.5%

Georgia

Race

• White:	59.7%
• Black:	30.5%
• Asian:	3.2%
• American Indian:	0.3%
• Native Hawaiian:	0.1%
• Two or more:	2.1%
• Other:	4.0%

Ethnicity

• Non-Hispanic:	91.2%
• Hispanic:	8.8%

Hawaii

Race

• Asian:	38.6%
• White:	24.7%
• Native Hawaiian:	10.0%
• Black:	1.6%
• American Indian:	0.3%
• Two or more:	23.6%
• Other:	1.2%

Ethnicity

• Non-Hispanic:	91.1%
• Hispanic:	8.9%

Idaho

Race

• White:	89.1%
• American Indian:	1.4%
• Asian:	1.2%
• Black:	0.6%
• Native Hawaiian:	0.1%
• Two or more:	2.5%
• Other:	5.1%

Ethnicity

• Non-Hispanic:	88.8%
• Hispanic:	11.1%

Illinois

Race

• White:	71.5%
• Black:	14.5%
• Asian:	4.6%
• American Indian:	0.3%
• Native Hawaiian:	0.0%
• Two or more:	2.3%
• Other:	6.7%

Ethnicity

• Non-Hispanic:	84.2%
• Hispanic:	15.8%

Indiana

Race

• White:	84.3%
• Black:	9.1%
• Asian:	1.6%
• American Indian:	0.3%
• Native Hawaiian:	0.0%
• Two or more:	2.0%
• Other:	2.7%

Ethnicity

• Non-Hispanic:	94.0%
• Hispanic:	6.0%

Iowa

Race

- White: 91.3%
- Black: 2.9%
- Asian: 1.7%
- American Indian: 0.4%
- Native Hawaiian: 0.1%
- Two or more: 1.8%
- Other: 1.8%

Ethnicity

- Non-Hispanic: 95.0%
- Hispanic: 5.0%

Kansas

Race

- White: 83.8%
- Black: 5.9%
- Asian: 2.4%
- American Indian: 1.0%
- Native Hawaiian: 0.1%
- Two or more: 3.0%
- Other: 3.9%

Ethnicity

- Non-Hispanic: 89.5%
- Hispanic: 10.5%

Kentucky

Race

- White: 87.8%
- Black: 7.8%
- Asian: 1.1%
- American Indian: 0.2%
- Native Hawaiian: 0.1%
- Two or more: 1.7%
- Other: 1.3%

Ethnicity

- Non-Hispanic: 96.9%
- Hispanic: 3.1%

Louisiana

Race

- White: 62.6%
- Black: 32.0%
- Asian: 1.5%
- American Indian: 0.7%
- Native Hawaiian: 0.0%
- Two or more: 1.6%
- Other: 1.5%

Ethnicity

- Non-Hispanic: 95.8%
- Hispanic: 4.2%

Maine

Race

- White: 95.2%
- Black: 1.2%
- Asian: 1.0%
- American Indian: 0.6%
- Native Hawaiian: 0.0%
- Two or more: 1.6%
- Other: 0.3%

Ethnicity

- Non-Hispanic: 98.7%
- Hispanic: 1.3%

Maryland

Race

- White: 58.2%
- Black: 29.4%
- Asian: 5.5%
- American Indian: 0.4%
- Native Hawaiian: 0.1%
- Two or more: 2.9%
- Other: 3.6%

Ethnicity

- Non-Hispanic: 91.8%
- Hispanic: 8.2%

Massachusetts

Race

• White:	80.4%
• Black:	6.6%
• Asian:	5.3%
• American Indian:	0.3%
• Native Hawaiian:	0.0%
• Two or more:	2.6%
• Other:	4.7%

Ethnicity

• Non-Hispanic:	90.4%
• Hispanic:	9.6%

Michigan

Race

• White:	78.9%
• Black:	14.2%
• Asian:	2.4%
• American Indian:	0.6%
• Native Hawaiian:	0.0%
• Two or more:	2.3%
• Other:	1.5%

Ethnicity

• Non-Hispanic:	95.6%
• Hispanic:	4.4%

Minnesota

Race

• White:	85.3%
• Black:	5.2%
• Asian:	4.0%
• American Indian:	1.1%
• Native Hawaiian:	0.0%
• Two or more:	2.4%
• Other:	1.9%

Ethnicity

• Non-Hispanic:	95.3%
• Hispanic:	4.7%

Mississippi

Race

• White:	59.1%
• Black:	37.0%
• Asian:	0.9%
• American Indian:	0.5%
• Native Hawaiian:	0.0%
• Two or more:	1.1%
• Other:	1.3%

Ethnicity

• Non-Hispanic:	97.3%
• Hispanic:	2.7%

Missouri

Race

• White:	82.8%
• Black:	11.6%
• Asian:	1.6%
• American Indian:	0.5%
• Native Hawaiian:	0.1%
• Two or more:	2.1%
• Other:	1.3%

Ethnicity

• Non-Hispanic:	96.5%
• Hispanic:	3.5%

Montana

Race

• White:	89.4%
• American Indian:	6.3%
• Asian:	0.6%
• Black:	0.4%
• Native Hawaiian:	0.1%
• Two or more:	2.5%
• Other:	0.6%

Ethnicity

• Non-Hispanic:	97.1%
• Hispanic:	2.9%

Nebraska

Race
- White: 86.1%
- Black: 4.5%
- Asian: 1.8%
- American Indian: 1.0%
- Native Hawaiian: 0.1%
- Two or more: 2.2%
- Other: 4.3%

Ethnicity
- Non-Hispanic: 90.8%
- Hispanic: 9.2%

Nevada

Race
- White: 66.2%
- Black: 8.1%
- Asian: 7.2%
- American Indian: 1.2%
- Native Hawaiian: 0.6%
- Two or more: 4.7%
- Other: 12.0%

Ethnicity
- Non-Hispanic: 73.5%
- Hispanic: 26.5%

New Hampshire

Race
- White: 93.9%
- Asian: 2.2%
- Black: 1.1%
- American Indian: 0.2%
- Native Hawaiian: 0.0%
- Two or more: 1.6%
- Other: 0.9%

Ethnicity
- Non-Hispanic: 97.2%
- Hispanic: 2.8%

New Jersey

Race
- White: 68.6%
- Black: 13.7%
- Asian: 8.3%
- American Indian: 0.3%
- Native Hawaiian: 0.0%
- Two or more: 2.7%
- Other: 6.4%

Ethnicity
- Non-Hispanic: 82.3%
- Hispanic: 17.7%

New Mexico

Race
- White: 68.4%
- American Indian: 9.4%
- Black: 2.1%
- Asian: 1.4%
- Native Hawaiian: 0.1%
- Two or more: 3.7%
- Other: 15.0%

Ethnicity
- Non-Hispanic: 53.%
- Hispanic: 46.3%

New York

Race
- White: 65.7%
- Black: 15.9%
- Asian: 7.3%
- American Indian: 0.6%
- Native Hawaiian: 0.0%
- Two or more: 3.0%
- Other: 7.4%

Ethnicity
- Non-Hispanic: 82.4%
- Hispanic: 17.6%

North Carolina

Race

- White: 68.5%
- Black: 21.5%
- Asian: 2.2%
- American Indian: 1.3%
- Native Hawaiian: 0.1%
- Two or more: 2.2%
- Other: 4.3%

Ethnicity

- Non-Hispanic: 91.6%
- Hispanic: 8.4%

North Dakota

Race

- White: 90.0%
- American Indian: 5.4%
- Black: 1.2%
- Asian: 1.0%
- Native Hawaiian: 0.0%
- Two or more: 1.8%
- Other: 0.5%

Ethnicity

- Non-Hispanic: 98.0%
- Hispanic: 2.0%

Ohio

Race

- White: 82.7%
- Black: 12.2%
- Asian: 1.7%
- American Indian: 0.2%
- Native Hawaiian: 0.0%
- Two or more: 2.1%
- Other: 1.1%

Ethnicity

- Non-Hispanic: 96.9%
- Hispanic: 3.1%

Oklahoma

Race

- White: 72.2%
- American Indian: 8.8%
- Black: 7.4%
- Asian: 1.7%
- Native Hawaiian: 0.1%
- Two or more: 5.9%
- Other: 4.1%

Ethnicity

- Non-Hispanic: 91.1%
- Hispanic: 8.9%

Oregon

Race

- White: 83.6%
- Asian: 3.7%
- Black: 1.8%
- American Indian: 1.4%
- Native Hawaiian: 0.3%
- Two or more: 3.8%
- Other: 5.3%

Ethnicity

- Non-Hispanic: 88.3%
- Hispanic: 11.7%

Pennsylvania

Race

- White: 81.9%
- Black: 10.8%
- Asian: 2.7%
- American Indian: 0.2%
- Native Hawaiian: 0.0%
- Two or more: 1.9%
- Other: 2.4%

Ethnicity

- Non-Hispanic: 94.3%
- Hispanic: 5.7%

Rhode Island

Race

• White:	81.4%
• Black:	5.7%
• Asian:	2.9%
• American Indian:	0.6%
• Native Hawaiian:	0.1%
• Two or more:	3.3%
• Other:	6.0%

Ethnicity

• Non-Hispanic:	87.6%
• Hispanic:	12.4%

South Carolina

Race

• White:	66.2%
• Black:	27.9%
• Asian:	1.3%
• American Indian:	0.4%
• Native Hawaiian:	0.1%
• Two or more:	1.7%
• Other:	2.5%

Ethnicity

• Non-Hispanic:	94.9%
• Hispanic:	5.1%

South Dakota

Race

• White:	85.9%
• American Indian:	8.8%
• Black:	1.3%
• Asian:	0.9%
• Native Hawaiian:	0.0%
• Two or more:	2.1%
• Other:	0.9%

Ethnicity

• Non-Hispanic:	97.3%
• Hispanic:	2.7%

Tennessee

Race

• White:	77.6%
• Black:	16.7%
• Asian:	1.4%
• American Indian:	0.3%
• Native Hawaiian:	0.1%
• Two or more:	1.7%
• Other:	2.2%

Ethnicity

• Non-Hispanic:	95.4%
• Hispanic:	4.6%

Texas

Race

• White:	70.4%
• Black:	11.8%
• Asian:	3.8%
• American Indian:	0.7%
• Native Hawaiian:	0.1%
• Two or more:	2.7%
• Other:	10.5%

Ethnicity

• Non-Hispanic:	62.4%
• Hispanic:	37.6%

Utah

Race

• White:	86.1%
• Asian:	2.0%
• American Indian:	1.2%
• Black:	1.1%
• Native Hawaiian:	0.9%
• Two or more:	2.7%
• Other:	6.0%

Ethnicity

• Non-Hispanic:	87.0%
• Hispanic:	13.0%

Vermont

Race

- White: 95.3%
- Asian: 1.3%
- Black: 1.0%
- American Indian: 0.4%
- Native Hawaiian: 0.0%
- Two or more: 1.7%
- Other: 0.3%

Ethnicity

- Non-Hispanic: 98.5%
- Hispanic: 1.5%

Virginia

Race

- White: 68.9%
- Black: 19.4%
- Asian: 5.5%
- American Indian: 0.4%
- Native Hawaiian: 0.1%
- Two or more: 2.9%
- Other: 3.2%

Ethnicity

- Non-Hispanic: 92.1%
- Hispanic: 7.9%

Washington

Race

- White: 77.3%
- Asian: 7.2%
- Black: 3.9%
- American Indian: 1.5%
- Native Hawaiian: 0.6%
- Two or more: 4.7%
- Other: 5.2%

Ethnicity

- Non-Hispanic: 88.8%
- Hispanic: 11.2%

West Virginia

Race

- White: 93.9%
- Black: 3.4%
- Asian: 0.7%
- American Indian: 0.2%
- Native Hawaiian: 0.0%
- Two or more: 1.5%
- Other: 0.3%

Ethnicity

- Non-Hispanic: 98.8%
- Hispanic: 1.2%

Wisconsin

Race

- White: 86.2%
- Black: 6.3%
- Asian: 2.3%
- American Indian: 1.0%
- Native Hawaiian: 0.0%
- Two or more: 1.8%
- Other: 2.4%

Ethnicity

- Non-Hispanic: 94.1%
- Hispanic: 5.9%

Wyoming

Race

- White: 90.7%
- American Indian: 2.4%
- Asian: 0.8%
- Black: 0.8%
- Native Hawaiian: 0.1%
- Two or more: 2.3%
- Other: 3.0%

Ethnicity

- Non-Hispanic: 91.1%
- Hispanic: 8.9%

71.5 Diversity

Based on the data of Census 2010, *USA Today* assessed diversity using a Diversity Index, defined as the probability that two people chosen randomly from a state will have different ethnic or racial backgrounds. The Diversity Index is a 0-to-100 score; a score of 50 means there is a 50% chance two randomly chosen people are of a different ethnicity or race.

The Diversity Indices are as follows:

- Hawaii: 81
- California: 73
- New Mexico: 67
- Texas: 66
- Nevada: 65
- District of Columbia: 63
- New York: 62
- Maryland: 61
- Arizona: 60
- New Jersey: 60
- Florida: 59
- Georgia: 59
- Alaska: 57
- Illinois: 55
- Delaware: 53
- Louisiana: 53
- Mississippi: 53
- Virginia: 53
- North Carolina: 52
- Oklahoma: 51
- South Carolina: 51
- Alabama: 48
- Colorado: 48
- Connecticut: 47
- Washington: 46
- Arkansas: 42
- Massachusetts: 41
- Rhode Island: 41
- Tennessee: 40
- Michigan: 39
- Kansas: 38
- Oregon: 38
- Pennsylvania: 36
- Utah: 35
- Indiana: 33
- Missouri: 33
- Ohio: 33
- Nebraska: 32
- Minnesota: 31
- Wisconsin: 30
- Idaho: 29
- South Dakota: 28
- Wyoming: 27
- Kentucky: 25
- Montana: 23
- Iowa: 22
- North Dakota: 21
- New Hampshire: 15
- West Virginia: 13
- Maine: 11
- Vermont: 11

72

STATE ECONOMIC PROFILES

72.1 Overview

First Research (www.firstresearch.com) compiles and publishes economic profiles for each state. This chapter provides a summary of personal economic data for second quarter 2013 and employment data for September 2013.

72.2 Personal Income

Personal income in second quarter 2013 was as follows (change from second quarter 2012 in parenthesis):

- Alabama: $ 175 billion (1.4%)
- Alaska: $ 37 billion (1.8%)
- Arizona: $ 243 billion (2.6%)
- Arkansas: $ 106 billion (2.1%)
- California: $1.80 trillion (3.0%)
- Colorado: $ 243 billion (3.1%)
- Connecticut: $ 217 billion (1.8%)
- Delaware: $ 41 billion (2.2%)
- District of Columbia: $ 48 billion (2.3%)
- Florida: $ 812 billion (3.4%)
- Georgia: $ 379 billion (2.7%)
- Hawaii: $ 64 billion (2.8%)
- Idaho: $ 56 billion (3.0%)
- Illinois: $ 602 billion (2.4%)
- Indiana: $ 255 billion (2.7%)
- Iowa: $ 139 billion (3.0%)
- Kansas: $ 127 billion (2.6%)
- Kentucky: $ 158 billion (2.0%)
- Louisiana: $ 188 billion (2.0%)
- Maine: $ 54 billion (2.2%)
- Maryland: $ 322 billion (2.2%)
- Massachusetts: $ 379 billion (2.6%)
- Michigan: $ 388 billion (3.1%)
- Minnesota: $ 257 billion (2.3%)
- Mississippi: $ 102 billion (2.0%)
- Missouri: $ 241 billion (2.8%)

- Montana: $ 40 billion (2.9%)
- Nebraska: $ 85 billion (2.5%)
- Nevada: $ 108 billion (2.7%)
- New Hampshire: $ 66 billion (3.0%)
- New Jersey: $ 498 billion (2.9%)
- New Mexico: $ 76 billion (1.6%)
- New York: $1.10 trillion (2.0%)
- North Carolina: $ 377 billion (2.0%)
- North Dakota: $ 40 billion (4.6%)
- Ohio: $ 473 billion (2.1%)
- Oklahoma: $ 160 billion (3.5%)
- Oregon: $ 156 billion (2.5%)
- Pennsylvania: $ 584 billion (2.2%)
- Rhode Island: $ 49 billion (3.1%)
- South Carolina: $ 168 billion (2.1%)
- South Dakota: $ 39 billion (3.5%)
- Tennessee: $ 256 billion (2.8%)
- Texas: $1.10 trillion (3.7%)
- Utah: $ 104 billion (3.9%)
- Vermont: $ 29 billion (2.7%)
- Virginia: $ 403 billion (2.5%)
- Washington: $ 325 billion (3.2%)
- West Virginia: $ 66 billion (1.2%)
- Wisconsin: $ 246 billion (2.5%)
- Wyoming: $ 30 billion (1.8%)

72.3 Unemployment Rate

The national unemployment rate in September 2013 was 7.2%. For each state, the unemployment rate was as follows:

- Alabama: 6.5%
- Alaska: 5.2%
- Arizona: 8.3%
- Arkansas: 7.0%
- California: 8.2%
- Colorado: 6.5%
- Connecticut: 7.6%
- Delaware: 6.5%
- District of Columbia: 8.6%
- Florida: 6.9%
- Georgia: 7.7%
- Hawaii: 4.5%
- Idaho: 6.0%
- Illinois: 8.5%
- Indiana: 7.0%
- Iowa: 4.1%
- Kansas: 5.4%
- Kentucky: 2.0%
- Louisiana: 6.5%
- Maine: 6.0%
- Maryland: 6.2%
- Massachusetts: 6.9%
- Michigan: 8.3%
- Minnesota: 4.6%
- Mississippi: 8.6%
- Missouri: 6.0%
- Montana: 4.5%
- Nebraska: 3.6%

- Nevada: 9.2%
- New Hampshire: 4.8%
- New Jersey: 8.2%
- New Mexico: 6.2%
- New York: 7.4%
- North Carolina: 7.6%
- North Dakota: 2.0%
- Ohio: 7.2%
- Oklahoma: 5.3%
- Oregon: 6.7%
- Pennsylvania: 6.9%
- Rhode Island: 8.9%
- South Carolina: 7.5%
- South Dakota: 3.4%
- Tennessee: 8.1%
- Texas: 3.7%
- Utah: 3.9%
- Vermont: 4.3%
- Virginia: 5.3%
- Washington: 6.3%
- West Virginia: 5.5%
- Wisconsin: 5.9%
- Wyoming: 3.8%

72.4 Job Growth

Job growth across the U.S. averaged 1.4% between September 2012 and September 2013. For each state, job growth was as follows:

- Alabama: -0.2%
- Alaska: -1.0%
- Arizona: 1.7%
- Arkansas: 0.9%
- California: 1.5%
- Colorado: 2.1%
- Connecticut: 0.4%
- Delaware: 1.7%
- District of Columbia: 0.1%
- Florida: 2.1%
- Georgia: 2.6%
- Hawaii: 1.5%
- Idaho: 2.5%
- Illinois: 0.8%
- Indiana: 1.4%
- Iowa: 0.9%
- Kansas: 1.2%
- Kentucky: 0.6%
- Louisiana: 1.6%
- Maine: 0.6%
- Maryland: 1.3%
- Massachusetts: 1.6%
- Michigan: 1.3%
- Minnesota: 1.4%
- Mississippi: 1.6%
- Missouri: 1.4%
- Montana: 1.1%
- Nebraska: 1.1%
- Nevada: 1.4%
- New Hampshire: 0.2%
- New Jersey: 1.6%
- New Mexico: 0.4%
- New York: 1.1%
- North Carolina: 1.8%
- North Dakota: 3.6%
- Ohio: 0.6%
- Oklahoma: 0.9%
- Oregon: 1.8%
- Pennsylvania: 0.5%
- Rhode Island: 0.8%
- South Carolina: 1.8%
- South Dakota: 1.9%
- Tennessee: 1.3%
- Texas: 2.5%
- Utah: 2.1%
- Vermont: 0.9%
- Virginia: 1.0%
- Washington: 2.0%
- West Virginia: 1.0%
- Wisconsin: 1.0%
- Wyoming: 0.2%

PART XI: COMMUNITIES

73

AMERICANS' VIEWS ON THEIR COMMUNITIES

73.1 Overview

A 2013 study by the Urban Land Institute (www.uli.org) assessed Americans' satisfaction with their communities, housing, and transportation and what they want for themselves and their families. The study was based on a survey of homeowners by Belden Russonello Strategists (www.brspoll.com).

This chapter presents a summary of the Urban Land Institute assessment.

73.2 Satisfaction With Communities

Quality of Life

- Ninety percent (90%) of American adults are satisfied with their community's quality of life, and few worry that these communities are in danger of deteriorating. Groups who are least satisfied with where they currently live, such as Latinos and big-city residents, tend to be the ones who are the most optimistic and who think their communities are on the upswing.

Community

- About a third of the American public live in what they consider small towns, a third in middle-sized or big cities, 21% in suburbs, and 15% in rural areas. If given a choice, a quarter say they would like to be living in rural communities.

Satisfaction With Residence

- Be it single-family houses, apartments, or other structures, most adults like where they live. Nine in ten adults report satisfaction with their current dwelling, and four in five are happy with the range of housing choices in their communities. Even among pockets of less contentment with housing, for example among Millennial adults (ages 18-to-34), Latinos, and big-city residents, dissatisfaction does not rise to high levels.

Single-Family Homes

- Two-thirds of the survey participants say they live in detached single-family homes and the remainder live in apartments, duplexes, row houses, and manufactured homes. Among those who believe they will move in the next five years, the appeal of the single-family home is strong, with two-thirds expecting to move into or remain in a detached single-family home.

Home Ownership

- Seven in ten believe that buying a home is a good investment for them, even in the aftermath of the housing and mortgage difficulties of the last few years. Two-thirds of survey respondents said they own their home and seven in ten renters are hopeful that within five years they will join the ranks of home ownership.

Migration

- Almost one-third of survey respondents said they moved to a different home in the last five years. The highest percentages of those who moved were young people, residents of large cities, and lower-income households. Most of those who moved did so because they sought larger homes. Two in five households anticipate moving within the next five years. Among Baby Boomers (ages 48-to-66), Caucasians, and Midwesterners anticipating a move, the majority say they would prefer moving to a rural location. Most Generation Yers, people of color, Westerners, and singles expressed an interest in urban living.

Commuting and Driving

- Most Americans travel by car, truck, or motorcycle nearly every day, and when the two-thirds who commute regularly go to their jobs or school, 85% travel in a car.
- Travel times to work or school divide in relative thirds: fewer than fifteen minutes, fifteen minutes to half an hour, and over half an hour. Rural and suburban residents and African-Americans have the longest commutes; about half need thirty minutes or more to travel to their employment or schools.

Public Transportation

- Overall, one in ten commuters use public transit to get to school or work. Reliance on buses and trains is highest among people of color and, naturally, residents of urban areas. The public that is served by buses and trains say the quality of their public transit systems is satisfactory; however, half of those who do not have access to trains and buses are discontent with the lack of public transportation.

The Appeal of Compact Development

- While much of the public expresses a desire for single-family homes and rural and small town life, there are competing pressures and needs that recommend compact development. Proximity to jobs, schools, and medical services, as well as a community's walkability, are powerful draws for many Americans.

Mixed-Use Development

- Two groups have a high interest in mixed-use development:
  - Young people and college graduates who are most enthusiastic about living in centers with shops and offices nearby.
  - Lower-income groups who would like to live in areas with more variety in housing type and economic diversity.

- Both of these groups share an interest in living close to where they work or go to school. They prefer to live in areas with public transit and would choose shorter commutes with smaller homes over longer commutes and bigger houses.

Walkability

- Americans place high priority on having communities that are walkable, and most are already at least somewhat content with this aspect of their own communities: 70% say their local sidewalks and crosswalks are satisfactory. One in five walk to a destination most days, and almost one-half do so at least once a week.

Job Market Dissatisfaction

- One area of some discontent with community life is the number and quality of job and career opportunities. More than two in five say this situation in their community is unsatisfactory. This is a problem most acutely felt by people of color and rural residents and, to a smaller degree, Millennials and Baby Boomers.

73.3 Generational Preferences

As Americans age and their incomes rise and then fall, their housing and community preferences vary.

Millennials (ages 18-to-34), half of whom are people of color, show the strongest preference for mixed-use communities. Most currently have an urban, apartment-living lifestyle. At the same time, Millennials are among the least satisfied with where they live and the most likely to be anticipating moving. They want walkable communities and use public transit more than others, although they are still very car dependent.

Many Generation Xers (ages 35-to-47) are in the child-rearing life stage and prefer single-family home ownership. While many members of Generation X are anticipating moving, they are not likely to be looking for mixed-use communities, nor to push for mass transit. This group has the largest percentages of high-income members and if they move they will be seeking to buy single-family homes.

Baby Boomers (ages 48-to-66) are the middle ground on housing and transportation preferences and behaviors, and live in a wide range of sizes of cities and towns. They are not as likely to move soon, but when they do, the Boomers desire smaller homes with shorter commutes. This cohort, as it eases into retirement, would like to be close to parks and apart from neighbors.

Seniors (ages 67 and older) are the most likely to stay in their current homes. These older adults, who are mainly out of the workforce, are especially likely to want to be in walkable neighborhoods and close to health services, family and friends, and shopping and entertainment.

73.4 Important Community Attributes

When asked what attributes they considered important in a community, survey responses were as follows (percentage of respondents):

• Neighborhood safety:	92%
• Quality of public schools:	79%
• Space between neighbors:	72%
• Walk or short drive to work or school:	71%
• Walk or short drive to doctors and hospitals:	71%
• Walkability: sidewalks/crosswalks:	70%
• Walk or short drive to shopping and entertainment:	66%
• Walk or short drive to parks or recreational areas:	64%
• Walk or short drive to family or friends:	63%
• Convenient public transportation:	52%

73.5 Market Resources

Belden Russonello Strategists, 1320 19th Street, Suite 620, Washington DC 20036. (202) 822-6090. (www.brspoll.com)

Urban Land Institute, 1025 Thomas Jefferson Street NW, Suite 500 West, Washington, DC 20007. (202) 624-7000. (www.uli.org)

74

WHERE AMERICANS WANT TO LIVE

74.1 Most Desirable Places To Live

A survey by the Pew Research Center's Social & Demographic Trends Project (www.pewsocialtrends.org) found that 46% of U.S. adults would rather live in a different type of community from the one in which they are presently living. There was no consensus, however, as to what is the ideal place to live. Survey participants responded as follows about their ideal community:

- Small town: 30%
- Suburb: 25%
- City: 23%
- Rural area: 21%

"Most city dwellers think the grass would be greener in a suburb, small town or rural area. But urbanites aren't alone in feeling mismatched with their surroundings. More than four-in-ten residents of suburbs, small towns and rural areas also report they would prefer to live in a different type of community."

Social & Demographics Trends Project
Pew Research Center

The following are other findings of the Pew study:

- By a ratio of more than three-to-one, Americans prefer living where the pace of life is slow. A similarly lopsided majority prefer a place where neighbors know each other well over one where neighbors generally are not acquainted.
- Over 60% of people prefer to live in a warmer climate.
- About seven-in-10 whites rate their current community as "excellent" or "very good"; only about half of Hispanics and four-in-10 blacks say the same. Rural and

suburban residents rate their communities better than do residents of cities and small towns.

- People who live in a city – as well as people who wish to live in a city – are more open than others to the idea of living with neighbors who are of different races. They are also more open to living among immigrants.
- When it comes to community involvement, there is no difference among those who live in cities, suburbs, small towns, or rural areas. About half of the residents in each place say they are involved in their communities.

74.2 Most Desirable States

A September 2013 Harris Poll (www.harrisinteractive.com) asked U.S. adults in which state, apart from their own state, they would like to live (ranking based on responses; one response per survey participant):

1. California
2. Hawaii
3. Florida
4. Texas
5. Colorado
6. New York
7. Arizona
8. North Carolina
9. Oregon
10. Washington
11. Virginia

12. (tie) Pennsylvania
12. (tie) South Carolina
12. (tie) Tennessee
15. Alaska

By demographic, adults identified the state they would most like to live in as follows:

GENDER

Female

1. Hawaii
2. California
3. Florida
4. Texas
5. Colorado

Male

1. California
2. Florida
3. Hawaii
4. Texas
5. New York

GENERATION

Millennials (ages 18-to-36)

1. California
2. Florida
3. New York
4. Hawaii
5. Texas

Generation X (ages 37-to-48)

1. Hawaii
2. Florida
3. California

4. (tie) New York
4. (tie) Texas

Baby Boomers (ages 49-to-67)

1. Hawaii
2. Florida
3. California
4. Texas
5. Colorado

Seniors (ages 68 and older)

1. Hawaii
2. Arizona
3. Colorado
4. Texas
5. (tie) California
5. (tie) Florida

74.3 Most Desirable Cities

In the 2013 Harris Poll, adults said that (excluding their own city) they would like to live in or near the following cities (ranking based on responses; one response per survey participant):

1. New York, NY
2. San Diego, CA
3. Los Angeles, CA
4. San Francisco, CA
5. Honolulu, HI
6. Seattle, WA
7. (tie) Denver, CO
7. (tie) Portland, OR
9. Miami, FL
10. Boston, MA
11. Las Vegas, NV
12. Chicago, IL
13. Austin, TX
14. Atlanta, GA
15. (tie) Nashville, TN
15. (tie) Phoenix, AZ

In the survey by Pew Research Center, people said they would like to live in the following cities or its surrounding metropolitan area (percentage of respondents; multiple responses allowed):

- Denver, CO: 43%
- San Diego, CA: 43%
- Seattle, WA: 38%
- Orlando, FL: 34%
- Tampa, FL: 34%
- San Francisco, CA: 34%
- Phoenix, AZ: 33%
- Portland, OR: 31%
- Sacramento, CA: 29%
- San Antonio, TX: 29%
- Boston, MA: 28%
- Miami, FL: 28%
- Atlanta, GA: 26%
- Washington, DC: 25%
- New York, NY: 24%
- Dallas, TX: 24%
- Philadelphia, PA: 24%
- Chicago, IL: 24%
- Houston, TX: 23%
- Las Vegas, NV: 23%
- Riverside, CA: 23%
- Los Angeles, CA: 21%
- Baltimore, MD: 20%
- St. Louis, MO: 18%
- Pittsburgh, PA: 17%
- Minneapolis, MN: 16%
- Kansas City, MO: 15%
- Cincinnati, OH: 13%
- Cleveland, OH: 10%
- Detroit, MI: 8%

75

RELOCATION

75.1 Overview

According to the U.S. Census Bureau (www.census.gov), about 5 million people, or 1.5% of the population move to another state each year. These moves, which are typically job- or retirement-related, shift where billions of dollars are spent annually. Keeping abreast of population shifts can help businesses with expansion strategies.

The rate of population migration, already in decline over several years, saw an even greater decline during the recession. According to the U.S. Census Bureau, the nation's mobility rates during the Great Recession were among the lowest since World War II.

The rate of migration typically increases as adults approach retirement. According to The Demand Institute (www.demandinstitute.org), a Nielsen company, more than 40% of Americans ages 50 to 64 plan to move within the next five years.

75.2 Relocation 2012

Allied Van Lines (www.alliedvanlines.com), Atlas Van Lines (www.atlasvanlines.com), and United Van Lines (www.unitedvanlines.com), the three largest U.S. moving companies, report annually on migration activity in the United States.

Allied Van Lines reported 2012 interstate household moves as follows:

	Inbound	Outbound
• Alabama:	854	870
• Alaska:	28	20
• Arizona:	2,369	1,936
• Arkansas:	405	333
• California:	6,178	5,967
• Colorado:	2,440	1,989
• Connecticut:	956	1,057
• Delaware:	393	355
• District of Columbia	370	331
• Florida:	5,582	4,916
• Georgia:	2,264	1,969
• Idaho:	484	359
• Illinois	2,690	3,572
• Indiana:	930	1,028
• Iowa:	634	864

• Kansas:	619	783
• Kentucky:	837	683
• Louisiana:	749	845
• Maine:	296	347
• Maryland:	1,273	1,442
• Massachusetts:	1,326	1,404
• Michigan:	1,396	2,173
• Minnesota:	1,190	1,199
• Mississippi:	368	443
• Missouri:	921	902
• Montana:	250	121
• Nebraska:	369	403
• Nevada:	948	951
• New Hampshire:	304	265
• New Jersey:	1,334	2,018
• New Mexico:	564	526
• New York:	2,330	2,867
• North Carolina:	2,836	2,681
• North Dakota:	184	243
• Ohio:	2,057	1,984
• Oklahoma:	663	833
• Oregon:	1,059	711
• Pennsylvania:	1,936	2,884
• Rhode Island:	178	214
• South Carolina:	1,687	1,376
• South Dakota:	186	218
• Tennessee:	1,505	1,555
• Texas:	5,990	4,405
• Utah:	864	718
• Vermont:	171	138
• Virginia:	2,800	2,859
• Washington:	2,182	2,065
• West Virginia:	279	449
• Wisconsin:	952	913
• Wyoming:	172	168

With a net relocation gain of 1,585 families in 2012 (inbound moves minus outbound moves performed by Allied Van Lines), Texas was the leading magnet state for the eighth consecutive year. Florida ranked second in 2012, with a net relocation gain of 666 moves.

Atlas Van Lines reported 2012 interstate household moves as follows:

	Inbound	**Outbound**
• Alabama:	1,151	1,019
• Alaska:	201	162

- Arizona: 1,936 2,038
- Arkansas: 452 535
- California: 6,918 5,960
- Colorado: 2,115 1,979
- Connecticut: 834 1,123
- Delaware: 265 304
- District of Columbia: 510 295
- Florida: 4,973 4,641
- Georgia: 2,818 3,119
- Hawaii: 125 127
- Idaho: 450 435
- Illinois: 2,458 3,174
- Indiana: 1,315 1,701
- Iowa: 623 603
- Kansas: 930 1,147
- Kentucky: 941 839
- Louisiana: 942 1,086
- Maine: 290 289
- Maryland: 2,042 1,944
- Massachusetts: 1,378 1,506
- Michigan: 1,511 1,474
- Minnesota: 862 1,142
- Mississippi: 482 463
- Missouri: 1,042 1,164
- Montana: 218 215
- Nebraska: 357 503
- Nevada: 713 717
- New Hampshire: 282 225
- New Jersey: 1,309 1,750
- New Mexico: 746 643
- New York: 2,367 3,291
- North Carolina: 3,273 2,225
- North Dakota: 216 136
- Ohio: 1,909 2,503
- Oklahoma: 854 790
- Oregon: 770 610
- Pennsylvania: 2,040 2,418
- Rhode Island: 229 192
- South Carolina: 1,676 1,932
- South Dakota: 185 202
- Tennessee: 1,904 1,467
- Texas: 7,120 5,585
- Utah: 434 505
- Vermont: 126 159

• Virginia:	3,411	3,262
• Washington:	3,024	2,309
• West Virginia:	243	305
• Wisconsin:	732	889
• Wyoming:	193	274

United Van Lines reported the states with the highest net inbound moves as follows:

- District of Columbia: 64%
- Oregon: 61%
- Nevada: 58%
- North Carolina: 56%
- South Carolina: 55%

The top five outbound states for 2012 were as follows:

- New Jersey: 62%
- Illinois: 60%
- New Mexico: 58%
- New York: 58%
- West Virginia: 58%

75.3 Interstate Migration Trends

A State-by-State Typology, an assessment by the Pew Research Center (www.pewresearch.org) based on the Census Bureau's *American Community Survey* (www.census.gov/acs/www/), found dramatic differences in states' abilities to to keep native-born residents.

The percentage of the population of residents living in a state other than where they were born is as follows:

- Nevada: 86.4%
- Arizona: 72.0%
- Alaska: 70.8%
- Florida: 70.1%
- District of Columbia: 63.0%
- New Hampshire: 62.9%
- Colorado: 62.9%
- Wyoming: 62.7%
- Idaho: 58.7%
- Oregon: 58.2%
- Delaware: 57.4%
- Washington: 54.3%
- Maryland: 52.0%
- Vermont: 50.1%
- Montana: 50.1%
- New Mexico: 49.8%
- Virginia: 49.4%
- Georgia: 44.3%
- Kansas: 41.5%
- South Carolina: 40.7%
- Arkansas: 40.1%
- North Carolina: 39.9%
- Connecticut: 39.9%
- Tennessee: 39.6%
- Oklahoma: 39.3%
- New Jersey: 39.1%
- Utah: 38.2%
- California: 38.0%

- Maine: 36.5%
- South Dakota: 36.3%
- Hawaii: 36.0%
- Missouri: 35.0%
- Rhode Island: 34.4%
- Texas: 33.4%
- Nebraska: 33.2%
- Indiana: 32.2%
- North Dakota: 30.1%
- Alabama: 29.4%
- Minnesota: 29.4%
- Mississippi: 28.8%
- Kentucky: 28.5%
- Massachusetts: 27.4%
- West Virginia: 27.3%
- Wisconsin: 27.1%
- Illinois: 26.3%
- Iowa: 25.8%
- Ohio: 25.2%
- Michigan: 22.2%
- Pennsylvania: 20.9%
- Louisiana: 20.1%
- New York: 18.8%

The percentage of the population of residents native to the state where they live is as follows:

- Texas: 75.8%
- North Carolina: 71.4%
- Georgia: 69.6%
- California: 69.0%
- Wisconsin: 68.6%
- Michigan: 67.5%
- Tennessee: 66.7%
- Minnesota: 66.3%
- Utah: 66.1%
- South Carolina: 66.0%
- Florida: 66.0%
- Ohio: 65.1%
- Louisiana: 64.4%
- Washington: 64.3%
- Pennsylvania: 63.8%
- Alabama: 63.7%
- Indiana: 62.8%
- Kentucky: 62.6%
- Virginia: 61.9%
- Missouri: 61.9%
- Arizona: 61.5%
- Maryland: 61.1%
- Oregon: 59.2%
- Illinois: 59.0%
- Massachusetts: 58.7%
- Hawaii: 57.3%
- Connecticut: 57.1%
- New Jersey: 55.6%
- Oklahoma: 55.6%
- New York: 55.5%
- Maine: 55.3%
- Mississippi: 54.9%
- Colorado: 54.7%
- Arkansas: 54.5%
- Iowa: 54.0%
- Delaware: 54.0%
- Rhode Island: 53.9%
- New Mexico: 53.5%
- New Hampshire: 52.8%
- Vermont: 52.5%
- Nebraska: 50.2%
- Kansas: 50.2%
- West Virginia: 48.9%
- Nevada: 48.7%
- Idaho: 48.6%
- Montana: 47.1%
- South Dakota: 43.4%
- North Dakota: 40.4%
- Wyoming: 35.7%
- Alaska: 28.2%
- District of Columbia: 13.0%

75.4 Metropolitan Relocation

In 2012, 2.2% of adults in metropolitan areas moved from outside that region, according to International Demographics (www.themediaaudit.com). The percentage was 3.5% and 4.4% in 2007 and 2005, respectively.

"The slowing of population movement is a common response to powerful recessions and has many negative economic consequences, particularly for job hunters who need to be able to move in search of work. But the social impacts are more mixed. One of the virtues of being stuck is that we can continue to rely on the friends and family nearby to help us get through hard times. Staying put may mean that we retain the strength of our ties to one another."

Katherine S. Newman, Ph.D.
Professor of Sociology
Princeton University

In 2012, 61% of adults reported that they have lived within a metro area for 20 years or more, an increase from 59% five years prior.

The following are the metropolitan areas with the highest percentage who have lived in the area for 20 or more years:

- Buffalo, NY: 83.5%
- Pittsburgh, PA: 80.7%
- Cleveland, OH: 79.4%
- Syracuse, NY: 77.2%
- Rochester, NY: 76.3%

75.5 Local Relocation

A February 2013 study conducted at the Luskin School of Public Affairs at the University of California Los Angeles (http://luskin.ucla.edu/public-policy) compared the reason that people moved within their communities prior to and after the Great Recession.

Primary reasons for moving before and during the Great Recession (2007-2009) were as follows:

	Pre-Recession	During Recession
• Demographic/life cycle:	28.2%	31.1%
• Own home/better neighborhood:	41.3%	30.4%
• Find cheaper housing:	20.8%	23.1%
• Look for work:	4.9%	7.8%
• Take a new job:	1.9%	2.3%
• Other:	2.8%	5.4%

"Typically, over the last couple of decades, when Americans moved, they moved to improve their lives. This is the shock: For the first time, Americans are moving for downward economic mobility. Either they lost their house or can't afford where they're renting currently or needed to save money."

Prof. Michael A. Stoll, Ph.D.
Chair, Public Policy
Luskin School of Public Affairs
UCLA, 2/20/13

76

ALL-AMERICAN CITIES

76.1 Overview

All-America City Awards are presented to U.S. cities each year by the National Civic League (www.ncl.org). Winners can be neighborhoods, towns, villages, cities, counties, and regions. Since the program's inception in 1949, more than 600 communities have been named All-America Cities.

76.2 Recent Award Winners

The following are recent award winners:

2013

- Birmingham, AL
- Downey, CA
- Montrose, CO
- Peoria, IL
- Dubuque, IA
- Owensboro, KY
- Dunn, NC
- Garner, NC
- Thomasville, NC
- Norfolk, VA

2012

- Baltimore, MD
- Dubuque, IA
- Louisville, KY
- Marshalltown, IA
- Pittsfield, MA
- Providence, RI
- Quad Cities (Bettendorf, Davenport, Moline, Rock Island), IA/IL
- Roanoke, VA
- San Antonio, TX
- San Francisco, CA
- Seattle and the South King County Cities, WA
- Southern Pines, NC
- Springfield, MA
- Tahoe/Truckee, CA

2011

- Belleville, IL
- Dublin, CA
- Eden, NC
- Fayetteville, NC
- Fort Worth, TX
- Kenai, AK
- Lakewood, CO
- Scott City, KS
- South Bend, IN
- Tupelo, MS

2010

- Acworth, GA
- Chandler, AZ
- Des Moines, IA
- El Paso, TX
- Gastonia, NC
- Lynwood, CA
- Mount Pleasant, SC
- North Miami, FL
- Rancho Cordova, CA
- Salisbury, MD

Communities winning this award more than two times comprise the All-America City Hall of Fame. These communities are as follows:

Five-Time Winners

- Cleveland, OH
- Des Moines, IA
- Kansas City, MO
- Phoenix, AZ
- Roanoke, VA
- Worcester, MA

Four-Time Winners

- Anchorage, AK
- Columbus, OH
- New Haven, CT
- Peoria, IL
- Philadelphia, PA
- Rockville, MD
- Tupelo, MS
- Wichita, KS

Three-Time Winners

- Akron, OH
- Asheville, NC
- Baltimore, MD
- Boston, MA
- Cincinnati, OH
- Dayton, OH
- Edinburg, TX
- Fayetteville, NC
- Fort Wayne, IN
- Fort Worth, TX
- Gastonia, NC
- Grand Island, NE
- Grand Rapids, MI
- Hickory, NC
- Independence, MO
- Laurinburg, NC
- Saint Paul, MN
- San Antonio, TX
- Seward, AK
- Shreveport, LA
- Tacoma, WA
- Toledo, OH

76.3 Market Resources

National Civic League, 1889 York Street, Denver, CO 80206. (303) 571-4343. (www.ncl.org)

77

BEST SMALL TOWNS

77.1 Award-Winning Towns

Since 2011, *USA Today* in conjunction Rand McNally's has designated small towns that excel in five categories: friendly people, great scenery, food, patriotic fervor, and fun. A sixth category, geocaching, was added in 2013.

Winning towns have been as follows:

2013

- Most Beautiful: Jefferson City, MO
- Most Fun: Corning, NY
- Most Patriotic: Gallup, NM
- Best for Food: San Mateo, CA
- Best for Geocaching: Helena, MT
- Friendliest: Kewanee, IL

2012

- Most Beautiful: Bardstown, KY
- Most Fun: Delray Beach, FL
- Most Patriotic: Gainesville, TX
- Best for Food: Santa Fe, NM
- Friendliest: Murray, KY

2011

- Most Beautiful: Sandpoint, ID
- Most Fun: Glenwood Springs, CO
- Most Patriotic: Rapid City, SD
- Best for Food: Lafayette, LA
- Friendliest: Walla Walla, WA

77.2 Top 20 Small Towns

Since 2012, *Smithsonian* has ranked the top 20 small towns in America.

In 2013, only towns with populations of less than 15,000 were considered, and selections were made based on exceptional concentrations of museums, art galleries, orchestras, theaters, historic sites, and other cultural resources.

The Top 20 Small Towns for 2013 are as follows:

1. Gettysburg, PA
2. Cleveland, MS
3. St. Augustine, FL
4. Baraboo, WI
5. Astoria, OR
6. Petoskey, MI
7. Fairfield, IA
8. Los Alamos, NM
9. Sitka, AK
10. Provincetown, MA
11. Galena, IL
12. Sausalito, CA
13. Hanover, NH
14. Oberlin, OH
15. Jackson, WY
16. Lexington, VA
17. Abilene, KS
18. Lihue, HI
19. Fredericksburg, TX
20. Glenwood Springs, CO

In 2012, only towns with populations of less than 25,000 were considered, and selections were made based on high concentrations of museums, historic sites, botanic gardens, resident orchestras, art galleries, and other cultural assets common to big cities.

The Top 20 Small Towns in 2012 were as follows:

1. Great Barrington, MA
2. Taos, NM
3. Red Bank, NJ
4. Mill Valley, CA
5. Gig Harbor, WA
6. Durango, CO
7. Butler, PA
8. Marfa, TX
9. Naples, FL
10. Staunton, VA
11. Brattleboro, VT
12. Princeton, NJ
13. Brunswick, ME
14. Siloam Springs, AR
15. Menomonie, WI
16. Key West, FL
17. Laguna Beach, CA
18. Ashland, OR
19. Beckley City, WV
20. Oxford, MS

77.3 Market Resources

Destination Marketing Association International, 2025 M Street NW, Suite 500, Washington, D.C. 20036. (202) 296-7888. (www.destinationmarketing.org)

78

GREAT PLACES IN AMERICA

78.1 Overview

Since 2007, the American Planning Association (www.planning.org) has recognized streets, neighborhoods, and public spaces that demonstrate exemplary character, quality, and planning with annual Great Places in America awards. Criteria include architectural features, accessibility, functionality, and community involvement.

78.2 Great Neighborhoods

The 2013 Great Neighborhoods in America award winners are as follows:

- San Francisco, CA: Chinatown
- Norwich, CT: Downtown Norwich/Chelsea Landing
- Decatur, GA: Downtown Decatur
- Evanston, Il: Central Street Neighborhood
- Mason City, IA: Downtown Mason City
- Covington, KY: Historic Licking Riverside
- Minneapolis, MN: Kenwood
- Beaufort, SC: Beaufort Historic District
- Norfolk, VA: West Freemason
- Madison, WI: Williamson Marquette

The following are previous award-winning neighborhoods:

- Atlanta, GA: Ansley Park
- Austin, TX: Old West Austin
- Baltimore, MD: Charles Village
- Baltimore, MD: Fells Point
- Baton Rouge, LA: Garden District
- Berkeley, CA: Northbrae
- Birmingham, AL: Highland Park
- Boise, ID: North End
- Boston, MA: Back Bay
- Brooklyn, NY: Park Slope
- Buffalo, NY: Elmwood Village
- Chicago, IL: The Pullman Neighborhood
- Cincinnati, OH: Hyde Park
- Columbus, OH: German Village

- Davenport, IA: Gold Coast & Hamburg Historic District
- Denver, CO: Greater Park Hill
- Denver, CO: Lower Downtown
- Fall River, MA: Lower Highlands and Historic Downtown
- Fargo, ND: Downtown Fargo
- Franklin, TN: Downtown Franklin Historic District
- Frederick, MD: Downtown Frederick
- Grand Rapids, MI: Heritage Hill
- Hattiesburg, MS: Hattiesburg Historic Neighborhood
- Houston, TX: Montrose
- Jacksonville, FL: Riverside Avondale
- Kenmore, NY: Village of Kenmore
- Lafayette, IN: Historic Ninth Street Hill Neighborhood
- Lake Oswego, OR: First Addition
- Las Vegas, NV: John S. Park Neighborhood
- Lincoln, NE: The Haymarket
- Los Angeles, CA: Echo Park
- Mariemont, OH: Village of Mariemont
- Memphis, TN: Cooper-Young
- New Orleans, LA: Faubourg Marigny
- Newport News, VA: Historic Hilton Village
- Oklahoma City, OK: The Paseo
- Omaha, NE: Dundee-Memorial Park
- Pasadena, CA: Bungalow Heaven
- Philadelphia, PA: Chestnut Hill
- Philadelphia, PA: Society Hill
- Pittsburgh, PA: Chatham Village
- Portland, OR: Ladd's Addition
- Providence, RI: College Hill
- Salem, MA: Downtown Salem
- Salisbury, NC: Downtown Salisbury
- San Diego, CA: Hillcrest
- San Francisco, CA: North Beach
- Salt Lake City, UT: Fairmont-Sugar House
- Seattle, WA: Beacon Hill
- Seattle, WA: Pike Place Market
- Sheridan, WY: Downtown Sheridan
- Sioux Falls, SD: The Cathedral Historic District
- Spokane, WA: Browne's Addition
- Syracuse, NY: Greater University Hill
- Tulsa, OK: Swan Lake
- Urbana, IL: West Urbana
- Village of Oak Park, IL: Frank Lloyd Wright Historic District
- Walla Walla, WA: Downtown Walla Walla

- Washington, DC: Eastern Market
- Wichita, KS: Old Town

78.3 Great Public Places

The 2013 Great Public Spaces in America award winners are as follows:

- Milford, DE: North and South Walnut Street
- Pensacola, FL: Palafox Street
- Honolulu, HI: Kalakaua Avenue
- Virginia City, NV: C Street
- Las Vegas, NM: Bridge Street
- Corning, NY: Market Street
- Jim Thorpe, PA: Broadway
- Philadelphia, PA: Ben Franklin Parkway
- Galveston, TX: The Strand (Avenue B)
- Staunton, VA: West Beverley Street

The following are previous award-winning public spaces:

- Bar Harbor, ME: Village Green
- Birmingham, AL: Charles W. Ireland Sculpture Garden
- Boca Raton, FL: Plaza Real
- Boston, MA: The Emerald Necklace
- Bowling Green, KY: Fountain Square
- Burlington, VT: Church Street Marketplace
- Charleston, SC: Waterfront Park
- Charlevoix, MI: East Park
- Chicago, IL: Chicago Union Station
- Chicago, IL: Lincoln Park
- Cleveland, OH: West Side Market
- Colorado Springs, CO: Garden of the Gods Park
- Dallas, TX: Fair Park
- Denver, CO: Washington Park
- Des Moines, IA: Gray's Lake Park
- Detroit, MI: Campus Martius Park
- Dover, DE: The Green
- Flushing, NY: Queens Botanical Garden
- Glencoe, IL: Chicago Botanic Garden
- Houston, TX: Buffalo Bayou
- Huntington, WV: Ritter Park
- Indianapolis, IN: Monument Circle
- Keene, NH: Central Square
- Lancaster, PA: Central Market
- Milwaukee, WI: Milwaukee RiverWalk
- Minneapolis, MN: The Grand Rounds

- Mobile, AL: Bienville Square
- Nashville, TN: Bicentennial Capitol Mall State Park
- New Haven, CT: New Haven Green
- New Orleans, LA: Jackson Square
- New York, NY: Bryant Park
- New York, NY: Central Park
- Olympia, WA: Percival Landing Boardwalk and Park
- Philadelphia, PA: Rittenhouse Square
- Pittsburgh, PA: Mellon Square
- Portland, OR: Governor Tom McCall Waterfront Park
- Portland, OR: Pioneer Courthouse Square
- Prescott, AZ: Yavapai County Courthouse Plaza
- Providence, RI: Waterplace Park
- Richmond, VA: Maymont
- Riverside, CA: Fairmount Park
- Sacramento, CA: Cesar Chavez Park and Plaza
- Saint Paul, MN: Rice Park
- San Antonio, TX: Main Plaza
- San Francisco, CA: Ferry Building
- Santa Monica, CA: Santa Monica Beach
- Savannah, GA: The Squares of Savannah
- Tacoma, WA: Point Defiance Park
- Virginia Beach, VA: Virginia Beach Boardwalk
- Washington, DC: Union Station

78.4 Great Streets

The 2013 Great Streets in America award winners are as follows:

- Anchorage, AK: Tony Knowles Coastal Trail
- Los Angeles, CA: Grand Park
- Hollywood, FL: Broadwalk
- Boston, MA: Norman B. Leventhal Park
- Cambridge and Watertown, MA: Mount Auburn Cemetery
- St. Louis, MO: Forest Park
- Newark, NJ: Essex County Branch Brook Park
- New York, NY: Grand Central Terminal
- Chattanooga, TN: Walnut Street Bridge
- Vancouver, WA: Esther Short Park

The following are previous award-winning streets:

- Alexandria, VA: King Street
- Ann Arbor, MI: South Main Street
- Annapolis, MD: Main Street
- Arlington, VA: Clarendon and Wilson Boulevards

- Bath, ME: Front Street
- Boston, MA: Washington Street
- Bozeman, MT: Main Street
- Charleston, SC: Broad Street
- Chicago, IL: North Michigan Avenue
- Clayton, MO: Wydown Boulevard
- Cleveland, Shaker Heights, and Beachwood, OH: Shaker Boulevard
- Collingswood, NJ: Haddon Avenue
- Culpeper, VA: Davis Street
- El Paso, TX: South El Paso Street
- Eureka Springs, AR: Spring Street
- Franklin, PA: Liberty Street
- Galena, IL: Main Street
- Greenville, SC: Main Street
- Hoboken, NJ: Washington Street
- Kansas City, MO: Ward Parkway
- Key West, FL: Duval Street
- Kingston, NY: Wall Street
- Knoxville, TN: Gay Street
- Lahaina, HI: Front Street
- Lawrence, KS: Massachusetts Street
- Little Rock, AR: President Clinton Avenue
- Louisville, KY: West Main Street
- Miami Beach, FL: Ocean Drive
- Middleburg, VA: Washington Street
- Milwaukee, WI: East Newberry Boulevard
- Nantucket, MA: Main Street
- New York, NY: 125th Street
- New York, NY: Fifth Avenue
- New Orleans, LA: St. Charles Avenue
- New Bern, NC: Middle Street
- Northampton, MA: Main Street
- Philadelphia, PA: Broad Street
- Pittsburgh, PA: Grant Street
- Portland, ME: Commercial Street
- Portsmouth, NH: Market Street and Market Square
- Red Lodge, MT: Broadway Avenue
- Richmond, VA: Monument Avenue
- Saint Paul, MN: Summit Avenue
- Salt Lake City, UT: South Temple Street
- San Diego, CA: 5th Avenue
- Santa Fe, NM: Canyon Road
- Saratoga Springs, NY: Broadway

- Savannah, GA: Bull Street
- Skagway, AK: Broadway Street
- St. Louis, MO: Delmar Loop (University City)
- St. Louis, MO: Washington Avenue
- Tampa, FL: 7th Avenue (Ybor City)
- Tempe, AZ: Mill Avenue
- Traverse City, MI: Front Street
- Wallace, ID: Bank Street
- Washington, DC: U Street N.W.
- West Hollywood, CA: Santa Monica Boulevard
- Wheeling, WV: North Main Street
- Williamsburg, VA: Duke of Gloucester Street
- Woodstock, VT: Downtown Woodstock Streetscape

78.5 Market Resources

American Planning Association, 205 N. Michigan Avenue, Suite 1200, Chicago, IL 60601. (312) 431-9100. (www.planning.org)

APPENDIX A

ACADEMIC RESEARCH CENTERS

Bowling Green State University, Center for Family and Demographic Research, Five Williams Hall, Bowling Green, OH 43403. (419) 372-7279. (www.bgsu.edu/organizations/cfdr/)

Carnegie Mellon University, Center for Behavioral Decision Research, Tepper School of Business, 5000 Forbes Avenue, Pittsburgh, PA 15213. (412) 268-2268. (www.cbdr.cmu.edu)

Columbia University, Graduate School of Business, 3022 Broadway, New York, NY 10027. (212) 854-5553. (www.gsb.columbia.edu)

Davenport University, Donald W. Maine College Of Business, 6191 Kraft Avenue SE, Grand Rapids, MI 49512. (www.davenport.edu/college-business)

Duke University, Fuqua School of Business, 100 Fuqua Drive, Box 90120, Durham, NC 27708. (919) 660-7700. (www.fuqua.duke.edu)

Duquesne University, Palumbo-Donahue School of Business, 600 Forbes Avenue, Pittsburgh, PA 15282. (www.duq.edu/academics/schools/business#/1)

Eastern Illinois University, Family and Consumer Sciences, 1032 Klehm Hall, 600 Lincoln Avenue, Charleston, IL 61920. (www.eiu.edu/famsci/)

Elon University, Imagining The Internet Center, School of Communications, Elon, NC 27244. (336) 278-2000. (www.imaginingtheinternet.org)

Georgetown University, Institute for Consumer Research, McDonough School of Business, Rafik B. Hariri Building, Georgetown University, Washington, DC 20057. (202) 687-0111. (http://consumerresearch.georgetown.edu)

Golden Gate University, Edward S. Ageno School of Business, 536 Mission Street, San Francisco CA, 94105. (800) 448-4968. (www.ggu.edu/programs/business-and-management)

Harvard Business School, Bloomberg Center, 25 Harvard Way, Boston, MA 02163. (www.library.hbs.edu/guides/demographicsconsumerbehavior.html)

Indiana University, Kelley School of Business, 1275 East Tenth Street, Bloomington, IN 47405. (812) 855-8100. (www.kelley.iu.edu)

Kansas State Olathe, Sensory & Consumer Research Center, 22201 W. Innovation Drive, Olathe, KS 66061. (913) 307-7354. (http://olathe.k-state.edu/centers-institutes/ConsumerResearch.html)

NYU Stern, Henry Kaufman Management Center, 44 West Fourth Street, New York, NY 10012. (212) 998-0100. (www.stern.nyu.edu)

Northwestern University, Kellogg School of Management, 2001 Sheridan Road, Evanston, IL 60208. (847) 491-3300. (www.kellogg.northwestern.edu)

Rochester Institute of Technology, E. Philip Saunders College of Business, 105 Lomb Memorial Drive, Rochester, NY 14623. (http://saunders.rit.edu)

Saint Joseph University, Center For Consumer Research, Erivan K. Haub School Of Business, 5600 City Avenue, Philadelphia, PA 19131. (610) 660-1645. (www.sju.edu/academics/centers/ccr/index.html)

Stanford University, Graduate School of Business, Knight Management Center, 655 Knight Way, Stanford, CA 94305. (www.gsb.stanford.edu)

University of California Davis, Center for Consumer Research, Davis, CA 95616. (530) 752-2774. (http://ccr.ucdavis.edu/)

University of California Los Angeles (UCLA), Interdisciplinary Group in Behavioral Decision Making, Anderson School of Management, Box 951481, Los Angeles, CA 90095. (310) 825-0003. (www.anderson.ucla.edu/x2271.xml)

University of Chicago, Center for Decision Research, Booth School of Business, 5807 South Woodlawn Avenue, Chicago, Illinois 60637. (773) 702-4877. (http://research.chicagobooth.edu/cdr/)

University of Chicago, National Opinion Research Center, 1155 E. 60th Street, 3rd Floor, Chicago, IL 60637. (773) 256-6000. (www.norc.org)

University of Georgia, Selig Center for Economic Growth, 110 East Clayton Street, Suite 608, Athens, GA 30602. (706) 542-4085. (www.terry.uga.edu/selig/)

University of Massachusetts Dartmouth Center for Marketing Research, 285 Old Westport Road, North Dartmouth, MA 02747. (508) 999-8000. (www.umassd.edu/cmr)

University of Michigan, Stephen M. Ross Business School, 701 Tappan Street Ann Arbor, MI 48109. (734) 615-9700. (www.bus.umich.edu)

University of Minnesota, Carlson School of Management, 321 19th Avenue South, Minneapolis, MN 55455. (612) 625-0027. (www.csom.umn.edu)

University of Pennsylvania, Wharton School of Business, Jon M. Huntsman Hall 3730 Walnut Street, Philadelphia, PA 19104. (215) 898-6183. (www.wharton.upenn.edu)

University of Pittsburgh, Joseph M. Katz Graduate School of Business and College of Business Administration, Mervis Hall, Pittsburgh, PA 15260. (412) 648-1700. (www.business.pitt.edu)

University of Rochester, Simon Graduate School of Business, 305 Schlegel Hall, Rochester, NY 14627. (www.simon.rochester.edu)

University of South Alabama, Mitchell College of Business, 307 University Boulevard, Mobile, AL 36688. (www.southalabama.edu/mcob/)

University of Southern California, Center for the Digital Future, Annenberg School for Communication and Journalism, 11444 West Olympic Boulevard, Suite 120, Los Angeles, CA 90064. (www.digitalcenter.org)

Vanderbilt University, Owen Graduate School of Management, 401 21st Avenue South, Nashville, TN 37203. (www.owen.vanderbilt.edu)

Yale University, Center for Customer Insights, School of Management, 135 Prospect Street, Box 208200, New Haven, CT 06520. (203) 432-6069. (www.cci.som.yale.edu)

APPENDIX B

ANALYSTS

American Customer Satisfaction Index (ACSI), 625 Avis Drive, Ann Arbor, MI 48108. (734) 913-0788. (www.theacsi.org)

America's Research Group, 810 Travelers Blvd, Suite G-1, Summerville, SC 29485. (843) 695-0090. (www.americasresearchgroup.com)

Arbitron, 9705 Patuxent Woods Drive, Columbia, MD 21046. (410) 312-8000. (www.arbitron.com)

Belden Russonello Strategists, 1320 19th Street, Suite 620, Washington DC 20036. (202) 822-6090. (www.brspoll.com)

BIA/Kelsey, 15120 Enterprise Court, Chantilly, VA 20151. (703) 818-2425. (www.bia.com)

Boston Consulting Group, Exchange Place, 31st Floor, Boston, MA 02109. (617) 973-1200. (www.bcg.com)

Brand Keys, 9 West 29th Street, 5th Floor, New York, NY 10001. (212) 532-6028. (www.brandkeys.com)

Chadwick Martin Bailey, 179 South Street, 3rd Floor, Boston, MA 02111. (617) 350-8922. (www.cmbinfo.com)

Concentric Marketing, 101 Worthington Avenue, Suite 190, Charlotte, NC 28203. (704) 731-5100. (www.getconcentric.com)

Economic Analysis Associates, 5 Glen Court, Greenwich, CT 06830. (203) 869-9667. (www.eaaresearch.com)

eMarketer, 75 Broad Street, 31st Floor, New York, NY 10004. (212) 763-6010. (www.emarketer.com)

Envirosell Inc., 907 Broadway, 2nd Floor, New York, NY 10010. (212) 673-9100. (www.envirosell.com)

EPM Communications, 19 West 21st Street, New York, NY 10010. (212) 941-0099. (www.epmcom.com)

ForeSee Results, 2500 Green Road, Suite 400, Ann Arbor, MI 48105. (800) 621-2850. (www.foreseeresults.com)

GfK, 75 Ninth Avenue, 5th Floor, New York, NY 10011. (212) 240-5300. (www.gfk.com)

Harris Interactive, 60 Corporate Woods, Rochester, NY 14623. (585) 272-8400. (www.harrisinteractive.com)

IEG, 350 North Orleans Street, Suite 1200, Chicago, IL 60654. (800) 834-4850. (www.sponsorship.com)

International Demographics, 10333 Richmond Avenue, Suite 200, Houston, TX 77042. (713) 626-0333. (www.themediaaudit.com)

Ipsos Marketing, 1600 Stewart Avenue, Suite 500, Westbury, NY 11590. (516) 507-3515. (www.ipsos.com/marketing)

IRI, 150 North Clinton Street, Chicago, IL 60661. (312) 726-1221. (www.iriworldwide.com)

J.D. Power and Associates, 2625 Townsgate Road, Westlake Village, CA 91361. (805) 418-8000. (www.jdpower.com)

Javelin Strategy & Research, 4301 Hacienda Drive, Suite 550, Pleasanton, CA 94588. (925) 225-9100. (www.javelinstrategy.com)

Kantar Retail, 585 S. Front Street, Suite 50, Columbus, OH 43215. (614) 355-4000. (www.kantarretail.com)

Leo J. Shapiro and Associates, 153 West Ohio Street, Suite 300, Chicago, IL 60654. (312) 321-8111. (www.ljs.com)

Luxury Institute, 115 East 57th Street, 11th Floor, New York, NY 10022. (646) 792-2669. (www.luxuryinstitute.com)

New Strategist, 26 Austin Avenue, P.O. Box 635, Amityville, NY 11701. (800) 848-0842. (www.newstrategist.com)

ORC International, 902 Carnegie Center, Suite 220, Princeton, NJ 08540. (800) 444-4672. (www.orcinternational.com)

Paramount Market Publishing, 950 Danby Road, Suite 136, Ithaca, NY 14850. (607) 275-8100. (www.paramountbooks.com)

Pew Research Center, 1615 L Street, Suite 700, Washington, DC 20036. (202) 419-4300. (www.pewresearch.org)

Prosper Business Development, 450 Old Wilson Bridge, Suite 370, Worthington, OH 43085. (614) 846-0146. (www.goprosper.com)

Richard K. Miller & Associates, 4132 Atlanta Highway, Suite 110, Loganville, GA 30052. (888) 928-7562. (www.rkma.com)

Riedel Marketing Group, 5327 East Pinchot Avenue, Phoenix, AZ 85018. (602) 840-4948. (www.4rmg.com)

Scarborough Research, 770 Broadway, New York, NY 10003. (646) 654-8400. (www.scarborough.com)

Sentier Research, 8 Mayo Avenue, Annapolis, MD 21403. (703) 764-0249. (www.sentierresearch.com)

Service Management Group, 1737 McGee Street, Kansas City, MO 64108. (800) 764-0439. (www.smg.com)

Teenage Research Unlimited, 222 Merchant Mart Plaza, Chicago, IL 60645. (312) 951-4100. (www.teenresearch.com)

Temkin Group, 48 White Oak Road, Waban, MA 02468. (617) 916-2075. (www.temkingroup.com)

The Conference Board, 845 Third Avenue, New York, NY 10022. (212) 759-0900. (www.conference-board.org)

The Futures Company, 1300 Environ Way, Chapel Hill, NC 27517. (919) 932-8858. (www.thefuturescompany.com)

The Gallup Organization, 901 F Street NW, Washington, DC 20004. (202) 715-3030. (www.gallup.com)

The Nielsen Company, 770 Broadway, New York, NY 10003. (646) 654-5000. (www.nielsen.com)

The NPD Group, 900 West Shore Road, Port Washington, NY 11050. (516) 625-0700. (www.npd.com)

Unity Marketing, 206 E. Church Street, Stevens, PA 17578. (717) 336-1600. (www.unitymarketingonline.com)

Urban Land Institute, 1025 Thomas Jefferson Street NW, Suite 500 West, Washington, DC 20007. (202) 624-7000. (www.uli.org)

uSamp, 16501 Ventura Boulevard, Suite 250, Encino, CA 91436. (877) 217-9800. (www.usamp.com)

WSL Strategic Retail, 307 Seventh Avenue, Suite 1707, New York, NY 10001. (212) 924-7780. (www.wslstrategicretail.com)

APPENDIX C

MARKET RESEARCH SOURCES

C.1 Consumer Surveys and Opinion Polls

Surveys and polls are popular tools identifying consumer attitudes, preferences, and behaviors relating to a broad spectrum of interests. There are a host of firms that specialize in this field; some of the major survey firms in the U.S. are as follows:

- Gallup Inc. (www.gallup.com)
- GfK MRI (www.gfkmri.com)
- Harris Interactive (www.harrisinteractive.com)
- Ipsos (www.ipsos.com)
- J.D. Power and Associates (www.jdpower.com)
- Kantar Retail (www.kantarretail.com)
- Leo J. Shapiro and Associates (www.ljs.com)
- Prosper Business Development (www.goprosper.com)
- ORC International (www.orcinternational.com)
- Scarborough Research (www.scarborough.com)

C.2 Retail Sales Reporting

Many companies develop comprehensive retail analyses based on sales data provided to them by major retail chains. Reporting companies provide data as varied as products that consumers purchase as well as how much they spend. In addition to receiving a fee for their data, retailers gain access to information that includes their competitors' sales figures. A few retailers, including Walmart, do not release sales data.

Companies that provide point-of-sale market research data include the following:

- Experian (www.experian.com/simmons-research/simmons-consumer-research.html)
- Market Decisions (www.marketdecisions.com)
- SportScanINFO (www.sportscaninfo.com)
- IRI Group (www.iriworldwide.com)
- The Nielsen Company (www.nielsen.com)
- The NPD Group (www.npd.com)

Such companies also develop retail market data based on statistical-sample monitoring of households. This approach (e.g., sampling and projecting) was the norm in the data gathering industry before scanner data became available.

C.3 Media Consumption Research

Several specialized companies offer survey-based data on consumer use of various media. This data is used by advertisers to guide marketing campaigns and ad placements. The following are leading companies in this field:

- Arbitron (www.arbitron.com)
- Audience Research & Analysis (www.audienceresearch.com)
- Kantar Media (www.kantarmedia.com)
- Media Management, Inc. (www.mediaaudit.com)
- PQ Media (www.pqmedia.com)
- Screen Digest (www.screendigest.com)
- The Nielsen Company (www.nielsen.com)

C.4 Geodemographic Segmentation

Information about consumers based on where they live guides companies in siting their new stores. The data is also used to guide direct marketing campaigns as well as the placement of local spot ads. Various geodemographic segmentation tools, primarily based on geographic information system (GIS) technology, are available for this type of analysis.

The following are companies specializing in this field:

- Acxiom (www.acxiom.com)
- Applied Geographic Solutions (www.appliedgeographic.com)
- ESRI (www.esri.com)
- Nielsen SiteReports (www.nielsen.com)
- Phoenix Marketing International (www.phoenixmi.com)
- Pitney Bowes Software (www.pbinsight.com)

C.5 Online Activities

Several companies track consumers' online activities, and the assessments are used by marketers to guide the placement of online ads and promotions. They also provide insight into consumers' ever-changing habits as they surf the net or shop online.

The following are some market research firms specializing in online tracking:

- Compete (www.compete.com)
- ComScore (www.comscore.com)
- Experian Hitwise (www.hitwise.com)
- Forrester Research (www.forrester.com)
- Juniper Research (www.juniperresearch.com)
- Quantcast (www.quantcast.com)
- Shop.org of the National Retail Federation (www.shop.org)
- The Nielsen Company (www.nielsen.com)

C.6 Consumer-Focused Market Studies

The following firms publish market research reports assessing consumer market segments and market characteristics:

- America's Research Group (www.americasresearchgroup.com)
- Prosper Business Development (www.goprosper.com)
- Datamonitor (www.datamonitor.com)
- EPM Communications (www.epmcom.com)
- Euromonitor International (www.euromonitor.com)
- GfK North America (www.gfk.com)
- Mintel (www.mintel.com)
- MMGY Global (www.mmgyglobal.com)
- New Strategist Publications (www.newstrategist.com)
- Packaged Facts (www.packagedfacts.com)
- Paramount Market Publishing (www.paramountbooks.com)
- Parks Associates (www.parksassociates.com)
- PKF Consulting, Hospitality Research Group (www.pkfonline.com)
- Richard K. Miller & Associates (www.rkma.com)
- Scarborough Marketing (www.scarborough.com)
- STR Global (www.strglobal.com)
- The Futures Company (www.thefuturescompany.com)
- The NPD Group (www.npd.com)
- The Yankee Group (www.yankeegroup.com)
- Unity Marketing (www.unitymarketingonline.com)
- WSL Strategic Retail (www.wslstrategicretail.com)

APPENDIX D

PERIODICALS

FYI, International Demographics, 10333 Richmond Avenue, Suite 200, Houston, TX 77042. (713) 626-0333. (www.themediaaudit.com/press/archived-newsletters)

Journal of Consumer Psychology, published by Elsevier Publishing Co. (www.myscp.org) and (www.elsevier.com)

Journal of Consumer Research, c/o University of Wisconsin-Madison (www.ejcr.org)

Knowledge@Wharton, published online by Wharton School of the University of Pennsylvania. (http://knowledge.wharton.upenn.edu/)

MIT Sloan Management Review, published by Massachusetts Institute of Technology. (www.sloanreview.mit.edu)

Multicultural Marketing News, 150 W 28th Street, Suite 1501, New York, NY 10001. (212) 242-3351. (www.multicultural.com)

Research Brief, Center for Media Research, MediaPost Communications, 15 East 32nd Street, 7th Floor, New York, NY 10016. (www.mediapost.com/publications/research-brief/)

REFERENCES

PART I: THE AMERICAN CONSUMER

Chapter 1: Demographic Overview

America's Families And Living Arrangements 2012, U.S. Census Bureau, August 27, 2013.

U.S. Population Clock, U.S. Census Bureau, November 27, 2013.

Chapter 2: Consumer Spending

Consumer Expenditures 2012, Bureau of Labor Statistics, September 2013.

Consumer Price Index Summary, Bureau of Labor Statistics, 2013.

Chapter 3: Retail Spending

Harris, Elizabeth A., "Thanksgiving Openings Take Sales From Black Friday," *The New York Times*, November 30, 2013.

Chapter 4: Use Of Time

American Time Use Survey - 2012 Results, Bureau of Labor Statistics, June 2013. (www.bls.gov/news.release/atus.nr0.htm)

Chapter 5: Use Of Media & The Internet

America At The Digital Turning Point, University of Southern California, Annenberg School for Communication and Journalism, January 2012.

Brenner, Joanna and Aaron Smith, "72% Of Online Adults Are Social Networking Site Users," Pew Internet & American Life Project, August 5, 2013.

"Demographics Vary Across Social Networks," eMarketer, March 11, 2013.

Duggan, Maeve, *Cellphone Activities 2013*, Pew Internet & American Life Project, September 19, 2013.

Duggan, Maeve and Aaron Smith, *Cell Internet Use 2013*, Pew Internet & American Life Project, September 16, 2013.

Goel, Vindu, "Our Daily Cup Of Facebook," *The New York Times*, August 13, 2013.

Loechner, Jack, "Demographic Divisions Among Social Network Users," *Research Brief*, Center for Media Research, April 19, 2013.

Loechner, Jack, "Social Networking Captures Almost 3/4 Of U.S. Adults," *Research Brief*, Center for Media Research, August 2, 2013.

Media Use Benchmark 2013, Temkin Group, April 2013.

"Most TV, Tablet Interactions Involve Another Screen," *eMarketer*, September 11, 2012.

Rainie, Lee and Aaron Smith, *Tablet And E-Reader Ownership Update*, Pew Internet & American Life Project, October 18, 2013.

State of the Media Democracy Survey, 7th Edition, Deloitte, January 2013.

The 2013 Digital Future Report: Surveying The Digital Future, Annenberg School for Communication & Journalism, University of Southern California, 2013.

"U.S. Time Spent On Mobile To Overtake Desktop," eMarketer, August 1, 2013.

Zickuhr, Kathryn and Mary Madden, *Older Adults And Internet Use*, Pew Internet & American Life Project, June 6, 2012.

Chapter 6: Consumer Income & Wealth

DeNavas-Walt, Carmen, Bernadette D. Proctor, and Jessica C. Smith, *Income, Poverty, and Health Insurance Coverage in the United States: 2012*, U.S. Census Bureau, September 2013.

Fry, Richard and Paul Taylor, *A Rise In Wealth For The Wealthy; Declines For The Lower 93%*, Pew Research Center, April 23, 2013.

Green, Gordon and John Coder, *Household Income Trends*, Sentier Research, November 2013.

Reich, Robert, *Inequality for All*, 72 Productions, September 2013.

Rampell, Catherine, "Median Household Income Down 7.3% Since Start of Recession," *The New York Times*, March 29, 2013.

Suddath, Claire, "Rich Man, Poor Man," *Bloomberg Businessweek*, September 26, 2013.

"Top Hats And Tails," *The Economist*, September 14, 2013.

Yen, Hope, "4 in 5 In U.S. Face Near-Poverty, No Work," Associated Press, July 28, 2013.

Chapter 7: Consumer Debt

Carey, Benedict, "Life In The Red," *The New York Times*, January 14, 2013.

Fry, Richard, *A Record One-in-Five Households Now Owe Student Loan Debt*, Pew Research Center, September 26, 2012.

Fry, Richard, *Young Adults After The Recession: Fewer Homes, Fewer Cars, Less Debt*, Pew Research Center, February 2013.

Quarterly Report On Household Debt And Credit, Federal Reserve Bank Of New York, November 2013.

PART II: SHOPPING BEHAVIORS

Chapter 8: Competition Between Shopping Channels

"Consumer Electronics Purchase Path Upended," *eMarketer*, October 5, 2012.

Dugal, Lisa Feigen, "The Future Of Retail," *Marketing Daily*, May 13, 2013.

Hale, Todd, *Retail USA: What's In Store for 2016*, Nielsen, March 2012.

Klaassen, Abbey, "CMOs Talk Personalization, Social, Mobile," *Advertising Age*, October 21, 2013.

Multichannel Consumer Survey, PwC, May 2013.

"Showrooming & The Price Of Keeping Buyers In-Store," GroupM Next, August 20, 2012.

"Showrooming Not Slowing Down," The Harris Poll, Harris Interactive, June 4, 2013.

Chapter 9: In-Store Shopping

Dugal, Lisa Feigen, "The Future Of Retail," *Marketing Daily*, May 13, 2013.

Hale, Todd, *Retail USA: What's In Store for 2016*, Nielsen, March 2012.

How America Shops, WSL Strategic Retail, 2013.

Loechner, Jack, "Shoppers Prefer Personalized Bricks-and-Mortar vs. Online," *Research Brief*, Center for Media Research, May 27, 2013.

Loechner, Jack, "Shopping Centers Morphing To Lifestyle Centers," *Research Brief*, Center for Media Research, June 7, 2013.

"Shoppers Like In-Store Experience," *Mass Market Retailers*, June 10, 2013.

The State Of The Shopping Center, Nielsen, May 23, 2013.

Chapter 10: Online Shopping

"Beauty And The Beast," A.T. Kearney, June 5, 2012.

Loechner, Jack, "Online Shoppers Want Choice And Convenience," *Research Brief*, Center for Media Research, June 13, 2013.

Loechner, Jack, "Shopping Sight Unseen," *Research Brief*, Center for Media Research, May 24, 2013.

"Main Reasons Young Adults Shop Online," *USA Today*, December 5, 2012.

"Monthly E-Commerce Research Initiative To Track Key Retail Trends," Shopzilla, May 13, 2013.

Online Shopping Customer Experience Study, comScore, May 2013.

Pulse Of The Online Shopper, UPS, May 2013.

Chapter 11: Mobile Shopping

"How Does Wi-Fi Affect Mobile Shoppers?" *eMarketer*, March 14, 2013.

Loechner, Jack, "10% Of E-Commerce Spending On Smartphone Or Tablet," *Research Brief*, Center for Media Research, September 5, 2013.

Mahoney, Sarah, "Tablets, Smartphones Gaining Retail Dominance," *Marketing Daily*, October 2, 2013.

"Majority Of U.S. Mobile Consumers Use Devices To Comparison Shop," eMarketer, May 20, 2013.

Mobile Audience Insights Report: Q4 2012, JiWire, February 28, 2013.

"SOASTA Survey: San Francisco #1 In Smartphone Shopping," The Harris Poll, Harris Interactive, October 14, 2013.

Chapter 12: Peer-to-Peer Shopping

"All Eyes On The Sharing Economy," *The Economist*, March 9, 2013, pp 13-15.

"Crowdfunding In America: End Of The Peer Show," *The Economist*, June 1, 2013, p. 74.

"Disrupters," *Forbes,* April 15, 2013, p. 90.

Elliott, Christopher, "Peer-to-Peer Travel Unnerves Traditional Companies," *USA Today*, September 30, 2013.

Geron, Tomio, "The Share Economy," *Forbes*, February 11, 2013.

Lev-Ram, Michal and Kurt Wagner, "Crowdfunding Tries To Grow Up," *Fortune*, May 20, 2013, pp 40-42.

"The Rise Of The Sharing Economy," *The Economist*, March 9, 2013, p. 9.

PART III: BEHAVIORAL ANALYSES

Chapter 13: At Home

15th Annual Household CE Ownership and Market Potential Study, Consumer Electronics Association, April 2013.

Corso, Regina A., "Is Working At Home Really Just Watching TV In Sweats Or Increased Productivity?" The Harris Poll, Harris Interactive, March 11, 2013.

"What Do We Like To Do Most In Our Yards? Relax, Says A New U.S. Poll," The Harris Poll, Harris Interactive, March 12, 2013.

Chapter 15: Brand Loyalty

Trejos, Nancy, "Travelers Get Stingier With Their Loyalty," *USA Today*, January 19, 2013.

"What It Takes To Drive Store Brand Sales, Retail Profits," *Mass Market Retailers*, November 4, 2013, p. 16.

Chapter 16: Buying American-Made

"Born In The USA Or Coming To America," The Harris Poll, Harris Interactive, March 6, 2013.

Clifford, Stephanie, "That 'Made In U.S.A.' Premium," *The New York Times*, November 30, 2013.

"Made In America," *Mass Market Retailers*, September 2, 2013, pp 1-2.

Sherman, Lauren, "Made In America: More Than A Marketing Stunt?" *Advertising Age*, February 18, 2013, p. 17.

Chapter 17: Buying Local

Ruehle, Jens and James Rushing, "Buying Into The Local Food Movement," A.T. Kearney, January 2013.

Suddath, Claire, "Whole Foods Local Forager Elly Truesdell Is a Grocery Tastemaker," *Bloomberg Businessweek*, May 2, 2013.

Steinmetz, Katy, "Shelling Out: Buy-Local Advocates Are Rallying Mobs To Shop," *Time*, November 5, 2012.

Chapter 20: Environmentally Conscious Consumerism

2013 Green Gap Trend Tracker, Cone Communications, April 2013.

Goldstein, David, "Green Still Follows Green: The Environment Retains Influence On Spending," The Harris Poll, Harris Interactive, May 30, 2012.

Neff, Jack, "As More Marketers Go Green, Fewer Consumers Willing To Pay For It," *Advertising Age*, September 24, 2012.

Russo, James, "For Many Consumers, Every Day Is Earth Day," Nielsen, April 16, 2013.

Steinberg, Kathy, "Fewer Americans Thinking Green," The Harris Poll, Harris Interactive, April 18, 2012.

Chapter 21: Gift Giving

Dunn, Elizabeth and Michael Norton, *Happy Money: The Science of Smarter Spending*, Simon & Schuster, 2013.

"Have-It-All-ers, Unclassified Love Interest and Frenemy Are Hardest To Shop For," BusinessWire, December 4, 2012

Chapter 23: Payment Preferences

2013 Online Banking and Bill-Payment Forecast, Javelin Strategy & Research, September 2013.

"How Does Wi-Fi Affect Mobile Shoppers?" *eMarketer*, March 14, 2013.

Mobile Audience Insights Report: Q4 2012, JiWire, February 28, 2013.

"Proximity Mobile Payments Set To Explode In U.S.," *eMarketer*, October 18, 2012.

Chapter 24: Post-Recession Consumer Behavior

Kochhar, Rakesh, *A Recovery No Better Than The Recession*, Pew Research Center, September 12, 2012.

Leonhardt, David, "Standard Of Living Is In The Shadows As Election Issue," *The New York Times*, October 23, 2012.

Mahoney, Sarah, "For Consumers, Small Luxuries Are Back," *Marketing Daily*, February 12, 2013.

Rampell, Catherine, "In Hard Economy For All Ages, Older Isn't Better, It's Brutal," *The New York Times*, February 2, 2013.

Rampell, Catherine, "Median Household Income Down 7.3% Since Start of Recession," *The New York Times*, March 29, 2013

Shannon-Missal, Larry, "Small Ticket Savings And Big Ticket Purchases Both On The Rise," The Harris Poll, Harris Interactive, July 25, 2013.

Chapter 25: Privacy Issues

Dolliver, Mark, *The Digital Privacy Dilemma*, eMarketer, December 12, 2012.

Loechner, Jack, "Adults Feel Personal Information Collected Online Unwarranted," *Research Brief*, Center for Media Research, February 13, 2013.

"Nearly Half of U.S. Adults Believe They Have Little To No Control Over Personal Info Companies Gather From Them While Online," Ipsos, January 24, 2013.

Purcell, Kristen, Joanna Brenner and Lee Rainie "Search Engine Use," Pew Internet & American Life Project, March 9, 2012.

Romanov, Alex, "The Big Data And Mobile Privacy Conurdrum," *Marketing Daily*, July 24, 2013.

Shannon-Missal, Larry, "Less Than Half Of Americans Trust The Federal Government With Personal Information," The Harris Poll, Harris Interactive, July 16, 2013.

Turow, Joseph, "Behavior Aside, Consumers Do Want Control Of Their Privacy," *Advertising Age*, January 28, 2013, p. 32.

"U.S. Web Users Concerned About Privacy, But Hold Themselves Accountable," *eMarketer*, September 12, 2013.

Von Drehle, David, "The Surveillance Society," *Time*, August 12, 2013.

Chapter 26: Purchase Decision Making

Brustein, Joshua, "JPMorgan Chase's Brian Tunick on Retail's Recovery via Value Pricing," *Bloomberg Businessweek*, October 3, 2013.

"Millennial Shoppers Favor Deals Over Brands," *eMarketer*, November 19, 2012.

Tuttle, Bran, "The Price Is Righter," *Time*, February 13, 2013.

Chapter 27: Response to Advertising

2013 Online Personal Experience, Janrain, July 31, 2013.

Loechner, Jack, "Almost Half Of Brand Emails Opened On Mobile," *Research Brief*, Center For Media Research, August 27, 2013.

Loechner, Jack, "No More Patience With Irrelevant Ads," *Research Brief*, Center For Media Research, August 5, 2013.

Loechner, Jack, "Target Email With Individualized Demographics," *Research Brief*, Center For Media Research, August 28, 2013.

Loechner, Jack, "Willful Email Subscribers Don't Read Much Of It," *Research Brief*, Center For Media Research, October 4, 2013.

"Study: Consumers Actually Like Advertising," *Advertising Age*, March 11, 2013.

Chapter 28: Response to Customer Service
"Customers Don't Care," *Forbes*, September 23, 2013.

"On The Web, Customer Service Stores Move Fast," *eMarketer*, April 23, 2013.

Chapter 29: Response to Reviews
Buy It, Try It, Rate It, Weber Shandwick, January 2013.

Chapter 30: Spending for Goods Vs. Experiences
Markman, Art, "Why Regret Makes Buying Experiences Better than Buying Stuff," *Psychology Today*, January 20, 2012.

Nobel, Carmen, "To Buy Happiness, Purchase an Experience," *Harvard Business School Working Knowledge*, August 5, 2013.

Rosenzweig, Emily and Thomas Gilovich, "Buyer's Remorse or Missed Opportunity? Differential Regrets for Material and Experiential Purchases," *Journal of Personality and Social Psychology*, February 2012.

Thompson, Derek, "Why Wanting Expensive Things Makes Us So Much Happier Than Buying Them," *The Atlantic*, June 11, 2013.

PART IV: AFFLUENT CONSUMERS

Chapter 31: Luxury & Affluent Markets
Affluent Market Tracking Study, American Affluence Research Center, September 2013.

Chapter 32: Population Centers of U.S. Affluence
2013 World Wealth Report, Capgemini, June 2013.

"Valley High," *Forbes*, November 18, 2013.

Chapter 33: Market Surveys
Affluent Consumers and their Travel Plans 2013, Unity Marketing, March 2013.

Affluent Market Tracking Study, American Affluence Research Center, September 2013.

"Affluent Shoppers Make Mobile An Essential Stop In The Purchase Funnel," *eMarketer*, June 10, 2013.

"At Least Affluents Are Optimistic," *Research Brief*, Center for Media Research, March 15, 2013.

Greenberg, Karl, "Affluents Will Spend With Optimism In Check," *Marketing Daily*, March 28, 2013.

Greenberg, Karl, "Affluents Worry About Purchasing Online," *Marketing Daily*, October 16, 2013.

Greenberg, Karl, "Meet The Rich At The Club," *Marketing Daily*, April 12, 2013.

Loechner, Jack, "Affluent Predictions," *Research Brief*, Center for Media Research, April 16, 2013.

"U.S. Affluents Use More Digital Devices," *eMarketer*, October 2, 2013.

PART V: CUSTOMER BRAND PREFERENCES

Chapter 40: Facebook Fan Brand Loyalty

Irwin, Tanya, "Study Reveals Brands With Loyal Facebook Fans," *Marketing Daily*, February 7, 2013.

Chapter 41: Online Retailer Shopper Satisfaction

"2012 Harris Poll Shopper Satisfaction Study Of Online Retailers," Harris Interactive, November 28, 2012.

PART VI: ETHNIC FOCUS

Chapter 42: African-American Consumers

The African-American Consumer: Resilient, Receptive, and Relevant - 2013 Report, Nielsen, 2013.

Chapter 43: Arab-American Consumers

Asi, Maryam and Daniel Beaulieu, Arab Households in the United States: 2006-2010, American Community Survey Briefs, U.S. Census Bureau, May 2013.

Chapter 44: Asian-American Consumers
"Asian Consumers Upscale, Light Media Users," *FYI*, The Media Audit, June 2013.

Demographics Of Asian Americans, Pew Research Social & Demographic Trends, April 2013. (www.pewsocialtrends.org/2013/04/04/asian-groups-in-the-u-s/)

Facts For Features: Asian/Pacific American Heritage, Census Bureau, March 2013.

Chapter 45: Hispanic- & Latino-American Consumers
Lopez, Mark Hugo, *Diverse Origins: The Nation's 14 Largest Hispanic Origins Groups*, Pew Research Hispanic Trends Project, June 19, 2013.

Motel, Seth and Eileen Patten, *Characteristics Of The 60 Largest Metropolitan Areas By Hispanic Population*, Pew Research Hispanic Trends Project, September 19, 2012.

Chapter 46: Jewish-American Consumers
A Portrait Of Jewish Americans, Pew Research Religion & Public Life Project, October 1, 2013.

Chapter 47: Muslim-American Consumers
Muslim Americans, Pew Research Center, August 2011.

Chapter 48: Native-American Consumers
Facts for Features: American Indian and Alaska Native Heritage, U.S. Census Bureau, October 2013.

Indian Americans, Pew Research Social & Demographic Trends, 2013.

The Multicultural Economy, The Selig Center for Economic Growth at the University of Georgia, October 2013. (www.terry.uga.edu/selig/buying_power.html)

PART VII: GENDER FOCUS
Chapter 49: Female Consumers
2013 Social Mom Report, Baby Center Solutions, April 2013.

Greenberg, Karl, "Marketers Should Take Women Seriously As Consumers," MediaPost.com, September 19, 2013.

"Mothers Share Their Brand, Coupon Preferences," eMarketer, September 17, 2013.

Silverstein, Michael J., Kate Sayre, and John Butman, *Women Want More: How to Capture Your Share of the World's Largest, Fastest-Growing Market*, Boston Consulting Group, August 2013.

"Smartphones Are Go-Everywhere, Do-Anything Devices for Mothers," eMarketer, October 9, 2013.

"U.S. Women Control the Purse Strings," Nielsen, April 2, 2013.

Wang, Wendy, Kim Parker and Paul Taylor, "Breadwinner Moms," May 29, 2013.

Chapter 50: Male Consumers

A Tale Of Two Fathers, Pew Research Center, June 2011. (http://pewresearch.org/pubs/2026/survey-role-of-fathers-fatherhood-american-family-living-apart-from-children)

"Men Do Like Shopping Online," MMR, June 10, 2013.

The Great Male Survey, AskMen.com, July 2012. (www.askmen.com/specials/great_male_survey/)

How Dads Are Different: Playing A New Role, But Only Up To A Point, eMarketer, September 2012.

PART VIII: GENERATIONAL FOCUS

Chapter 55: Millennial Consumers

Baar, Aaron, "Millennials Growing Up, Changing Attitudes," *Marketing Daily*, October 5, 2013.

Cohn, D'Vera, "Millennials: Only A Third Head Their Own Households," Pew Research Center, October 18, 2013.

DDB Life Style Study, DDB Worldwide, April 24, 2013.

Everything You Thought You Knew About Millennials Might Not Be True, Concentric Marketing, August 2013.

Lachman, M. Deanne and Deborah L. Brett, *Generation Y: Shopping and Entertainment In The Digital Age*, Urban Land Institute, May 2013.

Loechner, Jack, “Generation Y: A Complex Social Niche,” *Research Brief*, Center for Media Research, May 29, 2013.

Mahoney, Sarah, “Affluent Gen Y Spends Less, Invests More,” *Marketing Daily*, May 14, 2013.

“Millennial Men Keep Their Digital Lives Humming,” *eMarketer*, September 23, 2013.

Stein, Joel, “The New Greatest Generation,” *Time*, May 20, 2013.

The Teen Transition: Adolescents Of Today, Adults Of Tomorrow, Nielsen, April 16, 2013.

“Young with Money Atypical Media Consumers,” *FYI*, International Demographics, August 2013.

PART IX: SEGMENTATION

Chapter 56: College Students

Everything You Thought You Knew About Millennials Might Not Be True, Concentric Marketing, August 2013.

Locher, Jack, “Tech Products and Discretionary Spending Advancing With College Students,” *Research Brief*, Center For Media Research, June 27, 2013.

Chapter 58: Families With Children

“Bye-bye Boomerangs,” *The Economist*, August 17, 2013, p. 31.

Fry, Richard, “A Rising Share of Young Adults Live in Their Parents' Home,” Pew Research Social & Demographic Trends, August 1, 2013.

Sandler, Lauren, “None Is Enough,” *Time*, August 12, 2013, pp 39-45.

Chapter 59: Family Caregivers

Fox, Susannah, Maeve Duggan, and Kristen Purcell, *Family Caregivers Are Wired For Health*, Pew Internet & American Life Project, June 20, 2013.

Unpaid Eldercare In The United States, Bureau of Labor Statistics, September 18, 2013.

Chapter 60: Gay & Lesbian Consumers
Gee, Graham, "U.S. LGBT Households Make 16% More Shopping Trips Than The U.S. Average," Nielsen Newswire, January 30, 2013.

Rapkin, Mickey, "The Gay Retiree Utopia," *Bloomberg Businessweek*, May 20, 2013, pp. 83-85.

Chapter 61: Immigrant Consumers
Cohn, D'Vera, *Second-Generation Americans, By The Numbers*, Pew Research Social & Demographic Trends, February 7, 2013.

Chapter 64: Pet Owners
"Pets Aren't Just Animals; They are Members of the Family," The Harris Poll, Harris Interactive, September 13, 2012.

PART XII: COMMUNITIES

Chapter 73: Americans' Views On Their Communities
Americans' Views On Their Communities, Housing, And Transportation, Belden Russonello Strategists and the Urban Land Institute, March 2013.

Chapter 74: Where Americans Want To Live
Shannon-Missal, Larry, "California Stands Out As The State Where Americans Most – And Least – Want To Live," The Harris Poll, Harris Interactive, September 5, 2013.

Taylor, Paul, Rich Morin, Kim Parker, D'Vera Cohn, and Wendy Wang, *For Nearly Half of America, Grass Is Greener Somewhere Else*, Pew Research Center, January 29, 2009.

Chapter 75: Relocation
2012 Migration Patterns, Atlas Van Lines, January 2013.

36th Annual Migration Study, United Van Lines, January 2013.

45th Annual Magnet States Report, Allied Van Lines, January 2013.

El Nasser, Haya, "Americans On The Move Start Moving Down, Not Up," *USA Today*, February 20, 2013.

Lloyd, Janice, “Where Will Your Years Be Most Golden?” *USA Today*, March 13, 2013.

“Number Living In The Same City 20+ Years Rises,” *FYI*, International Demographics, June 2013.

Chapter 77: Best Small Towns

Bly, Laura, “The Five Best Small Towns In America: 2011,” *USA Today,* July 22, 2011.

Bly, Laura, “The Five Best Small Towns In America: 2012,” *USA Today,* July 20, 2012.

Spano, Susan. “The 20 Best Small Towns to Visit in 2013,” *Smithsonian*, April 2013.

Spano, Susan and Aviva Shen, “Best Small Towns In America Of 2012,” *Smithsonian*, May 2012.

Stapen, Candyce H., “Best Small Towns In America: 2013,” *USA Today*, October 14, 2013.